Roving Reuter Reporter

1959–61

For Jan
alles gute!
Peter S. Robinson
King's College Hospital, London
21/7/5

For my sister, Pat
and our nephew, Andrew

Roving Reuter Reporter 1959–61

Peter B. Johnson

Tagman
www.tagman-press.com

Acknowledgements

I am greatly indebted to David Childs, Emeritus Professor of Politics at Nottingham University, who edited my first volume, *Reuter Reporter in Divided Germany 1955–58*, and found me a publisher for it. I am also grateful to Reuters archivist, John Entwistle, who provided me with information on the agency's growth. My thanks go also to our two daughters-in-law, Angela and Janis Johnson, for solving some of my word-processing problems and to my computer guru, Alan Mitchell, for solving others.

The author and publishers are grateful to the following for permission to reproduce photographs: Associated Press; German Federal Press Office; *Life*; Press Association; The Reuters Archive; and to Dean Rusk for permission to use the quotation on p. 394. The quotation on pp. 271–3 from *The Jewish War* by Josephus, translated by G.A. Williamson, revised by E. Mary Smallwood (Penguin Classics, 1959, Revised Edition 1981) is reproduced by permission of Penguin Books Ltd. Every effort has been made to trace the holders of other copyright material.

Preface

Like my two previous volumes, this book owes its existence firstly to a forgotten experienced someone – probably an elderly newspaperman – who, in about 1946, told me that would-be journalists ought to keep diaries – mine is now more than 56 years old. This volume, like its forerunners, deals primarily with Germany, a country – then divided into two hostile states – which has played a major part in my life. But, as a roving reporter, I was also whisked to a variety of other countries, including Russia, Israel, Yugoslavia, Austria, Italy, France, Belgium, Algeria, Morocco and Czechoslovakia.

My fading secondary school reports dated between 1935 and 1939, from two schools in my hometown, Bradford, Yorkshire (the independent Methodist foundation, Woodhouse Grove, and a state school, Grange High), show that I was among the best in German. And as a Royal Naval Voluntary Reserve sub-lieutenant in the Mediterranean, I polished up my German in spare moments. I was thus fairly fluent in the language when, aged 21, I was posted to a shore job in Royal Naval Headquarters, Germany, in the summer of 1946.

At first the headquarters were in the former building of the well-known Melitta coffee company in Minden, Westphalia, but were moved a few months later to refurbished barracks in still largely devastated Hamburg. There I met an intelligent and beautiful East Prussian refugee, Elfi Kowitz, one of the headquarters' interpreters. As I related in my earlier volumes, she was at first reluctant to go out with the former enemy, but an old Anglophile aunt told her the British were human too, so she relented. We became engaged about eight days after we had first gone out together.

Our marriage in Bradford in May 1947 was one of the first Anglo-German marriages after the Second World War. Our elder son, Robin, born in 1948, eventually became a German teacher in Yorkshire. We had to wait until 1953 for the arrival of our younger son, Christopher, who studied electrical engineering at Bradford University and went to work in West Germany, where he settled.

A few months before our marriage I had started my journalistic apprenticeship, which took me to such colourfully named weeklies and dailies as the *Whitley Bay Weekly Guardian* in Northumberland, the *Cleckheaton Guardian* and its companion, the *Heckmondwike Herald*, the *Halifax Courier* and the *Bradford Telegraph & Argus*, all in my native Yorkshire. Then, in 1954, Reuters took me on as a sub-editor, quite a lowly post, in its Fleet Street headquarters and, a year later, I was happy to be sent off to the Cold War – to the main German office in Bonn. Reuters did not expect me to fight in the Cold War, but to write about it as fairly as I could.

I found myself in a West Germany on the verge of rearmament, emerging from occupation rule under the conservative leadership of Konrad Adenauer. The first book, *Reuter Reporter in Divided Germany 1955–58*, ends by detailing my first visit to the interior of Communist East Germany in late 1958.

My second volume, *Reuter Reporter among the Communists 1958–59*, reports on Nikita Khrushchev's 'Berlin Ultimatum' of 10 November 1958, which threatened to cause a major East–West crisis, including a repetition of the Berlin blockade of 1948–49. I describe my first (positive) first-hand impression of Khrushchev, when he visited Leipzig and East Berlin in March 1959. The main part of the book deals with my five-month assignment as the first non-Communist Western correspondent in East Germany, where I opened up the first Reuter office in that country and obtained some insights on the true nature of the Communist regime.

I hope – at 78 – to write a fourth volume reporting on my two years' assignment (1962–64) as Reuters chief correspondent in the Soviet Union, which ended suddenly when I was expelled for writing an exclusive eyewitness report about a surprising unauthorized demonstration by some 200 African students on Red Square – a report which harmed Soviet relations with some African countries.

Working for Reuters in the fifties and sixties was not merely interesting but – as my onetime boss in Germany, Gerry Long, once put it – rather like being a committed member of a religious order, thanks largely to the agency's striving to be objective. And the work was often fun. But it was not very well paid: Walton Cole, successively editor and general manager, was quoted as telling new staffers, 'Don't worry about the money, old man.'

Reuters was founded in London in 1851 by a German Jew, originally called Israel Beer Josaphat. Born in 1816, Josaphat converted to Christianity, married a blonde non-Jewish German, Clementine Magnus, the daughter of a Prussian Government official, and took the name Paul Julius Reuter. He became known as Julius Reuter, later Baron de Reuter, after he was given a barony in 1871 by the Duke of Saxe-Coburg-Gotha, a German duchy. Reuter retired as managing director of the agency in 1878 and was succeeded by his son, Herbert. Baron de Reuter died in 1899. Herbert committed suicide in 1915, ending the family connection with the agency.

In 1941 the Press Association, representing UK provincial newspapers, which had been the majority shareholder in Reuters Ltd – a private company – since 1925, became an equal partner in the company with the Newspaper Proprietors' Association, representing British national newspapers. In 1947 the main news agency of Australia and that of New Zealand were taken into the partnership. In 1948 the main Indian news agency, the Press Trust of India, was also brought into the firm, but withdrew in 1953. After the Second World War the South African Press Association (SAPA), a cooperative non-profit-making news agency, considered joining the Reuter partnership on terms similar to the Australians. But for political reasons this did not come about.

From the start, business news provided to bankers and stockbrokers produced most of Reuters revenue. That subsidized – and strengthened – the news service to the media. Initially the shareholdings of the news agencies and newspaper organizations were not seen as financial investments, but as way of ensuring a good news service as economically as possible.

However, by the early 1980s, thanks to the success of the agency's electronic systems in distributing news to business, it became clear that Reuters could become a big money-spinner. Some of the newspapers that held Reuter shares had financial problems. They realized they could obtain large sums if the firm were floated as a public company, enabling them to sell their increasingly valuable shares, or some of them. There was considerable opposition to the proposed change. But, after prolonged debate between shareholding companies and within Reuters management, the agency was floated in April 1984.

A main concern of the owners, management and staff was to maintain the principles of the 1941 Reuter Trust guaranteeing the agency's independence and objectivity. This was achieved; in fact, the trust arrangements were strengthened. The flotation, simultaneously in London and New York, provided the funds to enable Reuters rapidly to expand its business and its media services worldwide and also to make numerous acquisitions, particularly of firms in the computerized information sector.

Since the flotation, Reuters growth has been enormous. At the end of 1984, the firm had 3,865 employees (including me!) At the end of 2002 Reuters Group, including subsidiary firms, had 17,414 staff in about 90 countries, including some 2,400 editorial staff in 197 bureaux, making Reuters the world's largest international multimedia news agency.

In 1984 the 'old Reuters' revenue was £313 million and its profit before tax was £74 million. Ironically, that was a much better result than that achieved by the 'capitalist' Reuters Group in 2002, when revenue totalled £3,575 million, but there was a loss of £516 million, due largely to the slump in global markets. However, the poor 2002 result followed several profitable years. As I said in the preface to my second volume, I preferred 'my' Reuters, even if it was hard to get a wage increase! But I am glad that the 'old firm' still exists, even though general news – which was my sphere – now accounts for less than one-tenth of Reuters revenue.

Peter B. Johnson
London, April 2003

Map of Germany in 1959

1 Researching Reuters roots

4 November 1959 : Drove to Aachen, close to the Belgian and Dutch borders, on a Reuter history quest. An Aachen pub owner, Willi Brauers, had written to Reuters HQ saying he believed his pub was the building where, in April 1850, Julius Reuter, a German of Jewish extraction who founded Reuters, sited the Aachen end of his famous Aachen–Brussels pigeon post, which bridged the then gap of 76 miles in the telegraph line between Berlin and Brussels, enabling Reuter to beat his competitors. French news was reaching Brussels by train or pigeon, as the telegraph line from Paris was not opened for public use until April 1851. Thanks to his pigeons, Reuter could get the French news to Aachen in two hours, while the train took about eight.

In his letter to Reuters, Brauers asked if the agency would be interested in having a plaque fixed on the pub, which has the dialect name *Ajen Krüzbrüer,* which, I understand, means 'Aachen Monks of the Cross'.

Our HQ in London knew that Reuter had contracted with a Heinrich Geller, a brewer, distiller and pub owner, to set up the pigeon post early in 1850. But they did not know whether Geller's address had been the same as that of Brauers, who turned out to be a 35-year-old who had been a cook to a British Army unit after the Second World War. His pub had its fourth – top – storey destroyed in the war, but the remaining storeys date from 1737. The address is 117 Pontstrasse, near the centre of the historic city, once the seat of Charlemagne. By consulting the city archives I found that this was in fact Geller's address in 1850 – the first year that Aachen had an address book.

Brauers told me that the Geller family had been the previous owners of the pub. He showed me photocopies of newspaper cuttings referring to the pigeon-post contract Reuter made with Geller, who was also a pigeon fancier. Geller received one taler daily (quite a sum, then) for keeping 40 pigeons available, of which 12 had always to be in Brussels. Reuter paid for transporting them there (presumably by rail). Geller, or an assistant, used to wait on his roof to immediately detach from the pigeon's tail feathers the message, which had been sewn in. Without unrolling the message, he sent it by messenger in a locked container to Reuter's office in the city centre. Reuter then dashed off to the telegraph office at nearby Aachen station to send on his reports, including stock exchange prices, to Berlin, Vienna and St Petersburg. This gave him up to a day's beat over his competitors. There is evidence that he was also providing a service in the opposite direction, to London, including Berlin and Vienna stock exchange prices. According to the newspaper cuttings, he made a lot of money through stock exchange speculations, giving him the capital with which he founded the agency in London in October 1851, after the gap in the Aachen–Brussels telegraph line had been closed in March 1851, making his pigeon post useless.

Before he started business in Aachen, Reuter, who was born in 1816, had been a bookseller in Berlin, a sub-editor with the French news agency Havas in Paris, and the owner of a small news agency in Paris that went bankrupt in 1849. It's an interesting sidelight that one of the founders of the Siemens electrical firm advised Reuter to move to London. Now Reuters and Siemens have close business connections; Siemens supply us with telecommunications equipment. At that time, though, Siemens were building the telegraph cable, and Frau Reuter complained to one of the Siemens that they were putting her husband out of business.

24 November 1959 : Interesting to learn in talks with politicians of all the main parties, in preparing a special article for a

2

Canadian newspaper, that they were in the main not critical of Britain's attitude towards European unity. In a nutshell, their view was that Britain, in view of its Commonwealth commitments, had done more or less what it could, while they regarded France critically – first, for throwing out the European Defence Community project and, last year, for preventing a compromise between the Common Market and the countries which have now formed the European Free Trade Association under Britain's leadership. But my informants did think it was up to Britain to do all it could to reach a good arrangement between the two European economic blocs, though even here their view was that it depended more on France than on Britain.

On the train to Hamburg this evening an interesting talk with some businessmen. One of them, a New York Jew, agreed when I said there was less freedom in the United States than in Britain. He referred to hysterical anti-Communism in the USA and at the same time said he thought (which I don't) that the USA might become susceptible to Communism as, he claimed, there was no real middle class as a bulwark against Communism, and that the workers, though well paid, had amassed little property.

25 November 1959 : In Hamburg to report on a German-run international conference on the construction of nuclear-powered merchant ships. We were told a West German consortium hopes to have its first nuclear ship afloat, at anchor, within $2^{1}/_{2}$ to three years. It will be a converted tanker bought cheaply from Esso. It will not be commercial. No one has yet shown how to make the use of nuclear power in ships economic; at present the capital cost of the reactor far exceeds the likely savings from using uranium instead of coal or oil.

26 November 1959 : Have noted here and elsewhere new phone boxes linked to the direct dialling system, which means I can ring up Elfi, about 300 miles away, after 7 pm and speak to her for nearly a minute for the equivalent of fourpence *[1.6p]*! Time they extended this service to California. *[That's where my father was*

3

living.] An enormous amount of rebuilding in this handsome city since 1945, when it lay waste. At that time it seemed impossible that the reconstruction could happen so quickly.

27 November 1959 : An American told me that the world's first nuclear freighter, the Savannah, launched in July, was expected to make its first trial voyage next September. It's being built on the Delaware river, not far from Chester, Pennsylvania, home of my elderly American half-cousin, whom we know as Aunty Anne Webb. This congress has shown me what a lot of snags there are in developing a new form of propulsion. And in this particular case much attention has to be paid to safety measures, which cost such a lot.

Supper in our maternity clinic; not where either of our sons were born, but where Elfi and I did some of our courting, in her basement room in 1946. It is run by a Protestant sisterhood, the *Albertinenschwester*, of which Elfi's now retired aunt, Lieschen Gutzeit, was one of the founders before the First World War. She later became the matron of this clinic.

28 November 1959 : A British nuclear industry engineer told me at the close of the conference that we were in danger of falling behind West Germany in nuclear ship propulsion, though research in that sector was banned by the occupation powers until 1955.

My first look at a nuclear reactor: a (small) five-megawatt type built from American parts at Geesthacht, near Hamburg, by the consortium planning to build the West German nuclear-powered ship. This is a 'swimming-pool reactor' and does indeed look like a swimming-pool. Near the bottom of the pool at one end is a framework holding uranium rods and 'moderators' – shielding material which, when raised, allows the reactor to produce some power and increased radioactivity. There are lifebelts in case any-one falls into the pool – apparently not too dangerous – and a cou-ple of kiddies' plastic ducks floating on the water. The most dan-gerous radiation is emitted at the bottom of the roughly 14-feet-deep *[4 m]* pool. The radiation is shielded by masses of concrete and other material, but some of it is channelled to operate research apparatus. Signs here and there warned of radioactivity, and members of staff carried film packs to see if they were getting too much exposure.

29 November 1959 : On the train home, finished the second, final volume of the autobiography of 85-year-old Professor Emil Fuchs, father of nuclear spy Dr Klaus Fuchs, who gave me a widely printed scoop interview in June when he settled in East Germany after being released from Wakefield prison, Yorkshire. *[Details in* Reuter Reporter among the Communists.*]* Professor Fuchs, who originally became a Protestant pastor, like his father, is now a Christian Socialist, Quaker and theologian.

I think he was brave to move from West to East Germany in 1949 to become a theology professor there, for while he is a left-wing socialist, he is also a devout Christian and has by no means always had it easy in East Germany. From his book, and from what he told me when we met earlier this year, I think he wants a true socialist democracy and hopes that, somehow, some day, it will emerge in the Communist bloc. Most Communists must see him as an anachronism or as someone they can exploit to make East Germany seem more respectable to Western democrats. He in turn regards Communists as only half-persons because they don't believe in God. But he is also very critical of many church leaders who, he alleges, confuse Christianity with support for one form of society, namely capitalism.

In beautiful sunshine, drove my family some 80 miles southwards along the Rhine to visit the Ratzenbergers, Elfi's wine-growing relatives, in the village of Steeg, in a valley behind the small Rhineside town of Bacharach. *[In my earlier volumes I explain in detail how the Ratzenbergers, East Prussians, fled first to East Germany and then to the Rhineland, where they became successful wine-growers.]* The head of the family, 60-year-old Hans Ratzenberger, who at first had to eke out his income by working in a factory, is now working full time in the vineyard and not finding things easy. He lacks capital, needs a car, for instance, to deliver

5

wine. However, the harvest this year was so good that all their wine could be made without adding sugar which, in a normal year in their valley, is unavoidable. As I have (virtually) forsworn alcohol, we bought some grape juice, which they had specially bottled for us. Nectar.

1 December 1959 : We had an unusual caller this evening: Wilhelm Belz, who came to try to sell us a machine: basically a half-horsepower electric motor with attachments, which will act as vacuum cleaner, floor polisher, paint sprayer, kitchen mixer and various other things. Belz, who had a persuasive spiel, told us he was a missile expert. He showed us a newspaper cutting telling how he once had a four-hour talk with Hitler about missiles and also about a scheme Belz had for disabling aircraft by putting out a blanket of gas in the air, which was supposed to affect aircraft engines. Belz told us he had been annoyed that the Nazis (of which he was one, 'like all good Germans') had not taken up this idea. He told us he was against dictatorship, in favour of European Union, and even liked the Russians, whom he'd fought in the army for four years, though he did not like the Bolsheviks, of course. I said I thought there had been a lot of decent Bolsheviks, 'just like there were Nazis'. He had to agree. He described Hitler, whom he met shortly before the Nazis took power, as having been bossy and megalomaniacal, though Belz said he had not then realized to what extent. We didn't buy Belz's machine, but a friend of ours did, and was satisfied.

3 December 1959 : Had dinner with Bob Elphick, 30-ish, cheerful second man in our two-correspondent Moscow office. He told me about some of the snags of working there. Outgoing news is censored. Before cabling or phoning it, it must be handed to a girl at the censor's office (the censor is never seen) and checked. Meanwhile one puts in a phone call to London and hopes that the censor has finished by the time the call comes through, usually in about 45 minutes. But sometimes the censorship takes hours. If one has a supreme story and does not want to wait for the censor, one can try putting in a call and, while pretending to chat with someone at the other end, somehow pass the vital information. However, this may result in expulsion, so it is not to be advised. Normally one has to stay within 40 kilometres *[25 miles]* of Moscow, unless given a special pass, and your flat is guarded by a policeman. If you were to have appendicitis you would probably be operated on under local anaesthetic unless you were lucky enough to be flown out to a Western country.

6 December 1959 : In Wuppertal, east of Cologne, noted for its unique *Schwebebahn*, a suspended overhead railway, we called on one of Elfi's cousins, Fritz Gutzeit, whom she had met only once, in Berlin during the war. He turned out to be a 50-ish ex-navy meteorological officer who had served in North Africa and had enjoyed being a prisoner of the British in Egypt after the war. Now he is an executive of a screw-manufacturing firm and an organist and Sunday-school teacher at a Baptist church. A tubby, jolly chap, with a little moustache, making him look rather like Oliver Hardy of Laurel and Hardy.

8 December 1959 : Made what the Communists call a 'self-criticism' today to our chief correspondent, Gerry Long, and his deputy, John Bush, our news editor, after I had heard that the office had been trying since yesterday to get confirmation of a newspaper report that a statue bought from the British sculptor, Henry Moore, and sited in Wuppertal, showing a modernistic reclining woman, had been glued and feathered. Elfi and I had in fact seen the thing – with feathers – two days ago and I, cogitating on its newsworthiness, had dismissed it on the ground that this statue had been causing controversy ever since it was purchased by the city last year.

10 December 1959 : A recurring job on late turn this week is to ring up a castle or castles to find out what the Duke of Edinburgh has been doing during a week's hunting holiday. So far he's had a good bag. Tonight I had a nice story by phoning United States

Army Colonel Almquist, from Alabama, who had been invited to hunt with the Duke and some other noblemen, as he happened to command a local American artillery unit. He and his wife had been charmed by the Duke's lack of side.

12 December 1959 : How to translate that untranslatable word *gemütlich*, which all Germans, and many people elsewhere, know the meaning of? I opted for 'something between cosy and jolly'. I used that in relating what a castle spokesman had said of the atmosphere at a family evening in Langenburg, Württemberg, where the Duke of Edinburgh was present with some of his German relatives.

13 December 1959 : Over coffee in a friend's house, chatted with a German former landowner, whose estate was in the Polish Corridor south of Danzig (now Gdansk). He said he had got on well with local Poles. Thanks to the last war and Hitler's megalomania, this man has lost his farm and land. Obviously such land problems cannot be solved on the basis of competing nationalisms.

20–23 December 1959 : Drove around a large area of West Germany in the motorcade of British Transport Secretary Ernest Marples, who was viewing German bridges, mainly post-war ones, and multi-storey car parks. Marples, by trade a building contractor, is a cheerful little rosy-faced man with a friendly manner. Towards the end of his trip Marples, accompanied by one ministry engineer and two from the private sector, told me he had decided to change the method of tendering for some bridge designs. Until now, he explained, the local authority concerned had chosen a consulting engineer or one of its own engineers to design the bridge, and then contractors had been asked to tender for carrying out that design. Marples said that in future he intended, in some cases, to put the design out to tender too, as is usually done in West Germany. When Marples made some political remark I told him I was an old Labour supporter, but would vote for him if he would have a motorway built to Yorkshire, so that I could get home more quickly from Bonn. He assured me he would.

One of the numerous bridges I saw while following Marples was near Worms, in the Rhineland Palatinate. In Worms itself we popped into the 900-year-old Romanesque cathedral of red sandstone, next door to where the 'Diet of Worms' was held in 1521 – one of those history-book laughs – it was actually an imperial assembly at which Martin Luther, the Protestant reformer, refused to recant.

2 A break in the Alps

Christmas Eve 1959 : Being in Germany and as I have a German wife, we celebrate Christmas in the German fashion. Shortly before 4 pm we entered our Lutheran church, which was already packed. We were critical to see that young people who had seats made no attempt to get up for older people who came later, something that both Elfi and I thought would not have happened in Britain. The carol service, with choir, brass band and strings, was moving, bringing back childhood Christmases to me. Emotional, no doubt, but not to be sniffed at, I think. Two giant Christmas trees on each side of the central pulpit sparkled with lights.

Back home, it was time to open the doors to fairyland – the sitting room, which had been out of bounds while Elfi arranged our presents. First the boys each recited a poem for us and then Robin, who is 11, played a German carol on his toy clarinet – one of last year's presents. We all sang a carol or two and then the lads joyfully opened their presents. A highlight among my presents was a new book, *Deutsches Tagebuch (German Diary)* by Alfred Kantorowicz, a German-Jewish Communist and intellectual, confidant of Heinrich Mann. He fought against Franco in the Spanish Civil War, fled from Europe in about 1941 to escape the Nazis in France, and settled in the United States. In 1946 he moved from New York to East Germany, where he became a professor. Becoming disillusioned with East German Communism, he fled West about 18 months ago. I find the book fascinating.

27 December 1959 : A colleague, David Rees, claimed that his father, an Anglican vicar, had exorcized an evil spirit from a house after it had frightened five families from the house in turn. I don't believe in evil spirits.

28 December 1959 : With four pairs of colourful skis on our car's roof rack, we set off for the Austrian Alps. We dropped in at Hans Ratzenberger's vineyard in Steeg, near Bacharach. My present view on wine: not necessarily a bad thing, but I can do better without it. (This enables me to try to sell it for Hans while not drinking it myself.) We arrived tonight at the Stuttgart flat of Elfi's brother, Horst Kowitz, and family, where we are staying for three nights.

29 December 1959 : On the way to visit a friend in Stuttgart, I asked the way of a one-legged man on crutches. He turned out to be *(a)* drunk, *(b)* a foreigner, *(c)* looking for a refugee camp. As it appeared, from what he slurred, that his destination was in our direction, and as he did not seem to have an evil face, I gave him a lift. Elfi whispered that he might knock me on the head, so I asked her to sit in the back so she could knock him on the head. It turned out that he was *(d)* a Pole. I realized this because he started chattering away in a mixture of Polish and Russian and was pleased when I was able to answer him. We dropped him near the refugee camp and he thanked us profusely with Polish politeness.

30 December 1959 : Was most upset this lunchtime. Chris *[then aged six years and nine months]* refused to eat some sprouts. I insisted. After trying persuasion, and mixing the sprouts up with his potatoes, I eventually boxed his ears twice, making him cry, but not making him eat the sprouts. I couldn't bring myself to hit him any more, and intended to put him to bed and make him eat the stuff later when he had calmed down. Elfi suggested I let her try and so, with Chris already on my knee, I hugged him and asked him to be a good lad. Elfi was then able, after a short while, to coax him to eat the lot. Thinking this over afterwards, I was angry with myself for having hit Chris at all. I should have told him that he had to eat it up, and left him to it, explaining he would not be allowed to do anything else in the meantime.

En route to Austria for our first skiing holiday, we today drove to the small Baden-Württemberg township of Welzheim, to visit Herr and Frau Prang, old friends of Elfi's parents from her home village of Schönbruch. *[This, until 1945, was in Germany's easternmost province, East Prussia. In 1945 northern East Prussia was annexed by the Soviet Union, while the southern part was placed under Polish administration and later became part of Poland. The large village of Schönbruch was split by the new frontier between the Russian and Polish territory. In time the Russian part, including a Protestant church built around 1300, was gradually razed, apparently to make frontier control more easy. In my previous book,* Reuter Reporter among the Communists, *I describe a visit to the still-inhabited Polish part of the village in 1959. In 1991, as Soviet Communism was collapsing, Elfi and were able to see what little was left of the Russian part, mainly the ruin of one house and the foundations of others.]*

Before 1945 Herr Prang managed a 2,500-acre farm near Schönbruch, in an area now in Russia. The farm was owned by a noble family, the von Wrangels, for generations. Herr Prang said farm labourers were paid about 60 marks a month, half of it in produce, and, I gathered, had free housing together with a small plot of land they could farm for their own purposes. When Herr Prang told me that each farm labourer had been allowed to keep one cow and any number of pigs and poultry, this reminded me of the East German Communist collective farms of today, where a similar system is practised. In a sense the old landowner's farm was a collective farm, except that the profits of it went in the main to the landowner rather than to the farmers. Of course, the state takes its cut in both cases.

Sixty marks a month was poor pay, even before 1945. Herr Prang himself received only about 450 marks a month, some of it in kind. He told me that the farm was mortgaged, partly because the von Wrangels, in that generation, had been compelled to give large dowries to marry off several daughters to gentlemen of the right class. The von Wrangel family, he said, had lived simply.

I also talked with the Prangs' son-in-law, a 40-ish foundry worker with a tough but humorous face, who was an NCO in the *Waffen* SS, Hitler's élite troops, from 1936 until 1945. He told me he had been half-forced, as a member of the Hitler Youth, to join the *Waffen* SS. (That reminds me of the pressure today put on members of the East German Communist Free German Youth to join the army.) Discipline had been very tough.

He had served under both Panzer Meyer – then a captain and later a general sentenced to death for complicity in shootings of Canadian prisoners during the 1944 'Battle of the Bulge' in the Ardennes – and Sepp Dietrich, one of the two SS officers who carried out Hitler's order to shoot the chief of the SA, the Nazi stormtroopers, Ernst Röhm, in 1934, and who later became a renowned *Waffen* SS general. *[Hitler had allegedly suspected Röhm of planning a coup. As I report in my first book,* Reuter Reporter in Divided Germany 1955–58, *I attended the Munich trial of Dietrich and the other accused former SS officer, Michael Lippert, in May 1957. Each was sentenced to 18 months imprisonment.]* My informant said he found both Meyer and Dietrich good commanders.

He told me that he and his comrades had disliked Heinrich Himmler, the head of both the SS and the Gestapo secret police. When I asked him for his view of Hitler, he said he thought that Hitler had not been too bad at all, but some of the 'little Hitlers' under him had been bad. He agreed with me, however, that Hitler had never been satisfied with his conquests and had always wanted more. On the gassings of Jews, he said that while he had known there were concentration camps – another section of the SS, the 'General SS', provided the guards for them – he had been flabbergasted to learn of the mass killings. He argued that it was wrong to condemn all former members of the *Waffen* SS as having been war criminals. The majority had in fact been élite troops, thrown in when the front seemed likely to break. I agreed with him on that, on the basis of what I have learned previously.

31 December 1959 : Leaving our car behind, we took a train from Stuttgart at about 4 am. By dawn we were approaching the eastern tip of Lake Constance, some 130 miles south of Stuttgart. Here the Rhine flows into the eastern end of the lake from its source in Switzerland. Soon we were in Austria, with the snowy Alps of Switzerland, Austria and Bavaria in view. Little snow at lower levels, unusual for December. After about an hour amid this wonderful scenery, we left the train at Bludenz, a picturesque small town nestling between the mountains. Thanks to our package-tour deal, a Volkswagen bus took us some 20 miles up into the mountains, a rather scary ride on narrow and partly icy roads. Our destination was the Austrian ski resort of Partenen, a village of a few hundred souls, near the Swiss border and the Silvretta pass, which is closed at this time of year. The village has wooden or brick-and-wood houses with overhanging eaves: what we in Britain call Swiss chalets. Partenen lies in a narrow valley at about 3,200 feet *[975 m]*. Peaks around tower to about 7,400 feet *[2,255 m]*. We were pleased to see that snow lay everywhere, more than a foot deep, even in the village.

Partenen boasts a rack railway to higher levels and a ski-lift, where skiers are somehow attached to a wire which pulls them up a slope so they can ski down again. Elfi had done some cross-country skiing in her youth, Robin and I had been on skis once or twice before, Chris not at all. As a result, Chris fell down continually, chuckling as he did so and picking himself up. Robin and I fell repeatedly, Elfi only once or twice. Elfi and I saw in the New Year at a village dance but, thanks to our earlier exertions, soon went home to tuck ourselves in under our bulbous feather beds which, to the boys' delight, I have christened Humpty-Dumpties.

1 January 1960 : We had the first of six two-hour skiing lessons today, conducted by a 30-ish local lady, Frau Mattle, on a slope. *[More than 40 years later I can still remember some of her instructions:* 'Bergski nach vorne, hinunter zum Tal gucken.' *('Mountainside ski ahead of the other one, look down into the valley.')]* Skiing is almost the opposite of sitting on a sunny beach in summer, but the sensation of fresh air, closeness to nature and free-and-easiness are common to both. It certainly makes it feel good to be alive.

2 January 1960 : Found it hard to sleep for a while during the night as I was half-consciously practising diagonal skiing – and turning in my sleep. The movements woke me up!

During today's lesson, the sun peeped over the top of a peak at the near end of the valley and shone onto our slope. (It does not reach the village between sometime in November and about 2 February because of the surrounding high peaks.) The snow glistened – a fairyland scene. I felt elated.

4 January 1960 : After each day's instruction we feel a little more confident. Slopes which would have sent me hurtling downwards, out of control, a few days ago are no longer terrifying. However, when one spreadeagles into a drift, there is quite a feeling of impotence until one manages to get one's limbs out, one by one, after disentangling the skis and the sticks.

With the Gschaiders, the family who run our guesthouse, we've had a game of Scrabble. To hear them pronounce the word was itself a delight; something like 'Skraablay'.

5 January 1960 : Frau Mattle took our little school-group by cable car from about 1,050 to about 1,750 metres, and we returned to Partenen walking and skiing. At one point we could see peaks – some with glaciers – on the Austrian–Swiss border a few miles to our south-west: a glorious sight.

6 January 1960 : In one of several unserious films we've seen here, a girl slipped out of the bed she was sharing with her mother, to find her boyfriend in the night. One of the locals in the audience, obviously deeply involved in the story, called out in the local dialect, '*Zi go-at.*' ('*Sie geht.*' 'She is going.') This brought a burst of laughter from the audience.

7 January 1960 : We've been playing Scrabble with several German fellow skiers. It will be some time before Elfi will forgive me for using WOLLABEND (wool evening) as a word, and managing to gain majority acceptance for it through dialectics. I argued that it would be possible for, say, a ladies' meeting to decide to do something or other with wool one evening. In some respects German is a good language for Scrabble because of its propensity for giant words composed of several words stuck together.

3 East Berlin calls

11 January 1960 : Back at the office, I learned that the big story while we have been away has been a crop of anti-Semitic incidents – mainly remarks in pubs and slogans scrawled on walls – starting in West Germany, but spreading to other countries. I do not regard them seriously, as I believe the average German is not involved in this and that such things will die a natural death. But insofar as some of these incidents have been committed by young people, they do show the need for more education about Hitler's crimes.

13 January 1960 : Elfi's mother, who is holidaying with us, told me that, when she was helping Chris with his homework, he said to her in German, 'You are silly.'

She replied, 'It's you who are silly.'

Chris countered this by saying, 'One does not speak like that to little boys.'

That sounds like an echo of what he is sometimes told: 'One doesn't say that to Daddy (or Mummy).'

14 January 1960 : The recent crop of anti-Semitic incidents is a story which tends to be lapped up abroad because, I suppose, it makes other people think they are better than the Germans. Several sources, including the opposition Social Democrats, have suggested that basically more important than scrawled slogans is the presence of former Nazis in top posts in West Germany – such as Professor Theodor Oberländer, the minister for refugees, who undoubtedly was a Nazi, worked for Nazi projects in German-occupied Eastern Europe and wrote in support of racism. On the other hand, Oberländer claims he had always wanted non-German population groups to be allowed to develop in their own ways and that, because of his attitude in that respect, had been under arrest in the Nazi era for a time. He also claimed that, while in some post in occupied Poland, he had refused to carry out an order for the murder of several thousand Jews. Whatever the truth in his defence, I'd say he is not a man who should be occupying a ministerial post today.

16 January 1960 : By train to Saarbrücken, where the authorities had banned a planned meeting tonight of the extreme right-wing German Reich Party. The party had appealed to a local court to rescind the ban, but the judge concerned said it was technically impossible to convene the court, as it was a holiday. (I think this was a pretext.)

Local Christian Democrats, Social Democrats and trade unionists held a meeting to protest against neo-Nazism and anti-Semitism. Officials of the German Reich Party held a series of press conferences disclaiming any support for anti-Semitism. (One of them said there could not be anti-Semitism in Germany now, as there were not enough Jews – only 30,000 of them.) They also denied that they wanted an authoritarian state. They claimed they were only nationalists who loved Germany and wanted to restore the Reich. The local leader of the party, Willy Kallert, said that as a senior officer, a Standartenführer, in the brown-shirted Nazi SA stormtroopers, he had prevented planned attacks on a local synagogue during the 'Crystal Night' pogrom in November 1938. Because of this he had been classified as a Nazi of only minor responsibility after the war.

Former dive-bomber ace, ex-Colonel Hans-Ulrich Rudel, holder of the highest German decoration awarded in the Second World War – he knocked out about 500 Russian tanks and several warships – was to have been the main speaker at the banned meeting. At a press conference, he said he was not a member of the German Reich Party and was interested in politics only insofar as it affected the treatment of ex-soldiers. Rudel, a handsome, wavy-haired man with a charming manner, is involved in trade with Latin America. He appealed for the release of all former German military men held in prison for offences committed during military operations. He argued that similar offences – such as the shooting of hostages in attempts to combat partisan warfare – had been committed by Allied forces (and were being committed by the French in Algeria), but the victors had not been punished. In his view such acts were a military necessity and should not be punished at all. However, he said that such people as concentration-camp guards who had committed crimes should be punished. He urged that 'Free Europe' should join together against the Communist bloc. He added that, as a pastor's son, he had always opposed discrimination against religious and racial groups. As a career officer, he had not been a Nazi Party member. It was pointed out that, although Rudel had not been allowed to address a meeting in Saarbrücken this weekend, his memoirs had been a bestseller in the United States and France.

While I dislike the ideas of the German Reich Party, I do not consider it to be a threat to German democracy, as it lacks the necessary support. I think the authorities are making a mistake in banning its meetings, for they only make it more interesting to some.

18 January 1960 : To Essen for a Christian Democratic Party meeting at which Chancellor Konrad Adenauer said that anyone who caught a lout daubing swastikas should box his ears; something which, in my view, and in the view of some German newspapers, is against the law. Adenauer softened it a bit by adding that, in the current wave of swastika daubings, it would have been better quickly to convene a court to deal with the first group of offenders, instead of holding them under arrest for some time even after they had confessed, while anti-German feeling grew abroad.

Some people laugh at my woolly ski hat, with a pom–pom on it, but an old man in Essen today said, 'That's the right thing to wear for this weather.' The cap fits my head anyway, unlike most hats.

19 January 1960 : At a get-together with foreign pressmen tonight, two leading Christian Democratic Party officials said there was no hope of German reunification unless the Soviet Union surprisingly changed its policy. I argued later with Michailov of *Pravda* and a Polish Communist colleague that the Soviet Union was storing up trouble for itself by maintaining the division of Germany. They took the view that Germany was safer divided; that trouble could really begin if it were reunited.

22 January 1960 : The interior minister of North-Rhine Westphalia, Josef Dufhues, reporting on the recent anti-Semitic incidents, said they now appeared to be dying down. He said that in only seven out of 65 arrests in his state had there been clear political reasons for the actions; above all, reasons of a neo-Nazi character. Other main reasons were a desire to show off, and drunkenness. Most of the offenders were young, including even children (who might never have seen a Jew). Like Dr Nahum Goldmann, President of the World Jewish Congress, who gave a press conference here yesterday, Dufhues stressed the importance of educating people about Nazism. He also pointed to a difficulty, namely the reluctance of those teachers who had themselves supported the Nazis to teach children the truth about that era. In some areas school books are being reviewed and teachers of history re-screened.

26 January 1960 : Am standing in for a few weeks in Reuters East Berlin office, which I set up last year. The East German Government Press Office issued a statement saying that the East German Communist leader, Walter Ulbricht (East Germany's top leader), had written to Adenauer calling on him to abandon nuclear arming. Later the text of the letter was issued. It rated a high priority because it included the threat that East Germany would ask its allies for missiles if West Germany did not quickly stop nuclear arming and set an arms ceiling. On this issue I'm on Ulbricht's side. West Germany's effort to obtain nuclear arms is a dangerous policy and ought to be stopped. *[In the end West Germany became one of the countries which, in the Nuclear Non-Proliferation Treaty, which took effect in 1970, renounced the production, acquisition and use of nuclear weapons.]*

I don't accept Ulbricht's thesis that West Germany's leaders are planning to attack East Germany, but I do believe that their policy makes conflict more likely. One must, I think, accept the fact that Germany is divided in two and that the Communist world begins on the Elbe, and then get down to negotiating to make the best of it, on a basis of mutual self-interest.

I am currently standing in for our East Berlin correspondent, Brian Horton, who has taken leave to get married. I'm using his battered Volkswagen Beetle. It has only one trafficator working – on the left. So I have to try to do as many left turns, rather than right turns, as possible, especially at crossings where policemen are watching. Hope to have it fixed tomorrow.

28 January 1960 : East Berlin is at its dingiest at the moment, with dirty blobs of old snow, strewn sand and cinders making the pavements look worse kept than usual, which is normally not too good. Two old women – I put one at nearly 70 – in city uniforms swept away cinders and dirt on the pavement in front of our office building today. Pensions are so small that many old people, men and women, have to go out to work.

31 January 1960 : Sunday. Went to the East Berlin Quaker meeting. My present thinking about God and the purpose of the world is that we are not intended to know the answer, for if we did, we would ourselves be gods and everything would be too easy. Though my thoughts often wandered to the mundane, the quiet of the meeting, during which only one person, an old lady, spoke, was conducive to good thoughts.

Ulbricht and Prime Minister Otto Grotewohl today travelled

to Moscow. Possibly they will be preparing their moves for the planned East–West summit conference, including the question of a peace treaty for Germany. I am increasingly of the view that it is time for the West to recognize East Germany and for the two Germanys to negotiate an acceptable *modus vivendi*. Now that socialism is showing definite signs of becoming economically satisfactory one of these days, I believe that the average East German is more concerned about the right to visit his relatives in West Germany, or anywhere else, rather than whether the factory he works in is state-owned or private.

Wrote a report on the first trip of a 12,400-ton former Swedish luxury liner, bought by East Germany to be run as a workers' holiday vessel. Its first trips from Rostock via Gibraltar, Rhodes and Piraeus to Constanza, Romania – passengers returning by air from Bucharest to Berlin – lasting 14 days, will cost 250 marks for trade unionists (about a fortnight's industrial wage), compared with about 4,500 marks for a similar trip in a West German ship. I think to put on such trips is overdoing it when many things are in short supply in East Germany. One should make more efforts to provide first things first. However, I'm in favour of workers getting a chance to go on such ships instead of their being reserved (by price) for the (partly) idle rich. *[The East German scheme made me think of a similar one run by the Nazis, called* Kraft durch Freude *(Strength through Joy).]*

1 February 1960 : To the Berliner Ensemble, the East Berlin theatre company founded by Bertolt Brecht, to see his satire on Hitler's rise to power, *Der Aufhaltsame Aufstieg des Arturo Ui.* (*The Resistible Rise of Arturo Ui*). Brecht's company is now run by his Austrian-Jewish widow, Helene Weigel. *[Weigel died in 1971.]* In the play the main figures in the rise of the Nazis are given counterparts in an American city, concerned mainly with the greengrocery trade. The Nazis are cast as gangsters, who get into the business by blackmail and by keeping workers in a state of fear. Ekkehard Schall, who plays the Hitler character, puts him over as something between comic and awe-inspiring, which I believe he was. There is a touch here and there of Charlie Chaplin's *Great Dictator*. The play emphasizes the support of some industrialists for Hitler which is, of course, a fact. The printed programme is laced with some pretty damning information, none of it really new to me, about what many of Hitler's backers and aides are doing today in West Germany.

An East German Note to the three Western Allies was published tonight. It complained about what it called West German 'provocations' in West Berlin; that is, visits there by West German leaders and West German attempts to act as though West Berlin were part of West Germany. East Germany maintains it is not and even Western Allied spokesmen have said in recent months that it is not. *[When the West German state was set up in 1949, its Basic Law (constitution) declared West Berlin to be one of its* Länder *(states). However, the three Western Allies, who retained supreme occupation power in West Berlin, vetoed this provision. But they allowed West Berlin's integration into the legal, economic, fiscal, monetary and social welfare systems of West Germany. West Berlin was represented in the West German Parliament, but without a vote.]*

3 February 1960 : A long lunch with Gubanov, one of the *Pravda* correspondents, a man of great charm. We discussed religion and atheism. He said one needed something to live for; some had religion and he had Communism. Religion, he said, had been invented by men in primitive times, but was incompatible with science. I agreed there was much superstition and nonsense, but I said – and he agreed – that science had not been able to show what made the universe and thus had not been able to disprove the existence of God. If God were good, why was there so much badness in the world, he asked.

5 February 1960 : A senior West Berlin radio journalist, whom I met at a party, opposed the diplomatic recognition of East Germany, while not excluding negotiations with East Germany on certain issues. His attitude – and I can understand it – is that the West must hold on to its present position and hope, in regard to German reunification, that something will bring about a change in Soviet policy. To recognize East Germany would dash such hopes, he maintained. My view is that we cannot reasonably hope for a change in Soviet policy. Therefore, rejecting war, we must negotiate both with the Soviet Union and East Germany, showing the Communists that the capitalists or the social democrats in the rest of the world do not menace them, encouraging more and more exchanges in the hope that both world systems will in time rub the rough corners off each other.

At the same party a professional couple from East Berlin complained, among other things, about the ban on Western newspapers there. (Of course, unhappily, Communist newspapers are banned in West Germany.)

7 February 1960 : To the main East Berlin Protestant church, the Marienkirche, to hear the monthly Sunday sermon of 73-year-old Bishop Otto Dibelius, head of the All-German Evangelical (Protestant) Church, a confederation of regional churches, and Bishop of the Evangelical (Protestant) Church of Berlin-Brandenburg which, apart from West Berlin, has all its members in surrounding East German (and East Berlin) districts.

Several thousand people packed the church. Bearded Dibelius, who looks rather like the Communist leader, Walter Ulbricht, has recently been criticized by some churchmen, in both East and West Germany, for re-phrasing the church's view on temporal authority by saying that a Christian, in some circumstances, is not bound by laws passed in totalitarian states. One illustration he gave was, that as a Christian, one should not feel bound by traffic laws in a totalitarian state. He withdrew that and other illustrations later, but said, however, that he maintained the principle. Today Dibelius did not repeat his new interpretation of authority, but said, in broad terms, that the Ten Commandments and the Bible were above the law.

Dibelius has also been criticized, by East German figures, for his youthful anti-Semitism. He said today that, as a young student, he had supported criticisms of the Jews made at the turn of the century by a famous Berlin pastor, court chaplain Adolf Stöcker.

Dibelius said that Stöcker's criticisms had been directed at certain aspects of Jewry, which he did not detail. But he added that anyone who had known the situation in Berlin in that respect at the time in question would understand this. He said that this attitude had nothing in common with the racist aggressive attitude of the Nazis towards the Jews. As soon as persecution of the Jews had begun, he said, he and others had known they must go to the aid of the Jews and had done so. He felt, in view of that, that he had the right to express shame at the anti-Semitic graffiti which had recently appeared in West Germany. (I had read earlier that Dibelius did protect a number of Jews during the Nazi era. However, he supported Hitler's 'New Germany' as late as April 1933 – three months after the Nazis had come to power. At that time he appealed for a stop to Jewish immigration into Germany and for 'firmness' by the German race, so that it did not succumb to the Jewish race.)

The Soviet authorities have ended the jamming of BBC broadcasts to the Soviet Union – an important step. They have apparently not stopped jamming the Voice of America, but that is generally felt to be not as objective as the BBC broadcasts.

8 February 1960 : I recently took out to lunch Soviet Embassy deputy press chief, 45-ish Benjamin Sutulov. Today he returned the compliment at the Hungarian restaurant, Budapest, in East Berlin's Stalinallee. Sutulov told me he was a former teacher, which helps to explain why he is so good in helping me with my Russian. *[Another explanation was that he was probably working for the Soviet espionage service, the KGB. I learned later that he tried unsuccessfully to get a colleague of mine into a position where he could blackmail him.]* One of his duties is to sound out Western journalists and others on various political issues. At present there seems to be a fair amount of agreement on basic issues between the British Conservative Government, under Harold Macmillan, and the Soviet Government. By basic I mean the desire to negotiate rather than to shoot, and the desire to make agreements which would tend to reduce tension. Of course, that does not mean that Britain is ready to give up West Berlin in face of Soviet pressure, or that the Soviet Union is ready to hand over East Germany to the West.

10 February 1960 : East Germany's rubber-stamp parliament, the *Volkskammer* (People's Chamber), met today, and instead of repeating the intention to ask the Soviet Union for missiles, set up a new body called the National Defence Council, chaired by Ulbricht, to unify defence measures and keep a watchful eye on West German moves. It looks as though, for the time being at least, Moscow has decided not to go ahead with the missile plan, perhaps in the hope that reserve in this sphere will improve the atmosphere at the planned summit conference.

11 February 1960 : In my East Berlin hotel room, had what might well have been the first game of Scrabble to have been played in the Communist bloc. My opponents were our West Berlin correspondent, Alfred Klühs, and his doctor wife, Gaby. Alf won.

After a meal together in the hotel, I had to pay for what they, West Berliners, had eaten, in West German marks, while I, with a residence permit for East Berlin, could pay in East marks. This is a measure designed to prevent the smuggling of East marks from West Berlin, where they can be bought at an artificially cheap rate.

12 February 1960 : Discussed with two Swiss colleagues the issue of planned West German nuclear armament. Otto Frey of the *Neue Zürcher Zeitung*, a youngish chap, criticized British opponents of the West German plans, while Paul Werner, of the Calvinist *Tribune de Genève*, thought these opponents were right.

Werner, an older man, told me he had been in Berlin during the Nazi period and just did not trust the Germans with nuclear weapons after the way he had seen them act under Nazism.

By rail sleeper to Oberhof, a major winter-sports resort in

Thuringia, about 150 miles south-west of Berlin. Before turning in, chatted with a pleasant house painter, a member of the SED. He told me he had joined the party, fairly recently, because he felt the Communist state was being run in the interest of the majority. From his experience of SED discussions at lower levels, he considered the party to be democratic. He criticized some East Germans who, he said, were not in the least thankful for the social services they had in the Communist state, but just took them for granted and criticized other things.

13 February 1960 : Around 5 am, after we had passed through snow-clad fir forests, we emerged from a tunnel at our destination. A loudspeaker voice announced, 'Oberhof, station of German-Soviet friendship'. I stepped out to see a sign: 'Oberhof, workers' spa'. Another sign said: 'Photography forbidden'. A railway official told me photography is forbidden on all rail property, but he added with a grin that some people managed to take snaps at Oberhof station after all. Other posters gave a welcome to international sportsmen.

A bus took half an hour on winding uphill roads to reach the village of Oberhof itself, once a renowned holiday resort for the better-off. The houses were mainly faced with wooden tiles. Most of them were guesthouses named after Communist personalities or ideas, such as (Georgi) Dimitrov and *Einheit* (Unity).

At the regional office of the Communist trade union organization, which organizes workers' holidays throughout East Germany, I was received by a little grey-haired wiry man with a lined face: Werner Urban, 45, who runs the holidays organization in the region, about one-fourteenth of the country, but quite an important holiday area. Urban told me he had been a Communist before the Nazis came to power, had been briefly imprisoned by them and later served in the German Army. He joined the re-founded Communist Party after the war.

Urban said that, in this region, the trade unions and individual state-owned factories catered for 230,000 holidaymakers a year, of whom 30,000 came to Oberhof, a village of about 1,300 people.

The trade union holidays are heavily subsidized but, Urban added, Oberhof also had room for about 5,000 unsubsidized holidaymakers. Oberhof, which started to become a resort around 1800, had its last big pre-war skiing competitions in 1931, as the Nazis turned to Garmisch in Bavaria for the biggest events, perhaps because Oberhof was to some extent patronized – and owned – by Jews. Urban said the Communist trade union organization acquired quite a number of hotels through confiscation when, around 1950, the owners were sentenced for black-marketeering, though some of the owners either got their hotels back later, or were compensated, when it was proved that the court verdicts had been 'incorrect'. More hotels were bought by the trade union organization later, and others take trade union guests on a contractual basis. Six million East German trade union members and their families, out of the total population of 17 million, are eligible for the cheap holidays.

I was quartered in a miners' guesthouse, used mainly for foreign delegations. It serves proper coffee for breakfast, whereas those for the normal trade union guests provide grain coffee. However, the trade union guests, enjoying such cheap holidays, can usually afford to order a cup of real coffee at an extra charge.

In my guesthouse a middle-aged East German trade union official, Fred Goder, who had been a political refugee in Britain during the Nazi era, was minding four British trade union shop stewards who had been invited to come and see some of East Germany's 'socialist achievements'. During my two-day stay in Oberhof I had many talks with these chaps and found it valuable to hear their viewpoints. Basically they took the view that East Germany was on the right road and were doubtful that Britain could progress without going Communist. From their positions on the shop floor, they saw British capitalists as being in business mainly to cream profits from their employees' work. While they recognized that East Germany is a dictatorship, they considered it to be a dictatorship of the workers – the majority – working in the interests of the majority to improve life all round.

One of the shop stewards worked for the British Motor

Corporation. *[This firm was at that time a hotbed of disruptive left-wing trade unionism. After various ownership and name changes it was bought – then named Rover – by the German firm, BMW, in January 1994. After making considerable losses, BMW sold Rover to a British consortium in May 2000.]* This shop steward, Les – he would not tell me his second name, saying he had been misrepresented by journalists before – said that after touring several East German factories he believed that, for the effort the workers expended (far less than in a British private firm where working methods are highly organized), East German workers were earning more all round than British workers. *[There was some truth in this view. It was said of workers in the Communist bloc, 'We pretend to work and you pretend to pay us.']* I think that most British workers prefer to work harder and earn more than the East Germans do. One of the shop stewards told me he had been perturbed when members of a Czechoslovak delegation he had met were not allowed to give their addresses for an exchange of letters. He thought this was carrying security too far. These four men were impressed by the workers' holidays system and asked me if I had seen anything like it in Britain. Of course I haven't, but the average British worker – unlike the average East German worker – can afford a reasonable holiday at the seaside.

During the day, joined a ski class including a doctor and his doctor wife, a foreign trade official and an engineer. The elderly teacher was called Schweizberger, which almost means 'Swiss mountains'. Everything still looked very Christmassy, with snow frozen on the trees.

14 February 1960 : During talk in the dining-room with the British trade unionists and several East Germans, we discussed the question of journalistic objectivity. I maintained that Reuters tried to attain this, though admitting that this could not always be achieved. I said I should think more positively of the uniform East German press if they began, at least in their news columns, to print the full versions of important statements by Western leaders instead of printing only the parts which suited them.

By train to the large city of Erfurt, some 50 miles to the north-east, to visit my Communist friend, Wolfgang Warzok, an agricultural journalist on a paper which is designed to get private farmers to accept the idea of joining collectives. *[After the reunification of Germany in 1990, I learned that Warzok, a man I liked, had been one of the main informers about me to the East German secret police, the Stasi.]* Warzok and the editor of the Erfurt regional paper, *Das Volk*, a man called something like Czarplinski, who had studied journalism in Leningrad, discussed with me the East German allegation that West Germany was planning to launch a blitzkrieg against East Germany. They could not convince me that the East Germans really had any proof of that allegation.

15 February 1960 : Back in Berlin, Austrian Communist journalist, Peter Gellert, told me about an Italian Communist friend of his, who is bringing up his small son as an atheist, and was delighted when the boy came home from his Roman Catholic school to announce he had made a convert to atheism. His pal, Rodolfo, had told him that he no longer believed in the Guardian Angel – something they had been taught about at school. The Communist's son was pleased and told his Dad that Rodolfo had said, 'I don't believe in the Guardian Angel any more. I only believe in God.'

16 February 1960 : Lunched with Professor Pichotka, a West German, who heads the physiology faculty at the East Berlin Humboldt University. He told me he took the job partly because it is professionally important and partly because he wants to help the two sides of Germany understand one another. Not a Communist. Like me he feels the East German Communists are being utterly stupid in their petty harrying of scientists who are not party members. He said that the favouritism being given to those students who are politically loyal was causing educational standards to fall. While scientists were well paid, many of them were leaving for the West because they did not, for instance, want their children to be virtually forced to accept the atheistic youth dedication ceremony instead of confirmation in the Church, or because they were angry at not being allowed to read the books and newspapers they wanted. Pichotka said it had taken him several years to get permission for some of his assistants to attend scientific congresses in the West.

19 February 1960 : The Soviet Army authorities in East Germany have issued controversial new passes to the three Western Allied military missions (from the United States, Britain and France) which, since 1945, have been accredited to their forces in East Germany. (The Soviet Army has a counterpart mission in West Germany.) The new passes refer, for the first time, to the Western Allied missions being in the 'German Democratic Republic' and say they are registered with the republic's Interior Ministry. As the Western powers do not recognize the GDR, they have issued an official protest and declared the new passes to be unacceptable. The missions are staying put, either in their West Berlin headquarters, or in their branch offices in Potsdam, in nearby East Germany. They are travelling between these two offices, but are not making their normal journeys around East Germany to do their routine spying. Today I called at the three branch offices in Potsdam, each in a separate villa guarded by East German police who, however, are not allowed to check the mission members themselves. I was allowed to the door of the villas, but the occupants were tight-lipped, on instructions from above. All this byplay is, of course, linked to the Soviet intention to turn over control of all traffic between West Berlin and West Germany to the East Germans, including Western Allied military traffic along the autobahn, until now checked by the Soviet forces. Other traffic is already under East German control.

20 February 1960 : Interviewed several East Berliners on the street last night to get a little light reaction to the birth to Queen Elizabeth of a second son *[later christened Andrew]*. Got different views, ranging from 'Queens are no different from anyone else, so why make a fuss?' to 'a glorious day for Britain'. The most interesting point was that all those I questioned had heard the news on Western radio or television.

My spell of duty in East Germany ended this afternoon. On my roundabout way home, I called first on Elfi's cousin, Margot Schellberg, at the state farm of Gross Bäbelin, in the north-west of East Germany about 70 miles from the West German border. Her husband, Hans-Dieter, is an under-manager on this large farm, in charge of work on the fields as opposed to the dairy and poultry side of things. He told me that last year the farm was subsidized to the extent of about one-sixth of its income, but had recently got a new manager who seemed to be improving matters. There's a great drive on in East Germany to make state and collective farms pay their way.

After only a brief visit to the Schellbergs, I drove some 30 miles westwards to the large city of Schwerin, near the Baltic, to visit Elfi's only uncle, Hermann Engler, a dairy manager, his wife and their grown-up children. None of them is a Communist, but the trend of our chat was that they resent being regarded as poor relations by the West Germans, that they are not doing so badly and that you can't just dismiss Communism as rubbish. I stayed till around midnight.

21 February 1960 : Around 1 am today, as I made for the West German frontier at Lauenburg, south of Hamburg, I began to drive down a slope on a wooded stretch of road. (I was driving Brian Horton's Volkswagen coupé.) Thanks to ice on the road, the badly tyred car spun round at about 30 mph, out of control, and came to rest by banging its rear end on a whitewashed stone marking the edge of the road. There was moderate damage to the rear of the rear-engined car. The motor still worked, but the car would not climb the slope back on to the road proper. I got out. A motorbike came along. Stupidly I stood and waved. Result: he skidded on the ice too, threw himself and his pillion rider off. Neither hurt. They helped me get the car back on the road.

Was about to set off again when a car approached, braked slightly on seeing my lights, spun around and banged against a heap of sand. Its steering was damaged and it could go no further. Driver and three passengers smelled of alcohol. The result of it all: had to hang around for a couple of hours until the police took details of the German car driver's comprehensive insurance, and let me go. Glad they did not see Brian's car in daylight, otherwise they might have acted differently. Reached West Germany at about 5 am and, after some hours' sleep, drove home.

22 February 1960 : For a fortnight I am standing in for John Bush as news editor – deputy to the chief correspondent, Gerry Long. This means that, in consultation with Gerry when I think it necessary, I must arrange all our news coverage in West and East Germany and West Berlin, and to be generally in charge of the detailed running of affairs. The job is not my choice because it is too bitty and leaves too little time for writing, which is what I like doing. But it is interesting to see the problems involved in the job – problems I have previously seen from an underling's point of view.

29 February 1960 : An eleven-hour day, like most of them since I've been standing in as news editor. Wrote about the Cologne Rose Monday carnival procession and others in the Rhineland. Saw some of them on TV. On one carnival float Adenauer was shown accepting the verdict of the electorate after winning the 1970 election. I hope that does not turn out to be true. *[Adenauer resigned the chancellorship in 1963, aged 87.]*

4 Agadir: earthquake aftermath

2 March 1960 : With about ten other journalists, I boarded a United States Air Force C-130 turbo-jet this evening in Ramstein, Rhineland Palatinate, to be flown to the American air-base at Nouasseur, near Casablanca, Morocco – a flight of about six hours. We were going to report on the aftermath of an earthquake which, on 29 February, devastated Agadir, on the Atlantic coast about 240 miles south of Casablanca. About 5,000 people are believed killed or injured out of the total local population of 40,000. Our plane is also carrying a lorry and two trailers packed with rescue and aid materials. Our seats are against the side of the aircraft and some of us have our knees under the lorry or trailers. Being in this plane is like travelling in a flying ferryboat. One can't see out. Taking off produced just a roar, and it was impossible to tell when we had left the ground.

3 March 1960 : 'Welcome to Morocco', said a colourful fresco on the wall outside the arrival lounge at the United States base at Nouasseur. We arrived there at about 1.30 am local time (same as GMT), after covering about 1,250 miles. Ninety minutes later, refuelled, we flew another 350 miles southwards, winging over the 15,000-feet *[4,572 m]* Atlas Mountains and landing at a French naval base about five miles south of Agadir.

Resisting the desire to have a couple of hours' sleep, I interviewed a young US naval ensign, who told me the Moroccan authorities estimated the total dead at 5,000. Fresh water was still being taken into the city from the base. No epidemic reported, but there was a definite health hazard. About 100 airlift planes had landed in the past 24 hours, mainly American. Nations taking part in the aid operation, apart from French from the base, included Spanish, Portuguese, Dutch and British. No telephone contact with the outside world. Contact being kept with Casablanca and other bases by transmitters flown in by the voluntary US-Government-supported military affiliate radio system (MARS), manned by US Air Force 'hams'.

There are now about 250 American soldiers trying to remove more survivors from the rubble. An American captain, William R. Andrews of Jacksonville, Arkansas, had been in charge of one team digging in the rubble. He told me, 'The first batch we brought in were mostly injured. As we dug deeper in the rubble, naturally there were dead. Even up to last night we were picking out live ones.' His group had saved 19 people. Sometimes when bodies were brought out, half-crazed relatives would grab them and not allow them to be carried away for burial. The American team had come across a father sitting on the ruins of his house, knowing the rest of his family to be buried beneath.

From the Hotel Saada (Happiness), which had been housing about 80 European guests in this palm-lined sub-tropical paradise – average of 360 sunny days a year! – Mrs Sue Martin, the wife of a United States Air Force lieutenant, had been released slightly injured 38 hours after the quake. (I heard later that this woman had offered to recite Shakespeare to her rescuers.) Her husband and baby had got out unharmed earlier. About 50 people died in the Saada. Two young tourists saved their lives by going for a midnight swim. Their parents inside were killed.

Describing the scene in the city, Captain Andrews said, 'Buildings are laid in sandwiches on top of one another. I hope we never see anything like that again. The smell is awful.' Tomorrow, he said, spraying of disinfectant would start – to neutralize the odour of putrefying bodies – and soldiers would wear masks.

I hastily typed out the details of these interviews, so that Captain

Andrews could take my reports back to his base in Casablanca and have them phoned through to Finlay Campbell, my colleague there.

Shortly after dawn I was taken into the city in an American Army lorry. On the outskirts bulldozers were scraping out mass graves for the bodies, which lay on the green grass under coloured robes or drapes. Occasionally a camel was to be seen, and more often an ass. Women were mainly veiled. Men wore the Arab burnous. Inland the mountains, green and brown, with the clear, blue sky behind, made a beautiful sight.

We passed the tents and makeshift shelters of refugees and reached the southern outskirts of the city. The area we came to first was the New City, not more than 20 or 30 years old, composed of what were attractive modern buildings in pastel shades – hotels, offices, apartment blocks and the like – standing on broad avenues. For the first few hundred yards damage to buildings appeared minor, though virtually every building had been affected. Then we came to scenes of absolute destruction, where the quake shocks had completely torn down handsome buildings. The Hotel Saada on the seafront, which had been of three or four storeys, was a mere heap of rubble less than one storey high, still with the almost intact hotel sign in Latin and Arabic letters on the top.

Our lorry drove northwards, to the next main section of the city, the Medina, or old city. The Medina stands largely on a hillside sloping down to the sea and is, at a guess, 80 per cent destroyed, perhaps partly because its buildings were older. Soldiers from our lorry restarted their task of clambering on the ruins, calling to see if anyone replied and digging out the live and the dead. Some Moroccans in colourful Arab robes sat stunned by their belongings – primitive bedsteads, brass ornaments, bundles of clothing – which they had salvaged from their houses. An advert in English for a washing powder, still fastened to the wreck of a building, said something like, 'Tide washes whiter.' One row of houses, the backs gone, looked like a Hollywood set. But on the rubble stood a Moroccan who told us his whole family was trapped in there. Squashed cars peeped out from heaps of masonry. Seagulls circled above, almost like vultures.

Although I had a bad cold, I could smell the sweetish odour of decaying corpses, some of which, removed from the rubble, lay on the roadside. Maybe the world would be something like this after a nuclear war, I thought. But it was heartening to see men of several nations digging in the ruins. There were steel-helmeted Moroccan police and soldiers side by side with French sailors, between whom relations have been bad since Moroccan independence in 1955 and the French refusal to quit Moroccan bases. On the sea front I saw mud and water left by a tidal wave which swept up to about 200 yards inland in certain places after the quake.

A 20-year-old American aircraftman, Elmer Horne of Fort Worth, Texas, digging in the Medina, told me that he and some 30 comrades had found three survivors and six bodies within the last day or so. General opinion today was that it is possible, but not probable, that more persons are alive. (It turned out, in fact, that people were brought out alive until well into the next week.)

Though it is only early March, temperatures in the bright sunshine rise to about 36° Celsius. I got too much sun today, as I had no hat. If one forgot the destruction and the dead for a moment, the scene in the Medina, with the sunshine and birds twittering in the palms, was peaceful.

The third main part of Agadir, to the north, is the walled Moroccan Kasbah, or Arab city, on a hilltop. This, which I did not visit, is almost absolutely razed, having been built mainly of baked mud. Many hundreds are dead or trapped in its ruins. More than once I felt that I ought to stop collecting information and give a hand in the digging, but then I reasoned that it was also of use to the citizens of Agadir that the world should know of their plight and respond accordingly.

My task today was to concentrate on foreign angles – non-Moroccans affected by the quake – so I returned to the Hotel Saada, where the French manager, Henri Remaut, told us in what remained of its pleasant garden that about 24 persons had come out alive and four dead. I saw the bodies of what were believed to be a British couple brought out. (We were shown a letter apparently sent to the husband from Glasgow.) At Agadir's damaged hospital a friendly Moroccan doctor showed me a little silver medal, marked 'Rowdy', which a young German man killed in the quake had worn round his neck. I was told that mass burial of all Moroccan dead had been ordered to combat the danger of epidemic, even though mass burial is contrary to Muslim tradition.

Back at the air base by early afternoon, I typed three copies of my evening story while waiting to fly back to Casablanca. One copy was supposed to be transmitted via the American cruiser, *Newport News*, which had reached Agadir. That copy never arrived. The second copy I sent to Casablanca in a plane in which I was not allowed to travel, but I got to Finlay Campbell before that copy did. The third copy I took along with me. It seemed phenomenal to be flying nearly 300 miles to work each morning and back again at night. I was living off tinned American rations, reminding me of days in the Second World War when the motor torpedo boat flotilla in which I was a navigating officer was operating from Leghorn, Italy, with a flotilla of US torpedo boats.

At the modern El Mansour hotel in Casablanca's European quarter I met Finlay Campbell for the first time, a little dark-haired humorous hot-tempered Francophile and Germanophobe Scot from our Paris office, who had been in Agadir yesterday. Finlay was still struggling with communications to Europe – had been having hours of telephone delay. Fortunately a large British insurance and shipping firm, L. Barber Ltd – known by some in Casablanca as El Baba – kindly let us use their telex, giving almost immediate communication with Paris or Bonn, from where Reuters has private lines to London. Barber's office in Agadir had been wrecked by the quake and one of their seven employees killed – that young German whose medal I had been shown! After a meal with Finlay in a French restaurant with mock Tudor ambience I fell asleep, exhausted, in the second bed in the luxurious room Finlay had taken.

Cannot forget the German colleague who, given a pink wax earplug as we began our return flight from Agadir today, popped it in his mouth, thinking it was chewing-gum. Later, when I gave him a sweet, he pretended to stick it in his ear.

4 March 1960 : My turn to work in Casablanca while Finlay flew to Agadir again. He returned in the evening with the news that the search for survivors would end tonight, except where cries were heard during demolition and disinfecting operations. Spent part of the night arguing with Finlay about the merits and demerits of Germans.

5 March 1960 : Flew to Agadir again. A sign in the Casablanca air base took my fancy: 'Grill steak with everything.' That sounds like the United States. Am filled with admiration for the US Air Force, both as an organization and as regards the individuals I have met on this operation. They are doing their job with good humour, modesty and plenty of hard work. It is most inspiring, as though we were living in a future world where an international organization automatically jumps in with great resources to combat any catastrophes.

Since yesterday journalists have been forbidden to enter the city of Agadir, which is being put under strict quarantine in case of epidemic, while aid workers spray buildings with DDT and chloride of lime and bulldozers level the worst sections.

This evening the Moroccan Crown Prince, Moulay Hassan, gave the most picturesque press conference I have ever attended, in a garden at his headquarters, the reddish sandstone palace of the Caid (governor-cum-judge) at Inezgane, about six miles south of Agadir. A fairytale tent, embroidered with multi-coloured Byzantine-like designs, had been put up. A few yards away there stood Hassan's modern caravan, with an awning under which had been placed a couple of low divans and a colourful rug. Hassan sat on a step of the caravan while journalists lounged on the divans and rug.

Hassan, in khaki uniform with a general's red tabs, impressed me with the quick and clear way he answered questions in French. He said the present estimate of casualties was 10,000 to

12,000 dead, of whom about 5,000 had been brought out of the ruins. He said that where engineers, levelling off ruins, considered that someone could still be trapped in an air space, efforts would continue to get them out. Otherwise, rescue work had stopped. The last people to be rescued, so far as is known, were two women found by American engineers yesterday.

At the naval air base, where I overnighted on a camp bed, I came across a 37-year-old Frenchman, Jacques Strozza, who had lived in Agadir. He was having superficial cuts and bruises treated. He told me and some American officers that he, his wife Denise, aged 28, and their son Patrick, aged three, had been saved 14 hours after the quake, after being trapped in a double bed.

This was his story: 'My wife said, "Papa, we are dying," and just at that moment our bed – on the first floor of a four-storey block – dropped through to the ground floor and the block collapsed. We were saved only because a cupboard with some cases on it fell on the foot of the bed during the early tremors. When, later, the roof collapsed, the cupboard held it up over our bed, leaving a small space.' (In the next room his other son, Jacqui, aged 11, and his mother-in-law had been killed by falling masonry.)

'Dust filled the air. We breathed it in. I was on my side with my child partly under me. My wife was at right angles to us, with her head near my head. I could touch her. We spoke all the time. We never gave up, neither did Patrick. He cried from time to time, waking up and asking for something to drink. He said, "My glass is on the bedside table, give it to me."

'I told him it was broken and that the house was broken. He said it was not and told me to put on the light and give him something to drink. When one is lying there one thinks a lot. I thought, perhaps one of us has some injury and is losing blood and will die. I felt one of Patrick's arms, but could not reach the other. I asked him if anything hurt. He said his stomach hurt. I could touch that so I knew he was not injured. My wife said she was not either. I felt nothing.'

In the ruined second floor above them was a Frenchman

named Turpin. About ten minutes after the quake Turpin cried out, 'My wife is dead.'

Turpin had a watch on and kept calling out the time in answer to cries from Strozza. Patrick wanted to pass water and Strozza told him to do so in the bed, but the little boy said, 'No, I can only do that in the toilet.' He remained dry until rescued.

The hope of rescue began when a man in the ruins of the top floor, Tessier, pushed his way out of the rubble and got one of his two daughters out. Another daughter and his wife were dead.

Tessier heard Strozza calling out and said he would fetch help. He hurried to the nearby naval base and returned with a party of Moroccans who tapped around for a while but, finding no one quickly, gave up. But Tessier did not give up. He fetched French sailors and more Moroccans and in the end 12 people were saved; 19 died.

Strozza continued, 'At one stage my wife again said, "We are going to die," and Patrick answered, "Don't die." I said, "We can't die here." I told my wife we had air and that she should not give up hope. You know what women are; they get excited.'

Several hours later, Turpin was taken out alive and, after this, Strozza said, he noticed a pinpoint of light above his head. Excitedly he pointed this out to his wife and said, 'They are coming.'

Strozza went on, 'We heard orders in French, then tapping to the left and to the right. The nearer they came, the more we felt the tapping would bring the rest of the building down. The pinpoint of light grew larger and I could see shadows moving past it. I heard a Moroccan speaking Arabic. His face was near mine by the hole. I guided his tapping. The hole grew bigger. I said, "Be careful," because I did not want to die after 14 hours. He reached down with his hand. It was black. I thought, "We are saved." I grabbed bricks myself and passed them through to him.'

Then Madame Strozza and Patrick were pulled through the hole. But the hole – bounded by the square steel mesh of what had been a concrete floor – was not large enough for Strozza to get through. The mesh went near Strozza's ear and eyes, and had to be cut. Strozza told the rescuers, 'It doesn't matter if you cut my ear off, but get me out.' They cut the mesh without harming him. But he still could not get out, as he was held by a slab of concrete roof, about eight inches *[20 cm]* thick, resting partly on his chest. He told the rescuers to hit it with a sledgehammer. They put a paper bag over his head and hit the concrete several times. The slab broke. He was free.

After he had been released he saw a friend's house across the road, still standing, and said, 'That's not fair.'

Strozza's final rueful comment to us, 'That's life, and that's death.'

An American Navy chief petty officer, Charles Bordeaux, said he had been about to spend a holiday in Agadir to celebrate the silver wedding anniversary of his French wife's parents. But the quake killed both the parents. He and his wife had managed to salvage a few family mementoes, but no bodies.

6 March 1960 : Another slight earth tremor during the night. In the morning I was told that the tremor woke many soldiers, and some of them ran from their hangars or huts. I – and some of my journalist colleagues – did not wake.

Grey-robed King Mohammed, a handsome 50-year-old, flew in from his capital, Rabat, some 400 miles to the north, with the diplomatic corps, to view the ravaged city and refugee camps. I joined him as he inspected the West German and Italian military hospitals set up to tend the injured. Diplomats with the King were refreshed later at the Caid's palace with Coca-Cola cooled in a Moorish fountain. Morocco's chief geologist, Robert Ambroggi, a Frenchman, told me that Agadir lay on top of two geographical faults believed to extend westwards to the Canaries and eastwards to Tunisia, a total of some 1,300 miles. He said it would be dangerous to build again on the immediate fault area, as there might be more quakes, though no one could say whether they would come soon or in, say, 2,000 years.

In an open-air market, a biblical scene: Arabs mingled with blacks, perhaps the descendants of slaves. I bought a basket and two or three native pots.

7 March 1960 : On the first leg of my journey back to Bonn, a French Noratlas transport plane brought me to Casablanca in the night. At about 5 am, turned in at the El Mansour Hotel for about four hours. After what I'd seen in Agadir, glorious just to lie in the comfy bed of a luxurious hotel room, with a good breakfast to eat, Perrier table water to drink.

8 March 1960 : Got a lift to Paris in a West German Noratlas loaded with about 25 parents and children being evacuated from Agadir. A wonderful atmosphere on this flight, with German officers comforting French mothers and children who were air-sick when we took a buffeting south of Madrid, where we touched down. (I learned later that a plane carrying 85-year-old Sir Winston Churchill had been forced to land at Madrid this afternoon when it hit the same storm. Churchill was bound for Tangier, Morocco, where he sometimes does some painting.)

As we flew over Spain, I chatted with members of the German crew about the attempts of the West German armed forces to obtain the right to have bases in Spain, which is ruled by the dictator, Francisco Franco. In some Western capitals this had raised the spectre of West Germany using Spain as a training, testing or production area for nuclear weapons, which would not be against the letter of NATO and associated treaties. The German crew supported the idea of getting bases in Spain. One argument was that they needed areas for flying training, as a jet pilot flying over West Germany needs to nod only for two or three minutes to find himself over the Communist bloc. That seemed a valid reason to me.

One of the Germans asked me why there were so many attacks on West Germany in the British press. I replied that it was due to mistrust arising out of the war. As we passed over Bilbao, in northern Spain, I asked the Germans jokingly to point out the West German missile factory there – the non-existent brainchild of the British Labour MP, Bob Edwards. They smiled and said it was obscured by a cloud layer. 'Camouflage,' said one of them.

It was dark as we approached Paris Orly airport. It gave us a bit of a shock, when we were nearly down, to hear the engines rev up loudly again. Our plane had been about to land on the wrong runway. This airport is badly lit, one of the Germans told me. Later, as we taxied in, we got stuck in mud, which should not be possible at such an important airport.

The French taxi driver who took me from the Air France terminal to the Reuter office in central Paris was a former Agadir hotel-keeper who had left Morocco three years ago after it had become independent. 'M'sieu,' he told me, 'I know what has happened in Agadir. God has punished the Moroccans because they just would not give the French credit for anything we did out there.'

When I suggested his theory was somewhat shaky, as several hundred French people had also died in the earthquake, he retorted, 'Those were not good French people. They stayed merely to make money.'

As he had told me he was a Catholic, I argued that his view of God's role in the quake hardly accorded with the thinking of his Church. He grinned and said, 'You're right.'

Reuters editorial office, rue du Sentier 36, is a slum, with fittings no better than those at the *Cleckheaton Guardian*, the ancient weekly in West Yorkshire where I worked in 1947.

9 March 1960 : A thrill to see some of the Paris landmarks for the first time since 1946. With a small bouquet of tulips, I took a taxi to a 12-storey modern block in the rue du Val d'Or in the posh suburb of Saint-Cloud. There, on the top floor, I found tall blonde 30-ish Janik Heim de Balsac (*née* le Bomin), whom I first met on a Toulon–Paris train in 1946, when I was a 20-year-old RNVR sub-lieutenant returning home from the Mediterranean and she was a nubile 17-year-old, well guarded by her mother. However, her mother invited me to stay for a couple of days in the palace-like family home, standing in a small park in Saint-Cloud – on condition that I behaved myself. I did. Out of that chance contact arose a long friendship.

Today Janik introduced me to her husband, whom I'd not yet met: Gerald, small, dark and handsome, an impeccably-mannered economist, who works in the big contracting business of Janik's father who, I believe, is a millionaire, at least in franc terms. Also present were their 13-month-old son Michael and their intelligent dachshund, which obeyed my order in French to go into its basket, but apparently could not understand my request that it should come out again, for it stayed there.

The taxi driver who took me to the Reuter office later was a Communist who had the party organ, *L'Humanité*, spread out on his front seat. He said he had waited for years, without result, for Stalin to come to Paris and was now pleased that Khrushchev was planning to come shortly. I told him that if the Communists took power in France he would have to give up his taxi to a state concern or join a cooperative. He said he would not mind.

In the first-class carriage of the train which took me back to Germany was a Frenchman, Jean Letlas, of Algrange, in the Moselle region near the German border. He told me later he had got into the first-class compartment – Reuters is paying for my ticket – with a second-class ticket, hoping the ticket collector would not challenge him. He had festooned the compartment with his coat and bags to give him more room. He said he was a former colonial official who had been in the resistance during the Second World War and was later sent to Buchenwald concentration camp, near Weimar – the site of which I visited in 1958. He had retained a few German words, above all *andererseits* ('on the other hand', often used in arguments).

Today Letlas is a devoted Gaullist. *[De Gaulle had come back to power as Prime Minister during the Algerian crisis of 1958 and had been elected President in 1959.]* This Frenchman told me that whatever de Gaulle did was right with him, though he admitted that some things de Gaulle was doing were not what he, as an ex-colonial, would have done. But if '*le grand Charlie*' (pronounced 'Sharlee') decided on something, it was OK by him. A good thing that de Gaulle is not another Hitler, for in this type of person – of whom there are evidently millions in France – he has fanatically loyal followers. Perhaps, though, if de Gaulle were like Hitler he would not have so many followers.

We were joined in the compartment later by an American

serviceman of French extraction. After Letlas had been challenged by the ticket collector and had to pay the excess, the American told me, while Letlas was in the corridor, that I should not think that all Frenchmen were like that. We agreed that Letlas might have learned that kind of tricky behaviour while in Buchenwald. Letlas told us how Frenchmen at Buchenwald had pinched extra blankets from other prisoners. The Germans ordered prisoners to parade with all their blankets – officially, one each. So 40 Frenchmen appeared on the parade ground with one blanket each made into a turban on their heads. This so aggravated the German in charge of the parade that he did not think to have the Frenchmen's billet searched – where the other blankets were hidden.

As I came home I was filled with a feeling of goodwill to all humanity. Wish I always felt like that, maybe what I experienced in Agadir will help me to recapture that feeling more often.

11 March 1960 : During the night I was in a semi-dream, still trying to get information about Agadir on an imaginary telephone, speaking French. At one stage, when Elfi tried to shut me up, I asked her to help me.

12 March 1960 : Before John Bush returned this lunchtime, I worked out the office schedule for next week, giving everyone more days off than they would have had from John, who is more concerned about sending more news to London than giving everyone the minimum of days off we theoretically get here: that is, $1^1/2$ days a week, half a day less than in London, and our shifts are often longer than in London. I – and I'm not the only one – regard John's attitude as encouragement to Reuters to keep the staff at a lower level than it ought to be. Reuters tends to appoint news editors willing to cooperate in such a system. If anyone in Bonn complains, the answer is that they can go back to London, where the writ of the National Union of Journalists runs – a five-day week and overtime paid – but few want to do that as Reuters HQ is, for most of us, not a pleasant place to work in.

46

5 The Soviets and German unity

14 March 1960 : Talked to highly-decorated former *Wehrmacht* major, Dr Erich Mende, handsome chairman of the Free Democrats, a minor opposition party which is a mixture of liberals and conservatives. Mende had recently had dinner with the Soviet Ambassador, Andrei Smirnov. According to press reports Smirnov had said in effect at that dinner that there would be no German reunification if West Germany did not embrace Communism. On closely questioning Mende, I found that Smirnov had not said that at all; he had merely reiterated the known Soviet position, namely, that the two German states must negotiate on reunification and that West Germany must renounce revanchism and nuclear arms. Of course, it is better for Adenauer's propaganda to represent the Russians as saying what they didn't say; that way it is much easier to justify Adenauer's wrong policy.

16 March 1960 : When I took the boys swimming to the old Bonn baths for the first time in months, Chris, who is seven, was delighted to find he was bigger and had more of himself sticking out of the water in the shallow end. He said, 'I'm grown enough.' At home, having a slight argument with Elfi, was interrupted by Chris who said, '*Mutterquäler*' (mother torturer). We don't know where he picked this up.

18 March 1960 : After accepting a glass of slivovitz – plum brandy – from a Yugoslav diplomat the other day, broke my teetotalism for the second time this week by taking a glass and a half of champagne at the wedding reception of my Yorkshire-born colleague, Lionel Walsh, 29, who had married a Rhineland girl, Veronika Hoene. That champagne may have been the cause of a great stupidity I committed this afternoon when I used the word 'snap' as the tag – or slug, as we call it – for a story about a cold spell. 'Snap' is the code word for a high-priority message. Gerry who, of course, spotted this, asked me if I realized what I had been doing. I said, of course not, otherwise I wouldn't have done it. My mind must have been near-blank at the time.

21 March 1960 : Excellent cup of coffee in the Defence Ministry, where I gleaned some details of talks between the minister, Franz-Josef Strauss, and visiting US Defence Secretary Thomas S. Gates. One issue was, of course, West Germany's desire to obtain military depots in Spain, which the US seems to be half backing, at least. Militarily, I think the Germans have a good case, but there is the memory of Hitler's military and political support for Franco. It would be much better if the Germans were working for disarmament, and putting Central Europe under international arms control, than doing all they can to build up their military striking power within NATO.

23 March 1960 : John immediately accepted London's criticism of a story of mine which he had sub-edited and passed. I had quoted a West German spokesman as 'discounting' an Israeli report that Adenauer had promised the Israeli leader, David Ben-Gurion, a loan at a recent meeting. I went on to give the spokesman's actual words: 'The Chancellor has reported to us on his meeting with Mr Ben-Gurion, and we have not the slightest information about such a report (about a loan).' To me, that fitted well the meaning of the word 'discount'. Gerry has a much more independent – and acute – mind on such matters.

As a dinner guest at the flat of Boris Yurinov, correspondent of the Soviet news agency TASS, I felt obliged to compromise with Yurinov on alcohol, as he seems congenitally incapable of understanding why someone should not want at least a small drink. So I took a little whisky – of which I like the bouquet – with a large amount of soda. After, as usual, having far too much to eat, we surprised them by producing Scrabble, which we all proceeded to play in Russian, German and English, using a mixture of Latin and Cyrillic letters – some appear in the Latin alphabet – for the Russian words. Elfi won of course, with me a poor second.

Boris told us of a recent interesting assignment for his agency, TASS. He went to Munich to write about Lenin's associations with the city, on the occasion of the ninetieth anniversary of the birth of the founder of Soviet Communism, which falls on 22 April. Lenin lived in Munich for, I think, several months under an assumed name and published the first issues of his newspaper, *Iskra* (*The Spark*), from there. Lenin used to enjoy walking in Munich's 'English Garden', a park. *[During the Cold War the headquarters of the anti-Communist, American-financed Radio Free Europe, which broadcast to the Communist satellite countries, was on the edge of the 'English Garden'.]* Boris also visited Stuttgart, where Lenin attended a congress of the Second International in 1907 – along with Ramsay MacDonald, the Labour Party leader. I told Boris about my efforts in Aachen to dig up more of the history of Julius Reuter. While comparing the two tasks, I did not imply that Reuter was as great a man as Lenin. *[Today I would say that Reuter had a much more positive influence on the world than Vladimir Ilich.]*

25 March 1960 : Have read a history of Ackworth, a Quaker co-educational boarding school near Pontefract, Yorkshire, where we may send Robin. It seems to be imbued with a good Christian spirit, overriding the desire for mere examination successes. The school – with about 450 pupils – is also a mirror of changes in Quakerism. For a considerable time after its foundation in the late eighteenth century, dancing and music were forbidden as sinful. Those days are long gone. I particularly liked one quote in the history – what a master said to a girl: 'If thou can't be good, be as good as thou canst.' Much tolerance expressed there.

Chris graduated to his first pair of Bavarian-type real leather shorts, handed down from Robin. He was delighted. I tested their insulation powers by seeing whether it hurt when I smacked his bottom. He maintained it didn't.

26 March 1960 : Questioned Fritz Erler, deputy chairman of the Social Democratic *Bundestag* group, about the closed committee sessions at the current Anglo-German Königswinter Conference, an élite annual event attended by politicians, journalists, business-men etc. He told me that the German side, including Social Democrats, had been disappointed to find that most of the British, of varied political views, were ready to cement the *status quo* in Europe by means of treaties, including the diplomatic recognition of East Germany. The Germans oppose this on the ground that it would seal the division of Germany. German par-ticipants had warned the British that such action could cause a crisis of confidence between West Germany and the Western Allies and might result in West Germany turning away from democracy.

The situation is a particularly sad one from the Social Democrats' point of view because, for years, they have warned Adenauer that if he made no move towards relaxing tension in central Europe, by means of a regional disarmament scheme, the result would be to harden the division of Germany. Thus, in a sense, Adenauer himself is responsible for creating the present British viewpoint, which is based on the desire to reach some kind of *modus vivendi* with the Russians instead of continuing the arms race.

28 March 1960 : Had a worthwhile discussion about religion with Herr Arnade, a lawyer employed by the All-German Evangelical (Protestant) Church's office in Bonn. When I told him I couldn't believe in religious dogmas, as varying churches had varying dogmas, he said he thought the essence of

Christianity was helping one's neighbour. I replied that while I was glad to hear him say that, it could equally apply to other religions and to some Communists. He agreed. To be a Christian, he said, one had to believe in the Trinity and in Jesus as the Son of God. I passed over the Trinity and told him I did not know what the Son of God meant, and anyway did not believe in such a concept. He said he had learnt to believe as a child, and if he were to use his reason he would not believe any more. I don't go along with that approach.

What a contrast to that talk about religion when, later, I phoned US Army Warrant Officer Albert C. Schweikert, from Pacific Springs, California, to interview him about the stabbing, not fatal, of his wife earlier today by a 13-year-old German boy – a friend of his son. The boy, from a poor family, had learned that 700 marks (about £60) had been put away in the Americans' house and tried to find it. Coming across the wife in the house, he tried to kill her with a kitchen knife and by hitting her on the head with a tennis racket in a press, then fled. Neighbours rushed her to hospital, where her life was saved.

2 April 1960 : Wrote about the farming situation in East Germany, where in recent weeks nine out of the 14 regions have reported either total farm collectivization or a decision in principle to carry that out. Those announcements came after a campaign in which all kinds of pressure had been used, including arrests in a few cases, to get farmers to join the collectives.

Buttonholed Defence Minister Franz-Josef Strauss, the bulky Bavarian son of a butcher, as he waited at Bonn airport for Adenauer to return from the USA and Japan. He said the question of whether West Germany would need military depots in Spain, after already obtaining some within the NATO area, would need further study. He also said he hoped European NATO countries, in particular France, Britain and West Germany, would agree on a European tank design. Strauss was friendly but, I felt, sly. I don't like the look of him. *[He did, however, have much intelligence and charm.]*

Adenauer, looking cheerful, said nothing of note after Lufthansa's first polar-route flight from Japan. I was irritated by a couple of banners, obviously financed by some organization – I was told later it was the Catholic News Agency – welcoming him back. The banners were carried by four people who, unlike the general public, had been allowed through a police barrier.

At a party tonight given by *Baltimore Sun* correspondent, Bynum Shaw, I used my Russian to argue with a First Secretary from the Soviet Embassy, J.V. Siborov. I told the Russian he did not know the true facts about the situation in East Germany where, I maintained, a majority were against the government. He, in his turn, said it was I who did not know the facts. I said he perhaps knew the facts about the Soviet Union – where, I believe the majority today support the government – but not about East Germany. At least he was complimentary about my Russian.

3 April 1960 : Up at 5 am to start about a fortnight's leave by driving to England. After we reached Dover on the car ferry, Elfi firmly kept me on the left-hand side of the road. Once again, we found England quaint. This impression was underlined by the first stretch of road outside Dover, walled and rather narrow.

4 April 1960 : After a whopping English breakfast in our hotel on the outskirts of London, we drove into central London, where we found traffic heavy, but not as bad as recent newspaper reports had led us to expect. We even managed to park the car, without charge, on Blackfriars embankment. We lunched in one of Joseph Lyons' self-service restaurants, after taking the boys to see the changing-of-the-guard at Buckingham Palace from one busbied regiment to another. Roads near the palace were festooned with Union Jacks and French tricolours for General de Gaulle's state visit, beginning tomorrow. London looked wonderful, but I also remembered the smog I have suffered from there.

While Elfi and the boys were delighted at Madame Tussaud's waxworks – distorting mirrors gave them their biggest laugh – I had prospective job interviews at *The Times* and at Labour Party headquarters, Transport House. *[No job offers ensued.]* When we came back to our car, we found a note on our windscreen from two homesick Germans, unnamed, asking us to take greetings to 'Old Germany'.

6 April 1960 : In Halifax, Yorkshire, near my hometown, Bradford, bought an off-the-peg suit for £10 10s and a sports jacket for £7. At the *Halifax Courier*, the evening paper where I worked from 1947 to 1949, the boys were allowed to see the printing press working.

7 April 1960 : Calling at another of my former workplaces, the *Bradford Telegraph & Argus*, I learned more about last year's printers' strike, during which, at this and some other papers, the journalists were ordered out by the executive of our union, the National Union of Journalists. The executive felt that the journalists should not provide copy for a newspaper being brought out by managers and staff from other departments. Most of the journalists in Bradford, and in quite a number of other places, decided to carry on working. I feel that if I had been working at the *T. & A.* I would have come out. How would the journalists have felt if they were striking and the printers had accepted copy from non-journalists? Looking through back numbers of the paper, I found some of my reports from Agadir.

8 April 1960 : We visited my oldest friend, Peter Fox, a farmer at Elvington, near York (about 100 acres *[40 ha]*, 65 milk cattle). We chatted about the concept of farm collectivization. As a tenant farmer with capital, he is naturally against the idea, but said he could understand that farm workers might favour it, on a voluntary basis. It is, he told me, becoming increasingly hard for anyone to become a farmer in Britain without a large slice of capital. He argued that it was an efficient, and therefore good, thing that small farmers who became uneconomic were bought out by bigger ones, whereas I felt that such a situation could become unhealthy, reducing the wealth of one section of the population.

53

9 April 1960 : In Morecambe, on the Lancashire coast, visited an old family friend, 'Uncle' Stanley Ramsden, who had fought against the Germans in East Africa during the First World War. He was interested to learn from me that the German commander in that campaign, General Paul Lettow-Vorbeck, had recently celebrated his ninetieth birthday in Hamburg. Stanley had helped to escort the general into imprisonment in 1918. He showed me the programme of a ceremonial dinner from the later twenties at which Lettow-Vorbeck and his former opponent, General Jan Smuts, were the main speakers. *[Lettow-Vorbeck died in 1964.]*

13 April 1960 : Had an interview with Harry Whewell, news editor of the *Manchester Guardian* in that paper's homely office building. *[It had long been an ambition of mine to work for the Guardian, but the interview led nowhere].*

15 April 1960 : While we have been staying in Bradford with Mum, have appreciated her open fire – something I still miss in Germany, while appreciating the more modern heating there. Would like both if I designed a house.

17 April 1960 : On our way back to Germany today, we drove on Britain's first major motorway, the M1, which gives about 80 miles of crossing-free motoring from Lutterworth, south of Leicester, to the approaches of London near Elstree. The tarmac motorway has three lanes on each side, compared with two on the German autobahns. It was a strange feeling to be driving along an autobahn with *English* countryside around us, like being in a film about the future.

18 April 1960 : On our way through Belgium we spent a couple of hours in the pleasant flat of Communist journalist Martin Thijs, whom I got to know in East Germany in 1958, and his Social Democratic wife. *[My diary does not state where Thijs was living then, but I think it was in a suburb of Antwerp.]* As well as being a Communist, Thijs is also a Flemish nationalist, hating the strong influence in Belgium of the French-speaking Walloons. Just back from a congress of the Belgian Communist Party, he told me his party had now accepted the parliamentary way as one way to socialism. We did not have long enough to talk to clarify what is meant by this.

I spoke German, as Flemishly as possible, when buying some food in a shop. Thijs told me the shop lady had praised my Flemish!

23 April 1960 : Back at work, I overnighted in Altenbauna, near Kassel, at the home of one of my best German friends, ex-Nazi and now Social Democratic headmaster Henner Pflug. Henner, who since the war has been campaigning strongly against neo-Nazi tendencies, told me that the recent wave of anti-Semitic daubings or, rather, the reaction against them, had subdued local ex-Nazis who had gradually been opening their mouths more loudly. Some had argued, for instance, that there was no need to teach youth more about what happened under Hitler, that it was better to forget. But the daubings had removed that argument.

Henner's area is being transformed by the construction of a vast new plant of the Volkswagen company.

25 April 1960 : I kept on the heels of Britain's Aviation Minister, Duncan Sandys, as he toured West Germany's third post-war aircraft industry fair in Hanover. The fair featured such names as Messerschmitt, Heinkel, Dornier and Focke-Wulf, as well as many British firms. Sandys, who has been in West Germany since 20 April and has had talks with the Defence Minister, Franz-Josef Strauss, today issued a communiqué saying that West Germany had agreed to join with France and Britain in developing a vertical take-off and landing (VTOL) aircraft, the next 'generation' of fighter aircraft. Strauss told reporters he was concerned to avoid each of the three countries' trying to develop its own plane, as Britain and France had done in the fighter field previously. This kind of cooperation in such an important sector is new. It reflects the increasing integration in aircraft development in the West, conditioned partly by strategic needs and partly by ever-increasing costs.

26 April 1960 : In Karlsruhe, on the eve of the ninth annual congress of Adenauer's Christian Democrats, I obtained confirmation of a DPA story that Theodor Oberländer, the Christian Democrat Minister for Refugee Affairs, had agreed to resign after the party had acceded to his request for a parliamentary investigation of allegations made against him by Communists. They had accused him of complicity in wartime murders in Lvov, Ukraine. It looks to me as though Oberländer, an ex-Nazi, was not responsible for the murders, but his high-level position in the Nazi era in organizations promoting German expansionism to the east is more than sufficient to make him unfit to hold his present post.

27 April 1960 : At the Christian Democratic congress, I admired the vitality of 84-year-old Adenauer. But I was most depressed to once again hear his ideas – the Russians are the root of all evil, therefore make no concessions, stick to NATO – all the old tune. He's almost as uncompromising as the East German leader, Walter Ulbricht, and both of them are bad for world peace and for Germany. One slight sign of discontent was the demand of a handful of delegates that the vote on the re-election of the party chairman, Adenauer being the only nominee, be conducted secretly. Previously it has always been done by acclamation. This time he got 427 in favour, ten abstentions and four against.

Adenauer told delegates not to bother about the succession. Ludwig Erhard, Economics Minister and Vice-Chancellor, got the biggest clap of all ministers, apart from the old man. He still rates as the most likely choice to succeed Adenauer, even though Adenauer opposes him and dished him last year. Some are doubtful whether Erhard has the political acumen needed, but others say he could do the job with some strong assistants on the political side.

Dined well – roast halibut from the North Sea – with four Soviet correspondents including Yurinov, accusing them of holding the East Germans in subjection and thus storing up trouble, but also listening with some inner concern to their charge that the West is stalling on disarmament. I chuckled inwardly when they invited me to accompany them to the cinema to see a film with curvaceous Italian star, Gina Lollobrigida. I declined, saying I preferred to return to my hotel to read *Izvestia*, the Soviet Government newspaper.

29 April 1960 : Adenauer wound up the Christian Democratic congress with a speech urging that a real start be made to disarmament at the planned East–West summit conference. (He opposes discussion on Germany and Berlin, maintaining that this will only help the Russians to extort something.) I hardly think that his appeal is sincere, as one of his official spokesmen told me recently that the government had no expectations of anything more than a goodwill declaration being achieved at the summit.

Adenauer has repeatedly opposed an agreement on disarmament in central Europe, involving withdrawals of some distance by Western and Soviet troops. His remarks show he classes Khrushchev with the devil and refuses to believe there is any point in negotiating with him. I only hope that the Western Big Three are reasonable enough to reach an initial disarmament agreement with Khrushchev at the summit, on the issue of an end to nuclear weapons tests. The Russians have come a long way to meet the West, further than Adenauer and people of his ilk would ever have thought possible.

1 May 1960 : In picturesque Ellwangen, near Stuttgart, I was favourably impressed by a speech made by Adenauer to a large gathering of mainly German refugees from East Germany and Eastern Europe. Adenauer tacitly dissociated himself from the other main speaker, Hans Schuetz, a Christian Democratic *Bundestag* deputy, who called for the 'liberation of the enslaved peoples' of Eastern Europe with whom, together with the German refugees, he said a new order could be built. Adenauer, on the other hand, said many refugees had got jobs in West

Germany, and he appealed to Germans to offer the refugees and their children the friendliness and help they needed. As for the future, he said, it was too dark to make forecasts.

6 May 1960 : Elfi shed a few joyful tears watching on TV the wedding of the Queen's sister, Princess Margaret, to photographer Tony Armstrong-Jones. Watching the evening repeat, I almost wished the charming princess were going to be called Johnson instead of Jones. And I'm an anti-monarchist, in principle anyway.

9 May 1960 : Robin's twelfth birthday party was attended by six of his energetic strapping schoolmates. I could see little difference from English boys, except they were a shade tidier, a shade politer and not quite as jolly, though jolly enough. They drank just as much pop anyway.

10 May 1960 : Am applying for a Labour Party job – press relations officer to the Parliamentary Labour Party, that is, the Labour group in the House of Commons. I think I must be getting tired of journalism. At least, I find little attraction in the general run of my present work. It's like being a sausage machine. I feel I'm more like a tape-recorder than a human being, an overworked tape-recorder at that.

11 May 1960 : In a discussion with German friends, I argued that if Adenauer were to back a neutralist policy, the moral argument for German reunification would be unshakeable. But as things are one can ask, 'What will the Germans want next, if they get the unification of present-day East and West Germany and still have a big army plus nuclear weapons?'

15 May 1960 : We have adopted a baby hedgehog who comes round for milk and bread a couple of times a day, and is most tame.

6 Khrushchev wrecks Paris summit

16 May 1960 : I shot off to Berlin by car as the Paris summit conference ended before it started, after US President Eisenhower (rightly) refused to accept a Soviet demand that he apologize for the espionage flight of a United States plane over the Soviet Union and punish those responsible. (The plane was shot down near Sverdlovsk.) Eisenhower had already said that such flights had been stopped and would not be resumed. Khrushchev is expected to travel to East Berlin tomorrow.

17 May 1960 : Am staying at the Hotel Johannishof, where I lived for several months last year while opening up the Reuter office in East Berlin. The hotel porter handed me a parcel containing about a dozen eggs which I had forgotten to take with me after a visit to East Berlin about three months ago. I looked at this with distaste, but he took an egg, cracked it on the reception desk, smelled it and pronounced it still good! He intends to fry them all, saying that they had remained edible because it is cool in the hotel's luggage store.

Watched Khrushchev on TV giving a press conference in Paris before about 2,000 journalists, some of whom booed him at one point. He accused the booers of being West German 'riff-raff' or 'abortions' – the translators differed. Later, relaxed and smiling, he said he just loved to fight against such imperialist lackeys. I felt he gave no convincing explanation of why he broke up the summit. I cannot see what he hopes to gain by it, as he has already got an American promise not to fly over the Soviet Union again. Many people think there is some internal reason for his surprising attitude. Maybe we shall know some day.

19 May 1960 : Back in my old hunting grounds again. Drove out to East Berlin's Schönefeld airport, along a road lined by several thousand police and soldiers, and with civilians distributing paper East German and Soviet flags to people gathering on the route. Before leaving for the airport, chatted with Soviet Embassy officials and Soviet journalists. They maintain that Eisenhower's promise to stop overflights is not enough, as he will be President only until next January. Stephanie Roussel, veteran (anti-Communist) *France Soir* correspondent, who had been at the summit, said she thought I was being over-critical of the Russians on this issue. She had the impression that the British and French were hopping mad with the Americans.

At the airport Khrushchev waddled solemnly past a steel-helmeted army guard of honour. He raised claps and cheers from workers' delegations and children welcoming him with banners, paper flags and flowers. In a short speech he repeated his Paris accusations that the United States had torpedoed the summit, and his thesis that military circles were directing US policy, so it was no use holding a summit at present. He said he still favoured peaceful co-existence.

Khrushchev said he would discuss with East German leaders the question of a German peace treaty and, within that framework, the West Berlin problem. In our East Berlin office, Gerry Long, Brian Horton and Alfred Klühs worked from the TV, while I gave them some additional colour and some quotes from the speech which they had not got fully.

Returning to the centre of East Berlin, I drove slowly in the tail of Khrushchev's procession, some ten minutes behind him, hearing lots of comments about my West German numberplate and having a bouquet of lilac thrown at me. I'm getting used to this.

Khrushchev is staying in a nineteenth-century villa in the fenced-off and guarded East German Government enclave in the suburb of Pankow. Keeping watch to see if Khrushchev came out of the enclave again, I was lucky enough, an hour or so later, to bump into Horst Sindermann, press and propaganda secretary of the SED central committee, who was my top contact man when I was stationed in East Berlin last year. *[Sindermann later became Prime Minister, from 1973 to 1976.]* Sindermann told me that talks between Khrushchev and the East German leaders were to start this evening; preliminary talks on a peace treaty, I understood him to say. He forecast that there would be no action on a peace treaty until the postponed summit conference took place; Khrushchev had proposed it be put off for six to eight months. Sindermann said Khrushchev had enjoyed his brush in Paris, when some journalists – Khrushchev said they were West Germans, but we understand they were mainly Americans – booed him at his press conference and he called them 'imperialist lackeys'. Sindermann told me Khrushchev loves an argument and criticizes everything he sees. He certainly was rude to Eisenhower in Paris. At the same time one can understand Khrushchev's feeling hurt at Eisenhower's authorizing, or at least supporting, the sending of an aircraft deep into Soviet airspace, a month or two after their meeting at Camp David.

Sidelight: bought a couple of bottles of lemonade in a very trim self-service shop in East Berlin and noticed that the clientele were virtually as well dressed as their counterparts in Britain.

20 May 1960 : Am still wondering why Khrushchev wrecked the summit. There are, I think, three main possible reasons:

1 that he genuinely believes there is no point in talking to the Americans at the moment because, as he maintains, the Pentagon is directing policy and thus no agreement is possible – in another six months things may be different, if the Democrats get in;

2 that the supporters of a tougher line in Russia – and China – have taken the upper hand behind the scenes and forced

61

Khrushchev to find a pretext for not negotiating at the summit;
3 that it was a temperamental Khrushchev tantrum, combined
with Russian pride and Communist suspicion, and the desire
to teach the United States a lesson and, having done so and
let some time elapse, he may get down to talks.

Spent a pleasant hour with Elfi's West Berlin uncle and three
aunts, who are not too worried about Berlin's situation.

Around 9 pm we got word that the Associated Press was ahead
of us on a big story: a United States Air Force Dakota had landed
about 30 miles inside East Germany, near the West German border and the Baltic. We phoned around frantically and could raise
nothing official. Finally, around 11 pm, I managed to get a hotel
official in a place near where the plane was supposed to have landed, and had the story confirmed, with the additional fact that the
nine Americans on board, including one woman, had been taken
to the local Soviet *kommandatura*.

21 May 1960 : Armed with an official East German permit, I
drove the roughly 150 miles from Berlin to Grevesmühlen, near
where the Dakota had come down in a field. Whatever had happened during the recent forced completion of farm collectivization in East Germany, it had not made the countryside look less
lovely in springtime. I drove past lilac bushes in bloom and
through avenues of chestnuts with blossom like yellow fireworks.
On the way I passed several lakes.

I lunched hastily at a hotel in Kyritz, about 60 miles north-west of
Berlin, which sports a plaque stating that Wilhelm Pieck, then the
Communist Party leader and now East Germany's representational
president, announced the start of the post-war land reform there in
autumn 1945. That was when the big estates were split up and given
to landless farmworkers and refugees. Since then they have been put
together again, to a large extent, through collectivization.

After my months in this country last year, I find the East
German scene familiar: signs stating that collectivization has been
completed and calling for a German peace treaty. New signs

62

going up, attacking 'American air provocations'. Villages still in need of a lot of paint, but better than they used to be. Collective farm entrances with names like 'Red Banner' and 'First of May'. Soviet barracks – former German ones – surrounded by the inevitable green palisades which mark Soviet units in this country. A motorist's paradise, as the roads are quite good and there is very little traffic. Around 4 pm I neared Grevesmühlen. A fat farm woman, telling me where the plane was, said she thought it was English. Her daughter corrected her. In the centre of Grevesmühlen, half a dozen youths stood near a petrol pump with their motorbikes. They told me the plane was about eight miles further north. One of them said he thought the crew was in the local Soviet *kommandatura*, apparently once a German municipal office. This youth told me he had seen several Soviet jets force down the American plane by firing warning bursts and flying directly above it to make it descend. It had landed perfectly in a field and was being guarded by the East German People's Army.

At the entrance to the *kommandatura*, a sort of garrison office, I asked a khaki-uniformed Russian soldier, in Russian, where the Americans were. This round-faced, high-cheekboned chap smiled and said, 'Americans? What Americans. There were no Americans.'

When I told him there had been an official announcement about the plane on East German radio last night, he grinned again and asked me where I had learned Russian. He told me he was alone and added, 'My chief will be back later.'

'How long?' I asked.

'In an hour, or two, or three ...' he replied, like a character in a Russian novel.

I was highly amused, and dashed off round the corner into a little cobbled square to phone a story from a local tradesman's house. Gerry Long, who had postponed his return from Berlin to Bonn because of this story, sounded almost overcome with joy that I'd managed to get something. He had been very worried because AP had been ahead of us and Gerry had even received an urgent service message from the general manager, Walton Cole, on the matter.

After I had phoned, a woman told me she had seen two or three Americans earlier today sunning in the (green-palisaded) garden behind the *kommandatura*. I decided to take a look at the garden myself. As I arrived at the *kommandatura*, a green Soviet Army Pobyeda (Victory) limousine and a Soviet jeep drew up. From the car, about three yards from where I stood, there emerged what I took to be three American men, in civilian clothes, and an American woman.

I stepped forward and asked one of the men if they were American. He said, 'Yes,' and smiled. Then I asked his name. This made him suspicious. Perhaps he thought I was a new kind of interrogator. I told him who I was, but then it was too late. One of two East German civilians accompanying the Americans asked me, politely but firmly, to step to one side with him. He flashed his card identifying him as a state security official.

The official, who wore a check sports jacket and the badge of the ruling SED, told me he had been advised that I was coming, and that my travel permission had been mistakenly issued and was now cancelled. I must return to Berlin. I replied that I could not believe that the issue of the travel permission was a mistake as there had been full consideration beforehand. I told him that I merely wanted to apply for an interview with the Americans, whose presence in East Germany was by no means secret. I asked him to put this request to the Soviet commandant.

He told me to sit in my car, which was parked about 15 yards away, until the matter had been discussed in the *kommandatura*. As I waited, several girls and boys came and chatted to me, noting with interest an empty wrapper from Wrigley's chewing-gum, which they immediately identified. Not able to supply them with chewing-gum, I gave them some mints instead. Along came a little man in civilian clothes and shooed away the children. I protested and asked what he thought he was doing. He showed me his People's Police card. He said he thought the children had been pestering me. I asked him sarcastically if what he had done was intended to be a form of peaceful coexistence. After more quite friendly argy-bargy, he asked me not to put it in the papers that he had sent the children away. I shan't.

The state security man returned and told me, 'The commandant says you should return to Berlin. You will not be able to talk to the Americans.'

I asked if the Soviet commandant could order me around in an East German town. He replied that the East Germans were in charge, or words to that effect, and that my travel document had been cancelled. He said I should therefore leave the area, but might telephone my office to check on the situation if I wished.

I phoned another story, this time from the local post office, and told our East Berlin office the situation. While they consulted, I withdrew some miles down the road and ate a couple of *Bockwurst* (Frankfurters) in a state-owned village café much in need of decoration. With about half a dozen people in the café, including the friendly boiler-suited Communist burgomaster, I had a discussion on the abortive summit and on farm collectivization. One man agreed with me that Khrushchev ought not to have broken up the summit, in spite of the American provocation, which, we all agreed, had been grave. On collectivization, the burgomaster said no one had been forced in this village to join a collective, but he admitted that there had been 'excesses' elsewhere.

As an example of progress in East Germany, I was told that the café, which at present supplies only drinks and *Bockwurst*, would next year obtain the necessary apparatus for frying and boiling eggs. A new café was also to be built, as the present one was too small. Learned that people in this area can receive, not only East and West German TV, but also Danish TV. My feeling, that so much depends not on the particular form of society or dogma, but on the quality of the people who are in charge, received a fillip when one man told me that the burgomaster, though a Communist, was not a fanatic and was well liked. 'If they were all like him, life would be a lot better,' he told me.

Having been told to make my way back to Berlin, I overnighted in Schwerin, not far from Grevesmühlen, at the home of Elfi's cousin, Gerdi Goldenbagen and her husband Jochen, an official of the state bank. Jochen told me that mortgage debts owed by farmers to the state bank were cancelled if the farmers joined collective farms – just another part of the persuasion and pressure which led to the completion of farm collectivization a few weeks ago.

Gerdi and Jochen told me they were careful not to disagree openly with the things their daughter Angelika, a pretty and slightly plump ten-year-old, is taught at school, because she innocently repeats her parents' remarks.

They insist she takes religion, which is taught outside of the school curriculum by a teacher appointed by the Church, in their case the local Protestant church. Angelika told me she did not like the religious instruction, as she found it boring. She also mentioned she had been told at school there was no God. I asked her if the teacher had proved that and she said, 'No.'

Her parents told me they realized that the religious teaching was not interesting, as it was given by a desiccated spinster who, they said, did not always put her Christianity into practice, but was apparently the only person available to the local church to give the lessons. They want Angelika to decide for herself what she believes when she is older, but want her to have at least the basis of Christian teaching put over to her.

They agreed with me that, under the conditions of the East German regime, people who are religious are more likely to be really convinced Christians than the mass of habitual churchgoers in the West. Angelika showed me three letters from pen pals, one in German and two in Russian from two Soviet girls. She also corresponds with Robin.

Gerdi told me she had been surprised to get a vacuum cleaner – they are scarce – through a mail-order firm in Leipzig. Then her mother ordered one too. Sold out. That's what shopping for consumer goods is often like in East Germany.

22 May 1960 : Back in Berlin, was the guest tonight of George Turner, Yorkshire-born chief British information officer in Berlin. A former journalist, George appears to think that the East German regime is becoming more and more stable. Made him and his wife Marjorie laugh by presenting them with a paper East German hammer-and-dividers tricolour, handed to me during the welcome for Khrushchev. London were very pleased with yesterday's story; I was quoted by name in many German papers for part of it. Am thoroughly enjoying Reuters again at the moment.

7 Arguing with a Soviet colleague

23 May 1960 : Dinner in a restaurant with Oleg Yenakiev, correspondent of *Izvestia*, the Soviet Government newspaper, a chap I like. A 60-ish East German who took the third chair at our table and joined in our conversation, conducted in English, German and Russian, amazed me by openly criticizing the regime. He was some kind of professor, who said he admired Russian culture and had Russian friends, but was convinced that the Soviet Union was following a wrong policy towards Germany. He argued that the Big Four powers should agree on the security conditions to be imposed on a united Germany – no army or only a little one and no membership in an East or West military alliance. They should then allow a free vote on German reunification and the form of state to be set up.

Yenakiev agreed to all but the free vote and repeated the Soviet standpoint that the two German governments should negotiate on reunification. The professor, who said he was so fed up that he was not afraid to talk frankly, whatever happened to him, said that proposal was wrong as the East German Government had never been freely elected. As the argument went on, Yenakiev grew angry, his sallow face colouring and his eyes bulging a little. He recalled how he had fought against the Germans in the defence of Leningrad, and how his father had died in that battle. He passionately opposed a renewal of Nazism and referred to people in West Germany, who bore some responsibility for what had happened, again being in power and making revanchist demands. I tried to mediate, saying that the professor did not favour such people at all, but merely wanted an Austrian solution for Germany. I almost feared that Yenakiev would denounce the professor, but after a while he got hold of himself. Before the professor left, he said he had spoken out because he took us both for decent people.

Afterwards Yenakiev said to me, 'I wonder why he thought I was decent.'

I'm sure Yenakiev will take no action against the professor. *[I don't know whether he did.]*

24 May 1960 : Brian and I had a nice beat on a Soviet announcement that the Americans from the Dakota were to be handed back to a representative appointed by the United States military headquarters in Germany. In some previous cases, where American servicemen have strayed into East Germany, the Russians have made the United States in a sense recognize East Germany by making the American Red Cross negotiate with the state-run East German Red Cross. I think the Russians are trying to say, by their moderate handling of this case, that they can be gentlemen when someone makes a mistake, but not when it is a question of spying.

As soon as we got this Soviet statement, we started making efforts to obtain permits to travel to Grevesmühlen again, to be present at the handover of the plane and its occupants. The East Germans stalled us for about five hours, but gave in after we had remonstrated at various levels that our agreement with them provided for us to be able to travel where we want (unless, of course, the authorities closed an area to all civilians).

It was decided that I should go, partly because I have some Russian. Bad weather – driving rain – during part of the 180-mile drive. I gave a lift for some distance to a 45-ish former Hitler Youth leader who told me he was a factory book-keeper and would flee if it weren't for his old mother. He said at first that things were getting worse economically, but agreed when I interrupted him to say things were much better than a few years ago.

However, his general feeling of bad economic organization is one I have met many times. He told me that at a factory meeting he had criticized Khrushchev's attitude in breaking up the summit.

I kept touching wood that the plane would not – as had been forecast – have left before I reached the spot. I drove straight to Klütz, about three miles from the Baltic, north of Grevesmühlen. A villager showed me where the plane was, on a two-kilometre-long rolling slope of a collective farm field, sown mainly with rye and barley. The 50-ish man who showed me to the plane told me, 'What we have here is not freedom.'

He recalled that when he was serving in the German Army in Latvia late in the Second World War, the Russians were advancing, and a 14-year-old Latvian girl had hissed, 'I hate the Russians.'

Turning to me, the man said feelingly, 'And I hate the Russians too.'

I said he was wrong to do that. He agreed, and said, 'I hate the system.'

It was almost dark when I spotted the silhouette of the plane, parked on the field, near a small wood at the top of a rise. Two East German soldiers in steel helmets, who stopped my car about 400 yards from the plane, told me that it had been intended to have the plane take off today, but the ground was considered too soggy after rain. It was only after they had spoken that I noticed there was a third man with them, a little chap in a khaki greatcoat, looking like someone from World War One – a Russian.

I drove the eight miles back to the Grevesmühlen *kommandatura*. A friendly Soviet captain told me that members of the United States military mission accredited to the Soviet forces in East Germany had been at the *kommandatura* earlier in the evening and would return in the morning. He said I could not speak to the Americans from the Dakota as they were already asleep, and added, 'If I disturbed them, people would say, "Just look what Soviet officers do!"'

At the local state-owned hotel, the Bauernkrug (Farmers' Pub), I obtained a bed in a room with three beds, paying three marks – about the equivalent of three shillings' purchasing power *[15p]*. On the phone I took a call from a radio station in Cleveland, Ohio, which wanted an interview with the Dakota's captain, Captain Lundy, and a member of the crew, Morrison. I explained this was impossible tonight.

25 May 1960 : I shall long remember the piglike snoring of an elderly man who, with a younger man, occupied the other two beds in my hotel room, and also the pistol-like cracking of his bed as he turned over. Not a good night. Enjoyed breakfast, except there was no jam. I asked why. Apparently, few people had been asking for jam here so their stock became mouldy and no one would take the responsibility to order some more. I said this was not much of an advertisement for the German Democratic Republic. They agreed, and said they would have some in next time I came.

Persuaded the Soviet captain to let me at least see the Americans in their bedroom. I was allowed to say good morning to the one woman among them, a Mrs MacCash, who looked well and well made-up. She told me she felt fine. In spite of the fact that I was not allowed to interview the Americans, the details I gleaned from various Soviet and German sources were most useful. Around 9.30 am, four members of the United States Military Mission to Soviet Forces in East Germany arrived, headed by its chief, Lieutenant-Colonel Baldwin, followed by a Soviet colonel representing Colonel-General Ivan I. Jakobovsky, the Soviet commander-in-chief in East Germany.

For some six hours consultations went on between the Russians and Americans at various levels, on whether it was advisable for the plane to take off today, or at all. It is standing on the rolling collective farm field where it landed, just short of a boggy hollow. I learned that the Americans wanted to make the take-off attempt, but that East German and Soviet pilots were more than looking askance. I learned that the Americans had played volleyball with the Russians and had also been able to watch TV.

Meanwhile I washed the car, had some tasty horsemeat for

lunch – the first in my life – during which I had a friendly talk with a retired bricklayer, a lifelong Communist, who emphasized that it was necessary to be decent to people, for instance, to the farmers one had to persuade to enter the collectives. He saw no reason for allowing opposition parties, pointing to the Weimar Republic as an example of where that could lead (to Hitler). I again visited the 'air'-field, to find that a Soviet helicopter had arrived with an air force expert to advise on the best take-off line among the rye and barley. I also had a discussion with an East German radio reporter about the unfreedom of the effectively one-party state, from which I felt I emerged on top. (In typing this, I recall a talk with an East Berlin taxi driver, who appeared pro-regime, but agreed with me when I maintained that even if Khrushchev, in his last East Berlin speech, had announced that Soviet troops were marching into West Berlin, his audience would have jumped up and cheered just the same.)

In addition, I chatted with some grimy but cheerful motor mechanics in an apparently privately-owned garage, who told me they had to work wonders to keep some of East Germany's old vehicles on the roads in spite of a severe shortage of spares. One man showed me a differential gearwheel which had been worn out. A local welder had welded a blob of metal on to each worn tooth, and they were going to file down the teeth to the required size again. I asked if they knew whether the steel the welder used was of the right grade. They didn't. How long would the repaired gear wheel last? They didn't know that either. I said at least they had the satisfaction of knowing they were using a lot more craftsmanship than their West German fellows, where mechanics lightly throw away parts which are only slightly worn and take replacements from the shelf.

Around 6 pm, two East German reporters and I were called into the *kommandatura* for what the Russians called a 'press con-ference', held in a room about six yards square, decorated with pictures of Khrushchev, Voroshilov – recently replaced as Soviet President – and Lenin, and a bust of Marx. The Americans sat rather glumly around the walls, with a couple of Soviet officers, one of them called Kozlovsky, and an interpreter at a table. The whole thing was a farce, as Kozlovsky referred all questions to Baldwin, who said he had orders to say nothing. He would not even identify the Americans who had been on the plane. We gave up after about ten minutes. (Two signs in the *kommandatura*, in Russian, amused me. One said: 'Members of the Soviet Forces will salute each other when they meet.' Another, painted in white on a telephone, read: 'Be on your guard. The enemy is listening.' I was taken back to my days in the navy.)

Phoned more through to Brian from the garage, which I'd been using as my communications post all day, then drove up to the field. Kozlovsky at first forbade photos, then allowed them, and at my suggestion he and Baldwin shook hands warmly. Baldwin told me, not for publication, that Kozlovsky was a 'great guy'.

As the Dakota made its take-off run, about 30 East German firemen and several ambulance men stood tensely by their vehicles. The plane tore through about 450 yards of rye and barley, from ankle-deep to knee-deep, moving diagonally up a rolling hillside. It left the ground with 500–600 yards to spare before a small wood at the top of the hillside. Soviet and East German soldiers ringed the field, and several hundred local farming folk looked on as the plane gained height, circled the field once to waggle its wings in salute, and sped off to the west, five days after being forced down.

Phoned my piece from the house, about three-quarters of a mile away, of a bricklayer; not the Communist I had spoken to earlier, but a non-political man. He told me he thought that quite a lot of the 'new farmers' – people who were given land in the post-war land reform – were accepting collectivization readily, but it was hard on the 'real farmers', people who had owned land before that. He himself had little to complain about, except for the travel restrictions.

The plane took off at about 7.30 pm. I drove to the nearby West German frontier at Lübeck, following part of the route on which Elfi fled westwards from the advancing Russians in 1945. Just before leaving East Germany, on a country road where I'd lost my way, I spoke to a pretty young girl in drainpipe trousers, a modern artificial leather jacket and headscarf, walking with a young man, also well dressed. The girl, who pointed out the way, told me she was, of all things, an apprentice shepherdess. I felt the sheep were lucky. She told me life in the GDR was good.

28 May 1960 : Back home. A duplicated slip from the Labour Party told me I had not been short-listed for the post I had applied for on 10 May. Somewhat disappointing, but I know I have not much experience of that kind of press relations work. It does not mean the end of my ambitions regarding the Labour Party.

31 May 1960 : Elfi has become the proud possessor of an electric floor-polisher, very useful in our flat, as in many German flats, which have expanses of uncarpeted wooden blocks. About two-thirds of the polisher was financed by me to mark our thirteenth wedding anniversary – today – and Elfi provided the rest from her translations. I also gave her a dozen roses – thought I'd better avoid 13, though I'm really not superstitious. We had a little celebration tonight with friends on the terrace of the Rhineside Hotel Dreesen, where Hitler stayed and had talks with Chamberlain on 22 September 1938, as the Sudetenland crisis moved towards its climax – the Munich agreement which gave the German-speaking Sudetenland area of Czechoslovakia to Hitler and – for the time being – avoided war.

8 East German secret police on our heels

5 June 1960 : Driving through East Germany, north-west of Berlin, on a holiday trip, we stopped by a lake where I swam. As I saw the happy-looking people swimming I thought, not for the first time, what a damned shame that Communist and non-Communist politicians can't stop attacking each other and instead concentrate on doing positive things like increasing production – each in their own way – and removing restrictions on freedom of movement – these mainly imposed from the Communist side. I'm pretty sure it does not matter much to the average Herr Schmidt whether he works for a nationalized or private factory, providing his living standard is gradually improving and he is not unduly badgered by the state.

My view was doubtless not shared by a master baker and his fat wife, whom I engaged in conversation, rather hoping she would offer me one of many pieces of cake she had with her. (She didn't.) Although they were cautious in their remarks, it was clear they were fearing the evil day when, in all likelihood, they would have to hand over – perhaps with some small compensation – their shop and bakery to the state. I see no necessity for this being forced on them, but it's been done in Russia so, unless the party line changes, it will be done in East Germany too.

We overnighted with Elfi's Schwerin relatives *[see 21 May]*. It was the first time Elfi had seen them since the Second World War. Many flags out in Schwerin, which is celebrating its 800th anniversary, with the accent on the last eleven years of its history – since the East German Communist state was set up.

6 June 1960 : We drove Elfi's cousin Gerdi and her family for a day at the seaside at the little Baltic resort of Boltenhagen, about an hour's drive from Schwerin. The sandy beach was glorious in the sunshine, and the water was quite warm enough to swim. A patrol boat cruised past occasionally, not far from the coast, and rowers were ordered through a loudspeaker not to go more than 300 metres from the beach. The West German frontier is about 15 miles away. As we drove through Schwerin tonight Elfi remarked that a blue car which was driving near us had been near us before. Gerdi said she wouldn't be at all surprised if we were being shadowed.

7 June 1960 : Remembering the suspicious car of last night, I kept my eyes open when I drove from Aunt Lieschen's house across the city to pick up Elfi and the boys at Gerdi's flat. As I set off, a beige Wartburg (number BE 81 03), which had been standing in a nearby side street, also set off. I deliberately went by a roundabout route to Gerdi's and found that the Wartburg followed. It stopped about 300 yards away from her flat. I said nothing to the family then, not wanting to worry the Schweriners. It had been a most happy stay. All were so pleased that this family link had been re-established.

As we drove to the West German frontier, about 25 miles to the west, the beige Wartburg, containing two or three youngish men in civilian clothes, no doubt from the Ministry for State Security, stayed close to us all the way. It was joined by a blue Wartburg, containing three more young men, who looked rather scruffy. Normally one car stayed ahead of us – at a discreet distance, just coming into sight occasionally – and one stayed behind, at a similar distance. When, for fun, we stopped a couple of times, the car from behind came past us and stopped further down the road, on one occasion hiding itself partially behind a road-mending lorry.

After we had left Schwerin I told Elfi and the boys what was going on and they were tickled. On one occasion they even waved to the man in the blue car. It is, of course, quite possible that we were followed all day yesterday as well, and that I have been followed in this way previously, but this is the first time that I have noticed it. It may be that the East Germans were perturbed at my going to the area not far from where the Dakota landed. Of course, this kind of surveillance goes on everywhere, but it is usually done much more cleverly. On one occasion when we passed the beige car and Elfi and the boys waved, the driver smiled back, Elfi told me.

[When we developed our family cine-film, of the scene on the beach at Boltenhagen, we thought we recognized, in the background, several of the security men from the Wartburgs. And after the reunification of Germany in 1990, when I obtained copies of my Stasi secret police file, I came across the report put in by one of the young men who had been following us on 7 June 1960. The report, referring to my manoeuvres intended to check whether I was being followed, said I had acted 'very strangely', but did not suggest that I suspected I was being followed. As these secret policemen apparently did not know my name, they gave me a code name in their report – 'Mond' ('Moon'), perhaps a reference to my bald head. They described how we drove to the West German frontier, making several stops on the way.

In a special remark, the report said: ' "Moon" and his family waved to all cars which overtook them or which they overtook, including the car of the observers. "Moon" tried to take the number of one of the observers' cars, by driving towards the car that was parked at the side of the road, letting his car free-wheel and then suddenly accelerating. He did not succeed in getting the number, as the observers were standing by the boot.']

9 June 1960 : Back in Bonn, I learned that, of all things, an American civilian glider pilot competing in the world gliding championships in West Germany had strayed into East Germany and landed there yesterday, within a couple of miles from where the Dakota landed, and close to Boltenhagen beach where we bathed the other day. He was released today without trouble.

10 June 1960 : Left by car for a 750-mile drive to the northern Yugoslav port of Pula, south of Trieste, where, on 12 June, President Gamal Abdel Nasser of the United Arab Republic, a political union of Egypt and Syria, arrives to stay for a week with President Josip Broz Tito on the Yugoslav leader's private island, Brioni, off Pula in the Adriatic. Took with me Italian, Russian and French dictionaries and a Shell booklet giving some motoring phrases in Serbo-Croat, Yugoslavia's main official language.

Overnighted in Reutte, just inside Austrian North Tyrol, where I heard two middle-aged men and their wives talking in a familiar accent at the side of a Standard Vanguard car. Yes, they were from Yorkshire, garage owners from Leeds.

11 June 1960 : Covered my second 350 miles today, to Pula, port and tourist spot, treasurehouse of Roman remains on the southern tip of the Istrian peninsula, about 60 miles south of the big, but now largely idle, Italian port of Trieste. This was a wonderful journey, taking me over several Alpine passes. The drive through the Alps, and then the pink Dolomites, reminded me of trips through the Yorkshire Dales, though the scale was greater. But there were the same rushing torrents near the road, and the wind and the steep inclines. Once again I came across those hair-raising Italian drivers who blow their horns before entering each blind curve, a frightening habit which I think is almost worse than crashing.

In Austria, noted several scrawled signs calling for the return to Austria of South Tyrol, Italian since 1918, largely Germanic in population. One sign near a church said: 'Pray for South Tyrol.' The German-speakers accuse the Italians of trying to flood the area with Italians so as to change its ethnic balance. I hope the European spirit will solve this problem in time. *[Much of the heat was taken out of the situation thanks to a 1969 agreement between Austria and Italy, giving the region a special status and guaranteeing language rights to the different communities.]*

It had been easy to drive into Austria – a frontier official did not even want to see my passport. It was a little more complicated to get into Yugoslavia, which starts on the edge of Trieste. I had to fill in a form (90 seconds), get a stamp in my passport and have my valuables, particularly typewriter and camera, quickly checked. Very friendly, though.

In under two hours, I drove in the dark to Pula on good (former Italian) roads. Pula, formerly Pola, was once a big Austro-Hungarian naval base, later Italian and since 1947 Yugoslav. Two of the now-Yugoslav nationalities, Croats and Slovenes, lived mainly in the small towns and villages, the Italians in the big towns. Most of the Italians left when the Yugoslavs took over the region.

My seafront hotel, the Riviera, was described in an official brochure as high-class. It is clean and the personnel are friendly. But it is not too well kept. The cold tap in my room has a faulty washer, and there are three holes in the wall where it had apparently been intended to fix electric plugs, but the job had not been done. The lavatory in the nearby bathroom is broken. Food, however, is good.

12 June 1960 : Phoned an advance story via Belgrade and enjoyed a swim in the crystal-clear Adriatic, 20°C, with several Belgrade correspondents of international agencies. In the evening drank a slivovitz (plum brandy) as teenagers jived in happy abandon in a café not far from a well-preserved 1,900-year-old Roman amphitheatre, like the Rome Colosseum, with room for 23,000 spectators.

The Yugoslavs appear to be rather small people, just like Elfi finds the older Bradfordians (stunted in textile mills). They are, here at least, more Italianate than the average Russians; not so many high cheekbones, for instance. As for language, I'm managing with Italian, French, German and English in that order of usefulness.

13 June 1960 : President Nasser arrived in his large official yacht, *El Horreya*, to be received by a young-looking Tito, 68, in a cream civilian suit. Nasser, in grey suit and sunglasses, looked very brown compared to his host. Each leader was accompanied by his pretty wife. Bugles, boatswains' pipes and a 42-gun salute from four Yugoslav naval batteries accompanied Nasser's descent from the gangway.

I'm pleased I have seen Tito at last, as I have long had a soft spot for him after his wartime partisan struggle and his courage later in defying Stalin and trying to work out a different form of Communism suitable for his country. Tito and Nasser drove to Fazana, about four miles north of here, from where they took a launch to Tito's private island, Brioni, about 1$^{1}/_{2}$ miles off the coast. It is a low-lying, largely pine-clad island, described as idyllic, about half a mile by two miles. It was formerly a holiday spot for the rich.

Now that the two leaders are on Brioni, our only source of information is a Yugoslav Foreign Office spokesman, Mr Vujica, who travels to the island once or more daily and then comes back to tell us something, or nothing, as the case may be. Fortunately our Belgrade correspondent, Bane Petrovic, is able to glean some information there. Together we put together a story on the phone and he teleprinted it to London. Another glorious swim today.

Late tonight Mr Vujica handed me the Serbo-Croat texts of toasts proposed by Tito and Nasser at lunch today. Ulrich Schiller, friendly West German radio correspondent, translated the toasts for me, but by the time he had done that Petrovic had them in Belgrade from the official Yugoslav news agency.

14 June 1960 : Have been feeling tired since my drive down here, and dissatisfied at our lack of news sources. However, am grateful to be able to bask in the beautiful sunshine and swim in the warm Adriatic. Today Tito and Nasser began political talks on the islet of Vanga, near Brioni. Photographers were allowed to snap them at a long table in an open-sided villa. In a café, listened to an unintentionally funny band, singing mainly in Italian, one of whose numbers turned out to be *Danny Boy*, performed in what passed for English. This was greeted by lots of cheers and 'Viva's and what a colleague assured me were shouts of 'Moreagain', all in one word.

15 June 1960 : Another day of waiting and swimming, with virtually no news. Several men at a garage, Croats and ethnic Italians, told me there were still 8,000 ethnic Italians in Pula, out of a total population of 35,000. All these men said there was no discrimination against the Italians, who could travel freely to Italy.

Dmitri Dymov, correspondent of the Soviet news agency TASS, took me for a fish dinner served on a lino-covered table in an open-air café. Dymov, a little fair-haired chap, argued with me about the question of forced farm collectivization. He could not deny that it had been shown in Poland and Yugoslavia, when freedom was granted to farmers to leave collectives, that the majority were against it. He tried to equate those farmers in Russia who had opposed collectives with the 'White' counter-revolutionaries, but I pipped him by quoting from Mikhail Sholokhov's book, *Virgin Soil Upturned.* Sholokhov makes it clear that some farmers who opposed collectivization nevertheless supported the Soviet system. I recently finished this most powerful book – no doubt approved by the Soviet authorities because it is basically pro-Communist – in which there is not only some excellent characterization, but also details of brutalities in the collectivization campaign of the early thirties.

16 June 1960 : A petrol pump attendant told me his wage was 13,000 dinars a month, equal to about £130 a year at the official rate. *[The purchasing power was almost certainly higher.]* Labourers, he said, got only 10,000 dinars. A journalist told me he got 35,000. However, I have seen no really poor-looking people in Pula, and many who were well dressed. Colleagues tell me no one goes hungry, but Dymov insisted that the standard of living in the Soviet Union was markedly higher. *[I believe he was wrong. I was able to judge for myself a year later when I first worked in the Soviet Union.]*

Started the day with a 150-mile drive in my Beetle through countryside of wild beauty, with breathless glimpses of the blue

Adriatic as we wound our way up and down good mountain roads towards Rijeka (Fiume) – both words mean river. Then into the interior for another 120 miles or so to Karlovac, through less mountainous though rolling farming and vineyard areas, rather like parts of Austria, in places like a wilder Somerset.

At Karlovac, we followed Tito and Nasser as they walked round a modern turbine factory. I liked the absence of more than the odd slogan, and the undrilled clapping which greeted the two leaders as they walked past grimy workers in blue overalls and black berets. It was not good of me to be quietly amused on the car journey to Karlovac as poor old Dmitri, who has been drinking too much vodka, had to jump out several times because of car sickness on the mountain roads. He, poor chap, wanted the window open, but one of two Yugoslavs who also travelled in my car said he had just had flu and asked for the air supply to be restricted. They had to compromise.

The roads were excellent. Good food at lunch in Karlovac. The general standard in restaurants seems much better than in Poland. What is more, no poultry wandering on the roads as in Poland, though I'm told there is in Serbia. This is Croatia. From Karlovac another 50 miles to Plitvice, scene of a natural wonder, some 16 connected lakes with about 30 waterfalls set in wooded mountains at about 2,000 feet *[610 m]*. Tito and Nasser are to tour the area tomorrow – my 35th birthday. A nice present from Reuters.

17 June 1960 : From Plitvice I drove some 220 miles to Bled, an Alpine lakeside tourist spot near the Austrian frontier. Dymov came with me again and, for part of the way, we had a hitch-hiking forestry official, whom Dymov questioned about workers' self-government in Yugoslav factories. He put the questions in Serbo-Croat and told me afterwards in Russian that in each factory, the man said, there was a workers' council, elected by all the employees, and a factory directorate, comprising the manager and some technicians and foremen. The directorate was responsible for technical questions and the workers' council for others, with cooperation between them.

Have been enjoying the Turkish coffee which is served, with the grounds, in little copper or brass pots, tinned inside, looking like large inkwells with handles, except that they are wider towards the bottom instead of the reverse. *[Part of Croatia was in the Ottoman Empire until the nineteenth century.]* You pour the coffee – called '*kava*' here – into a cup and let the grounds settle, and then drink until you start tasting grounds. Then, reluctantly, because it is so tasty, you stop, and drink the water which is normally served with the coffee.

In a restaurant, Dymov wished me many happy returns of my birthday and added that he hoped I would spend part of my life under Communism. I laughed and said I did not know whether that would be good for me. *[I think I was trying to be polite.]*

On the way to Bled we drove to Ljubljana, the handsome little capital of the most northerly Yugoslav republic, Slovenia. The Slovenes and Croats are both Slav races and speak similar languages. Ljubljana has quite an Austrian look, and when Dymov asked people the way in his excellent Serbo-Croat they replied in equally excellent German, having noticed we were in a Volkswagen. In a modern exhibition hall, Tito and Nasser walked round a motor show. Yugoslavia is now producing quite a large range of motor vehicles, most of them under licence from foreign firms, with increasing percentages of locally produced parts.

Overnighted in a very good hotel, the Grand Hotel, Toplice, which was packed with American, British and German tourists.

18 June 1960 : The passenger in my Volkswagen today was Mrs Biro – not sure of the spelling – a 40-ish Jewess who runs the photo service of the Yugoslav news agency. She told me she was a Communist whose father had been gassed in Auschwitz. She had escaped the same fate because the train taking her and other Jews to Auschwitz (Poland) from Hungary had to turn back because Soviet bombers destroyed the railway lines ahead. She was put into an Austrian concentration camp and had to work on a farm for a year until the war ended.

She told me that the murder of her father, a good man, had

destroyed her Jewish religious faith. She had told her father not to worry when they had to part, because she was sure that God would not allow such a good person to suffer unduly. I asked what she was living for. She said she was inspired by human progress, of which there had been much in Yugoslavia since the last war. This is something which plays a large part in my philosophy too.

This little, quite jolly and fairly pretty woman, who spoke good English, said that Tito's greatest achievement was workers' self-government, which was making the workers in nationalized firms much more interested in their work. *[The only private firms are small craftsmen employing just a few workers.]* She said that if the workers made their firm more efficient they got a share of the profits.

The emphasis had changed over from state-subsidized production to making things which are saleable and fixing economic prices. Even publishing houses wanting to put out Communist classics had to finance this unprofitable side of their business by publishing tripe.

As for agriculture, she said that at present there were no direct efforts to increase collectivization at all. Instead, private farmers were being encouraged to make contracts with state and collective farms to grow certain needed crops. In return the state and collective farms helped them by operating machinery on the small private holdings. Two land reforms in Yugoslavia since the war have cut private farms to a maximum of 25 acres *[10 ha]*.

The state and collective farms account for only a few per cent of the land at present. Mrs Biro said that in the period of attempted collectivization until 1953 production fell, because the farmers just did not want to be collectivized. I was amazed to hear a Communist putting that so simply and so truly. In Yugoslavia, she added, much of the land, which was hilly, would not gain economically by collectivization anyway. She told me that virtually every Yugoslav was free to travel abroad – another glaring contrast to East Germany.

From Bled, a picture-postcard resort, we drove first up into the Julian Alps which, with peaks around 8,000 feet *[2,400 m]*, run along the Austrian and Italian frontiers. We stopped on the

7,000-feet Vrsic pass. There were large patches of snow near the road. I snowballed with Yugoslav journalists and the Foreign Office spokesman, Mr Vujica. Staggering view of bare stone peaks, like the Dolomites, but greyish instead of pinkish, and with lots of snow in crevasses. We had to drive ahead of Tito and Nasser and, owing to a stupid official arrangement, we reporters were not allowed to see the two leaders up in the mountains; only the photographers were permitted there. I had to pick up information hours later from photographers about how Nasser played in the snow with his 15-year-old daughter, Hoda, and three young sons, while Tito looked on.

On the far side of the pass, which was Italian territory until 1945, we drove through a mountainous area which was the scene of tough fighting between Austrian and Italian Alpine troops in the First World War, described by Hemingway in *A Farewell to Arms*.

As the two leaders approached the small town of Korabid, the local siren blew, and hundreds rushed from cafés to catch a glimpse of them. On the way back to Pula, near Trieste, Mrs Biro pointed out that we had passed close to the once Austrian and now Yugoslav village of Lipica, once the site of the Austrian Imperial Stud, which bred the white Lipizzaner horses, made famous by the exquisite dressage of the Austrian Imperial Court's 'Spanish Riding School' in Vienna. We saw several Lipizzaner being ridden along a road.

19 June 1960 : After waiting for the final communiqué, which did not come, I swam with colleagues near Pula. Bright sun played on light-coloured rocks which, underwater, looked yellow, then green, gradually dissolving into the greeny-blue of the Adriatic. Who could resist having another swim there in spite of the feeling of sunburn on one's bald, 35-year-old head? Not me. We ate tasty fish in the open air on a veranda by the sea. The journalists, including the Yugoslavs, are getting fed up at being kept hanging around.

20 June 1960 : Seeing the mountains this week has awed me and given me comfort. The Alps are so wonderful that they help to prove the existence of an equally wonderful (or more wonderful) Creator.

Today was our pay-off day. Around 10 am we embarked in a trim launch from a village near Pula to cross the lovely blue strait of about $1^1/2$ miles to the small, neat harbour of Tito's private island, Brioni, which is only occasionally seen by journalists. The two-mile long, fairly low-lying island, about half a mile wide, is largely covered with pinewoods. From a hotel, reserved for official guests and staff, we walked across the island to Tito's modern two-storey villa of about ten large rooms. We soon realized why so many politicians go to visit Tito there. Apart from the sun, sand, sea and peace, there are sub-tropical flowers, tame deer roaming in the woods and open spaces, a zoo, Roman ruins and a former Roman Catholic church now used as a museum.

From a tastefully furnished anteroom we were ushered through glass doors into a large, long room. Tito, in a cream suit, as smart as ever – he has been numbered among the world's best-dressed men – and Nasser in a dark blue suit, came towards us from a terrace. After the photographers had had their chance, we began to ask questions. The answers were not very revealing, as the two leaders in most cases referred us to their final communiqué, which we did not yet have. Tito ticked off one of his subordinates for not having let us see it before the press conference. Nasser, who is dark brown, has an appealing smile and speaks good English. Tito also spoke some English, but did not say as much as the Egyptian. He ended the exchanges after a few minutes, after asking the waiters to give us reporters drinks so we would not ask so many questions. Tito has humour and a commanding presence; is handsome too.

Afterwards we were given the communiqué, which was notable for not taking up the Indonesian proposal for a 'neutralist' summit conference. Tito had apparently favoured that, but had bowed to opposition from the Indian leader, Nehru, and Nasser. Apparently the consensus among the 'non-aligned countries' now is that such a conference would not be able to achieve much during the present East–West stalemate, but might be worthwhile in the event of a world crisis.

This evening I took my leave from colleagues who have helped to brighten up this half-holiday week, and drove through the mainly moorland countryside of Istria, past donkey carts and chirping crickets, back to Italy – Trieste.

21 June 1960 : No problem to have my Beetle quickly serviced at the Trieste Volkswagen garage; another advantage of this car. Had an efficient Italian haircut – lots of faff with powder, perfume and other little touches of virtuosity. The barber told me life was going on reasonably well in Italy, in spite of 20,000 unemployed in Trieste alone. Another Italian, manning a souvenir stall at San Giusto castle, built by the Venetian doges in the sixteenth century, told me things had been in some respects better when Trieste was part of the Austro-Hungarian Empire before the First World War, as it then had a large hinterland.

Regretfully had my last Adriatic swim near Trieste. Wishing to lunch a few miles further north, I asked for fish and was told they only had some small fish which the waitress thought I would not like. So I ordered some veal. But the waitress returned to tell me she had found out they had a second kind of fish. I asked her what kind. She said, '*Rani.*' Although I have some Italian I did not know this word, so asked her to describe them. She said something like, '*Quelle che vivono nelle fosse e dicono "quaak quaak".*' ('Those that live in ditches and say "quack-quack".') I said, no thank you very much, and later confirmed from my dictionary that she had indeed been talking about frogs. *[Some years later, having become more used to Continental cuisine, I tried frogs' legs and found them excellent, like delicate chicken.]*

My nerves are again becoming accustomed to that terrible Italian habit of having one's car fitted with a klaxon and using it on all possible occasions, even in a '*zona di silenzio*'.

22 June 1960 : Driving through Switzerland, I picked up a slightly bearded 19-year-old engineering student from Wanne-Eickel in the German Ruhr area, who told me he had cut his studies to go hitch-hiking for three weeks through France, Spain and Italy and said he had been robbed of most of his money in a Milan youth hostel, so was now making for home. At the West German frontier, an official gave my companion a grilling, took him inside his office and searched his baggage closely. The student grinned at me and admitted ruefully that he did look rather scruffy. At a camp site, I offered him my tent for the night and fixed up a bed for myself in the car. The student told me his father was the deputy director of a nitrogen factory and there had been a family storm when he announced he was going to make his trip. He said his conscience had pricked him a little about missing some lessons; he was nevertheless confident he would pass his exams.

23 June 1960 : Argued about religion with the student, a Catholic. He said he did not agree with everything he had been taught; he was particularly concerned about the Pope's riches, to me a subsidiary matter. He said that on religion one would never find a complete answer, so it was better to concentrate on one's job and so on. Dropped the student north of Freiburg in Baden-Württemberg, near where he intended to visit friends. Back home this evening. Elfi was delighted with a pair of blue leather Yugoslav moccasins.

9 Touring Austria with Khrushchev

26 June 1960 : I left my folks again to cover a visit to Austria by Khrushchev. Comforted Chris by telling him we shall be having a whole month together in Berlin shortly after my return in a fortnight.

Overnighted in Ulm in Baden-Württemberg, which boasts the highest church in the world (161 metres), a handsome Gothic structure. Churches, taken as a whole, are perhaps the most beautiful buildings in the world. *Ergo*, there must be something in what inspired them. Of course, one could use the same argument about beautiful modern buildings in the Communist world, but I doubt if there are many up to now.

In a café, watched a satirical TV film about the past of many average Germans in the Nazi era and since. One crack that brought the house down in my café was when one of the three heroes, who has been put into a lunatic asylum, insists that he does *not* think that he is Hitler. Have bought a car radio, which helps me to keep awake while driving.

27 June 1960 : Onward via the Salzburg area to Vienna, another 350 miles, but easy going as most of it is now motorway. At the frontier I gave a lift to a young Hungarian student who'd fled to Austria with his father after the abortive 1956 revolt. His father had been a local leader of the revolt. The student was amused when I told him he could thank Khrushchev for his lift today.

Although this young man has every reason to hate Khrushchev, he agreed with me that Khrushchev has introduced a certain liberalization in Communism.

30 June 1960 : Called at the luxurious Imperial Hotel, a Soviet secret police headquarters until the four-power occupation ended in 1955. Staff were busy polishing for the arrival of Khrushchev, whose party will fill most of the hotel. By a twist of fate, among the guests still in the hotel this morning was Edgar Eisenhower, a lawyer who happens to be the eldest brother of the American President. He was to have stayed in the hotel tonight, but left this morning. He did not admit he was leaving because of Khrushchev. Half jokingly, he turned to another reporter and me and asked us what we would ask Khrushchev. Then he said, 'Ask him to explain Hungary.'

To Vienna's modern airport with Bill Krasser, Czech-born chief assistant of our chief correspondent in Vienna, 62-year-old Englishman Hubert ('Harry') Harrison, a veteran of pre-war and wartime journalism. Khrushchev was greeted by a largely silent crowd and exactly three Soviet flags put up by the authorities. Austrian leaders shook hands with him warmly. Speeches on both sides emphasized Austria's neutrality, and Khrushchev described this as a fruit of co-existence. On the 15-kilometre road to the hotel there were thin crowds, and a few people waved paper Soviet and Austrian flags distributed by the local Communists. About 4,000 people near the hotel produced some scattered cheering and clapping.

Later Khrushchev waved and smiled from the hotel balcony, where Hitler was cheered after the 1938 annexation of Austria. A man in the crowd said, 'Hitler!' and a group of Communists near him muttered angrily. But their leader told them not to let themselves be provoked and the incident passed off quietly.

After protocol visits and wreath-laying ceremonies this afternoon, Khrushchev and his appealing, motherly wife, Nina Petrovna, saw Mozart's *The Magic Flute*, one of my favourites, at the opera. It was a fascinating sight – the ex-miner in his black suit in the royal box, the glittering candelabra and the plush red-and-gilt decorations. I wondered what would happen were I to pretend to point a pistol at Khrushchev; I knew the place was packed with Austrian and Soviet plainclothes men. I decided not to pretend. The libretto was changed at one point to make Papageno, the comic bird-catcher, say when he was given a drink of water, 'It's not even vodka.' I shall probably never know whether Khrushchev was told of the joke.

1 July 1960 : At 7.40 am I took up position in the pavement café outside the Imperial Hotel. We know Khrushchev's habit of taking surprise walks. Other journalists were also on the watch.

The Soviet leader came out at 9 am and waddled off along the busy, tree-lined Ringstrasse with his wife, Foreign Minister Andrei Gromyko, top Soviet woman Communist, Yekaterina Furtseva – rather haggard-looking, but not unattractive when she smiles – other leaders, a dozen or so Austrian and Soviet security men, an equal number of pressmen and a posse of green-uniformed Austrian police.

This time Khrushchev got a friendly reception from the crowds, who responded to his waves and smiles. A few people clapped. Khrushchev patted small children's heads, chatted with one or two people and plunged down a pedestrian subway at the busy Opera crossing. Underground, he darted into a coffee bar, where I was amused to watch Austrian policemen mishandling plainclothes Russian security men who were trying to keep up with Khrushchev in the crush. Shortly after that the 20-minute walk ended and Khrushchev drove off for talks with Austrian leaders.

Later this morning he walked round a formerly German-owned truck factory, which was run by the Soviets after the Second World War and in which the Austrian state is now the majority shareholder. Here, in a speech to the employees (who, in this factory, unusually include a large Communist element), he offered to 'buy the whole of Austria' – providing the Austrians bought goods of similar value from the Soviet Union. (Next year the Austrians are due to complete the main deliveries of goods to the Soviet Union in payment for Soviet-appropriated former German assets which the Russians handed over to Austria when the Soviet Union decided at last to withdraw from Austria in 1955 – a decision for which the Austrians are publicly giving Khrushchev a lot of the credit, no doubt correctly.)

Khrushchev also gave impressive figures on Soviet economic progress. For instance, he said that this year the Soviet Union is building more dwellings than Britain, France, Sweden, Belgium, West Germany and Switzerland put together. *[That figure did not look quite so impressive if one realized that the total population of the countries referred to was roughly equal to that of the Soviet Union – 218 million. Further, Khrushchev did not state the size of the dwellings being built in the Soviet Union, where the average living space per family was much smaller than in Western European countries.]*

Khrushchev argued that the Soviet Union's large housing construction was one factor showing that it could not possibly want war. Khrushchev was well received at the factory and was in good form. When people in the audience shouted to his interpreter to speak up, Khrushchev smilingly slapped the man on his back and said, 'You are young. You ought to be able to speak loudly.'

Tonight there was another scrum with the security men, when the Soviet party arrived at the eighteenth-century baroque palace of Schönbrunn, the former imperial summer residence in the Vienna suburb of Hietzing. Officials shouted, 'It's impossible ... no discipline,' as pressmen and other guests elbowed a way into the front ranks of the 1,500 waiting in a gilded gallery to catch a glimpse of the Soviet leader and his wife as they were shepherded into a supposedly private room where, I was told, one or two journalists had already managed to secret themselves. I was stopped at the door with other colleagues.

Later, after phoning some copy, I learned that correspondents of the American agency, United Press, and the French agency, AFP, had managed to get past the door, perhaps being taken for someone official. I got in soon afterwards. I was wearing a dinner jacket. Holding a plate in the air, like one of the waiters, who were also wearing dinner jackets, I followed a waitress into the sanctum.

Several colleagues were allowed to follow me later, after protesting to the head of the Austrian state police that we could not do our job if we could not see Khrushchev.

Khrushchev had a really jolly time with the Austrian leaders, who look like a lot of pleasant fat uncles and treat Khrushchev like another one. He evidently likes this. No doubt this sort of treatment – compared to Adenauer's view of Khrushchev as the devil personified – helped in persuading the Russians to withdraw from Austria. Before he left, after about $2^{1}/_{2}$ hours, Khrushchev put his arm round Chancellor Julius Raab, of the (Catholic) People's Party, on the sofa where they were sitting, and Social Democratic Vice-Chancellor Pittermann put his arm round Furtseva.

A tipsy Austrian ex-minister shook hands with Khrushchev, and an art professor sketched him, to his delight.

Gromyko, who is amazingly like US Vice-President Nixon, gave an impromptu press conference. He provided a good line for my report when I asked him if the Soviet Union would accede to Prime Minister Macmillan's request that it should return to the Geneva disarmament talks. He replied, 'Not at all.'

A feature of the slap-up buffet: eggs with edible (Soviet) red stars on them.

2 July 1960 : After six hours sleep – more than I thought I would get on average this week – another day following Khrushchev in and near Vienna. In the evening he made a speech in the Hofburg, the former imperial palace, to the Communist-dominated Austro-Soviet Society. There were 1,200 inside the hall where he spoke and another 5,000 or so outside. He departed from his prepared text to make an impassioned appeal for peace, in which he said that anyone who thought it necessary to have a war to bring about the final victory of Communism –which he said he was convinced was coming anyway – belonged in a lunatic system. We Western correspondents took that as a jab against the Chinese who have suggested in recent months that they think a war might be necessary.

Khrushchev illustrated the present world situation by recalling that, as a boy, he had been one of the top scholars in a Bible class. He said he still remembered the story of how Noah put in the Ark seven pairs of 'clean' animals and seven pairs of 'unclean' ones. He compared these two sets with the capitalist and Communist worlds, and said that the animals were ordered to keep calm so as not to rock the boat. Today, he said, with sputniks and moon rockets, the world was so small that it was like Noah's Ark, and if we rocked it we would all be annihilated.

I agreed with that, but was not convinced by his arguments on disarmament controls. The Western position is that the control measures for each step in disarmament should be worked out in advance. The Soviet position is that the two sides should sign a complete disarmament agreement, including controls, but that the controls would not be immediately put in force.

3 July 1960 : Khrushchev and we – some 150 journalists – left Vienna today for a five-day tour of Austria. Police cars and motor-cycles escorted the Soviet leader's convoy on the road, helicopters did the same in the air, police boats on lakes and rivers, and foot police on the roads and in the woods.

After a visit to a power station, we drove westwards by the (not blue) Danube to the site of Mauthausen concentration camp, a fortress-like complex of buildings on a small hill. Of about 350,000 people from all over Europe who were imprisoned here during the Second World War, about 123,000 died, mainly from maltreatment or being shot in the back of the neck. They included about 32,000 Soviet citizens, 34 Americans and 17 Britons.

In a speech outdoors, near a stone memorial, tubby Austrian Interior Minister Afritsch said Nazism had shown what happened when government slipped out of the hands of the people, and a government thought it could disrespect human dignity. *[Khrushchev could have taken that as veiled criticism of the Soviet Union.]* Afritsch was followed by former Foreign Minister, Leopold Figl, now Speaker of the Austrian Parliament, who played a major role in the negotiations which resulted in the

Austrian Peace Treaty. Figl, himself a former inmate of Mauthausen, said the inmates' crime had been to love freedom. Meanwhile Khrushchev, his panama hat still on, had been seated in the front row of the audience. He rose to shake hands firmly with Figl. He then made a short speech, referring to the suffering under Nazism, particularly in Mauthausen, and going on to express concern about 'revanchism and militarism' in West Germany.

On to Linz, about 140 miles west of Vienna. A city of about 190,000, Linz is the capital of Upper Austria, one of the states of the Austrian Federation. *[Near Linz is Hitler's hometown, Braunau-on-the-Inn, just inside Austria. Hitler planned to have a gigantic art gallery built in Linz, which would have contained German and other European art treasures, bought or stolen by the Nazis. Many works of art were collected and stored, but the gallery was never built.]*

In Linz I pecked at an exquisite dinner, put on in a local hall to honour Khrushchev. An orchestra played Strauss waltzes. I felt I was taking part in some operetta film. Later Khrushchev said, at an impromptu press conference, that he still hoped for an understanding with the West on disarmament, but felt this would be impossible with the present United States Government, which goes out of office at the year-end. The question which prompted this newsworthy reply was put by the doyen of Moscow correspondents, Romanian-born Jew Henry Shapiro, chief correspondent of United Press, a little moustached man. It gave me pleasure to beat Shapiro's assistant to a phone. *[I had no idea then that I would face tough competition from Shapiro in the early sixties, when I was Reuters chief correspondent in Moscow.]*

During the dinner, a noted American correspondent, Eddie Gilmore of the Associated Press, told me how he got to Russia in a British convoy in 1941. It took him 20 days to reach Moscow from the northern port of Murmansk. In 1943 he married a Bolshoi ballet dancer, but after the war Stalin would not let his wife leave. For a time she was sent to Siberia for having had relations with him, but a leading American Republican politician,

Wendell Willkie, intervened with Stalin on the Gilmores' behalf and his wife was released. Gilmore stayed on with her until 1953 when, after Stalin's death, Khrushchev allowed her to go. Later today Khrushchev visited Austria's biggest industrial plant, the Vöest steelworks in Linz, which employs 18,000. In an impromptu lunch speech, Khrushchev gave us the old, but still quite impressive, story of his father who was poor and his grandfather who was a serf. 'And who am I?' he went on, 'I am the Chairman of the Council of Ministers of the Soviet Union, and what a Council of Ministers, that of the largest country on earth.'

He puts it over with lots of punch, as though he means it, in a homespun way.

At Wels, where Khrushchev visited an agricultural research station, the Soviet leader was buttonholed by a weeping woman who wanted a visa to visit her parents in Russia. Khrushchev's unattractive daughter Yelena, a 23-year-old spectacled brunette, pleaded with him to do something. He promised he would.

An afternoon break in a spa building at Bad Ischl, favourite spa of Kaiser Franz-Josef and a residence of Franz Lehar. An orchestra played Lehar and Johann Strauss for Khrushchev as he drank his coffee. Through the beautiful mountain and lakes scenery of the Salzkammergut – ironically Austria's salt-mining area – passing the Wolfgangsee, where stands the White Horse Inn of operetta fame, to an old country house hotel overlooking Lake Fuschl, where Khrushchev overnighted in the room which had been used by Nazi Foreign Minister Joachim von Ribbentrop, who had owned the house until 1945.

Crowds, not very large ones, came out in places *en route*. Some people smiled, a few clapped and waved. I'd describe his welcome as friendly without being demonstrative. I was annoyed at a report in the *New York Herald Tribune*, describing the reaction of the people who thronged around Khrushchev in the Vienna pedestrian subway two days ago. I saw most of them smiling and many clapping and waving, but this American paper called the reaction 'frigid' – pure Cold War writing.

From Fuschl, Khrushchev drove to Salzburg, where he first

visited Mozart's birthplace, a six-storey house. Some of the several hundred people waiting there cheered and clapped while others whistled – a sign of disapproval in Austria. Salzburg is strongly Catholic, but there were thousands on the streets to see Khrushchev. After an official reception in the former residence of the local archbishop, he led Chancellor Raab onto a balcony at about 11 pm, took Raab's hand in his and raised it in a joint wave to a crowd of several hundred outside. There was quite a bit of cheering and a few more whistles.

In a short chat in Russian with Furtseva, I told her I was from Reuters. She threw her head back slowly, opened her mouth and said throatily, 'Oh!' in an awed tone. A former textile worker, she is reputed to have been Khrushchev's mistress.

5 July 1960 : To the Glockner-Kaprun, Austria's most important hydro-electric complex, in the north-west close to Switzerland. On the way up to view a dam, Khrushchev's delegation and accompanying journalists travelled part of the way on a large open platform lift, some 15 yards square, which moved up the mountainside. Suddenly Khrushchev, leaning against an outside rail of the lift, said to Henry Shapiro, 'Give us a song!'

Shapiro excused himself, saying he was not in good voice. So Khrushchev, rather hesitantly and, for the first time in my experience, looking a shade shy, broke into the strains of *Stenka Razin*, a famous song about the leader of a seventeenth-century abortive revolt of Cossacks and peasants, who was executed in Moscow in 1671. Members of the Soviet party on the lift, and others who knew the song, joined in. They included the Vienna correspondent of the French news agency AFP, Latayev, who hails from an exiled Russian family. He told me afterwards he did not like Khrushchev, but decided, after all, to sing along with him. The singing lasted for just a few minutes, until the lift reached the top. I don't think I shall ever forget it. *[I think that, sadly, no one recorded Khrushchev in song; there were not so many portable tape-recorders in those days.]*

6 July 1960 : By flaunting a copy of the Soviet Government newspaper Izvestia, I managed to get past the police and gain access to the warm mineral baths at the city of Villach, in southern Austria, to which we drove last night. The baths were visited by Furtseva and Khrushchev's daughter Yelena, who was seen for the first time today to be wearing lipstick. I was asked to leave before the two women started to swim. We had all hoped that Khrushchev would go for a swim, but he didn't. The police had taken terrific precautions to see that no one got in to take a picture of tubby old Khrushchev in his bathing trunks.

On through more beautiful countryside to Klagenfurt, capital of the state of Carinthia, which borders on the Yugoslav republic of Slovenia. Until 1954, during the four-power occupation of Austria, Klagenfurt was the garrison town of the West Yorkshire Regiment. Khrushchev ate in a hotel there which had been an officers' club of that regiment. *[Carinthia is currently in the news, as its premier is Jörg Haider, former leader of the Freedom Party and a right-wing populist.]*

Eddie Gilmore and a number of other correspondents are wearing lapel badges showing an eagle, similar to those worn by the Soviet delegation. This enables them to get past the security men. They bought the badges at kiosks.

After Khrushchev was presented with a sporting rifle in Klagenfurt, he said he had never shot anyone in his life, to his knowledge. He had used a gun only as a soldier and, like most soldiers, had not known if his shots had killed anyone.

Later several hundred guests attended a sumptuous dinner given for Khrushchev at Eggenberg Castle, near Graz. Around 10 pm we journalists boarded the tail-end of Khrushchev's special train for the last four-and-a-half-hour lap back to Vienna. I asked Mr Lebedev, Khrushchev's quiet and handsome private secretary, if he could get a few words of comment on the death of Aneurin Bevan, deputy leader of the Labour Party and, in my opinion, one of the few real British political personalities of recent years. Lebedev said he would try, but Khrushchev had gone to bed.

7 July 1960 : During a Soviet Embassy reception tonight – one of the final events in Khrushchev's Austrian visit – the Soviet leader's senior security officer, Major-General I.S. Zacharov, half humorously dressed me down for reporting that he had been buffeted by Austrian police when unrecognized in a street mêlée caused by Khrushchev walking through a welcoming crowd in Graz yesterday; one of the warmest welcomes Khrushchev has had. I told Zacharov that my report had been correct. I was worried when Zacharov said he had a 'present' for me, apparently in response to what I had written. I expressed my concern to a Soviet Embassy official who told me not to get the wind up. *[I never received Zacharov's 'present'.]*

8 July 1960 : Khrushchev left today, after saying at a press conference that if the West German *Bundestag* (Lower House) goes ahead with its plan to hold a meeting in Berlin in September, the Soviet Union might conclude its threatened separate peace treaty with East Germany. That, he said, would require members of the *Bundestag* to ask for East German visas to return to Bonn. *[That was mere polemics, as the* Bundestag *members could have flown back to West Germany.]* Khrushchev said recently that neither side should change things in Berlin for six to eight months until a new summit meeting was held. He apparently regards a *Bundestag* meeting in Berlin as rocking the boat, though such meetings have been held there before and have been allowed by the three Western Allies, the occupying powers in West Berlin.

9 July 1960 : On my way home, overnighted in Merklingen, near Stuttgart. Had just booked in at a small hotel, when Bonn office told me I might have to fly to the troubled Congo Republic in a United States Air Force plane. As no one in the hotel could hear the phone at night, I got permission to sleep in the hotel's telephone booth on my airbed. As I was dozing off, a great Alsatian loomed in the open doorway but, disdaining me as a morsel, moved away. I was already asleep when the phone rang, causing me to wildly disturb my bedclothes. I grabbed the phone in the dark and found it was someone on the autobahn wanting to know if there was a room free. There wasn't. In the morning I was told that the cleaning woman had thought there was a body in the booth. The things I do for Reuters.

15 July 1960 : Found I was pictured in the Soviet Government newspaper, *Izvestia* – along with a man called Khrushchev, of course, as he was kissing a baby near Salzburg.

10 An unnatural lifestyle

17 July 1960 : It has been lovely to be home for a week and have
nearly four days off. It makes me realize what an unnatural life
I have been leading this past 18 months. Last year, for instance, I
was away from home for more than six months. Naturally, I have
enjoyed many of the jobs which have taken me away, but I yearn
for a more ordered existence, say with a house of our own where
we would stay for years and years. Of course, if we had that, I
would probably be restless, that's me. *[That did not come about for
more than ten years.]*

24 July 1960 : Holidaying on the southern Netherlands island of
Walcheren, we have been introducing sundry Germans and
Dutch to the ancient game of cricket. Robin was bucked because
he scored 24 in one innings today. He asked me what the world
record was. Later the attraction of cricket was demonstrated by a
German, aged about 40, who watched us playing, but declined an
invitation to join in. But after a while he started asking technical
questions and, about an hour later, when one of our fielders went
home for lunch, he signalled from the boundary – the sea – that
he would step in. We picked up several players this way, including
a young Dutchman trained on baseball who wanted to bowl like a
pitcher, which of course is *verboden*.

Showed Robin a sausage packet which in Dutch
'*gegarandieerd tot*'. He easily guessed that the first word meant

'guaranteed', but as '*tot*' in German means 'dead', he really thought it meant that the sausage had given up the ghost. But in Dutch '*tot*' means 'until' and, next to the word, was the sell-by date.

An extract from the foreword to *Essays in Labour History* – a collection in memory of G.D.H. Cole, Oxford professor and socialist theorist, by an American, Stephen K. Bailey:

> Life in midpassage is too filled with demands and routines to permit much personal reflection. One is conscious that the years are ticking by; that the children are mushrooming; that parents and other older friends are now gone, or have themselves become dependent; that sooner than expected the sharp, cutting edge of one's own psyche has been slightly dulled by time and fate; and that the great questions of purpose and meaning of life remain as intractable as ever ...

I like that, as much of it reflects my feelings.

28 July 1960 : I get a further rise of £150 a year from next month, bringing my total emoluments to £1,850, which sounds astronomical. In a letter giving me this news, Gerry said I had been making a 'splendid contribution' to Reuters. I took over today as John's holiday relief as news editor, finding, as usual, colleagues clamouring for days off they had been bilked of. It made me, in spite of my rise, once again annoyed at Reuters and reinforced my determination to seek a better job.

30 July 1960 : An 11-hour day yesterday and 10¾ hours today. Had a talk with Gerry in which I told him that the staff as a whole was fed up at their lack of time off, and repeated my earlier plea that we should not cast the news net quite so widely. He advised me not to worry so much about 'the boys', but to begin to realize that, with my status in the firm, I had interests more akin to those of the management. He maintained Reuters could not afford to give proper time off, but agreed that things had been worse than

102

usual in recent months. He said things were even worse in the Paris office, where he had worked previously. That is a disgrace. I just don't believe that Reuters cannot afford to give reasonable time off.

Took Elfi and Chris to Cologne-Bonn airport to see in Adenauer, returning from talks with de Gaulle in Paris. He would say nothing about the content of the talks, so I asked him what effect they had had on relations with Britain. He looked annoyed, half turned away, then turned back and smiled slightly as he said, 'I take it we are all friends.' *[While Adenauer was Chancellor, between 1949 and 1963, there was frequent friction with successive British governments.]*

1 August 1960 : A senior official of the Federal Press Office indicated to me that Adenauer and de Gaulle, at their weekend talks, had agreed to consolidate, rather than press on quickly, with European economic link-ups. They had also agreed to work for some kind of political co-ordination with Britain and other countries which are outside the Common Market.

De Gaulle has apparently made it clear that he does not want a supranational Common Market, for the time being anyway. (It would go against his ideas of France's grandeur.) Adenauer is now using the situation to seek a *rapprochement* with Britain, which he also needs because of the increasing tension with the Soviet Union. The fact that de Gaulle and Adenauer are shelving the supranational side of the Common Market design for the time being will make it easier for Britain to get into the Common Market, if it wants to.

6 August 1960 : A friendly discussion with John Adams, Bonn correspondent of Radio Free Europe (RFE), the Cold War radio station which broadcasts to the satellite countries of the Soviet bloc. *[In that era RFE claimed to be financed from voluntary contributions, but years later it was officially admitted that it was a CIA (Central Intelligence Agency) operation.]* Adams, a quiet-mannered Englishman, maintained that RFE was there to provide an opposition voice to the government propaganda radios of the Communist countries. I am in favour of this, but it all depends on how it is done and from what standpoint. He thinks it forces the Communists gradually to become more liberal, by giving way to arguments put forward by RFE and taken up by the peoples in the Communist countries. I hope he is right. Judging by some American propaganda about Communist countries, the result might be to make conditions harsher still, by strengthening Communist extremists rather than the less extreme forces.

11 August 1960 : British Prime Minister Harold Macmillan flew home today after two days of talks with Adenauer in Bonn. The main result was an agreement that, in attempts to bridge the gap between the six Common Market countries and the seven other European countries belonging to the European Free Trade Association (EFTA), there will be inter-governmental talks instead of talks between the two groups. (EFTA members are Austria, Britain, Denmark, Norway, Portugal, Sweden and Switzerland.) Macmillan described this decision as 'historic'. This new approach reduces the importance of the supranational Common Market Commission, which is apparently not in favour of bridging the gap.

Macmillan and Adenauer have evidently decided that, in face of the Soviet threat, one should not allow the two blocs which are forming in Western Europe to become final. The question remains whether de Gaulle agrees with them. Khrushchev's policy since the U-2 spy plane incident has done a lot to bring Macmillan and Adenauer together. Before that, Adenauer thought that Macmillan was 'soft' towards the Russians, while Macmillan, no doubt, regarded Adenauer as too much of a Cold War warrior.

One of the main arguments used in Britain against its joining the Common Market has been that Britain, due to Commonwealth ties, could not join a supranational political organization. This argument has now been largely removed because of de Gaulle's unwillingness to submit France to such a supranational organization, as was envisaged by the founders of the Common Market (and still is, in the long run).

13 August 1960 : A letter from my Dad – who lives in California – referring to my recent grouses about my job, tells me that 'the pluses in your business outweigh the minuses. You are doing something I would have like to have done, never made it. Am sure that there are many people who would give their high teeth to be in the position you are. All of which is not to discourage you to try something else, if that's the way you feel.'

14 August 1960 : Today's sermon in our local Lutheran church was on a text from Joshua in which the Israelites were exhorted to follow the right god, because he had dealt firmly with their enemies and, if they didn't follow him, would do the same to them too. The pastor did not bring out that this god was not the Christian God as conceived today, but the old Jewish tribal god. Even the Communists, today, do not threaten people with death if they do not join the party.

Elfi told me that, because of some of the things I have said about religion, she – brought up as a Lutheran – now feels a cheat when she says the whole of the creed in church. And, on the other hand, she sometimes feels ashamed for not believing it all, thinking that she is breaking her loyalty to the Church, ingrained since childhood. I told her she ought not to feel ashamed for using her brains, and that the church's exhortation to 'believe', whether one is really convinced or not, was unfair.

11 To the Rome Olympics – and the Pope

17 August 1960 : On my way, in my Beetle, to join the Reuter team at the Rome Olympics, I was accompanied by Rainer Wiegel, the 20-year-old dental technician son of our respected family dentist, Otto Wiegel. We called in Milan on 35-ish Sicilian plastic surgeon, Giuseppina (Geppi) del Duce, a stunning slim brunette whom I and a fellow sub-lieutenant, Joe Holder, used to take out when we were based in Messina, Sicily, in 1945. (In accordance with local tradition, she was always chaperoned by her younger brother.)

Geppi lives with her parents. Since Elfi and I visited her five years ago, time has drawn a few lines across her dark Latin features, but she remains a beauty. She has not married. Her mother told me that Geppi, since breaking off an engagement some years ago, has not found any man to her liking. I used my still-operative wartime Italian to chat with Geppi, who has just about forgotten the English she used to know. She told me she was one of only four Italian women surgeons specializing in plastic surgery. She works mainly on accident cases. Last summer she gave a lecture at an international surgeons' congress in London. She liked London, describing it as 'more honest' than Paris because it was not so tourist-oriented.

I collected tourist petrol coupons, allowing me to buy petrol at

4s 4d *[about 21p]* per gallon – locals pay about 20 per cent more. We drove along a new *autostrada* to Parma. Then the road took us up into Italy's backbone, the Apennines, where cypresses, wild-looking scrub, peeling hill towns and modern petrol stations provided local colour.

I picked up a German theology student, a Roman Catholic, from Münster University. As a good reason for believing in God, he referred to the evident order in the universe; a good reason, I think, for believing in some god, open to all kinds of arguments as to the nature of this god. Arriving at the Tyrrhenian Sea, on Italy's west coast, we plunged into the warm water at Marina di Massa. The shore is spoilt by ramshackle fences marking off private beaches belonging to hotels and hostels. We swam from what appeared to be a small communal patch. Near us a swarm of children played under the eyes of white-robed nuns. We overnighted in modern bedrooms let by a grocer who charged ten shillings *[50p]* a night, without breakfast.

18 August 1960 : After dropping Rainer about 40 miles north of Rome, where he was to have a few days' holiday, I drove along the Aurelian Way into the 'Eternal City' – founded, according to myth, in 753 BC. I caught a glimpse of the dome of St Peter's as I looked for the Reuter team's Olympic quarters in the Domus Pacis, normally a Roman Catholic youth hostel in north-western Rome. (All the Catholic organizations scattered about Rome made me think, not for the first time, of the resemblance between the all-embracing Catholic Church and the Soviet Communist Party.)

Was welcomed by Ranald McLurkin, our London chief reporter and manager of the Olympic team, and our elderly sports editor, moustached Vernon Morgan, a sporting 'blue'. *[I forget in which sport.]* Was handed various advertising items, including toothpaste, several cakes of soap, an inflatable rubber cushion for sitting on hard stadium stands, and a maroon tie embossed with the symbol of a Lambretta motor scooter.

Driving in Rome – I can compare it only with being at the wheel of a dodgem car in a very rollicking fair. One must forget most traffic rules and be ready to turn and twist at any moment, or to put brakes on hard when someone sweeps across your bow from right or left, particularly the former. The Continental priority-from-the-right rule applies, as in Germany, but much more so, because few side streets have 'Halt' or 'Slow' signs, so that, say, a motor scooter coming out of a small street into a main road often has the right of way over vehicles approaching from its left along the main road – and usually tries to insist on it. Vernon Morgan told me he had soon realized why we are all insured by the Olympic authorities during the games.

I am quartered in a tiny room about 10 ft by 7 ft *[3 m by 2 m]*, containing two single beds, one of which will soon be occupied by Bill Krasser from our Vienna office, fortunately someone I like a lot. Tonight I was a target for Roman flies. Vernon told me later that he, who has rather better accommodation, has ants as well as flies.

19 August 1960 : My main tasks during the Olympics are to cover rowing, canoeing and gymnastics. Today I drove out to the Olympic Lake, a two-mile wide, roughly circular crater lake called Lake Albano, beneath the wooded or wine-growing slopes on which stands the papal summer residence, Castel Gandolfo – a lovely venue whether for popes or oarsmen. Contacted Britain's oarsmen and canoeists at their modern boathouses and did a story on their first workout.

Am finding it fascinating driving in and around Rome, past so much history: the Forum, the Colosseum and the ancient Appian Way, flanked by the remains of Roman graves, many of them partially preserved with latter-day brick, with the Roman pieces looking grey like an unfinished jigsaw. On this road also are some of the catacombs associated with the early days of Christianity. Robin should be here for Latin practice.

This is my second look at Rome, but my first proper one, as I was here for only three or four hours one day in late 1944, during my naval service.

21 August 1960 : When I see the five Olympic rings, they remind me that I have that same symbol on a small photo album – a present from Dad after he had watched part of the 1936 Olympics in Berlin. (My future mother-in-law was also there, I learned after the war.)

Today I met a link with the 1936 Olympics, Gerhard Stöck, *chef de mission* of the German team, who in 1936 won a gold medal in the javelin and a bronze in putting the shot. One thing I had to ask him about was a report in *The People*, a mass-sale British Sunday paper, that there had been protests because a British woman athlete had changed sex, and that Germany was among the protesters. The Reuter team did not believe the story and Stöck said he knew nothing about it. I spoke to Stöck in the Olympic Village, a closely-guarded complex in central Rome, consisting mainly of smart brick-built blocks of flats, many of them on stilts, providing shade on the ground.

23 August 1960 : Looked in at the Germans and found, sure enough, there had already been some trouble in the all-German team. The East German officials, Communists, would much rather have a separate team, as part of their fight to gain international diplomatic recognition. But up to now the International Olympic Committee (IOC), while recognizing the two separate Olympic Committees of East and West Germany, has required them to form an all-German team.

The East Germans' tactics at present are to seek absolutely equal treatment. They had threatened to boycott the German flag-raising ceremony last night. (Each nation has its flag raised when a fair number of its team has arrived in the Olympic Village.) Their reason was the Italians had appointed a West German as liaison officer between the Olympics Organizing Committee and the all-German team, and had decided that he should stand in front of the German squad during the flag raising. In the end the East Germans accepted a compromise under which Gerhard Stöck and his East German deputy, Manfred Ewald, stood side-by-side, in front of the team.

Had some heart-warming chats with Nigerians and Ghanaians, jolly black chaps and so English in their mannerisms. One of them, Hogan Bassey, Nigerian former world featherweight champion, told me he'd had a chat with Pope John XXIII at Castel Gandolfo on 20 August. Bassey, a Protestant, had been much pleased by the Pope's friendliness. I then pointed out that the Catholic Church disapproved of boxing, and Bassey said, 'Yes, the Pope is very religious. He would not like anything ...' He struggled for a word, so I gave it to him – 'rough'.

Tonight to a party given for visiting journalists by Reuters chief correspondent in Rome, Patrick Crosse, and his wife Jennie. Crosse is also one of the agency's three deputy general managers. The party was held in the Crosses' flat, the most magnificent city home you could imagine. It occupies several floors of a thirteenth-century tower, the Torre del Grillo, slap in Rome's centre. Within a few hundred yards are the twin small hills named after Romulus and Remulus, Rome's legendary founders, with the Capitol – a squarish city hall – standing on one of them, the floodlit Colosseum where Christians were thrown to the lions, and several of the ruined forums. At this spot the imperial order to kill Jewish babies at the time of the birth of Christ was announced.

25 August 1960 : Today the seventeenth Olympics of the modern era – the first one was in Greece in 1896 – were opened in the Flaminio Stadium, which was specially built for the games a few hundred yards from the Tiber. It was my job to walk for 25 minutes in the sunshine – shade temperature around 35°C – by the side of that part of the British team – 120 out of about 320 – which has already arrived.

The march began with an unscripted tribute to Italian womanhood: whistles and appreciative murmurs from the British sportsmen when they glimpsed a pretty girl, her skirts ruffled by the breeze. The British women, in red hats and pale blue costumes, who headed the team after the officials, raised cheers and claps, especially among Italian men, who have an eye for a nice-looking female. I felt a little patriotic – in the nice sense, of course – as I walked alongside our team.

After phoning my story to our Olympics office, I managed to reach my press seat in the wonderful stadium – marble walls in the staircases leading to the press boxes – in time to see perhaps two-thirds of the teams march in. I missed Nationalist China, whose team displayed a banner marked 'under protest', because they have been ordered to compete under the name 'Formosa'. This is apparently a step towards admitting Communist China. In my view Communist China should have been admitted long ago if it is true that the Olympic authorities take no account of politics.

It was moving to watch the teams from all over the world march around in their differing Olympic costumes, including male Tahitians wearing grey cloth skirts which extend modestly below their knees. At about the time that Italy's President, Giovanni Gronchi, declared the games open, a young Italian athlete ran in with the torch bearing the Olympic flame, which came by ship from Greece to Sicily and was then run in relays to Rome. (Occasionally they cheated by taking it for short distances by car or lorry.)

The athlete stood silhouetted against the skyline at the top of the far side (from us) of the stadium. He then plunged the torch into an urn. A flame shot up. It will burn until the games end on 11 September. A member of the Italian team then recited the Olympic oath, pledging sportsmanship and amateurism. An impressive ceremony.

26 August 1960 : The first sport I am covering – canoeing – got under way today on Lake Albano, with heats. I found it very hard work sitting in the hot sun and phoning through descriptive and results. Even an Italian from Trieste, in the north, complained that the sun was too much for him.

Discussed religion with the trainer of the Soviet canoe team, a fattish tanned man whose name I have forgotten. In dealing with the question of the Virgin Birth, the Russian said this contravened the principle that there must be a cause for everything. I countered this by asking whether it was not God who was the cause of the universe. He was not able to answer that one, not that it answers anything really, but said, 'I am a Communist. Sport is my god.'

He did not say that boastingly. I told him I thought that, at any rate, there were worse gods than sport.

On this job Reuters is treating us pretty handsomely from the money standpoint. We have breakfast, one meal and our accommodation paid, and in addition receive £3 a day for our remaining meal and odds and ends. I have already sent home about £28 that I have saved.

28 August 1960 : To a reception given by President Giovanni Gronchi in the presidential palace, the Quirinal. It was nearly sunset, and the dome of St Peter's was silhouetted against the horizon as we marched over about 200 yards of red carpet in a zigzag, from room to room and over several terraces until we reached the palm garden where the reception was held. The sixteenth-century palace, which used to be successively a papal and royal residence, has some six storeys. I saw several courtyards with round-arched colonnades and cobbled floors.

We went on to another reception held by some industrial federation in a museum of Roman statues and inscriptions, housed in the vast remains, some 50 ft *[15 m]* high, of the baths of the Emperor Diocletian, who ruled from AD 284 to 305. I tried to decipher some inscriptions and was moved by the humanity of the statues, including one of a man with a pleasant face (except that some vandal had knocked off his marble or stone nose), with his arm round his wife's shoulders – sculptured on their own coffin lid. Wished I knew more Latin – had only a year of it at school.

29 August 1960 : Covered the canoeing finals today. Our remaining man, Ronald Rhodes, a glazier from Fulham, London, was unplaced. The Soviets and Hungarians remain dominant in canoeing, with the Germans the next strongest. Are we British soft?

30 August 1960 : Temperatures these past few days have topped the 100 Fahrenheit (38°C) mark. Carbon paper left in my car has partly melted – the first time I've known that to happen.

In the rowing heats, our best hope in today's programme, the coxed four from Molesey, London, made a false start. After the second start they did not row as well as expected and failed to get into the semi-final. I learnt later that the false start was caused when our coxed four had – deliberately, I was told – started to move their oars very slowly in the water before the final word – '*Partez*' – of the starting phrase had been said. The oarsmen, quite against Olympic rules and spirit, had been given this tip by an Australian colleague, I learned. I was told this on condition that I did not publish it, so I didn't.

31 August 1960 : Britain's leading oarsman, Chris Davidge, Old Etonian and member of Lloyds, stroked the Molesey coxless four to victory in its heat today – the first, and probably the only success of any note for Britain in the rowing. Davidge stroked Oxford to victory in the 1952 Boat Race – his third attempt.

Lunching in Castel Gandolfo, near the Pope's residence, I chatted with an elderly German, a retired insurance agent from Remscheid, Rhineland. Though himself not a churchgoer, he had been asked by Catholic friends to attend a papal audience, and had done so in a new hall built for this purpose in Castel Gandolfo a few years ago. He had seen the Pope carried in on a ceremonial chair and had heard him speak in Italian, now and again causing some laughter. A little of what the Pope said had been translated into English for some American sailors. The German said he had not been able to stand the heat and the crush inside so he had soon left.

This man told me he could not believe in the Christian idea of a loving God in view of some of the nasty things which happen in the world. He believed that scientists were very close to solving the secret of life. I think he's more than optimistic there. I don't think men will ever crack that one.

1 September 1960 : Had a delicious lunch of *stracciatella* (raw egg dripped into soup), *pollo arrosto* (roast chicken) and *insalata mista* (mixed salad), with an *aranciata* (orangeade) and *caffè con latte* (white coffee). It cost, including tip, 1,060 lire, about 11 shillings *[55p]*.

2 September 1960 : Was given a nice story by Gerhard Stöck, the greying German *chef de mission*. He told me that, last night, he had given a fatherly warning to the *enfant terrible* of German sport, 23-year-old Armin Hary, a Frankfurt shop assistant, who yesterday won the gold medal in the 100 metres, in which he already holds the world record at 10.0 seconds. Stöck said he had taken the young athlete into his office and told him, 'I once stood on the pedestal where you stand now. I have realized that sporting fame passes away. Don't regard it as too important. Be fair and decent. That is more important in life than a gold medal.'

Stöck said he had warned Hary, who has often been accused of unsporting behaviour, that when he was no longer a great runner he would need good friends, and should therefore behave accordingly. Hary had responded by shaking hands and promising he would do his best. But today he scratched from the 200 metres on the ground that he wanted to concentrate on the 4 × 100 metres relay. Stöck told me he found this not very sporting, because Hary had won a place in the 200 metres event after severe trials, and by scratching he was in effect depriving the runner-up of an Olympics chance. Stöck said he thought that Hary, who knew he would not win the 200 metres, wanted to bask in his fame.

3 September 1960 : Interviewed British long-distance runner Gordon Pirie, 1956 gold medallist in the 5,000 metres, who was knocked out in the heat of that event on 31 August. Pirie attributed his defeat to being brought to Rome only four days before the race – a decision of the British Athletics Board – instead of a fortnight before which, he said, would have enabled him to acclimatize. I learned later that this interview was splashed in the *London Evening News*, as it was the first time Pirie had really opened his mouth about his tragic defeat.

Reported on the rowing finals today. Disappointing to see our remaining finalists, Chris Davidge, Britain's leading oarsman and his coxless four crew, come in fifth. Germany came out on top, with three gold medals, the Soviet Union next, and the United States – top in 1956 – third.

5 September 1960 : Did something I was keen to do while in Rome: visited one of the most interesting catacombs, San Callisto, about two miles south of what was the old city wall of Rome. The elderly Irish priest who took us round, whose humour reminded me of Chesterton's Father Brown, told us that this catacomb had become forgotten several hundred years ago but was rediscovered in the nineteenth century. One enters down steps. The floor of the catacomb is perhaps 25 feet *[7 m]* below the ground.

Much of the catacomb consists of narrow passages lined with graves cut out of the stone. Nearly all the skeletons were removed earlier and buried in churches or elsewhere. In this catacomb, the priest told us, several early popes were buried, including one who was believed to have been an African. He showed us the grave niches of two of these popes, who are now buried elsewhere. There are several chapels where persecuted Christians used to come to worship before Christianity was adopted by the Roman state. Christians who were put to death by the Romans were buried here by their fellows.

Perhaps the most fascinating objects for me were stone fragments showing the fish, the secret sign of the Christians. The word 'fish' in Greek – some of the inscriptions are in Greek, then the church language – has letters which, the priest told us, stand for 'Christ the Lord is risen.' Other stones had swastika and arrow signs, which were ways of displaying the cross while at the same time concealing it. The priest suggested that if there were any Scots in the party they might like to stay the night in one of the grave niches for nothing. On another occasion, he said, 'Watch out, there are seven steps and a lot of empty graves at the bottom.'

8 September 1960 : Did interviews with the miraculous black United States sprinter, Jesse Owens, who angered Hitler by winning four gold medals at the 1936 Berlin Olympics, and with elderly crooner Bing Crosby, still good-looking, who both called on the American team.

Pirie was not placed in the 10,000 metres final today, poor chap, and is considering retiring.

10 September 1960 : I was given the morning off and used it by going to see the Pope – at one of his twice-weekly audiences at Castel Gandolfo. My press card gave me a seat on a wooden bench near the front of the long audience hall, which holds about 5,000. The hall is quite simple, except for a red-and-gilt throne on the platform, ornate curtains behind it and a canopy above bearing the papal coat of arms – crossed keys and a mitre, I think.

On each side of the throne stood a Vatican Swiss Guard, in pointed mediaeval helmet and orange-and-blue uniform, holding a halberd – a combined spear and battleaxe. Attendants in crimson uniforms ushered people to their seats. Some very favoured persons were seated on the sides of the platform. An excited rustle, followed by a burst of clapping, greeted the arrival of the Pope. Shortly before that an Irish Dominican nun, sitting behind me, told me that Pope John XXIII, who has a habit of leaving his official car and going on foot to meet people regardless of protocol, had been nicknamed 'Johnnie Walker' (a brand of whiskey). I was impressed by this bit of *lèse-majesté*.

In front of us sat Franciscan nuns, in black-and-grey – some French, some British – a pleasing example of the international bonds of the Church. Next to me was a German-born South African priest, who sold a rosary to a South African journalist who sat near me. The rosary was later blessed by the Pope, along with others brought by people present.

Several of the crimson-suited attendants carried in the Pope on a gilt-and-red chair. He wore a white skullcap and white habit, quite simple, with a kind of brocaded scarf round his neck, with its two ends descending to his chest. I believe he wore a simple

116

crucifix too. The applause continued as the chair was carried all the way down a central aisle. The Pope acknowledged it with a slight smile on his broad peasant's face, and by waving gracefully, like royalty in Britain.

When the Pope had taken his seat, which has two microphones nearby, a priest stationed at his side began to read out in Italian the names of perhaps eight or nine groups from different parishes or organizations in Italy who were present. As each name was mentioned there was a burst of clapping, sometimes with a shout or two. Then the priest stopped and the Pope began to speak. He spoke most naturally, with lots of gesture, like any Italian might do in a pub, if not quite so explosively. He smiled now and again and once or twice he had people laughing slightly. I think that in another life he would have made a good comedian; his big ears would have helped him in that role. But his jokes, I feel, would have been kind ones.

[Years later, in the early sixties, when Khrushchev was planning a visit to the Pope – a visit which never took place as Khrushchev was deposed in 1964 – a joke circulated in the Soviet bloc according to which the visit did go ahead. And, the story went, these two peasant types quickly solved all the problems between the Roman Catholic Church and the Soviet Communist Party, and then issued a communiqué saying: 'God created the world, under the direction of the Communist Party.']

I made a few notes of as much as I could understand of the Pope's address in Italian. The gist was that we are all here together on earth, we humans, including the Pope, and that we are all moving towards the same goal of eternal life, and that no matter what may happen to us we may be assured of God's love: a comforting message for those who believe.

After this address, delivered without notes, there was a long burst of applause. Then the Pope read, from texts, short messages in French, Spanish and English – the latter with a heavy accent – and a priest read a message in German for him.

The Pope's message in English: 'With paternal affection we welcome all the English-speaking pilgrims here present. We pray that your visit to the holy place of Rome may obtain for you an abundance of grace and favour from Almighty God. We give our blessing to each one of you and to all your dear ones at home, especially all those who are sick or suffering.' A few more words I missed. (I particularly liked the way the Pope, during his unscripted Italian address, wiggled his feet quickly as he referred to us mortals walking on life's journey.)

John XXIII ended the audience with the papal benediction, which he delivered while standing. He spoke the benediction in Latin, as a priest on either side of him held one edge of a parchment-covered prayer book. Applause rose to new heights as the Pope was carried out down the aisle. There were shouts of '*Viva il Papa!*' amid the clapping. I was not repelled by the obvious enthusiasm, but the thought crossed my mind that Catholics among the crowd would support persecution of others if the Pope ordered it, just as Communists do when one of their leaders announces some harsh policy.

This afternoon, with elderly Walter Davies, who has been with Reuters for over 30 years, and normally does parliamentary stuff in London, I had my last job of the Olympics: reporting on the positions of the leaders during the marathon, the last athletics event, run over about 45 kilometres *[28 miles]*, starting and finishing in central Rome. At the first stage we checked, about one-third of the total distance, we found a couple of Britons among the leaders, but by two-thirds they had dropped back to around tenth place. As it grew dark, soldiers held up torches in eight-feet-high metal tubes to light the way towards the end of the race, as the runners entered Rome again along the ancient Appian Way, the sight of which has given me so much pleasure.

The winner of the marathon was a barefooted unknown from Abyssinia, Abebe Bikila, one of the Emperor's guards. His name had appeared on the programme backwards, as B. Abebe, which caused us some trouble. We only got what we believe is his correct name from his Finnish trainer, who acted as interpreter when Bikila gave us an interview in his native language, Amharic.

Later, after a farewell drink in a *trattoria* with some of our

118

team, I retired to bed around 11.30, hoping to be restored for my drive home, which starts tomorrow.

11 September 1960 : The XVII Olympiad of the modern era ended this Sunday – but I wasn't there to see it. Around 7.30 pm, with a Reuter colleague, New Zealander Nick Turner, I drove out of Rome. Was happy to be going home, but a little sorry to be leaving Rome, Italy and the warm-hearted, responsive Italians.

We soon picked up a bearded Capuchin monk, in brown habit, aged about 50. He told us he had never doubted God's existence. He had apparently never doubted much of Catholic dogma either. He spoke about unity between the Christian churches, which he saw merely as the non-Catholics coming back into the fold – rather like the Communist attitude towards political unity with socialists.

Driving inland, through Viterbo and Siena to Florence, we were amazed by the large numbers of people with shotguns. It was as though mobilization had been ordered. They were all going hunting. We picked up one of the hunters, an electricity linesman, who proudly showed us the rabbit he had shot. He told us he had four children, earned the equivalent of £350 a year and usually shot a rabbit each Sunday.

We passed through much barren-looking countryside, mainly hilly, with signs of serious erosion. Later the colour of the earth turned from greyish-brown to reddish and there were fertile areas as we approached Florence. There we viewed Giotto's cathedral, dating from the twelfth and thirteenth centuries. It is faced with white, green and reddish marble. I did not like it much, as it reminded me of children's building bricks of not very good quality.

My main delight was to look again at the Piazza della Signoria – with the beautiful town hall, the tower of which, or one like it, I think, was the model for the town hall of my hometown, Bradford. But this town hall is not smoke-blackened, like Bradford's, but has a glowing sandy colour. *[Some years later Bradford Town Hall also took on a sandy colour, when its sandstone was sand-blasted.]* We admired, too, the bridges over the River

119

Arno, on the banks of which Dante and Beatrice walked.

We covered about 400 miles today, to Milan, where I spent the evening with Geppi. Over a meal she told me that recent months had been unhappy, as her father was ill, and she had not played the piano for months. We walked round the square surrounding Milan's great Gothic cathedral, and through an arcade where hundreds of people promenaded or sat in cafés – far more life late in the evening than in a British provincial city, or even in London. As I drove Geppi home, we recalled old times by managing to sing one verse of 'Santa Lucia'; we couldn't remember any more of that Neapolitan song.

12 September 1960 : Nick and I shared a double room in the little Hotel Nuovo, paying the equivalent of about 13 shillings *[65p]* each. Then we went onto the roof of the cathedral, where we could see at close quarters some of the detail: gargoyles, shapely statues on pinnacles, flying buttresses. It was typically Italian to find a kiosk on the roof selling Coca-Cola and other refreshments, and an elderly man renting a telescope through which one could view a gilded statue on the highest pinnacle.

North to Lake Como, where I swam in not-too-cool but nevertheless autumnal water, and onwards into Switzerland again, my fourth time this year. Our route took us over the Maloja and Julian passes, each around 2,200 metres. There was fresh snow on the peaks and we had stunning views of the mountains in the sunset.

13 September 1960 : We overnighted in St Moritz – Hotel St Moritzerhof, about £1 each a night including breakfast, trim single rooms – but could see little of the town and its lake owing to morning mist.

We made our way along the Upper Rhine valley and into Liechtenstein, that little independent principality which has a customs and currency union with Switzerland. We spent a few minutes in Vaduz, its capital, which looks no different from many neat, picturesque Swiss towns, except that there are plenty of Liechtenstein flags to be seen.

Soon we were in Austria and, not long afterwards, we entered Germany at Lindau on Lake Constance. Two hours' drive from there brought us to Ulm. From Ulm, some six hours' driving, including a break for eats, brought us home to Godesberg – a total of about 500 miles covered today. Elfi was waiting, and cups of tea were served around midnight.

14 September 1960 : Shortly after midnight I gave Elfi birthday greetings on her 36th; have brought her several presents from Italy, including a silk scarf with Rome scenes. Eleven guests, journalists and their wives, came to her jolly birthday party in our house tonight, when greetings were sung in German and English.

16 September 1960 : As expected, our chief correspondent, Gerry Long, 37, has been promoted. He has been made an assistant general manager, based in London. *[From 1963, after the death of Walton Cole, until 1981, Long was chief executive of Reuters. He did much to modernize the agency, but left it in 1981 when he accepted the offer of the Australian-born American media magnate, Rupert Murdoch, to become managing director of Times Newspapers, a post from which Murdoch removed him in 1982. As a result of the move to Times Newspapers, Long missed the chance, unlike at least two of his fellow Reuter executives, of becoming a millionaire when the agency, which had been a private company, was floated on the London stock exchange in 1984, with great financial success – a success for which Long had laid much of the basis. But Long publicly showed no bitterness about what had happened; he was reportedly not that much interested in money and, anyway, no doubt had an adequate amount. He was vice-chairman of Times Newspapers until 1984, when he moved to France.*

When Long took over as chief correspondent in Bonn in October 1956, after postings to Paris and Istanbul, a reputation for abrasiveness preceded him. Having drunk rather too much at his introductory cocktail, I asked him gaily if he was really as much of a shit as he was supposed to be. Perhaps because, like me, he was a straight-talking Yorkshireman, he never held that remark against me. (I don't remember how he answered.) In fact, at my request, he helped me to be appointed in 1962 as Reuters chief correspondent in Moscow – a burning ambition of mine. Long died in November 1998.]

19 September 1960 : Sometimes I think I am earning my money too easily, and at other times – when I am bored and uninspired by the work – I think that it is not easy at all. At times I have a desire to be working on my own, instead of being dependent on a big organization. But, of course, big organizations give more security for family men.

22 September 1960 : Am finding the philosophical writings of Marcus Aurelius, who was the Roman Emperor between AD 161 and 180, very helpful in my present – uninspired – state of mind. Though he was a pagan, he believed in the great design of the universe, in being thankful to the gods for one's blessings and in bearing life's trials with good nature and steadfastness. He is classed as a stoic.

12 More Berlin friction

24 September 1960 : Wove together stories done by our East and West Berlin offices on recent East German moves to restrict freedom of movement in Berlin. The East Germans are clearly seeking to show the strength of their position regarding West Berlin and its links with West Germany in the months leading up to the next Big Four conference, expected to take place after the American elections in November. So far they have banned West *Germans* (as opposed to West *Berliners*) from East Berlin unless they have East German permits, which are being freely issued for a start. Further, they have stopped recognizing West German passports held by West Berliners (thus reinforcing their claim – which is true – that West Berlin is not part of West Germany). Finally they have banned diplomats accredited in Bonn from East Berlin unless they, too, hold East German permits.

Whatever the West may say about Berlin's four-power status, which still exists on paper, the West tacitly allowed the Russians virtually to end the four-power status of the city in June 1948, when they did not fight back against the Soviet moves which split the city administration, leaving undemocratically appointed Communists in power in the Eastern (Soviet) sector, which later enabled the East Germans to proclaim East Berlin as their capital.

26 September 1960 : To a reception for a Ghana parliamentary delegation, which has come here after visiting East Germany. Was happy to learn that one of these cheerful black politicians – some in robes, some in European suits – had gained the impression that the majority of East Germans were being oppressed. But when I said that it was the West German view that Communism in East Germany would collapse if the Russians removed their troops, he replied, 'Oh, there are Russians there?'

Several hundred thousand, I told him.

Two German businessmen, whose plastics firm is setting up a subsidiary in Ghana, told me they had been put out to learn that in Ghana you can get things done only by means of 'tips' – a nice word for bribes. They said it was not out of the ordinary for a cabinet minister to accept the agency of some foreign company. The businessmen agreed with me that, as regards the threat of Communism in Africa, Guinea seems to be the worst infected at the moment.

27 September 1960 : Our most notable event was that Chris, who is $7^1/_2$, got top marks in German dictation, the first time he has managed this. He was overjoyed. Elfi kissed him and I gave him something extra for his moneybox.

28 September 1960 : At another reception attended by the jolly Ghanaians, a West German Foreign Office expert on Africa told me it was almost beside the point to consider whether African countries appeared to be going Communist, as Africa was a different world. The Africans would take what they needed from one or the other system, he said. He did not think that in the main they would go Communist, because they were very keen on private property and were religious. In his view Africans are in some respects superior to Europeans. He said, for instance, they had a great regard for human dignity – one reason why they are so keen to have their independence. He also liked the Africans' desire not to be tied to an employer. Some of them, he said, would work just long enough to earn a little money, with which they would buy things that pleased them, such as balloons and trinkets, and would then retire to their homes in the bush until they felt the need for money again.

29 September 1960 : Suffering from a fluey cold, I chased around after Willy Brandt, West Berlin's governing mayor. He had come to talk at the Foreign Office and with Western Allied envoys about the critical Berlin situation. The East Germans, followed by other Communist countries, have stopped recognizing the use by West Berliners of West German passports for travel abroad. Instead they are stamping visas in West Berliners' identity cards. This move is intended to weaken West Berlin's close links with West Germany, of which it is virtually though not officially a part. *[When the West German state was founded in 1949, the three Western Allies vetoed a planned clause in its constitution declaring Berlin to be one of its constituent states. West Berlin, though effectively part of the West German economic, legal and social welfare system, remained under the occupation rule of the three Western Allies. That rule ended only when Germany was reunified on 3 October 1990.]*

I learned that the Western Allies are particularly concerned at a new Soviet Note, published on 27 September, which declares invalid not only the wartime and immediate post-war agreements on Germany, but also the 1949 agreement between the Foreign Ministers of the Big Four (the United States, the Soviet Union, Britain and France) re-establishing the right of free access to West Berlin from the West. The note claims that all these agreements have been outdated by the Soviet grant of sovereignty to East Germany in 1955.

30 September 1960 : A counter-measure to the Soviet Note: West Germany announced it was giving provisional notice to end its trade agreement with East Germany on 31 December this year. This will enable it to stop East–West German trade from that date unless the East Germans talk turkey over Berlin. *[Because West Germany refused to recognize East Germany, trade agreements between the two countries had been handled since 1949 on the West German side by a subsidiary agency, the Trustee Office for Inter-Zonal Trade, which was subject to the Economics Ministry, and on the East German side by the Ministry for Foreign and Inner-German Trade. For West Germany, trade with East Germany was a potential*

means of political pressure, as it was of considerable economic impor-
tance to East Germany while of little economic importance to West
Germany.]

My view on this dispute is that the West Germans are fighting at the wrong time on the wrong issue. Effective power in East Berlin was ceded by the West to the Soviets and the East Germans when, in 1948, the Western Allies allowed the Communists to split the city administration. It is no use now saying that was all legally wrong. So if the East Germans, at Moscow's behest, start hindering travel into East Berlin, we cannot stop that. It is certainly nothing to fight a war on. Vastly different, however, is the position of West Berlin, which the West must defend to the last. So far, the East Berlin measures have been no threat to West Berlin.

Am impressed by the new Gillette 'Extra' razor blades. I was able to use the first one for 12 days, that is, until the centre of the blade started to rust – you must not wipe them, the instruction says. Previous blades normally lasted me two or three days.

Robin, who was 12 in May, had a small part in a fairytale play at his secondary school, the Nikolaus Cusanus Gymnasium, many of whose pupils are drawn from Bonn's international community. The play was written by two girls, one a Finn and the other a member of what used to be a German princely family, the Zu Löwensteins. Several foreigners at the school put on acts, including two tiny Indonesian girls in shimmering kimono-like garments, who sang a song. Good to think that all these nationalities get along together.

3 October 1960 : Having sold my old Volkswagen for the equivalent of £260, am buying a new '1961 model' which will cost about £410.

5 October 1960 : Am preparing to write a background report about the phenomenal Wankel rotary internal combustion engine, being developed jointly by the West German firm, NSU, and the US firm, Curtiss Wright. It was invented by the West German,

126

Felix Wankel, and first ran in 1957. The four-stroke petrol engine works without pistons, crankshafts, valves and some of the other working parts in traditional internal combustion engines. Instead of a piston, moving backwards and forwards, there is a metal rotor which turns in a chamber. Viewed in section, the rotor has a roughly triangular shape, though the three sides are convex. A mixture of petrol and air is sucked into the chamber and, as the rotor turns, the mixture is in turn compressed and ignited, and then the exhaust gas is expelled.

The basic idea had been thought of long ago by engine designers, as far back as James Watt (1736–1819), but no one had solved the problem of confining the gases, which is much harder to do than in a conventional cylinder. Wankel, an expert on confining gases, solved the problem. The engine has a much higher power-weight ratio than traditional types and is much simpler. It looks as though it could have a great future. *[Although the Wankel engine is still used in both motor vehicles and aircraft, problems with rotor seals and with cooling have been factors in preventing its widespread use. Wankel, born in 1902, died in 1988.]*

13 Offered Moscow job, but ...

6 October 1960 : I was ordered to phone Gerry Long, now assistant general manager for Europe, based in London, at 4 pm today. I imagined this meant my hoped-for move. Where would it be, I wondered; Vienna, Brussels, Warsaw came to mind. Gerry told me he had recommended to Walton Cole, the general manager, that I should replace Bob Elphick, our chief correspondent in Moscow – there are only two – when he returned home in about 18 months. The general manager had been very taken with the idea. What did I think of it?

I told Long that, of course, he knew that I had long been keen on that job, but that I would have to discuss it with Elfi.

Gerry said the job would bring a salary increase and a good living allowance. Then the blow fell. Gerry told me that our news editor (his deputy), John Bush, was being appointed chief correspondent, Vienna. I'd been thinking Gerry might want me to replace John; not that I would enjoy the job, but it would be experience. However, Gerry told me that Brian Horton, of all people, should be given John's post because the higher-ups desired that he should have this type of experience.

Gerry asked me what I thought about that decision, adding that he thought I was a good reporter who would be wasted in the post. (I agree with him there, but ...) I replied to the effect that I thought that the appointment of Horton as news editor – deputy to the chief correspondent – would be hard for such experienced staffers as Terry Davidson and Lionel Walsh to accept. (Brian is an intelligent young man, but no brilliant journalist, and has in my opinion been pushed on too fast by the powers that be, perhaps because he is the scion of a New Zealand newspaper-owning family.)

[Horton had an impressive career in Reuters, culminating in his appointment as editor-in-chief and as an assistant general manager in September 1968, when Long was general manager. Horton resigned from Reuters in December 1973.]

Back home, I told Elfi the news. The prospect of Moscow was a blow to her but, after collecting her thoughts, she said she realized how much the post meant to me. After a while she said, with a rueful grin, 'It will cost you a fur coat anyway.'

It is hard for Elfi, after the war and the loss of East Prussia to Russia and Poland, to think of living in Moscow without some apprehension, but our friendship with Boris and Inna Yurinov has done something to show her that even Communists can have human traits.

8 October 1960 : French Prime Minister, Michel Debré, a small dapper man who appears to be little more than an office boy for General de Gaulle, arrived in Bonn yesterday for a two-day visit. The West Germans have become most perturbed by de Gaulle's apparent desire to break up NATO integration, and by his intention to stop any further moves towards supranationality in Western Europe. *[As I write this, 40 years later, France remains not too friendly towards NATO, but some of today's greatest opponents of further supranationality in the European Union are the majority of British Conservative politicians.]*

West German sources told us Debré had toned down what de Gaulle has been saying. These sources say France has realized it is vital that the United States should keep troops in Europe, and that this depended on a certain amount of integration by the European powers. De Gaulle, in his way, is a much more tricky customer than, say, Khrushchev, whose general line is clear enough.

Have informed Gerry, in London, by phone that I have

consulted with Elfi and would be ready to go to Moscow if it were finally decided I should get the post. *[I was given a trial assignment in Moscow between June and August 1961, and was chief correspondent there from early 1962 until early 1964, when I was expelled. I write about my first two months in Moscow later in this volume.]*

9 October 1960 : On our Sunday walk we fulfilled a long-held resolve by climbing another of the nearby Siebengebirge (Seven Mountains), the Wolkenberg, only some 1,000 feet *[300 m]* high; the highest, the Ölberg, is a little over 1,500 feet. Enchanting in the wonderland of trees, with Cologne cathedral on the horizon 20 miles to the north, then the Rhine snaking towards us, and sunshine flashing through the leaves as we clambered up or slithered down.

At the recent annual conference of the Labour Party, a resolution, saying that Britain's defence should not be based on the threat to use nuclear weapons, was passed by a majority of about 300,000 out of 6,500,000 votes. Another resolution, stating specifically that Britain should not possess any nuclear weapons, was carried by a similar majority. Though this may not do the Labour Party's electoral chances any good, I find it heart-warming that there are so many people ready to denounce the use of nuclear weapons. I believe that, if only nuclear weapons can hold off Communism, it would be better to have Communism than resorting to them. They are absolutely evil, on whatever grounds they may be used. *[Looking back, I think that the possession by NATO of nuclear weapons may have deterred possible Soviet plans to invade Western Europe. But it would have been a terrible crime to use them.]*

12 October 1960 : Visited the boomtown of Wolfsburg, northeast of Hanover, near the East German border, the site of the main works of the Volkswagen concern, Europe's biggest motor vehicle producer. Planned production for this year is 850,000 units which, in number, is about half of West Germany's total motor vehicle production.

130

I was filled with a pleasant feeling of expectation (resulting from the acquisitive instinct), for I'd come to pick up our new car – the first new car we've ever bought. *[Our first car, bought in 1947, was a 1932 Jowett saloon, made in my hometown, Bradford. It had been standing, no doubt for a long time, in the open air at a second-hand car dealer's. Grass was growing on its dirt-strewn roof. We had more fun with that car – maximum speed about 30 mph – than with any other.]*

Before taking delivery of our new car, I interviewed two of the firm's press spokesmen and was given a tour of the works. Volkswagen was founded, as one of Hitler's schemes, to produce 'People's Cars' for which many thousands of Germans paid subscriptions before the Second World War. The prototypes were tested around 1934–36. Production was about to begin when Hitler started the war, and the works were used for various kinds of military production, including a military version of the Volkswagen. I walked around part of the vast works, made of redbrick in a stark functional style. (Hitler laid the foundation stone.)

A man aged about 22, working on the final assembly line, told me he earned 450 marks (about £40) monthly. Held up by my questions, he had to run after a car on the conveyor to fasten down a bolt. But he told me he did not have to work hard. He has only downed tools once, for a warning strike of two or three hours, protesting against the original partial privatization plan for the works, which was later modified. Work is paid according to the job, not the worker's sex. Quite a lot of women on the belt were mainly doing upholstering work.

VW is winning sales from people who are moving up from motorcycles and bubble cars.

In 1945 the badly-bombed works, bereft of some of the machines, which had been handed over to the Russians as reparations, started to tick over again under British occupation rule, delivering small numbers of the, then, very noisy cars for British forces and West German official bodies. A delegation of British motor manufacturers, who visited the works in 1945 and could have had it for nothing, called the Volkswagen 'ugly, out-of-date and with no future'. But under the management of the American-trained German, Heinz Nordhoff, a former Opel executive, the works became one of West Germany's major post-war industrial successes.

As the Nazi Labour Front, which had owned the works, no longer existed, the works were made the property of the Federal Government. Early next year 60 per cent of the company's share capital of 600 million marks is to be offered in the form of 'people's shares', while 20 per cent will remain the property of the Federal Government and 20 per cent will become the property of the state of Lower Saxony, where Wolfsburg is situated. It is part of the ideology of Chancellor Adenauer's Christian Democrats to 'spread prosperity' by offering 'people's shares', and this is the first major test of such a measure. For two months the shares will be on offer only to people with relatively low incomes. Each buyer will be limited to five shares, sold at a discount of 10 or 20 per cent according to the buyer's income. During a further two months these 'people's shareholders' will be allowed to increase their holding to ten shares each. If, after four months, there are still shares available, which is highly unlikely, they will be put on the stock market in the normal way.

The spokesmen told me that a critical situation on the West German car market was approaching. Even in the case of the phenomenally successful Volkswagen, delivery periods dropped from several months to a few days during the year ended 31 August 1960, though they have risen again to two or three months after the introduction of the improved 1961 model on 1 September. In the first eight months of 1960, according to official statistics, 25.2 per cent more motor vehicles were registered in West Germany than in the same period of 1959.

The average wage at Volkswagen is between 500 and 600 marks gross monthly (£500–600 annually). The normal working week has fallen from 48 hours after the war to 40 (five days) now. Reconstruction of and extensions to the factory, which was 70 per cent destroyed in 1945, have been financed entirely from reserves earned by the firm itself.

I asked the spokesmen for their views on safety belts, as I am considering buying one.

'We are for safety belts,' said one of them, 'but the fact that only very few people buy them shows that people do not like them.'

He argued that if VW were to supply safety belts with each car, the idea might get around that the Volkswagens were only safe if fitted with belts. He added, 'I think the whole industry would welcome them, but only if they were made compulsory.'

Volkswagen has subsidiary or associated plants, mainly for assembly, in Brazil, Australia, South Africa, Dublin, Brussels, Mexico, New Zealand and the Philippines. The establishment of such plants boosted exports. No such plant is planned for Britain, to which VW exported 9,227 cars last year, and 9,178 in the first eight months of this year. They expect to sell 180,000 VWs to the United States this year, compared with 150,000 in 1959. I read later that the Volkswagen engine can be seen as the descendant of an aircraft engine from the First World War which the VW designer, Ferdinand Porsche, a Sudeten-German, designed for Austro-Hungary.

Volkswagen exports this year are expected to remain at 58 per cent of total production. VW produces about twice as many motor vehicles as Italy and two or three times as many as total Soviet motor vehicle production. The Soviet Union 'compliments' Volkswagen by making a car with a VW-type front axle, a pirated VW engine and a rear axle and bodywork like some Fiats. VW staff call it a 'Volksfiatovitch'.

Around 4 pm, it was time to take over our new pastel-blue Beetle. It had been hard to wait so long, but the giant works is a fascinating place. As I drove southwards to the autobahn near Brunswick, I found the car even quieter than the last one, which I had already found phenomenally quiet. Springing and cornering better, too. And the car is, of course, more powerful: 34 instead of 30 brake horsepower. Automatic choke. All four gears are synchronized, instead of only the three higher ones. Indicator lights, instead of trafficators, and they switch off automatically after you have made the turn. A good buy for a little over £400 including the sunroof.

16 October 1960 : In West Germany car numberplates are issued in each municipality, rather than centrally, and if you move to another area you have to get a new numberplate. By a happy coincidence we have been given BN-AK-895. BN stands for Bonn. AK is just a random group, but happens to be the original British numberplate letters denoting my hometown, Bradford!

17 October 1960 : Visited Kurt Heintze, an elderly friend in the Ruhr mining town of Bottrop, where my widowed mother-in-law, Helene Kowitz lives. Heintze, a First World War naval officer, witnessed the scuttling of the German High Sea fleet at Scapa Flow in the Orkneys in 1919, an act of defiance against the terms of the harsh Versailles Treaty. Kurt is now the owner of a cinema. He is managing to keep his head just above water because his cinema is in the town centre and attracts courting couples. Many German cinemas are being made into supermarkets now, as television is gripping everyone.

This afternoon I drove to the city of Hagen, in the south of the Ruhr area, to visit a Lutheran pastor, Manfred Schloenbach, whom I had got to know about three years ago when he was on a visit to the West from his then parish in East Germany. Last year he and his wife were allowed by the Communist authorities to move to West Germany, after his wife fell seriously ill. Schloenbach and I talked for about six hours, his wife excusing herself after about four, around midnight. Aged about 35, Schloenbach has delicate features – and, thanks to war wounds suffered in Russia, two artificial lower legs, on which he walks without a stick. He comes from a long line of Prussian soldiers.

We talked mainly about religion. He put with burning sincerity his view that life was pointless without Christ; that one might as well, like the Romans, get into a hot bath and have a servant cut one's wrists. I replied that I found many beautiful things in life.

He implied that compared with him I had been lucky, for he told me about losing many relatives during the war, about his injuries and his wife's illness, and about wartime comrades who had lost not only arms and legs but eyes as well. He even went so far as to say he hoped that God could justify such things; in other words he hoped that Jesus was right in believing that God was a god of love.

Much of our discussion circled around his contention that, if one accepts the hypothesis that there is a god, one can scientifically show, through ethics and logic, that the Christian concept of God is the best. I didn't accept this view because I think it is so much a matter of personal taste, depending to a large extent on one's upbringing. He accused me of shirking a decision on what to believe, and said one ought to consider taking a risk by plumping for the thesis that Christ was right in his belief that there was a God. Even if it should turn out that there is no God, Schloenbach said, you have not lost anything anyway.

I told him that at present I was finding the Roman stoic (and emperor) Marcus Aurelius, more simple and more satisfying than Christian dogma. I went away feeling moved – and tired. Schloenbach now teaches religion at a technical college, with pupils aged from about 14 to 22. He thinks these young men are better, morally, than the Germans of the late 1930s who, he said, were corrupted by supporting Hitler. However, he added that the present generation of middle-aged Germans was being corrupted by economic prosperity. He maintained that about 80 per cent of Germans had supported Hitler after the defeat of France in 1940. *[That may be true as, by then the Germans were subjected to the jingoistic propaganda of the dictatorship, trumpeted by the state-run media. But, before Hitler came to power, his Nazi Party never won an overall majority of the votes in a democratic* Reichstag *election. In the last free* Reichstag *election, on 6 November 1932, the Nazis won 33.1 per cent of the votes cast and were able to come to power only by obtaining support from conservative politicians in the formation of a coalition government.]*

21 October 1960 : Dad, in a letter from his home in Los Angeles, has told me not to take the promotion of Brian Horton too hard; these things could be expected in life, and so on.

I have decided that: *(a)* although the thing smacks of favouritism, and very likely nepotism, there is no point in making a stink about it, for this would merely make the powers-that-be less well disposed towards me; *(b)* I am extremely lucky to be in the running for Moscow and have been well treated, as far as assignments and pay are concerned, during the last couple of years, thanks to Gerry; and *(c)* the promotion of Horton is not a personal slight against me alone, as John Bush, Terry Davidson and Lionel Walsh can feel equally badly done by – and have no Moscow to look forward to.

Depressing news from London: closure of the national daily, the *News Chronicle*, which has backed the Liberal cause since it was founded in 1855, with Charles Dickens as its first editor. The Liberal Cadbury family has sold the paper to the Tory Rothermere group and it has been nominally incorporated into the Conservative *Daily Mail*. About 3,500 employees of the *News Chronicle* have to seek new jobs. They get minimal compensation of one week's wage for each year worked for the firm. The left-liberal *News Chronicle* was one of the papers I would really have like to have worked for; good thing I never applied to it. Liberal Party leaders say they were ready to try to save the paper, but the Cadburys – Quakers at that – never gave them a chance.

22 October 1960 : Drove to Iserlohn, about 100 miles to the east of us, to hear the outcome of a British Army court martial I had attended a few days ago. A 22-year-old private, Kenneth Adshead, was acquitted of the murder of a sentry during a drunken brawl when he grabbed the sentry's weapon, a pick handle, and hit him on the head with it. The sentry died four days later from a brain haemorrhage.

The defence, led by the famous Queen's Counsel, wiry, bespectacled Christmas Humphreys, initially claimed that Adshead only punched the sentry who, they maintained, received his fatal head wound beforehand when he was trampled on by other men. However, it was stated in evidence that Adshead grabbed the pick handle from the sentry after the sentry had hit Adshead's friend with it. While acquitting Adshead of murder, the court found him guilty of striking a sentry and sentenced him to one year's military detention. Like some other British Army crimes on which I have reported, this one occurred after men had been drinking – this time it was lashings of beer and vodka. *[The British military authorities effectively encouraged heavy drinking, and smoking, by authorizing the sale of alcoholic drinks and cigarettes free of duty.]*

23 October 1960 : A Sunday climb with my family up one of the nearby Seven Mountains (Siebengebirge), just across the Rhine eastwards from us. This time we chose the Hirschberg, beautiful with the coppery autumn leaves and the green undergrowth, topped by a small ruin of no great age and a rotten seat with people's names carved on it.

The other day Robin was allowed to stay up with Elfi to see the first instalment of a 700-minute television film, being shown in 50-minute instalments, depicting the Nazi regime from a democratic point of view. His main comment was that Hitler had a horrible voice, and I must say that Hitler, viewed at this remove, seems rather like a caricature of a man, but I suppose that, with unemployment, Versailles and all that it was a cartoon of an era.

24 October 1960 : There are persistent reports of an improvement in West German–Soviet relations, despite an incident on 21 October in the *Bundestag* when Soviet Ambassador Andrei Smirnov jumped up in the diplomatic gallery and shouted a protest when the Economics Minister, Professor Ludwig Erhard, attacked 'Communist imperialism' as being worse than old-style colonialism. Smirnov was grabbed by an attendant, who began to hustle him out, until the *Bundestag* President (speaker), Dr Eugen Gerstenmaier intervened and said the Soviet diplomat had diplomatic immunity. The attendant then let go of him and accompanied him out.

Dashing after the Ambassador with other reporters, I asked him to repeat what he had said. White, and shaking with anger, he spluttered in broken German that he had said that the West

Germans would not give freedom to the Africans; look what the 'gold pheasants' (Nazi officials with gold braid on their uniforms) had done in Russia. They had killed 20 million Russians.

Smirnov mentioned in particular General Adolf Heusinger, West Germany's top soldier, (Inspector-General of the forces), who was the German Army's chief of operations during part of the Second World War. He was present at last week's meeting here, in the presence of distinguished African politicians, to launch an 'Africa Week'. It seemed to me that Smirnov's anger was genuine (though unjustified – just part of the way that Russians and West Germans keep mutually misunderstanding each other). Perhaps Khrushchev's rumbustious shoe-banging behaviour at the United Nations stimulated Smirnov to let his anger run away with him.

Adenauer immediately had a junior minister call on Smirnov to express 'regret' at the initial attempt to expel Smirnov from the chamber, though not an apology. It has since come out that Adenauer responded in this way because Khrushchev, in a recent meeting with West Germany's Moscow Ambassador, indicated he wanted to raise West German–Soviet relations from their all-time low. He even went so far as to promise to leave out some attacks on Adenauer from a planned speech.

14 Near miss of Queen's plane

25 October 1960 : We *nearly* had one of the biggest news stories in history today. The Queen's Comet airliner, taking her back to Britain from Denmark, was – according to its co-pilot, Flight Lieutenant F. Stevens – missed over northern West Germany by only about 50 feet *[15 m]* by two US-made Sabre jet fighters displaying 'damned big iron crosses' on their wings.

The near miss started mass investigations in West German fighter bases, with pilots possibly concerned being kept up till late at night for questioning, and senior officers on call through the night. Spent most of the night getting statements from here and there, but nothing firm.

26 October 1960 : Off I shot to Oldenburg, near Bremen, about 240 miles north-north-east of Bonn – one of three bases regarded as being the likely home of the near-miss Sabres. Arriving at the base around 9 pm, I was told in the guardroom, as expected, following a news black-out imposed last night, that nothing could be said. But while I was waiting for an officer to tell me this by phone, one of the men on duty in the guardroom mused that it was possible that one of the Sabres had been piloted not by a German, but a Canadian. He explained that Canadian instructors were training German pilots in squadron tactics, and sometimes an instructor went up in one Sabre with a German in another! This was a good line of approach. I got the man to tell me where the Canadians lived, just outside the base. I arrived in their street around 10.30 pm and started knocking on doors where lights were on. Finally got hold of not a Canadian, but two Britons, an RAF officer and a civilian technician, who ruled out the 'Canadian-in-Sabre' line and told me that a German pilot based at Oldenburg was suspected of having led the two-man flight. This pilot had denied being nearer than about 2,000 feet *[600 m]* from the Queen's plane. My sources said they did not know what the second German pilot had said. This gave me a good story for tonight.

27 October 1960 : Today the trail took me about 100 miles south-east to Hanover air traffic control centre, the civilian side of which had been responsible for the passage of the Queen's aircraft over Germany. By a great stroke of luck, a hitchhiker I picked up outside Oldenburg was a former *Luftwaffe* man, now a student, who had just been to visit his onetime *Luftwaffe* superior, head of the military air traffic control unit at Oldenburg base. His former superior had been talking about the incident, so the student was able to give me some useful details.

Overnighted near Hanover in a dilapidated pub whose proprietor, aged about 68, was a former *Wehrmacht* major who had been taken prisoner at the battle of Stalingrad, which ended in February 1943. He told me he had been released from Soviet imprisonment at the early date of 1948 because, working as an untrained vet, he had saved the lives of three cows owned by a high Soviet officer. The officer had promised he could go home if the cows pulled through, and kept his promise. The pub keeper said he had become a 'vet' simply by volunteering, though he had no academic qualifications, merely practical knowledge gained as a farmer in his youth. But he was so successful that he eventually had 20 Russians under him and was able to travel widely. His signature alone was valid to certify the death of a collective farm cow.

28 October 1960 : After talks at the Hanover air traffic control centre, I now have this rough picture. The Queen's plane, flying at about 35,000 feet *[10,700 m]* – economical for a Comet jet – had been handed over by Hanover to the next control centre, Amsterdam, when the alleged incident occurred. The plane was then still just inside West Germany, in the country's north-western tip, over the River Ems estuary.

This was not the safest place for the Comet, for it was 10,000 feet *[3,050 m]* above the top of the normal air corridor. Aircraft inside the air corridors are in the main directed by the traffic control centres, which have to keep them at different levels, at least 1,000 metres apart vertically and several miles (I don't know how many) horizontally. If other aircraft wish to pass through the corridors, they have to follow visual flight rules: that is, they have to keep out of the way of planes in the corridor, and those in the corridor have to keep out of their way.

Above the air corridor is a space which is part of a whole region used by many military aircraft for training and other flights. The military aircraft mainly avoid the air corridors, and their movements are not known to Hanover and Amsterdam. The job of the air traffic control centre as regards the Comet, at that height, was to keep in touch with it, note its position and warn it of any impending dangers.

Pilots flying from Oldenburg on military training flights had been warned of the Queen's flight, though I do not know if they were given full information. In any case, as the Comet was in 'uncontrolled air space', the military planes had just as much right to be there as the Comet. It was equally incumbent on all aircraft to keep a good lookout and take evasive action if necessary. Flight Lieutenant Stevens, who was at the controls of the Comet at the time of the alleged incident, said he did not find it necessary to take such action. But experts told me that in such cases one would normally take such action.

From what the German pilot at Oldenburg has said, it appears that the British officer was mistaken about the shortest distance between the Comet and the Sabres. *[That is, the officer thought the Sabres were further away than they actually were.]* Judging by remarks of some British officials, they thought the Queen was travelling in a 'Purple Airway' – a 20-mile-wide box, which should have been cleared from 30 minutes before the Comet entered it until 30 minutes after it had passed through it. This method is adopted for VIP flights in Britain but, I was told, is not done in Germany and was not done on this occasion.

Back to Oldenburg tonight to await the arrival of a six-man joint Anglo-German commission which is probing the incident.

29 October 1960 : Not long after midnight, the commission kindly received me in the officers' club of the Oldenburg base; an RAF station until 1957 and now the headquarters of a West German fighter unit and an advanced training unit. Had not expected information from its members, headed by RAF Group Captain Ian Spencer, and hardly got any. Over a beer (bought by Spencer) in the base mess, I told the commission the result of *my* findings and pleaded with them to tell me at least whether they were terribly out of line. One of the members – a British wing commander called Barber – grinned and said, 'Could be worse.' I took that as something like confirmation.

I hung around during the day with several other journalists. The commission indicated they were questioning pilots.

30 October 1960 : A seven-hour drive in my car brought me to the headquarters of NATO's 2nd Allied Tactical Air Force in Mönchengladbach, west of Cologne. In the officers' bar tonight a *Luftwaffe* air traffic control officer told me that when US President Eisenhower came by Boeing 707 to visit West Germany last summer, his plane, when it reached European air space with its heavy military traffic outside the air corridors, was told to descend into the air corridors.

A British air safety expert, who did not identify himself *[evidently a member of the investigatory commission]*, agreed with my contention that it would have been safer for the Queen's plane to have flown in the air corridor at the point where the incident occurred. He added that, bearing in mind the extreme rarity of air collisions, corridors only improved safety slightly, while in certain circumstances they might even make collisions more likely by collecting planes within a restricted space.

31 October 1960 : The commission completed its work early today and dispersed. Nothing is due to be published until the two governments have considered its report *[see 9 November]*.

1 November 1960 : The boys have had their first anti-polio shots, something we had considered for some years. It seems to me to be absolutely clear that inoculations prevent much illness.

A very special visitor tonight: George Craddock, Labour MP for South Bradford, part of my hometown. He is attending a conference of 11 MPs from the opposition Labour Party with 11 Social Democratic members of the *Bundestag*. Craddock, a semi-pacifist, is pleased that supporters of unilateral disarmament have the upper hand in the party at the moment. He does not want us to lay down our arms just like that, but believes that unilateralism may bring about a psychological atmosphere conducive to disarmament. His main hope is for the strengthening of the United Nations, to be provided with an international military force, as disarmament goes ahead.

Craddock would like Britain to give up its nuclear arms now, but realizes it would be a long process for NATO to discard its nuclear deterrent, and admits that this would have to happen in the course of disarmament negotiations. I've always liked Craddock because he is so obviously not on the make, but is trying to do his bit to make the world a better place. He was alone in his views at this conference. *[George Craddock was MP for Bradford South from 1949 to 1970. He died on 28 April 1974, aged 77.]*

15 Assignment in Czechoslovakia

2 November 1960 : By train to Prague. At 8 am, after six hours in a sleeper, I was in Nuremberg, once the scene of Nazi Party rallies and long noted for its tasty Christmas gingerbread. After changing trains, found myself in a French carriage which had come from Paris. Reached the German–Czechoslovak frontier at Schirnding in north-eastern Bavaria, among rolling fir-clad hills in sunshine and autumn winds.

Before (I think) the train crossed the frontier, I chucked out of the widow a pamphlet sent to me by Dad from California, containing some anti-Communist jokes.

The usual wooden watchtowers at the frontier, the sign of many Communist states. At the frontier we were held up for about 90 minutes. Overalled men looked under the train. One of them came into my compartment and looked under the seats. Khaki-uniformed guards with pistols in holsters patrolled near the train.

A sign at the main Czech frontier station of Cheb (German name: Eger) extolled world peace in red letters; in Czech it's almost the same as in Russian. I read a piece in the Soviet Government newspaper, *Izvestia*, contrasting rich men's hunting privileges in Britain with the eviction of people unable to afford recent rent increases.

The countryside looked better kept than in East Germany, houses in better repair. One or two German signs to be seen – this was part of the mainly German-speaking Sudetenland, which was part of Austro-Hungary until Czechoslovakia was created in 1918 after the First World War. *[The Sudetenland – which was annexed by Germany in 1938 on the basis of the Munich Agreement, after Hitler had threatened to take it by force – was returned to Czechoslovakia in 1945 and most of its German inhabitants were expelled.]*

A good lunch: vegetable soup, a cutlet with potato salad, and a chocolate dessert, washed down by Pilsener, for the equivalent of just under ten shillings *[50p]*, not dear for continental railways. Passport and currency formalities conducted with charm. From the frontier it is some 120 miles eastwards to Prague, which is still well within the western half of Czechoslovakia. Through hilly wooded countryside, with some craggy areas where the train ran through cuttings and tunnels, we made our way to Plzen (Pilsen) where the famous beer – best in the world, I'd say – is brewed. It looked a nondescript industrial town.

Some of the train conductors were women in dark-blue uniforms. They seemed cheerful. One of them had locked my compartment when I went to eat – a thoughtful idea. Altogether more signs of a decent service on the Czechoslovak railways, compared with the East German ones. I mean that people seem willing to offer their services, whatever their job may be, instead of being surly.

It was dark as we came into Prague around 6 pm. The street scenes reminded me somewhat of Vienna, with the same red trams of ancient vintage. People all decently dressed, rather better than in East Germany, and the city much less run-down than East Berlin.

I went first to Opletalova, a street named after a student killed by the Nazis in 1939, to call on Mr Fischer, one of the deputy directors of the Czechoslovak news agency, Ceteka, a 40-ish, rather sallow man with a friendly manner. Over a cup of strong Turkish coffee – a custom here as in Yugoslavia – he told me Czechoslovakia had a higher standard of living than East Germany, and argued that this was due only partly to the fact that Czechoslovakia was an advanced country when the Communists took power in 1948.

On to my nearby hotel, the Ambassador, which Fischer described as one of the second-best – there had been no room in one of the best. It is on Wenceslas Square – a long, thin square with a slight slope at one end, where stands a statue of the Bohemian duke, Wenceslas, patron saint of the Czechs, the same one who, in the English carol, 'looked out on the Feast of Stephen'. *[Wenceslas, who ruled from AD 909 to 929, attempted to Christianize his people and was murdered by his brother.]*

I found the hotel in a better condition than was generally the case in East Berlin. Everything in my *en-suite* room appeared to work, except that the shower lead was missing. The furniture was pleasant period stuff and the floors well carpeted. I looked at the back of an etching hanging in my bedroom and found the German words: '*Eigentum des Hotel Ambassador*' (Property of Ambassador Hotel) – another relic of the German occupation.

I walked up to the Hradcany, the area around the once-royal castle which stands on a hill across the Vltava river from my hotel. The castle is now the seat of Communist President, Antonin Novotny. I was much taken by the atmosphere of the quarter around the castle, with ancient gabled houses reminiscent of some German towns.

In a steeply sloping street beneath the castle, I went into a little old pub – state-owned or publicly-owned, but you would not have known that by the look of it. It was just a friendly little pub, with an elderly couple attentively looking after the dozen or so customers. The customers, mostly office workers or labourers judging by their clothing, sat at wooden tables chatting animatedly and quaffing large amounts of Pilsener beer from glass tankards like those we use in England. Also there were two khaki-uniformed young soldiers.

After eating some salami and cheese, with dark partly-rye bread like that in Germany, I said something I supposed to be the Czech for 'Good night' and departed. Later I found the historic pub, U Kalicha (At the Chalice), where Jaroslav Hasek's character, the Good Soldier Schweik, used to take his beer during the First World War and make cracks at authority – then the Austro-

Hungarian monarchy. On the walls are illustrations from the book, and on sale are various sizes of dolls depicting Schweik himself.

I joined three young men, students of railway engineering, and found they were best accessible in Russian. All said they were very content with their lives. All appeared sure that West Germany was an aggressive state – the tone of all propaganda here. I tried, at least, to give them a few facts: for instance, that it is not West German policy to lay claim to the Sudetenland.

3 November 1960 : Attended an official Czechoslovak press conference on the case of Adolf Eichmann, the Nazi official who organized the deportation of Jews from Eastern Europe to the death camps. *[Eichmann, who had been living in Argentina, was abducted from there to Israel by Israeli secret service agents in May 1960. Later in this book I report on his trial in Jerusalem in 1961 which ended with a death sentence. After an unsuccessful appeal he was hanged in 1962.]*

I found nothing basically new in the press conference, which was largely an attack on the maintenance in public office in West Germany of some people connected with Eichmann, such as Adenauer's State Secretary, Dr Hans Globke, a lawyer who wrote a commentary on the Nazis' racial laws which laid the basis for later crimes against the Jews.

The witnesses who spoke today had but fleeting knowledge of Eichmann, perhaps because they were Czechs, while the main Nazi measures for murdering Jews took place in Poland. We were shown a photocopy of a document, held by the Union of Czechoslovak Anti-Fascist Fighters, referring to 93 children from Lidice and Lezaka. These were two Czech villages whose adult inhabitants were murdered by the Nazis as a reprisal for the assassination in 1942 by the Czech underground of Reinhard Heydrich, the Nazi occupation ruler of the Czech lands.

In this document it was stated that some Nazi office was asking for instructions as to 'the future use' of the children, just as though they were things. We were told that these children were deported to Poland and did not return. Seven other children from the same villages were classed as 'suitable to be Germanized' and were therefore spared.

This afternoon I saw a performance of the new second programme of the internationally famous *Laterna Magica*, a Czechoslovak stage revue which is a mixture of ballet, theatre, opera and wide-screen film. The first programme was prepared for the Brussels International Exhibition in 1958. I did not see that. The second programme has been put together for two foreign tours, the first to Russia and the second to London.

One scene in the programme has a pretty girl *commère* with a microphone in her hand, standing in mid-stage. On each side of the front of the stage are screens on which are projected moving pictures of the same girl – pictures which were filmed earlier. First one sees the girl speaking on the left-hand screen, announcing in French the next part of the programme. Then her second self on the right-hand screen announces the same thing in German. Then the girl in the flesh – occasionally pausing for a bit of backchat with her two screen selves – announces the same thing in Russian.

I was given some background on the *Laterna Magica* concept from the company's art director, Zdenek Mahler, 31, a distant relative of the composer Gustav Mahler. He said the concept was developed from pre-war techniques used by the Czechoslovak director, poet and composer Emil F. Burian who, however, had not the same modern techniques at his disposal. The basic idea – combining theatre with film – had been used in several countries, including West Germany and the Soviet Union. When I asked Mahler whether one could call *Laterna Magica* a form of 'socialist realism', the officially approved form for the arts, he said party leaders had seen the new show in September and had applauded. He argued that socialist realism should not be regarded as dogmatism. (It certainly used to be.) He added that party and government officials had looked very carefully at their production 'and hold their protective hand over it'.

Met up with the three railway engineering students I had

chatted with in the pub, and together we walked over one of Prague's main landmarks, the Charles Bridge, built in the era of Karl IV (1346–78). *[Karl, scion of a Luxembourg dynasty, was not only the King of Bohemia and Moravia, the Czech lands, but also the Emperor of the Holy Roman Empire, largely composed of German-speaking states of western and central Europe. Founded in 962, it broke up in 1806 as a result of the Napoleonic Wars. For the Germans this was the 'First Reich', called in Germany the 'Holy Roman Empire of the German Nation'. The Second Reich was created by Bismarck in 1871 after the Franco-Prussian War, while Hitler ruled over what he called the 'Third Reich'.]*

The long bridge over the Vltava is an imposing structure, partly because of its age, but also because of a tower which stands sentinel at the end nearest to the old city, and the groups of statues dotted along its balustrades.

After crossing the bridge, we walked past a former bishop's or archbishop's palace, now part of Prague University which, when it was founded in 1348, was the first university in the first German Reich.

I asked the three students about their attitude to religion. Only old people believe in such stuff today, they told me. Still, they were not able to tell me how the world had been created, and why. Had a farewell beer with the students in another pub, The Two Black Cats, which had a couple of stuffed ones on show. The place was packed and everyone seemed in good spirits.

Later I was taken out to dinner by Mr Fischer, who was accompanied by his rather thin but not unattractive wife. We went to a beautifully furnished and decorated Chinese restaurant; state-owned or municipally-owned, of course. Chinese had been sent to start it up, to show the Czechs how to cook Eastern delicacies, but now it is entirely Czech-run. Prices seemed extremely high – obviously a place for top people.

We ate 'black eggs' which, I was told, are kept underground for two or three months in a special way. They tasted rather like Camembert. After getting over the idea, I enjoyed them. Then came some swallow-nest soup with chicken in it, followed by carp done in a tasty slightly fruity sauce. We drank a tot of ginseng liquor ('the root of life', which comes from Korea), and Chinese tea, with a spot of heavy red wine to finish off, along with a creamy dessert.

In response to a political joke from me, Fischer told me one about Stalin's will. Well, he left two of them, the story went. He instructed that one should be opened if things looked black and the other if things looked good. After he died, Khrushchev and the other leaders decided things looked black, and opened the first envelope. It said: 'Dear comrades, blame it all on me.' They did, and things improved a lot. So then, after a year or two, they opened the second envelope. It said: 'Dear comrades, now do as I did.' However, Fischer added that the joke was not true because Khrushchev had not followed Stalin's policy.

I raised the question of Communist restrictions on freedom of movement. Fischer said this was sometimes necessary in the interests of the state. That may sometimes be true – the United Sates occasionally refuses its citizens the right to travel abroad – but I think it is highly overdone by the Communists.

Fischer made a point of emphasizing the strong support the Czechoslovak Communist Party had before Czechoslovakia became a Communist state in 1948 *[through a coup]*. He implied that in his view that strong support had made it more justified to set up a Communist dictatorship.

4 November 1960 : For a couple of hours, before I took the train back home this morning, I tried to get some idea of the standard of living here. I learned that the average wage was around 1,100 crowns monthly for a 46-hour week. That's about £7 a week at the tourist rate of exchange. *[More meaningful than such figures was the fact that a Czech had to work for about 50 minutes for a two-kilogram loaf of bread, while the average West German had to work about 40 minutes for such a loaf.]* A young woman working as a hotel receptionist said the price of food was 'high enough'. A head waiter said he earned 1,400 crowns plus 600 crowns in tips – officially regarded as 'unsocialist'.

A waiter told me that miners and other heavy industrial workers got up to 3,000 crowns monthly, five weeks' holiday a year and free holiday accommodation. The waiter said of the miners, 'They live like lords, but I would not like to do their work.' He said rents were very low: about five per cent of wages compared with about 25 per cent he had to pay before the war. On this basis people who still owned accommodation to rent were receiving very little, he said. Apples were plentiful as there had been a bumper harvest.

A railwayman told me he earned 1,100 crowns monthly, of which 170 were an allowance for two children. After first inquiring whether I represented a Communist newspaper, he said, 'If you are in the party you are all right. I am not in it.' He said he did not go hungry. He was smoking.

In the train I sat next to the Czech-born wife of a West German businessman. She was returning to Germany after a visit to her sister and brother near Prague. She had waited eight months to get her visa. Four years ago she had had her first trip home in 13 years, after being refused visas earlier. She said her relations had a good supply of food and consumer goods, though certain things were more 'primitive' or not as attractively packaged as in the West.

I had a similar report from two elderly West German women, refugees from the Sudetenland, who boarded the train at Cheb, in the former Sudetenland, after being allowed into Czechoslovakia for only four days to attend the funeral of their mother. Their father and mother had not been allowed to leave Czechoslovakia when most of the German inhabitants were expelled after the Second World War, because her father was a key worker in the pottery industry.

These two women had with them a few of their mother's belongings, including an oil painting of the Virgin Mary, which had been in the family for about three generations. I was glad to hear they had been well treated by Czech customs officials, who had to approve the removal of some of their mother's chattels.

Also in our carriage was an old Polish woman, resident in

France, who was nearly refused entry into West Germany because her transit visa had run out. But the officials relented and gave her a gratis extension when they realized she had hardly any money. This carriage was a living example of what wars, frontiers and ideologies bring people in terms of sadness. Back home late tonight.

16 New US President: Kennedy

9 November 1960 : John F. Kennedy, 43, a Democrat, is the new US President. I preferred him to his Republican opponent, Richard Nixon. The Communists seem to have preferred him too. What a responsibility he has! I ought to like Nixon, I suppose, as he is said to be a Quaker. However, I am somewhat doubtful about his Quakerism, as he was an officer in the Second World War, while Quakers are usually pacifists.

A phone call from the Bonn CID, telling me they had been instructed by the Chief Prosecutor in Cologne to ask why I was receiving regular deliveries of Russian newspapers. There had been a suggestion, I was told, that these might be 'a danger to the state'. When I explained that I was a Reuter correspondent, everything was OK, as journalists are allowed to receive such material, as being necessary for their work. Ordinary people are not.

That sort of thing leaves a nasty taste. It is going too far to prevent people from reading what kind of publications they wish. It amounts to restricting freedom of thought to some extent. This does not happen in Britain.

Persuaded the chief Defence Ministry spokesman, Colonel Gerd Schmückle, to give me an advance copy of the communiqué on the alleged 'buzzing' of the Queen's plane. Schmückle gave me the copy, on condition we would not issue a word until an announcement was made shortly at a press conference. This enabled me to read the text, write the story and have it punched

153

onto teleprinter tape, so that we were ready to start it running to London as soon as it was released officially. This gave us a good start on the other agencies.

The communiqué did not go into much detail, but as far as it went, it confirmed the stories I had done. It said that while it had not been possible to establish the exact distance at which the Queen's Comet and the two jets had passed by each other, there had been no danger because the jet pilots had been watching the Comet for some time.

11 November 1960 : Our family watched part of the St Martin's Day procession, commemorating a fourth-century French saint who gave to the poor. In the procession children walked carrying paper lanterns, with candles inside, to a bonfire, and a man on horseback dressed as St Martin rode by. Afterwards Robin and Chris followed tradition by singing St Martin songs at the doorsteps of neighbours, returning with pocketfuls of sweets, a few pfennigs and some pears and apples.

12 November 1960 : Adenauer, in an interview with one of the papers today, said Khrushchev was different from Stalin and was a man one could talk to; something I have thought for a long time, but had not credited Adenauer with thinking. When asked if he would meet Khrushchev, Adenauer said it was up to the Soviet leader to come to Bonn as he, Adenauer, had gone to Moscow in 1955.

14 November 1960 : Brian Horton arrived today to start the take-over procedure as news editor (deputy chief correspondent) from John Bush, who is going to Vienna. I had a talk with Gerry, who told me that Brian had been informed that I was to go to Moscow later, which makes my position less awkward. While I repeated my criticism of Brian's appointment, I added that I would do my best to make things go smoothly. Gerry said he had been sincere in telling me earlier that I would have been wasted in the news editor's job. He went so far as to say he thought I was the best reporter Reuters had in Europe. *[I would never have made such a claim.]* Have received three letters from colleagues in our London head office criticizing Brian's appointment. But my mind has been set at rest, more or less, and now my task is to prepare myself for the Moscow assignment.

15 November 1960 : Elfi and I saw a German colour film of Goethe's *Faust*, directed by and starring Gustaf Gründgens, one of Germany's greatest actors who, sadly, showed some sympathy for the Nazis. In this film he played a frightening, but at times rib-tickling Mephistopheles to Will Quadflieg's Faust. Many of Goethe's ruminations in this work remind me of some of my own musings. This film made me feel what wonderful complexity there is in the world and the human mind – surely not all a joke. It made me feel I wanted to be good to people. Of course, such feelings do not always last.

18 November 1960 : Watched the third of the 14-part German TV programme on the rise of Nazism, very well done from a democratic point of view. In such films Hitler appears laughable to us, impossible to take seriously, if we did not know what he had brought about.

19 November 1960 : Gerry gave a cocktail party, attended by about 70 people, to mark the changes in the office. For me, the most important person present was Reuters general manager, burly Scot, Walton A. Cole, who, I believe, came up the hard way after leaving school at 15, like me. He took me aside, spoke to me about Moscow and said words to the effect, 'I'll see you get there' – providing, of course, that the Russians give me a visa.

20 November 1960 : Robin, who is 12, beat me at chess. 'You don't watch your queen enough Daddy,' he told me, forgetting that I had saved his for him a couple of times by pointing out proposed wrong moves. He's certainly improving though. *[I have never been much good at chess, though it's given me much pleasure.]*

23 November 1960 : Two days of important German–American talks ended yesterday. The American side, led by Treasury Secretary, Robert Anderson, failed in its aim to obtain direct cash payments to offset some of the dollar outflow caused by stationing about 350,000 members of the US armed forces, with about 190,000 dependents, in West Germany. This outflow totals over 600 million dollars annually and is nearly one-sixth of the current annual US balance of payments deficit.

It is difficult to say whether it is justified for the rich United States, where most families have two cars, to ask hardworking and not very well-off ordinary Germans to fork out something so that the Americans may continue to live as well or better than before. On the other hand, the United States was generous to West Germany with the aid it gave in the Marshall Plan, helping West Germany to get on its feet. So it is perhaps just that West Germany should pay back that moral debt now when the United States, due to its large foreign aid and defence contributions, is facing financial difficulties.

One reason why the Germans refused to offer cash was because they feared that would bring similar demands from Britain and France. And they did not want to increase taxes in the run-up to next September's federal elections.

Instead of offering direct cash payments, they made several offers which would have reduced the burden on the US balance of payments. For instance, they offered to pay more for NATO infrastructure, if the Americans paid less, and to repay immediately about 800 million dollars of outstanding post-war debts to the United States, instead of repaying them by instalments. The Americans made no decision on any of the German proposals.

The Germans indicated they just would not discuss making further direct cash payments. Such an important disagreement is unprecedented in West German–US relations. I take the view that the Americans were ill-advised to conduct the talks with so much emphasis on direct costs, because the Germans are, I think, ready to do quite a lot in other ways because they genuinely want to help the US, to which they feel much gratitude, and also because it is in the German interest politically and economically to do so.

Incongruous contrast tonight: packing Christmas parcels while watching a TV feature about the development of nuclear weapons and their danger to the world.

30 November 1960 : On a railway sleeper to East Berlin, chatted with a 50-ish Russian woman who left Russia legally 30 years ago to marry a German engineer. She now translates for a German firm which trades with Russia. She said she believed most Russians were for Communism, and that Khrushchev had colossally improved life there by taking away the 3 am knock on the door. She said the Russians violently opposed war and that this tendency would even increase as the new élite of highly educated people takes over gradually from the old revolutionaries.

17 Ulbricht back from Communist summit

2 December 1960 : To East Berlin's airport to report the return of the East German delegation from the Moscow summit conference of 81 of the world's Communist parties. The delegation was headed by the SED leader, Walter Ulbricht, who – since I was last in East Berlin – has become head of the State Council (collective presidency) following the death of the former President, veteran Communist Wilhelm Pieck.

The arrival turned out to be a good story, for Ulbricht disclosed that the Communist summit agreed that war was not inevitable as, in their view, the balance of forces had turned so much in favour of Communism. This looks like confirmation of the Khrushchev line, as opposed to the Chinese line, which has been much more sceptical about the chances of avoiding a war with the 'imperialists'.

Some observers even consider that in the world's basic interest – avoiding a nuclear war – the interests of the Soviet Union coincide at the moment more closely with those of the West than with those of China, because of China's allegedly belligerent attitude and its reported willingness to risk the deaths of millions, because it has such a large population.

Called on East Berlin friends, a skilled worker and his wife, living with two children in a four-room flat. Some months ago they had ordered a small East German car, a Trabant, which costs 14,000 marks. (Purchasing power equivalent would be about £700, but the sum represents more than two years' wages for the average industrial worker.) They will have to wait about two years for it. *[A few years later ordinary East Germans often had to wait ten to 15 years to obtain a new car.]*

4 December 1960 : I have learned that East Germans today appear to have worse supplies of some consumer goods, textiles for instance, than a couple of years ago. And one East German complained to me that there was less to buy at the annual Christmas fair on the Marx-Engels-Platz in East Berlin than in previous years.

5 December 1960 : Had learned that the expected declaration of the 81 Communist parties, after their Moscow summit, would be published in Communist Party organs around the world tomorrow.

The chiefs of the East German party organ, *Neues Deutschland*, had forbidden the issue of advance copies of the paper before official publication time, early tomorrow. But around 11 pm I managed to obtain a copy, and was apparently the first Reuter correspondent in Europe to break the story.

As soon as my 'snap' (very urgent) first paragraph had reached London, London started to issue a prepared version of the declaration from the British Communist organ, the *Daily Worker*. Perhaps they had an agreement with that paper allowing them to transmit the story when it came out elsewhere.

Later I wrote a piece comparing the declaration with that made in 1957 on the fortieth anniversary of the Soviet Revolution. My analysis was that today's declaration held the balance between the believed Soviet and Chinese viewpoints, with the Russians maintaining that the Communist bloc is so strong that war is no longer inevitable, while the Chinese are more sceptical and more rabid against the 'imperialists'.

The new document contains far more attacks on US 'imperialism' as the alleged main cause of everything that is bad – that's the

Chinese line all right. It also attacks the Yugoslav Communists by name as having betrayed Marxism–Leninism. In 1957 the attack was against the sin of 'revisionism', without the Yugoslavs being named. This is also more like the Chinese than the Russians who, while disapproving of the Yugoslavs, are not quite so harsh in their judgement.

A new Communist-bloc joke: Khrushchev applies to Peter for admission to heaven. Peter consults with the Almighty, who agrees to a six-month's probation, providing Khrushchev makes no anti-religious propaganda. After six months the Almighty asks how Khrushchev is behaving. The answer, 'He's settled down remarkably well, Comrade God.'

6 December 1960 : Erdmute Behrendt, our young East Berlin office assistant, played the role of St Nikolaus, who in Germany comes on the night of 5–6 December, bringing goodies to good children. She left a plateful of biscuits and sweets on the table for me.

7 December 1960 : Chatted in a café with three young men, whom I first took for students, as they were quite well dressed. They turned out to be two bricklayers and their labourer – what the Communists call a 'brigade'. They earn about 600 marks (£60) a month each. The labourer gets the same as the other two, to egg him on, because if he is slow in bringing bricks they don't earn as much on the piecework system used.

These chaps, in their early twenties, told me they were quite happy to stay in East Berlin – though they often see films in West Berlin – and felt they could live as well here as in the West. However, one of them said that would not apply to self-employed people like his father and mother, who were shopkeepers who had gone West and set up shop there.

These three young men disclosed that they worked only for six months of the year – because they liked having the rest of the time off. When they have saved up some money, they give notice and go on holiday, making their money spin out as long as they can.

One of them said, 'That wouldn't do for everyone. Some people would go to the dogs. But we can stand it. We look decent, don't we?'

Another explained, 'If I work, I have to spend more money – for fares and extra food. So what it amounts to is that when I work I have little and when I don't work I have little. So why work?' And after finishing their bowl of lentil soup, a beer I bought them and one they bought themselves, they set off to go on amusing themselves until their money ran out again.

Tonight went to see the German musical, *Dreigroschenoper* (*The Threepenny Opera*) with lyrics by Bertolt Brecht and music by Kurt Weill. It was put on by the Berliner Ensemble, the company founded by Brecht – who died in 1956 – in the East Berlin *Theater am Schiffbauerdamm*, where the original production was staged in the late twenties. It was produced then and now by Erich Engel, born in 1891. Set in London, it is based partly on John Gay's *Beggar's Opera*, which was first staged in 1728.

Ever since I got to know the music and some of the words of this wonderful work several years ago – 'Mack the Knife' is the popularized version of one song – I've been captivated, so it was a memorable experience to see this production.

Brecht's main point in this work, written when capitalism was in a much worse state than now, is that the capitalists as a class are just as much robbers as Mack was. That is why, at the end, he has Mack reprieved on the scaffold and given a title, a doctorate and a pension, which makes him accepted by the upper classes.

8 December 1960 : An East German Government press conference gave a few more alleged details of the role of Dr Hans Globke, now Adenauer's State Secretary, in connection with the Nazis' racial laws which prepared the way for the mass murder of the Jews. It is, I think, not denied in West Germany that Globke, as an official of the Prussian Interior Ministry and later of the Reich Interior Ministry, helped to prepare the racial laws and wrote an authoritative commentary on them.

Today it was alleged, with some evidence, that Globke had

visited Slovakia in 1941 in connection with the application of similar laws in that Fascist puppet state. Globke has been defended in West Germany by Catholic dignitaries, and by some Jews, on the ground that he allegedly stayed in office when the Nazis came to power in the hope of making some of their laws less inhuman, and also to enable him to warn the Catholic Church of impending new moves; he was and is a Catholic. Even if this defence is true, I think he should not be allowed to hold his present office.

An East German joiner told me that more and more East Germans were working in West Berlin. 'They are obeying Marx's injunction to sell your labour for the highest price,' he quipped.

Have been gripped by what I believe is the best book by the 60-year-old East German Communist writer, Anna Seghers: *Das Siebte Kreuz* (*The Seventh Cross*), about the escape of seven prisoners from a concentration camp near Mainz, Seghers' hometown in West Germany. Some fine descriptive and real feeling in this book, which she wrote in France while a refugee from Nazism. Some of her later books are said to be party-line stuff of much less literary merit. She returned to Germany in 1947, settled in East Germany, joined the SED and became chairman of the East German Writers' Union. She is praised officially here as East Germany's leading writer. *[Seghers later played a part in efforts by the SED to 'discipline' dissident writers. She died in 1983.]*

9 December 1960 : In one of East Berlin's better restaurants tonight I was told I could have no tea as, for some reason, deliveries had stopped a couple of days ago and, evidently, no one had done anything about it. There's plenty of tea in the shops.

12 December 1960 : Did a few paragraphs about Christmas preparations in East Berlin, where children have been employed to help out in one big state-owned store during the rush, and part of a history museum has been taken over to sell clothing. Clothing and textiles are apparently scarcer than last year. Though religious symbols are generally avoided in the shops, one can buy the traditional German circular Advent wreaths made of fir twigs, with four candles, one for each Sunday in Advent. Lots of Christmas trees, but these, of course, are not a religious symbol as such.

Chatted with an old friend and onetime Reuter colleague, David Rees, who is now working for Notley's, a London advertising firm which obtained a contract from the East German authorities to do public relations for East Germany in Britain. One main aim is to increase trade between the two countries. David is touring East Germany to pick up material which he will then try to place in British newspapers by writing articles.

13 December 1960 : Spent over two hours at a large radio works in the East Berlin suburb of Köpenick, questioning about ten managers and workers, mainly Communists, about a proposed new labour law. We sat around a table in an office of the old works, which were nationalized in 1946.

The German group was headed by Kurt Bräsemann, the 40-ish wiry director of a department employing about 950. He is an ex-mechanic who studied at a technical school and, of course, a Communist. He said he regarded as one of the main points in the proposed new law, provisions emphasizing 'that our workers have a role in the management of the works and bear full co-responsibility for what is their property. Management is not just by orders; the workers must understand the orders.'

Bräsemann said that 'old traditions', carried over from capitalism, under which the workers had no say in the management, were still evident among some people. He conceded that in capitalist firms workers had sometimes been encouraged to make suggestions to improve productivity, but said they had no say in the production plans.

The new law makes it rather easier to fine workers if, through negligence or on purpose, they turn out defective goods. Bräsemann said the previous power to fine workers in such cases had not been imposed harshly in this factory. Such a step was mainly intended for the otherwise unteachable.

One of the workers interposed to say that a worker who turned out rejects would first of all be tackled to find out the reason:

whether he was unhappy in his work or had family trouble etc. The works SED party secretary, Otto Bachmann – who in a Communist state plays an important role alongside the manager – underlined that point.

Another of those present was the non-party, but obviously pro-Communist, leader of a workers 'brigade' of 28 people working mainly in a milling machine section. Members of the brigade told me they were on average over-fulfilling their norm by 60 or 70 per cent. When I suggested that the norm might be too easy, they grinned. This year, they said, they had increased production by 45 per cent, partly by mechanization and better planning and partly by 'improving political consciousness' – that is, acceptance of the official line that, now factories have been nationalized, it's up to everyone to do their best for the common good instead of slacking, as when they worked for capitalists who were merely exploiting them to the largest extent possible.

One entirely new point in the proposed law is that, in future, not only manual workers, but also white-collar workers, right up to the director, can be fined for faulty work. In the past such people could of course be disciplined, but not fined. The law makes it general practice to hold 'production discussions' between management and representatives of the workers. In the Köpenick works these have been going on for a year already. They had normally been held once a month, partly in working time, partly not.

I tackled them about the right to strike, which is not mentioned in the proposed law. I referred to the 1953 uprising, which began with strikes. Bachman said that the people who had struck in 1953 'did not understand'. Under capitalism one had the worker and the capitalist, two conflicting parties, whereas a Communist state was organized for the benefit of all. I was told that 'almost all' their workers no longer contemplated striking, but the idea remained in some heads, out of old trade-union tradition, bolstered by ideas brought in from West Berlin.

Bräsemann declined to give an estimate of the percentage of his workers who supported the East German state, but he said that none of the workers wanted to give up their state-owned factory.

There were some workers, he said, he had no idea how many, who might be 'enemies of the state' and who would 'raise their heads if they thought things were going their way'.

The wages in this factory varied from 1,820 marks a month for Bräsemann, 570 marks for a skilled worker and 300 for the lowest-paid factory hands. Holidays were from 12 to 24 working days a year, according to type of work and position.

14 December 1960 : Professor Pichotka, a West German who has headed the Physiology Institute of East Berlin's Humboldt University for the past 18 months, told me at lunch the other day that, although his family had joined him about two months ago, he was almost certain he could stick it no longer.

Pichotka said university professors were not free to teach according to their scientific convictions if these conflicted with the party line. Further, promotions in university institutes were made partly on political grounds. The general standard in East German universities was lower than in West Germany, because the East Germans were being taught to become technicians rather than scientists.

On a visit to Russia, Pichotka said, he had found things much freer there. Russian academics were tending to become proper-tied. Professors he had met had a house in town and a dacha in the countryside.

On the reported Soviet–Chinese squabble, he told me that when he visited the Dubna Nuclear Institute, near Moscow, one of the leading officials, speaking to him in German, said they had about 180 Chinese students out of a total of about 250 foreigners, and urged Pichotka to try to have more Germans sent there, from East or West, the implication being that they could then cut down the number of Chinese.

Today I interviewed two officials of the state-owned taxi firm which runs 300 of East Berlin's 470 taxis; the rest are privately owned. A taxi driver had told me that moves were afoot to per-suade the private taxi-owners who, in some cases, are also the dri-vers, to take the first step towards nationalization by putting their vehicles under contract to the state-owned firm, which would then organize their use.

Kurt Werner, 38, traffic manager and a deputy director, told me the state-owned firm was founded in 1951 and equipped with two-litre EMW taxis built at Eisenach, Thuringia, in a factory formerly owned by the BMW company in Munich, West Germany. The East Germans were forced to change the name from BMW (*Bayrische Motorenwerke*) to EMW (*Eisenacher Motorenwerke*), but the cars remained basically the same. They went out of production in 1956 as part of a scheme to co-ordinate car production in the Communist bloc.

East Germany is now concentrating on the medium-size two-stroke Wartburg and the small two-stroke Trabant, apart from lorries and tractors. The average age of the taxis used at present is eight or nine years, though many of them have been renovated.

Werner told me that it was estimated that East Berlin needed 900 taxis, instead of the 470 available at present. But the present situation tended to push up earnings for the firm's drivers, who averaged about 660 marks a month, plus 150 marks in tips. Tips used to be frowned upon in Communist countries. They are now allowed as part of the trend to use material interest in improving efficiency. The firm's party secretary, Alfred Kindler, 40, himself a taxi driver, told me, 'We have a generous public. It is not obligatory to tip, but we say "thank you" when we get something.'

The firm's drivers work a 45-hour week – six days of 7½ hours. It is planned gradually to change over from the EMWs to Russian Volgas and Moskviches by 1967. Tests had shown that the engine life of a Volga was about 100,000 kilometres *[62,500 miles]* and that of a Moskvich about 110,000, compared with 180,000 kilometres for the EMWs. The firm uses a few Wartburgs, but they are too low-powered and not robust enough for effective taxi use.

The taxi drivers are organized in 'brigades' of 27. There are competitions between the brigades for bonuses and also between the individual drivers. One factor taken into account in awarding bonuses is the drivers' behaviour towards passengers. How was their behaviour judged, I asked. Werner smiled, 'It is very subjective. But if we get complaints about drivers they cannot be awarded bonuses. We also get letters praising our drivers.'

Kindler said that when a driver made a 'mistake' – had an accident or gave bad service – the matter was investigated in his brigade. 'We tell him, putting it crudely, "You are a lout. If you go on like this we shall chuck you out."'

When I questioned Kindler about the efforts being made to persuade private taxi drivers to work under contract for the state-owned firm, he indicated that one of the main forms of 'persuasion' was to give contract drivers the right to buy an unlimited amount of petrol, whereas private drivers could buy petrol for only 2,000 kilometres *[1,250 miles]* a month. The state-owned taxis do on average between 6,000 and 7,000 kilometres a month.

Kindler conceded that the petrol factor would tend to bind the private drivers to the state-owned firm. He added, 'But we say we must meet the needs of the population and not just to go out when we want to earn.' Private taxi drivers, he said, tended to be on the streets mainly at rush hours.

Kindler argued that the efforts to persuade private drivers to conclude contracts with the state-owned firm were intended 'to meet needs better'. However, he added, 'At the same time, of course, we are convinced that socialism is the right road.'

So far one private driver had signed up and 15 others had said they were willing to sign.

I asked why it was forbidden, with a few exceptions, for private persons to start up as individual taxi drivers. Kindler replied, 'Because under socialism we proceed from the collective, and we do not want new private businessmen.'

When I asked whether he thought the existence of private taxi drivers would prevent the establishment of socialism, he said, 'No.'

Another important means of pressure which the state-owned firm can use is its influence in helping private taxi drivers to obtain new or renovated taxis, which are extremely scarce. A private taxi driver told me earlier that, for him, the only difference between working for a private taxi owner and working for the state-owned firm was that, with the latter he would not be able to do overtime as a rule, and would have to go to meetings – political ones, he meant.

Lunched with 79-year-old East German historian, Bruegel, a former *Wehrmacht* officer who told me he had been linked to the July 1944 plot to assassinate Hitler. *[I did not note his first name.]* Some months later he had been arrested. In February 1945, while being driven through Berlin under guard, to go for questioning, he escaped when the car driver was killed in an air raid and another guard in the car was injured. Bruegel was apparently presumed dead. He was hidden in turn by a Communist, a Social Democrat and a Catholic, who all lived in East Berlin. The Catholic was Dr Heinrich Krone, who is now the chairman of the *Bundestag* group of Adenauer's Christian Democratic Party.

After the war, Bruegel stayed in East Berlin and worked at a Communist historical institute. He is now on quite a good pension. His view is that there is a great deal wrong in East Germany, but that the world is moving towards some kind of socialism, which he supports.

Bruegel has met a lot of the East German high-ups. He gave me this description of Ulbricht: 'He is not a nasty person, but is mediocre, though hard-working. He has an inferiority complex due to his mediocrity, and surrounds himself with other mediocre people – or sycophants.'

Bruegel said the Russians were aware of Ulbricht's mediocrity. He is convinced that the then Soviet High Commissioner in Berlin, Vladimir Semyonov, now a Deputy Foreign Minister, had tried to engineer Ulbricht's downfall by encouraging some disturbances in June 1953, but was himself disowned by Moscow when the disturbances developed into a near-revolution. According to Bruegel, Semyonov wanted to replace Ulbricht by the Dahlem-Zaisser group, who favoured a more elastic line.

Ulbricht's first wife, a French Communist known as Rose Michel, whom he married and divorced in Russia during the Second World War, is now the East Berlin correspondent of the French Communist Party organ, *Humanité*. Ulbricht is now married to a German Communist, Lotte (*née* Kühn).

15 December 1960 : Pre-Christmas dinner in one of East Berlin's best restaurants, the Budapest in the Stalinallee, with Erdmute Behrendt and Reuters new East Berlin correspondent, Adam Kellett-Long, 25, Oxford graduate, thin, friendly, boyish, small too. Seated near the orchestra, we had to shout our conversation amid wailing violins and planging cembalos. After one of the violinists, who came to our table, had played a Hungarian melody I asked for, the orchestra followed up with an uncalled-for encore, 'Daisy, Daisy', of which they knew the first two words and then relapsed into Magyar mouthings.

17 December 1960 : With Adam to a press conference given by Comandante Ernesto Guevara, one of the leading Cuban revolutionaries, now president of the national bank. He has been negotiating trade agreements with several Communist countries, including East Germany. He wore the usual Cuban revolutionary outfit, an open-necked khaki shirt and a beard, and looked like a latter-day prophet; most handsome, I thought. He answered questions clearly and without side-stepping.

I think, on balance, the Americans have themselves to thank for the Cuban situation, because they bolstered up the right-wing dictator, Fulgencio Batista in the old days. Be that as it may, it is a very tricky situation indeed now, because the United States can feel threatened by Cuba's presence as a back door for the agents – and missiles – of world Communism, though no doubt world Communism could easily put the missiles on ships if Cuba were not there. *[In retrospect that sentence looks prophetic in view of the 1962 Cuban crisis, caused by Khrushchev's action in siting Soviet missiles on Cuba, which nearly caused a Third World War.]*

Thanks to our special position as the only Western news agency accredited in East Germany, ADN gave us, a day in advance, the embargoed partial text of a speech by Ulbricht. In it he appealed for an agreement with West Germany on a ten-year non-aggression pact.

Nothing will come of this. But I hope the Big Four start getting somewhere on Germany at the next summit, as the situation is getting more and more dangerous. In my view the main danger at present comes from West Germany, which has rejected all proposals, whether from East or West, designed to relax the Central European situation without weakening one side more than the other.

For late lunch in the East German Press Club, Adam and I chose fried frogs' legs, done like fried chicken and tasting rather like it. Adam is surprised to find East Berlin much more cultivated and the people much less inhibited (frightened) than he had imagined.

18 December 1960 : The rest of Ulbricht's speech, published today in *Neues Deutschland*, included indirect references to the Sino-Soviet differences at the Moscow summit. Without mentioning the Chinese by name, he made it clear that there had been differences on the question of whether a world war would – as the Chinese reportedly argued – end in victory for Communism and was therefore not such a bad thing.

Ulbricht attacked that view as 'incorrect and harmful'. I understand that the Chinese put forward that view several months ago. Perhaps they have dropped it, in face of the opposition of most of the other Communist parties.

Ulbricht said the Communists wanted the 'class struggle' to continue in the form of 'peaceful coexistence', with the Communists gradually taking over more of the world, but without causing the 'capitalists' to start another war.

If they stick to that, I don't think it is an unreasonable policy. Whether they will be successful in taking over the world is another matter.

Paid a farewell visit to Elfi's East Berlin cousin, Margot Schellberg, whose husband Hans-Dieter, is the 30-ish deputy director of a state farm, but not a Communist. He told me the farm would this year make a profit for the first time in several years. Then I said my goodbyes to Elfi's three West Berlin aunts, before thankfully dropping into a sleeper which took me home. I was to have stayed another day, but a plane crash in Munich, killing about 50, has depleted the Bonn office and they asked me to return sooner.

19 December 1960 : Elfi, wearing what I call her pussycat fur coat – made from the fur of some wild cat – was waiting in the car at Bad Godesberg station, as I lumbered up the steps with my case swelling with a fresh pile of Russian books, bought cheaply in East Berlin. Lovely to be home in nice time for Christmas. When Chris came from school, he gave me a delightful grin through the front door pane, and Robin grabbed me for chess after lunch.

20 December 1960 : Elfi and I attended a Christmas social held for local Lutheran church lay helpers – we do a little voluntary work for the church. My doubts about Christian dogma were with me throughout the evening, but so was my conviction that there are wonderful elements in Christianity, which represent the striving of the advance guard of humanity for a better life and better people. At events like this, I notice one of the national differences between Germans and English: the Germans are more serious and do not relax into jollity so easily.

21 December 1960 : When my mother-in-law, whom I call *Mutti*, arrived to spend Christmas with us, she said I had more grey hairs – I shall be 36 next June. I told her I needed them to reinforce my authority.

24 December 1960 : At the office we wrote mainly Christmassy stories, one of them about British troops in Germany having their Christmas dinner served by their officers – a hardy annual. Lionel Walsh said he wondered what would happen if the Russians attacked in the middle of Christmas dinner.

Our local Lutheran church was almost full when we went in half an hour before the first Christmas service began at 4 pm; in Germany Christmas begins on the afternoon of Christmas Eve. Chris bubbled with happiness as the verger lit two large candles on each side of the central pulpit and then switched on the electric candles on two large Christmas trees. In a rather overlong service, during which I had to shush Chris several times, the pastor's main theme was that we should try to show in our behaviour the meaning of Christian love.

When we arrived home, Chris could hardly contain himself – Robin is now more 'mature' – until we were admitted to the lounge, where Elfi had lit the candles on the tree and laid out the many presents. We sang a German carol, '*Ihr Kinderlein kommet*' ('Come, Children'), which is traditional at this juncture. Then Robin and Chris rattled off the German Christmas poems they had learned – another German custom – before we unwrapped our presents.

Christmas Day 1960 : Among the guests at our goose-laden dinner table were our new chief correspondent, David Sells, and his wife Pauline, one of the few English wives of Reuter correspondents. *[I found it enjoyable to work with David Sells, partly because his sense of humour prevented him from taking things too seriously. He and Pauline had two sons, but divorced in 1982. David, born in Birmingham in 1928, had an impressive career in Reuters from 1952 to 1966, when he joined the BBC. He has worked as a reporter and presenter for several top BBC television and radio programmes, specializing in Europe and the Middle East. In 2002, as I write, he still works for the BBC, principally reporting for* Newsnight *on BBC television.]*

18 To strike-ridden Brussels

26 December 1960 : I was sent off to Brussels, about 200 miles west-north-west of Bonn, to help our correspondents, elderly Serge Nabokov (cousin of Vladimir, author of *Lolita*) and younger Derek Wilson, to cover a widespread strike called by the socialist-led trade unions, representing about half of Belgium's workers. The strike is a protest against an austerity law tabled by the Catholic–Liberal Government, partly to offset Belgium's expenditure caused by the effects of granting independence to the Belgian Congo.

When I crossed into Belgium, just beyond Aachen, I had my first experience of the effects of the strike. A Belgian frontier official, explaining that most of Belgium's trains were at a stand-still, asked me if I would give a lift to an elderly Greek couple who had come all the way by train from Greece, intending to visit a relative in Brussels, 80 miles away, and who were now stranded. As I drove towards Brussels, the Greek couple chatted with me in French, good practice for this assignment. We saw lots of police in cities on the way and hammers-and-sickles in whitewash at Liège station. As I had a fluey cold, it was no fun to work until 11 pm, mainly translating Belgian news agency reports from all over the country on the progress of the strike, which is tightly gripping the left-wing French-speaking south (Wallonia), but which has not taken a strong hold on the Flemish-speaking and largely Catholic north.

28 December 1960 : As the strike continued, had a long chat with Serge Nabokov, partly in Russian (for practice). Serge told me that his grandfather, Dmitri Nabokov, had been Minister for the Kingdom of Poland, then under Russian rule, and later Minister of Justice under the liberal Tsar Alexander II, who reigned from 1855 to 1881.

Serge's family fled at the time of the Bolshevist revolution in 1917. But when the Communists took power in Romania after the Second World War, Serge's sister – who is now aged about 57 – was working at the United States consulate in Bucharest. The Communists tried to enlist her as a spy, but when they failed, she was flown to Russia, put in Moscow's Lubianka gaol and sentenced to 15 years' labour camp.

Physically frail, she was given the comparatively light task of filling in holes in Kazakhstan potato fields made by small central Asian animals which, Serge told me, look rather like little kangaroos and are called *mushkanchiki*. His sister was released last year and now lives with them. Serge ascribed her release to intercession by Belgium's Dowager Queen Elizabeth, who is pro-Communist, a 'Red Queen' as a Belgian politician once described her.

A cousin of Serge, Ignatiev, now a Canadian Under-Secretary, once travelled through the Soviet Union with Canadian Foreign Minister Lester Pearson. Khrushchev asked Serge's cousin if one of his relatives had served in the post-Tsarist but pre-Bolshevik Government led by Kerensky. Serge's cousin replied, 'My relative only served the Tsar.'

Serge has quite friendly relations with Soviet diplomats and journalists, but he told me he was scared to visit Russia.

29 December 1960 : Police clashed with strikers in Brussels and Ghent yesterday, but no one was killed.

Today I was out in Brussels to get some eyewitness stuff, as about 15,000 demonstrators wound their way through the city to present a petition to Catholic Premier Gaston Eyskens, calling for the withdrawal of the austerity bill. Most of these people – men bareheaded or wearing flat caps or berets, women mainly with headscarves – appeared in good humour, but a small, rowdy element smashed a score or so of windows in two large banks by hurling stones as the demonstrators passed by. Under the broken windows of one bank were two posters advertising bank credits for buying television sets.

Demonstrators also overturned two private cars and damaged a bus whose driver was a strike-breaker. The strikers are demanding the withdrawal of the bill and its substitution by other measures designed to expand the Belgian economy rather than to cut workers' earnings. The marching demonstrators, some of them grinning, shouted in French, 'Eyskens to the gallows' or 'Eyskens, resign'. One burly leather-jacketed man told me he did not really want Eyskens to go to the gallows, but he should withdraw the bill.

Later, in gathering darkness, I waited with a bunch of other reporters and photographers at Brussels military airport to see the 31-year-old King Baudouin and his 32-year-old bride, Fabiola, a Spanish noblewoman, return from their honeymoon three weeks earlier than planned because of the crisis. Small knots of people waved and called a welcome to them.

The King is thought likely to help pacify the situation. He has more power than the British monarch, including the power to dismiss the government.

30 December 1960 : I did more eyewitnessing today and it was not nice, or very safe. First, for about half an hour, I walked alongside an orderly demonstration of perhaps a couple of thousand printing industry workers, which broke up without incident. A few of its younger members jeered at a poster on a church referring to the glory of God.

Some of these demonstrators then joined a larger march, including lots of postmen in uniform. Some postmen had stuck over their badges oval stickers issued by the strike committee showing the skeleton of a herring and a belt (for tightening), to depict the alleged effect of the austerity bill.

Today several thousand strikers broke through a police cordon and reached the modern multi-storey building of the state airline,

Sabena. A minority of young men in the procession, ignoring orders from strike orderlies, had earlier grabbed bricks and gravel from a building site. They first used them against the state tourist office, where they smashed three or four panes. Then it was the turn of the Sabena building, chosen, I understand, because of bitterness about an earlier strike involving Sabena personnel. There were cheers and jeers as half a dozen bricks went through plate-glass windows of the Sabena building, while office staff lined the top windows, out of range of the brick throwers.

Then two evil-looking mobile hoses, each with two nozzles, looking like machine-guns, poking from their dark-blue turrets, slid out from a side street and started spraying the marchers. I retreated with some of the demonstrators down the sloping square, managing to keep dry.

A fight broke out between two gendarmes and several strikers. As one gendarme fled, mounted gendarmes in black steel helmets, waving old-fashioned but frightening sabres, galloped from a side street and scattered some of the demonstrators. I had heard what sounded like thunder flashes, which demonstrators sometimes throw here. But the bangs were evidently partly shots. I saw a man with a blood-spattered pale face carried out from a *pâtisserie* on a stretcher, his body covered by a brown blanket. He and another man, who had blood spreading on his shirt, were rushed away by ambulance. I quickly phoned what I knew from a barber's shop, as this was the first apparent fatality in the 11-day strike. I suppose I am somewhat hardened by now, but this business left a nasty taste in my mouth. I returned to the barbers and had a haircut while the square gradually returned to normal.

It was announced later that the man I had seen carried out on the stretcher had been shot dead by another civilian as he tussled with a gendarme. The civilian, who was arrested, said he had fired shots in the air from his pistol to frighten strikers away from the hard-pressed gendarme. Then, as no one took any notice, he had fired at men who were grappling with the gendarme. One shot killed the man I had seen, a 30-year-old housepainter.

Prime Minister Eyskens, his face twitching convulsively as he smoked a cigar on the steps of his office, later told Serge about the killing. Before that Eyskens addressed a press conference of about 150 foreign journalists, saying his government would not 'abdicate' in the face of a strike with 'insurrectionary aspects'. He appealed to the opposition to 'return to legality'. Eyskens made it appear that the government felt the Communists were the driving force in the strike movement, which few experienced observers believe. He was by no means polite about the King, saying that the government had not advised his return and emphasizing that the King could not take political actions without consulting the government. This does not apply to the King's right to dismiss the government. However, the King must be very careful in using this right if he does not want to have the monarchy kicked out, as nearly happened in the forties before Baudouin's father, Leopold III, abdicated.

31 December 1960 : Today, happily, was more peaceful. The strikers staged a sombre silent march of mourning through central Brussels to mark yesterday's killing, which their leaders attributed, indirectly at least, to police repression. Some of them had black tapes on their lapels in memory of the dead house-painter who, according to his wife, was neither a striker nor a trade unionist.

The slow plodding of the marchers through the boulevards hung with Christmas decorations produced an eerie atmosphere. Hundreds of police lined the route, and scores of mounted gendarmes, their sabres today in their scabbards, looked on.

It's the first time since we were married in 1947 that Elfi and I have spent New Year's Eve apart, but we did manage a telephone chat.

I celebrated the coming of 1961 in the comfortable flat of Belgian Communist journalist Martin Thijs, whom I first met in East Germany in 1958, and his Social Democratic wife Julia. Martin is a Flemish nationalist as well as a Red. Their other guest was Sam Russell, bulky foreign editor of the British Communist Party organ, *Daily Worker*.

Much of our talk concerned the problem of combining Communism with something like the freedom which, I maintained, was the treasured possession of, for instance, the British. Russell agreed that this was indeed a problem, and was unable to prove that, under the Communist system as it is at present, there is a guarantee that the crimes of the Stalin era could not be repeated.

On the other hand I conceded that Communism, even as it is at present, brings larger freedom for certain peoples – such as China, some of the Eastern European countries and part of Latin America – than they have had under previous corrupt semi-Fascist regimes. Russell claimed that the British Communist Party, in its programme 'The British Road to Socialism', had taken account of the desire of the British people to hold on to their traditional freedoms. But he was not able to show me that the Communist Party, should it be elected to power, would not keep itself in power by force.

Julia sang us a British First World War song which her father taught her: 'Come into my garden of parsnips' – a sort of 'Dig for Victory' song.

New Year's Day 1961 : Belgium observed a semi-truce for the New Year, though there were a few minor scuffles in Brussels.

Tonight I was Serge's guest at his tastefully furnished flat. I noticed a print of his great-great-grandfather, Field Marshal Mikhail Kutuzov, victor over Napoleon. For the first time I met Serge's sister. *[I did not note her first name.]* She was allowed to come to the West about three months ago after 12 years in Soviet prisons and labour camps. She looks in better fettle than Serge who, for his part, has had 15 years with Reuters.

She told me that it was as an emigrée that she had been working in the US Embassy in Soviet-dominated Romania in 1948, when she was approached by the Russians to spy for them. When she refused, she was flown to Moscow and put in the notorious Lubianka secret police gaol, a former hotel. Food was not bad, the place was clean and she was not physically ill-treated, apart from regularly being taken out of her cell at night for hours of questioning by investigating judges, who tried unsuccessfully to make her confess she had been an anti-Soviet agent in Romania.

After several months in the Lubianka, being questioned alternately by what she described as a 'nasty' and a 'nice' investigating judge, she decided to help the 'nice' one by signing a statement saying that while she had not been an anti-Soviet agent she would have gladly been one had she had the chance.

She told us with much laughter how she once called the 'nasty' interrogator '*Golubchik*' – literally 'My little dove' but meaning 'My dear' – and he retorted, 'I am *not* your *golubchik*,' to which she replied, 'You certainly aren't, are you?'

The outcome of her interrogation was the sentence, passed in her absence by some kind of semi-military tribunal, of 15 years in a labour camp. Before being moved to the camp in Kazakhstan, her cellmates in prison had included the wife of the Soviet Ambassador in Peking, who was accused of 'links with foreigners' for having called in a British doctor to attend to her child, and a female army major, who was under arrest for lending a military revolver to someone and who tried unsuccessfully to hang herself in the cell they shared.

19 Referendum in Algiers

2 January 1961 : Drove the 200 miles from Brussels to Paris without incident, though in Belgium I saw some places where paving stones had been dug up and roughly replaced.

Around 5 pm, I arrived at the grimy Reuter office in the rue de Sentier, off the bustling, brassy Boulevard de Montmartre. I had been sent to Paris to accompany Basil Chapman, deputy news editor in our large Paris office, to Algiers to report on events there during the national referendum, starting on 6 January, on the question of whether Algeria should receive self-determination. The chief correspondent in Paris, the much-admired – and much-feared – Harold King, confidant of de Gaulle, gave me a friendly welcome.

3 January 1961 : Basil took me home for lunch with his pretty brunette wife Hildegard, an East German, and his *'Mutti'*, Hildegard's white-haired mother, who was allowed to leave East Germany in 1958 after much pleading.

Another of our Paris staffers, dour Scot Finlay Campbell, with whom I reported on the earthquake in Agadir, Morocco, last March, showed me a little of Paris at night, including Finlay's favourite small bar, where an elderly Brit, apparently stranded in Paris after the First World War, played old English hits rather badly on the piano, which I found nostalgically enjoyable. After dropping Finlay, I lost my way driving round the great Opera

House, not far from my hotel. As I stopped to look at my street guide, a smart Karmann-Ghia Volkswagen coupé drew up beside me and two dusky women inside it made inviting gestures and jolly grins. They had obviously taken me for someone on the look-out for more than the right turning. I had to stop several times as I drove round the Opera, and several times the swish car with its enthusiastically giggling occupants drew up alongside, until they gave up and I was able to concentrate on my orientation.

4 January 1961 : Lunched with 32-ish millionaire's daughter Janik Heim de Balsac (*née* le Bomin) and her mother in Janik's luxury flat on the 13th (top) floor of a great block in the suburb of St Cloud, with a wonderful view of the nearby Bois de Boulogne and, beyond it, the Eiffel Tower. *[I described, under 9 March 1960, how I got to know Janik.]*

I had kept in touch with Janik, who was initially critical when I told her I was to marry what she called a '*bochesse*', but she and Elfi later became friends when Janik visited us in Yorkshire.

Today Janik and her mother explained that the latter was present as a chaperone because Janik's husband of about four years, Gerald, is extremely jealous, as there have been several divorces in his family. Gerald, on a business trip in the south of France, rang up while we were lunching, and Janis told him that I – and the chaperone – were present. He seemed to take it well.

Janik and, probably, her mother will vote 'No' to de Gaulle's plans for Algerian self-determination. I tried to argue the case for voting 'Yes' – namely that the alternative is continuing war and causing the Algerian rebels to become more Communist-influenced. Anik, one of Janik's two sisters, has lost her fiancé in the Algerian fighting.

Hildegard drove Basil and me along the modern motorway to Orly airport where, as we went through the formalities, we were asked if we had arms. A policeman looked in one of my bags to make sure.

The 50 or 60 persons on our aircraft, a wonderful new twin-jet Caravelle, included about ten soldiers returning to service in

Algeria, some of whom were kissed goodbye by fathers or mothers.

A very smooth flight whisked us 1,000 miles south in two hours; a loudspeaker announcement pointed out the lights of Marseilles. The pretty stewardess who served us a tasty cold meal seemed to think my French pronunciation was funny or, at least, fetching.

A little girl, perhaps 2½, who waddled along the aisle, made me think of the terrible human problems involved in the Algerian situation. At least 120 people were killed in rioting between Europeans and Muslims on or around 11 December, when de Gaulle was touring the province.

In our hired Dauphine car we drove for 20 kilometres *[12½ miles]* along partly palm-fringed roads into the city, where I stayed for one night in 1944 while in the navy. As I went to bed in the luxury Hotel Aletti, I felt a little uneasy about the Muslims who, I imagined, might be waiting to send a hail of bullets through the hotel windows. So I got up and pulled down the main shutter somewhat.

Actually that sort of thinking is overdoing it, for the security forces are very strong in this area, particularly after the recent incidents and in view of the coming referendum. Muslim liftboys and waiters at the hotel told me of the atmosphere of fear hanging over Algiers because of the mistrust about what each community might do next.

The present situation is partly the result of the greed of the Europeans, who were much too late in giving the Muslims a fair chance in society here, and the procrastination of successive French governments, which have always made offers of reforms too late. Maybe de Gaulle, with his immense prestige internationally – though much less prestige among European Algerians, who think he is selling them down the river – can do something to prevent a disaster.

5 January 1961 : We made contact with officials at the multi-storey building of the Delegation-General, Algeria's administrative and military headquarters, which stand on one of the hills rising behind this most attractive, mainly European city. Today, by midday, in the brilliant sunshine it was like a warm English summer day. Outside the Delegation-General building there is a beautiful garden of palms, and from there one has a fine view of the blue Mediterranean.

By day in this bustling city it's hard to believe that the country is an armed camp with some 340,000 soldiers combating the rebels. But, as one moves around, it is not long before one comes across a patrol of gendarmes or soldiers armed with submachine-guns.

Basil introduced me to several officials, friendly fellows, most of whom, I should think, are going to vote 'No' to de Gaulle's proposals for Algerian self-government. One official showed us a bunch of passionately phrased leaflets, appealing for a 'No' vote. One came from Spain, from the former commander-in-chief in Algiers, General Raoul Salan, and other supporters of the anti-de Gaulle revolts of last January.

Later, searching for a teleprinter we might use, I talked to a Monsieur Gerbaud, the office manager of a forwarding firm. He told me he was born in Algeria and was prepared to die to stay here; he is a reserve officer who fights the insurgents for a month each year. An appealing chap, but the supporter of a wrong and hopeless policy.

Four out of five male clerks in a similar firm told me they would vote 'No', while the fifth, the only one not born in Algeria, was undecided. The four made it clear they were not worried about living in an independent Algeria, but living in an Algeria in which, overnight, they could lose their jobs, their homes and their safety if the Muslim majority so willed it. They agreed with me that by voting 'No' they would solve nothing, but they were not satisfied that if they voted 'Yes' there would be firm guarantees of their future.

Later I walked through a few streets to the Arab quarter of this great city, the Kasbah, which starts in some former European flats and continues in smaller Arab-type buildings with narrow hilly lanes between them. Some Arabs, perhaps new arrivals, live in filthy conditions under packing cases or makeshift tents at one end of the Kasbah. Looking at them made me feel ashamed to be eating good food in my posh hotel.

The street scene, particularly near the Kasbah, is attractive, with Arab and European elements mingling. Next to a windowless alcove used as an Arab shop, stocked perhaps with grain or fruit, you can find a smart European shop selling the latest gadgets. And next to well made-up European girls you can see white-robed Muslim women, whose veils of white cloth sometimes have a jolly little frill at the bottom, looking almost like a decorative beard.

The main post office is built like a mosque, with twin towers, and lots of extravagant Arab curlicues in relief inside. Little Arab boys, often ragged, and wearing flat cylindrical caps, offer dead thrushes for sale. They may taste nice, but this is one delicacy I have no desire to sample because I like little birds. Silly, I know, when I like eating pheasant or chicken. Basil wrote most of our first story tonight, as he is the expert. I made a few suggestions and added a few paragraphs.

6 January 1961 : The first day of the three-day referendum. Around 7 am, in our hired Dauphine, and accompanied by middle-aged *Manchester Guardian* correspondent Clare Hollingworth, I drove into the Bled, the Arab name for Algeria's country districts. We travelled eastwards on a good tarmac road, a few miles south of the coast. In the sub-tropical sunshine we drove past well-cultivated fields and vineyards. In the distance to our right we saw the brownish silhouette of the Atlas range. We passed through several mainly Arab-populated but French-looking towns, and stopped at Hassounvillers, a township of about 6,000 Muslims and 80 Europeans, some 40 miles east of Algiers.

Here we spoke to Aimé Melmoux, the 47-year-old European mayor, a schoolmaster, who was supervising the start of polling. In a bare room in the small town hall, two young European schoolmistresses and four bearded old Muslims, in grubby white headcloths and robes, sat at a table as scrutineers.

Up to then about 30 of the 1,300 voters had arrived to cast

their votes by taking a white paper for 'Yes' and a mauve one for 'No'. They then put one of the papers in a blue envelope in the secrecy of a blanketed-off booth in a corner and dropped the envelope into a wooden ballot box.

The mayor told us he thought about 75 per cent of the Muslims would come out to vote, with the remainder abstaining, mainly to show their sympathy with the Algerian 'liberation army' – the insurgents – whose leader, Ferhat Abbas, has called on the Muslims to abstain.

But when, with the mayor, we visited another polling station in a rough village school three miles away, a Muslim election official, speaking out of earshot of the mayor, said he thought the mayor was a fool because, in the Muslim's view, most of the people in the village supported the insurgents. About half the local population are people who have been forcibly resettled by the French, who have forbidden Muslims to live in separate isolated houses and have grouped them in villages, some of them new or partly new, to make it easier to protect them – and to check on them.

This man said that in spite of the widespread sympathy for the insurgents, he thought most people would come and vote because of the presence of many French military personnel. About 150 marines are stationed in this small place and nearby to help keep order. Several were patrolling near each of the polling stations, carrying submachine-guns.

In its campaign against the insurgents the French Army, in the last couple of years, has divided its units into small groups, usually linked by radio, so that there are a few soldiers in virtually every village. There are far fewer battles taking place than there used to be, especially in the coastal areas, and the army says there are only small groups of insurgents in these areas.

However, even the main road we had travelled on was closed at night for fear of attack, and big towns have curfews, altered at will –10 pm in Algiers last night.

I drove on about six miles further eastwards, to the township of Camp du Marechal, where a friendly major, le Duc, a veteran of Indo-China and an obvious right-winger from his talk, ordered a jeep with four armed soldiers, who had rifles or submachine-guns at the ready, to escort Clare, Bill Millinship of the *Observer* and me, in a car driven by Millinship up a winding mountain road for about three miles to the hilltop village of Beni-Ouarze Dine, a picture-book place of one-storey houses, with a new prefabricated school, a small army post and a big sign on a wall saying in blue paint: 'The army will stay for ever.'

Another sign, giving the name of the village, had underneath the words *'Village de France'*. I wonder how long that will be there. The soldiers we met were charming and friendly, and I only hope that, with de Gaulle's aid, it may be possible at least to arrange a bloodless transition to an Algeria in which the Muslims are the bosses.

Half the population of about 550 are children, garbed in multi-coloured robes. Many gathered around us, laughing. Voting was over, and we were told that between 70 and 80 per cent had voted, which shows the army pretty strongly in control here, in spite of the fact that the nearby forests are a hide-out for insurgents who, one day, may come along and cut the throats of Muslims who have allegedly collaborated with the French. The place looked very poor, but the kiddies were pretty clean, and it seemed that things were being done there; we saw a new washhouse with real taps.

We drove back to Camp du Marechal, where Major le Duc invited us to what turned out to be a superb lunch with several of his officers and one of their wives. We had some discussion on the Algerian problem, and again the key point was the guarantees for the European population which, the major maintained – and, I think, rightly for the time being – could only be given by the army.

There is much less terrorism now than a couple of years ago, partly because of army successes in killing or capturing terrorists and partly because of new tactics by the rebel leadership, which is now in a stronger position politically with the apparent approach of self-determination, and probably does not want to waste men or alienate sympathies by more terrorism.

On our way back to Algiers we passed one of the numerous 'training camps', which look just like Nazi concentration camps, where captured rebels are subjected to brainwashing and given job training. I'm told that the worst evils of the real concentration camps the French set up here earlier have been cleaned up following exposures in the media.

A bearded soldier from the French West Indian colony of Martinique, who works at the camp, wanted a lift so I took him along and asked him how the rebels were being treated. 'Better than me,' he replied with a grin.

His view was that the Algerians – I presume he meant the Muslims – should be allowed to run their own affairs.

This evening a big bang shattered the near-calm of Algiers. Basil and I found broken windows and lots of police and soldiers in an office about 100 yards from our hotel. The bomb which had gone off was made of plastic explosive which, the experts said, pointed to the work of French extremists wanting to demonstrate their opposition to de Gaulle's policy, which they regard as a sell-out. No one was hurt. There were similar blasts in Paris tonight.

7 January 1961 : Today it was the turn of larger townships to vote in the referendum. In general things were calm, but there was a nasty clash at Aflou in the southern Amour mountains when, according to an official spokesman, a rebel group suddenly attacked a polling station, killing a soldier and wounding three others. The army counter-attacked, killing about ten of the assailants and wounding another two.

Tonight, in the mainly European Algiers suburb of Hydra-Birmandreis, I was the dinner guest of a cousin of Janik's husband, Jean-Louis Siben, a 35-ish bank official. He maintained that the rebels were but a small minority of 30,000 to 50,000, out of a Muslim population of eight million. However, the rebels' threats to cut the throats of pro-French Muslims influenced many more people.

Siben claimed that the broad mass of the Muslims were not anti-French, but very much hoped the French would not leave, because this would result in the murder of pro-French Muslims and economic disaster. He said he had been at university along with Muslims, some of whom were his friends. He maintained there was no colour bar in the country, but agreed that the economic distinctions were tremendous.

Siben opposes self-determination, as he thinks it is conceived by de Gaulle. Though people of Siben's sort brought de Gaulle to power in 1958, they now think de Gaulle cannot be trusted to maintain a French Algeria, nor even to ensure that if Algeria becomes independent there will be a gradual peaceful transition.

Siben forecast that the referendum would take place quietly, with a majority of 'Yes' votes, but that in a month or two, when de Gaulle would install the first semi-autonomous Algerian Government there would be trouble, as the insurgents would seek to show their strength and the Europeans would reply. All the Europeans have somehow got themselves arms.

One very knotty point he raised was the Muslim birth-rate, which is expected to increase the present Muslim population of eight million to about 20 million within ten years. Though he and his wife are Roman Catholics, they said they favoured birth control. I wickedly suggested they wanted to apply this only to Muslims and they laughed. I also suggested that if Siben were a Muslim he would be an insurgent. His wife agreed.

Siben said the Muslims would suffer much more than people like himself if the insurgents took power, for he and his wife could go to France, where he had money. If Muslims came to France they would be very poor refugees.

It was an eerie feeling to drive through the curfew-cleared streets, lined with lots of modern cars, as I returned to my hotel around midnight, having to show my curfew pass once to a patrolling soldier.

8 January 1961 : The last day of the referendum. Shortly before 8 am, when polling began in Algiers, I walked to the lower edge of the Kasbah, the old Muslim town covering part of a hillside and housing about 150,000 people in mainly squarish houses sited in narrow alleys.

The Algerian rebel movement, the FLN, had called on

Muslims to boycott the referendum – they demand immediate independence.

The FLN's call was in the main not obeyed in the countryside and small towns, where voting took place in the past two days, because the army is in control in such places. However, in the Kasbahs of the larger cities the Muslims are packed together and – I take it – the army does not get in among them. Furthermore, the city Arabs are the more modern and politically conscious.

The Kasbah almost reaches the sea front, near a square bordered by a white mosque and a mosque-like Roman Catholic church. On the square about 350 blue-uniformed riot police, in grey vans, had taken up station, ready to rush into the Kasbah if need be.

On the fringe of the Kasbah proper, a school was being used to house half a dozen polling stations, one in each classroom, with voters both European and Muslim, but mainly the latter. Two steel-helmeted khaki-uniformed air force men, toting submachine-guns, stood at the door, and a civilian searched voters for arms as they arrived.

Outside, red-capped members of a Zouave (Algerian) colonial regiment patted children's heads in the warm sunshine, near portable barbed-wire fences, which could have been used to bar the Kasbah if needed. But all was calm this morning, and in Algiers the calm lasted all day. In other areas there were two or three clashes between troops and pro-FLN Arabs who were demonstrating, causing a death toll of six or seven, bringing the total death toll – all outside Algiers – to about 25 in the three days of voting. For troubled Algeria this is very minor stuff.

Later Basil and I drove around other parts of Algiers. We saw hundreds of soldiers ready for action, including green-bereted Foreign Legion men in armoured cars. There are believed to be about 40,000 soldiers and police in the Algiers area, and something like 400,000 in the whole country.

By making checks at two polling stations, and getting information from others, we were able to say, in the early afternoon, that the city Muslims were largely following the call of the FLN to abstain. Most of the Europeans are expected to vote 'No', as they want France to continue fighting the FLN and keep Algeria as part of France: a hopeless task in the opinion of most observers.

Vote counting started this evening, in well guarded buildings. I obtained a small specimen result, out of a few hundred votes, by looking over a scrutineer's shoulder, after jumping on to a counter in Algiers City Hall. That specimen was mainly 'No' and, in fact, Algiers – predominantly Muslim, though with several hundred thousand Europeans – voted about 70 per cent against de Gaulle, partly because most of the Muslims abstained.

9 January 1961 : Basil and I turned in at around 3.15 am, after reporting an official announcement stating that, after one third of the votes counted, there were about 72 per cent 'Yes' votes in Algeria and a similar response in metropolitan France. The announcement appealed for unity 'to build a new Algeria together'.

Some Muslims in a Muslim-run gift shop made it clear to me they were for independence, but they did not want all the French to leave. Basil told me the fact that Muslims were now prepared to say something about their political opinions was a great change; it indicated they realized they were on the winning side. It could have meant being clapped into gaol or worse not long ago.

I gained an insight into the minds of the French 'ultras', when one of them, Demolière, who has let us use his office telex, invited Basil and me for drinks in his exquisite home. He had helped to build barricades in the riot of the 'ultras' last month against de Gaulle's policies.

Demolière told me, more or less, 'Now we shall have to fight again. If de Gaulle comes here he will be killed. To stop now, when we have nearly won the war (he is optimistic) would be madness, betrayal, after all the lives that have been lost. We must declare an independent Algerian Republic and seek for allies. Perhaps there are some Fascists left in West Germany, or maybe they have become too bourgeois with their televisions and so on. But in South Africa we could find allies. We must win back Tunisia and Morocco.'

190

Demolière seemed to ignore the fact that the Muslim insurgents are part of a worldwide movement for independence from colonialism, which cannot be held back and, indeed, should not be held back.

10 January 1961 : Back to Paris in a Caravelle in that lightning two hours, passing over the blue Mediterranean, partly clouded Majorca and Spain's Costa Brava, France's snow-covered Massif Central, and down through the clouds to Orly.

This evening our Paris chief correspondent, Harold King, a greying lively 62-year-old with a sardonic humour, asked me out along with his number two, David Reid, a 38-year-old ex-intelligence officer, who seems to be one of the few people who can handle King.

King, who insistently pumped us full of excellent Beaujolais in a bar, took out a little piece of poetry describing a great man, and said he had sent it along to his idol, de Gaulle. He denied the allegation (made by many) that he is unobjective in his reports about de Gaulle, and said, 'When you see the sun rising gloriously, and describe it, that is objectivity.'

On to a restaurant where, after more wine, King's elderly head bent down towards the table, and he was silent for a few minutes. His head then jerked up and he began to talk again about all and sundry with lots of humour and life. Wish I could have taped it all. He said once or twice – I think he is a Catholic – that he was thinking about his after-life.

I was exhausted when, around 11 pm, King decided it was time for him to go home, but David insisted I come with him to a really very nice night club run by a Spaniard, who plays and sings, with two or three other instrumentalists, some genuine Spanish stuff, none of which I could appreciate in my state of bemused tiredness.

11 January 1961 : Verdict on Paris traffic, which I left today to drive to Germany: faster than in Germany, good reactions, not as erratic as in Italy, great reliance on the priority from the right

191

rule, with much forcing by drivers who nose out and make you give way even if signs give you the right of way.

Driving eastwards, passed through the sites of several First World War battlefields – my father fought on some of them – Châlons-sur-Marne, Verdun and Metz, where many Lorraine people still speak German. Entered Germany again south of Trier, Germany's oldest city, founded by the Romans. Overnighted near Trier.

12 January 1961 : It was bad judgement to take the mountain road from Trier, but fortunately there was not much snow on the road. Home shortly after midday to see Eliana Davidson, Palestinian wife of a colleague, emerging from our house with Elfi. With two pretty women at my home and, bearing in mind where I'd been, I felt like a polygamous Muslim.

20 Winter delights in the Sauerland

13 January 1961 : Starting our postponed holiday, we four drove some 70 miles eastwards to the Sauerland hills, which rise to about 2,200 feet *[670 m]*. The snow there was two to three feet deep. Near a ski lift, we found accommodation in a half-timbered farmhouse: 20 marks (£1 15s) for four beds-and-breakfasts. We were soon trying out our skis on easy terrain, which is what we need.

14 January 1961 : Glorious to revel in the snow and the quiet, and we are all loving staying at a farm. It's a dairy farm with about 15 cows, not as economic as farms lower down. The farmer is called Huhne – which sounds a bit like *Hüne*, meaning 'giant' – while his parents-in-law, who also live in the farmhouse, are called Huhn, which means 'hen'. They have all made us feel at home.

Wrote a background piece about the 'ultras' of Algiers, suggested by Harold King, and posted it to our Paris office.

15 January 1961 : 'Our' cows all have names, and some are more intelligent than others. The most intelligent is Hannchen, who leads them all when they go out on the fields in summer. I always chat to her and pat her when I go through the cowshed to the lavatory. She calmly chews her cud and belches. Another of the cows likes to eat banana skins. They are all tuberculosis-free and are milked electrically.

We went to the Sunday service at the nearby Lutheran village church of Langewiese. On a plaque commemorating the fallen of the Second World War was the name of Herr Huhne's son, who was a convinced Nazi and volunteered for more army service after already losing one eye. He was killed defending the autobahn near Hamm, on the eastern edge of the Ruhr area, in April 1945. He was to have taken over the farm. Instead, Herr Huhn, the son-in-law, who was a mechanic, took it over. It was history repeating itself, for Herr Huhne had taken over the farm in the First World War after his brother-in-law, who was to have had it, had been killed at the front in France in 1914.

I liked the sermon of the elderly pastor, who spoke about Jesus turning water into wine. He said all of us had experiences which we could call miracles, even if we regarded this particular story as legend. He said some people perhaps thought it had been wrong of Jesus to provide people with the chance of getting drunk, but one should not look at it like that. It was, on the contrary, a sign that God wanted people to be merry and enjoy life at times, and not to go around with sour faces.

17 January 1961 : Chris, who will be eight in March, did well to keep up with us three on a ten-mile ski trek. His latest choice of occupation when he grows up: ski instructor.

18 January 1961 : A drive of a few miles over snow-covered roads brought us to Winterberg, the main skiing centre in this area, also the site of a British Army leave centre. I tried out a few steep slopes, falling a few times, but safely. During the night it was minus 15° Celsius (about 27 degrees of frost Fahrenheit), but today in the sunshine it's a few degrees above freezing. One of the delights of this holiday is the sight of snow and fir trees in the sunshine, with the myriad light effects.

This afternoon we drove to a forestry station belonging to Prince Wittgenstein, a local big landowner, where we paid a small sum to enter a large hut with a lot of other people, and stand against a window overlooking a snow-covered valley. Near the hut had been placed troughs of cattle feed and, on the ground, chestnuts without shells were strewn.

After about 40 minutes – it was about 4.40 pm and beginning to grow dark – a gasp went up from the onlookers. Then we saw, trooping out of the fir forest across the valley, and edging cautiously towards us, about 30 stags and hinds, the oldest of the stags with about 18 points on its antlers, which means 18 years old, we understand. Some of the animals came to within a few feet of the hut to gobble up chestnuts. This feed takes place nightly in winter.

19 January 1961 : Having introduced the Huhnes to Scrabble, we've been playing in German. Here is an example of word building from a game we played today: AUF, KAUF, EINKAUF, EINKAUFT, EINKAUFTE, EINKAUFTET. *[Easier to do in German than in English.]*

21 January 1961 : We reluctantly said goodbye to our most excellent hosts – Robin and Chris patted all the cows and fondled dog and cat – and drove home on largely snow-covered roads, with about 15 marks of our holiday money left.

23 January 1961 : Reported on the arrival of a delegation from soon-to-be-independent Tanganyika, British-administered United Nations trust territory and, until the First World War, a German colony. The delegation is led by Chief Minister Julius Nyerere, 38, a slight, cheerful-looking chap who is regarded as one of the African moderates and is cooperating amicably with the territory's small white minority – around 40,000 out of eight million.

24 January 1961 : At a Foreign Office reception for Nyerere, Willy Wood, a white Briton who is Under-Secretary in the Tanganyika Ministry for Commerce and Trade, told me he had been doing his best to convince Germans that Britain would not resent it, but on the contrary would welcome it, if West Germany offered lots of aid to Tanganyika.

My bedtime reading: *Naught for your Comfort* by British Anglican priest, Father Trevor Huddleston, who has been campaigning against apartheid in South Africa. After reading part of that book, it is as clear as day to me that the South African Government's policy is doomed to disaster, like that of the Algerian 'ultras'. It is even worse than that.

29 January 1961 : I did not feel like church this Sunday morning. I am not as drawn towards the Lutheran Church as, for instance, to the Quakers, but there is no Quaker Meeting in Bonn. Church life in Germany does not seem to be as pally as in Britain. I'm very interested in religion, but church here in Germany often leaves me semi-bored.

The new American President, John F. Kennedy, seems to have made a good start. He has let it be known he would not be averse to meeting Khrushchev informally, if the Soviet leader comes to the next UN General Assembly session. Kennedy's cabinet-making seems most reassuring. He looks to have chosen a very competent, intelligent and, in general, liberal team.

A six-hour train journey, including about 20 minutes at the frontier, took me to picturesque Strasbourg, in Alsace, another mainly German-speaking French frontier province. A taxi driver told me he was German until the First World War, then French, German again from 1939–45, and now French again – a mirror of the province's change of sovereignty this century.

Some old people have even had an additional change of nationality – they were French before the Franco-Prussian War of 1870–71. When I asked the taxi driver how he felt personally about nationality, he grinned and said, 'I am a European. It's better that way.'

Strasbourg houses the headquarters of the Council of Europe, Europe's embryo political assembly.

30 January 1961 : I am in Strasbourg to cover a conference, which started today, intended to set up a European organization to develop a heavy satellite launcher. In the modern, but rather

LEFT *The pub in Aachen which used to house Julius Reuter's pigeon loft – Peter Johnson (right) stands with the pub proprietor (Photo: Foto Forschelen, Aachen)*

ABOVE *Nineteenth-century sketch showing Reuter in his pigeon loft and Men of the Day: Baron Paul Julius Reuter (*Vanity Fair, *1872)*

LEFT *Peter, Elfi, Robin and Chris at Bad Godesberg, 1 November 1958*

LEFT *Dr Konrad Adenauer, West German Chancellor, 1949–63 (Photo: German Federal Press Office)*

BELOW *Agadir earthquake – corpses line the roads, March 1960*

ABOVE *American (left) and Soviet officers shake hands near Klütz, East German Baltic resort, after resolving the incident caused when the US Dakota transport plane strayed into East German airspace and was forced to land, 25 May 1960*

RIGHT *Johnson closely follows Khrushchev as he makes a walkabout in central Vienna, accompanied by Foreign Minister Andrei Gromyko, 1 July 1960*

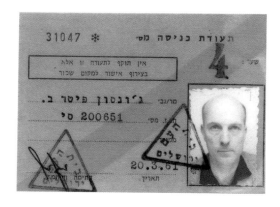

LEFT *Johnson's Hebrew identity card for the Eichmann trial, 20 March 1961*

BELOW *Johnson's sketch of Eichmann made at his trial: March 1961*

BELOW *Johnson's sketch of Mount Zion, in Jordan-occupied East Jerusalem, seen from Israeli West Jerusalem, May 1961*

ABOVE *Johnson at Capernaum, northern Israel, where Jesus is reputed to have done much of his early preaching, 22 April 1961*

RIGHT *Johnson (second from right) with colleagues at the Israeli Red Sea resort of Eilat, May 1961*

BELOW *Johnson with Bedouin and camel in the Negev desert, May 1961*

BELOW RIGHT *In Jerusalem's orthodox Jewish quarter, Mea Sherim, May 1961*

ABOVE *Difficult rocky descent from the ancient Jewish fortress of Masada, May 1961*

ABOVE *Temporary Soviet press card, July 1961*

ABOVE *In Red Square, with the Lenin Mausoleum in the background, 1961*

ABOVE *The Kremlin, as seen from the British Embassy, 1961*

RIGHT *A luxury Moscow underground station – Elektrozavodskaya, 1961*

ABOVE *Khrushchev with journalists, Henry Shapiro (left) and Johnson (centre), at US Independence Day reception in Moscow, 4 July 1961 (Photo:* Life*)*

BELOW *British Prime Minister Harold Macmillan chats with Yuri Gagarin, London, 13 July 1961 (Photo: Associated Press)*

RIGHT *Johnson's Reuter report of Khrushchev's badinage at the US reception, (*The Times*, 5 July 1961)*

MR. KHRUSHCHEV AT U.S. RECEPTION '61

Moscow, July 4.—A smiling Mr. Khrushchev brought six Soviet marshals to the American Embassy's July 4 Independence Day reception here today and not once mentioned Berlin in 90 minutes of joking with diplomatists and journalists.

The Soviet leader followed up his friendly telegram to President Kennedy by attending the reception with about 800 other Soviet guests—the first time he has done so for three years.

When one journalist had questioned Mr. Khrushchev, another commented "The attack has begun". The Soviet leader, smiling as he held a largely untouched glass of whisky, countered: "We shall repel it, but we will not use rockets".

TONGUE AS WEAPON

He added jokingly that he did not need a uniform and suggested that his brain would be sufficient by pointing to his head. But Mr. Mikoyan, a first deputy Prime Minister, interposed: "His weapon is his tongue."

Then Mr Khrushchev recalled how on a visit to Kazakhstan he attended a ceremonial meal of a sheep. "I took the eye and ear and gave it to the local party secretary because he needed to see and hear better" he said. Then he took the brains and gave them to a scientist.

Asked what had been left for him of the sheep, Mr. Khrushchev laughed so loud that the three Orders of Lenin on his chest shook and he replied: "I am Prime Minister of the Soviet Union. I do not need anything."

Mr. Khrushchev, who only sipped lightly at his whisky, finally handed the glass to his wife and made her try it. Mr. Boris Klossen, first secretary at the embassy, told the Soviet leader: "You know who is boss."—*Reuter.*

ABOVE *Johnson's biggest scoop: an advance copy of the Soviet Communist Party newspaper* Pravda *with details of the party's new programme, signed by Johnson and several colleagues* (Pravda, *30 July 1961*)

LEFT *Johnson's sketch of onion domes in Zagorsk, 1 August 1961*

RIGHT *Gerald Long (Photo: The Reuters Archive)*

LEFT *The Brandenburg Gate, just inside East Berlin – East German police and 'factory fighting groups', with water cannons, start to seal off the East Berlin sector border with rolls of barbed wire, 13 August 1961 (Photo: German Federal Press Office)*

neglected, Council of Europe building, workmen were uncovering the two-ton propulsion unit, weighing about 15 tons, of a British Blue Streak rocket. This was dropped from Britain's defence programme last year, mainly, I think, because it was not mobile enough.

At the start of the conference this afternoon, Peter Thorneycroft, the British Minister of Aviation, appealed to the 80 delegates from 16 nations to support an Anglo-French proposal for a launcher. Britain would provide free the results of its 60 million sterling Blue Streak programme, and Blue Streak would be the first stage of the necessary three stages.

France, it is planned, would build the second stage, while the third stage would be built largely by other countries. Another 70 million sterling, contributed by countries which join, would be needed over five or six years to complete the project, which would make Europe independent of the United States or the Soviet Union in launching satellites.

There seems to be a growing realization that satellites can become a commercial proposition, especially in the telecommunications and TV-relay field.

An Alsatian told me today he preferred being French to German – 'I get on better with the French' – but said he nevertheless felt 'occupied', whoever happened to be the boss in Alsace. However, he said that moves towards European union were tending to remove that feeling.

2 February 1961 : Most of the conference has been in closed session, but we have got a good idea of what's going on by questioning delegates after the sessions. There has also been another method. Near the conference room is a table marked 'distribution of documents' where, earlier, it was possible to take what one required. This included a summary of the previous day's proceedings, part of which were in private.

I took a copy of this, though I knew it was supposed to be for delegates only. Since then I have taken no more, because I decided it was not worth the risk of being expelled from the place and causing trouble for Reuters – and me. Several other colleagues, however, have continued to take documents – pretending to be delegates to do so, as a guard has been put on the table. They have been good enough to let me look at most of them.

Today the man from United Press International, Peter Robinson, and I pretended to interview one of our colleagues, a Dutchman called Raedeker, in order to convince the guard that Raedeker was a delegate. Raedeker then went over to the table and filled his bag with documents.

To do this sort of thing is obviously not moral – although the information should not have been kept secret anyway. But I felt impelled to behave in this way, as others were doing it, so that my stories would be equally as 'well informed' as theirs.

The conference ended tonight. It had not been intended to take final decisions, but Thorneycroft said it had been a success. After talking to a number of delegates, I quoted a majority as believing the project would be realized. Europe cannot, I think, stay out of such an important field of modern technology, allowing the Russians and Americans to go it alone. *[The Strasbourg conference led to the foundation, in October 1961, of the European Launcher Development Organization (ELDO), which was to construct a three-stage launcher of which Blue Streak was to be the first stage. However, because of budgetary restraints and technical problems, that plan was not realized.*

In 1975 ELDO and the European Space Research organization (ESRO) amalgamated to form the 14-nation European Space Agency (ESA), which uses the largely French family of Ariane launchers, fired from Kourou, French Guiana. ESA develops satellites and instruments for exploration, designs experiments and collects data. In the end little Blue Streak technology was used to construct the Ariane launchers, because of licensing difficulties.]

Around midnight, when I was trying to write an 'overnighter', directed at tomorrow's British evening papers, I kept being interrupted by jolly Angus McPherson of the *Daily Mail*. I picked up an ashtray and, after warning McPherson that I might throw it, I tossed it diagonally across the table towards him. He hadn't believed me and the thing struck him on the bridge of his nose, without his making any move to stop it. I admired the way he kept control of himself, grinned as a cut on his nose began to bleed a little, and immediately accepted my apology for the unintended injury. I bought him a drink later to clinch it.

Our Strasbourg correspondent, Frenchman Roger Stock, who has helped me during the conference, has a colourful history. Born in Lorraine, he was a soldier in the French Army and was taken prisoner when the Germans swept into France in 1940. He spent most of the war as a prisoner, working on farms, in sawmills and factories, mainly in East Prussia.

He was not badly treated, on the whole. Things were toughest at first when the Germans were filled with their early victories. He smiled as he told me how simple East Prussian farm workers would ask him his nationality. When he said, 'French,' they said, 'Oh, French, that's quite a cultured people, almost up to our standard.'

They spoke quite differently of the Poles and Russians, whom the Nazis regarded as sub-human.

As the war wore on and the locals gradually realized it was lost, the French prisoners became more accepted by the population and were even in demand for amorous adventures, because of their national reputation in that sphere.

Stock said he fell in love with a farmer's daughter, who obeyed his instructions not to go out with Germans. This was in Ribbenau, near Goldap, East Prussia. On one occasion when Germans suspected (rightly) that he was with the girl on the farm, a party of soldiers searched the place. He hid in a hayloft.

After the Russian forces entered East Prussia in late 1944, Stock fled with the farmer's daughter, her mother – her father was in the army – and others from the farm. As Soviet planes strafed refugee columns on the Kurische Nehrung, a long, sandy spit bordering the Baltic, he fell flat and was trampled on by bolting horses pulling a farm cart.

His shoulder was dislocated. A German doctor gave him an injection. 'I thought that was the end for me,' Stock grinned. 'But I came round with my shoulder back in its socket.'

When the group reached Danzig – now Gdansk – he was allowed to travel westwards with them by train. They reached present-day West Germany near Brunswick. He supervised a Russian and an Albanian on a farm, where the only inhabitant was one woman. After the Americans occupied that area in April 1945, they arranged the transport home of the former prisoners.

3 February 1961 : I travelled home by train, second class – I am entitled to claim first class – to save a little extra for our fund towards Robin's schooling in England.

6 February 1961 : The government press office issued a semi-denial that Defence Minister Franz-Josef Strauss had said that to develop the Blue Streak project would be a waste of money. We are all pretty well convinced he did say so, but that is not bound to be the final government decision, as there are other aspects making cooperation with Britain in the project worthwhile.

At the American diplomatic community's cinema, we saw a film of Kennedy's inauguration. Somehow the man inspires confidence.

8 February 1961 : The other day slogans were daubed on the wall of the Italian Embassy, across the street from us, saying: 'Freedom for South Tyrol'. Many German-speaking people live in South Tyrol, which was taken from defeated Austria after the First World War and given to Italy. Hitler let Mussolini keep it as thanks for the Italian dictator's help in other respects.

Now a police guard has been put on the building and Chris has dropped the idea of becoming a skiing instructor and has plumped for the police. I think the fact that the police have pistols attracts him.

10 February 1961 : To a costume carnival dance in the modern press club. Elfi used a khaki shirt of mine (ex-navy or ex-scout) in her rig as cowgirl. More than one person asked her if it was a former Nazi brownshirt! I went as a schoolboy, in short pants, German braces and with Chris's slate and Robin's cap. Among

200

the costumes were lots of pirates from the *Santa Maria*, the Portuguese liner recently captured temporarily by rebels, many Red Indians and quite a body of Russians.

12 February 1961 : I am slowly wading through several pages of *Izvestia*, the Soviet Government newspaper, reporting on a meeting of the Soviet Communist Party Central Committee, held about a month ago to discuss agricultural problems. Production results appear to be very patchy. No one, as far as I have read, went into the important question of incentives for the farmers.

At the meeting Khrushchev keeps interposing remarks, almost invariably greeted with what the newspaper refers to as 'applause' or 'laughter and applause'. I always enjoy reading what Khrushchev says, for he speaks directly and often with humour. Those present almost always agree with what he says, though some do not merely accept his criticism but try to explain away their shortcomings.

Some of the farm chiefs blamed problems on a shortage of the right machines. There was mention of a strain of soya used in the United States, which was better than the one used in the Soviet Union because the beans grew higher up the stalk, making it easier for machines to harvest them.

13 February 1961 : Called on 45-ish Willi Fingerhut (Thimble) in Korbach, Hesse, the husband of a childhood friend of Elfi, Waltraud, whose maiden name was Schneider (Tailor). Willi, a fuel wholesaler, is a right-winger. He spoke contemptuously of Willy Brandt, the Social Democratic governing mayor of West Berlin, because Brandt had fled Germany in the Nazi period and worked for Germany's defeat. Willi said he admired some men who had stayed at home and worked against Hitler, but regarded Brandt as a coward. *[This was a view frequently expressed by German right-wingers.]* Willi was not able to back up his allegation. In fact, Brandt was a left-wing youth leader when Hitler took power, and cannot be said to have been cowardly in leaving the country, or lacking in courage in returning to it in the grim days after the Second World War.

15 February 1961 : At breakfast-time Elfi and I watched, through sunglasses and some cloud, an almost total eclipse of the sun. A television commentator rightly stated that such a happening would have caused much fear in the olden days, particularly as today is Ash Wednesday. It grew pretty dark here. Later, when the moon had passed by, birds started twittering.

Drove to Brussels – three hours – to help Serge Nabokov and others cover the crash this morning of a Boeing 707 jet airliner from New York. All its 72 occupants were killed, plus a chicory farmer whom it hit when it nose-dived into a field near Brussels. The dead included 18 crack American ice-skaters bound for the world championships in Prague.

Some of the people I spoke to at the scene were Flemish villagers whom I managed to interview partly by understanding their Flemish through my knowledge of German, or by getting French-speaking Belgians to translate tricky bits.

Later I met for the first time our former Belgrade correspondent, tall dark Bane Petrovic, who has been appointed Nabokov's assistant. He finds the Belgians dissatisfied people, not seeming to know what they are living for. He thinks the British are different, inspired by their traditions. I'm not sure he's right. Many Britons today think more about their TV and football pools than their traditions.

20 February 1961 : Saw another instalment of the German TV series on Nazism, this one on the Blitzkriege in Poland and France, bringing back to me those days in summer 1940 when I was a schoolboy evacuee in Todmorden, which nestles in the Pennine hills on the western edge of Yorkshire. As the German Army spread out into France, I marked the battlefront on my school atlas.

Later I saw begrimed and bandaged soldiers passing through Todmorden by train after escaping from Dunkirk. Seeing Hitler on film today, one can scarcely understand why Germans followed him.

21 Adenauer flies to London

22 February 1961 : To Cologne-Bonn airport to see off Adenauer to London, where he is to have two days of talks with Prime Minister Harold Macmillan. Adenauer, 85, is not looking too well, rather yellowish, but that in my experience does not mean anything. He declined my request to say a few words, and said, 'When I get back.'

Though Adenauer and Macmillan are now friendly, the talks are not expected to produce much. Few think the time is ripe for Britain to join the Common Market. But there is a general desire to harmonize, as far as possible, the two Western European economic blocs, so as to make possible the eventual entry of Britain and other countries into the Common Market. This seems to me to be absolutely necessary, just as it was necessary for the North American states to become the United States. The main bars at the moment are de Gaulle's apparent unwillingness to have Britain as a competitor for a leading role in Europe, Britain's Commonwealth trade preferences and Britain's cheap food policy.

Adenauer flew to London in a plane of the civil airline, Lufthansa. When he goes to Paris he normally flies in a *Luftwaffe* aircraft. Is that significant?

23 February 1961 : The London talks resulted only in the rather useless idea of using the Western European Union (WEU) for political consultations with Britain, so that Britain is not left entirely out of the political consultations which the Common Market six are expected to start in May. *[The WEU was founded in 1955 with the Common Market six and Britain as members. Its task was to co-ordinate defence and other policies.]*

It is not necessary to use the WEU for consultations. The crux is whether the six – above all, France – want Britain to be in the consultations or not.

Oleg Yenakiev, *Izvestia* correspondent, invited me with a few other Westerners to a mainly Russian cocktail at his detached house. After two vodkas, I felt, not for the first time, that Communists are not the worst people in the world – not only because of the vodkas. Nevertheless, I argued that Soviet elections are not free, and also pointed to the agricultural shortcomings which show that Communism is by no means the answer to everything, at least in its present form. One thing the Soviet Union must have some day is a freer press and other checks and balances, as in the US and Britain. It is striking to see the 'normal' appearance of today's young Soviet journalists and diplomats, a far cry from the early revolutionaries. I had to take quite a grip on myself on the short drive home, as I had drunk too much.

27 February 1961 : Early shift, up at six, in the office two minutes late at two minutes past seven. Then reading two days of back files, then the bulky morning papers to pick out likely stories for follow-ups, at the same time reading stories coming up on the three teleprinters: the East and West German news agencies by the desk and the Czechoslovak news agency brought in from the next room.

Between times, several phone calls to tie up loose ends on stories or obtain information for new stories. Certainly, with Reuters, one can hardly ever complain there is too little to do.

28 February 1961 : Brian banged the news desk with a large pair of scissors and told me off heatedly for inserting a line of background in a story about the Constitutional Court decision quashing Adenauer's plans for a second television programme. I had inserted a line stating that the opposition had accused Adenauer of trying to press ahead with this scheme in order to use the second television programme to influence voters before this autumn's federal election.

I don't mind being ticked off when this is justified, but I'll be damned if I'll let Brian talk to me in the way he sometimes talks to waiters if they don't jump quickly enough. So I answered back with just as much force, but without losing my temper, and he finally calmed down. In fact, this particular piece of background has been used before without complaint from anyone.

1 March 1961 : Brian and I got on very well today. He was most complimentary about my work. He has also made complimentary remarks to others about it. I must say he is doing a good job as news editor. (Of course, I don't think he is doing the job as well as I could!)

Tonight I interviewed Alfred Servatius, who owns a small Rhineland hotel. *[My diary does not say just where it was.]* I was after background on his brother, Dr Robert Servatius, the 66-year-old lawyer who is to defend the former Nazi SS officer, Adolf Eichmann, at his trial in Jerusalem, which is to start in April. *[Dr Servatius had been tight-lipped.]* I am to be in the Reuter reporting team. Eichmann was kidnapped in Argentina in May 1960 by Israeli secret service agents and taken to Israel. *[The main charge against Eichmann, who organized the transport of Jews to the death camps, was that he enabled the murder of millions of Jews by gassing and other means in the extermination camps of Auschwitz, Chelmno, Belzec, Sobibor, Treblinka and Maidanek.]*

Alfred Servatius, a cheerful bespectacled chap, was canny enough not to tell me anything until I had agreed to pay him a sum which, after some haggling, was fixed at 75 marks (about £7). This will be chickenfeed for the *New York Sunday News*, which has ordered a story on the lawyer.

From what the brother told me, it appears that Dr Servatius, who was not a member of the Nazi Party, is a fairly unpolitical but patriotic German of the old school, a Catholic, an artillery officer in both wars, keen on languages, and with a spirit independent enough to cause him to learn Russian shortly before Hitler came to power and make a one-year visit to Moscow in 1932–33.

The Americans roped him in after the Second World War, as one of the few German lawyers who had not become Nazis, to defend Fritz Sauckel, a senior Nazi who was responsible for the treatment of foreign forced labourers and was sentenced to death in one of the Nuremberg trials. Dr Servatius agreed with the sentence, his brother said.

In another case at Nuremberg, Dr Servatius succeeded in having local Nazi leaders (*Ortsgruppenleiter*) removed from the categories automatically classed under occupation law as criminal. This brought him much business from little Nazis seeking the restoration of their property or jobs, which had been taken from them under the old ruling.

The brother hinted that former Nazis, who escaped to Switzerland with large amounts of money, were contributing towards Eichmann's defence. I felt a bit squeamish about paying a man's brother to give information about him, but the lawyer is definitely a figure of public interest, and I think newspapers have the right to try to find out some details about him. However, I don't think much of the brother; if he wanted to give some information he should have given it free.

3 March 1961 : It was announced after a cabinet meeting that the Federal Government (i.e. Adenauer) was dropping its plans to start a second television programme, thus bowing to the decision of the Federal Constitutional Court, which ruled on 28 February that the states alone have the right to authorize such a programme, as in the case of the existing programme. Adenauer has tried to run roughshod over the constitution in order to start a second programme, which would have been under his control, unlike the present programme, which is run cooperatively by the regional radio corporations which are overseen by boards representing all parties and various social groups and organizations.

4 March 1961 : The *Deutsche Mark* is being increased in value by about 4.75 per cent. This will cheapen West Germany's imports and make its exports more costly to others, thus tending to reduce its large favourable balance of payments. It is a step which experts in other countries, and here too, have suggested. The pound will now be worth about 11.1 marks compared with about 11.7 until now. This decision is quite a big gesture on the eve of a three-day visit by Averell Harriman, President Kennedy's roving ambassador, who is to discuss among other things the harmonization of balances of payments in the Western world.

5 March 1961 : Reported on a complicated press conference given by the Economics Minister, Professor Ludwig Erhard, the chubby cigar-smoking symbol of West German prosperity. He detailed the decision to revalue the mark upwards by about 4.75 per cent.

Erhard explained that one reason for the step was that a new boom is on the way in West Germany, with the fear of inflation. To combat inflation you can restrict credit by raising the bank rate. But if West Germany raises its bank rate, this attracts more speculative foreign money, as the bank rate in some other Western countries is lower than in West Germany.

Speculative foreign money, on top of West Germany's favourable trade balance, would increase its payments surplus even more, which is internationally undesirable at a time when the United States and Britain have balance of payments problems.

Chris, who will be eight tomorrow, has until recently not liked being called Christopher. But today he insisted that Elfi mark his full name on a box of paints, a birthday present. Growing up?

Robin this morning made the mistake of using toothpaste to do his hair with – the two tubes are similar. His hair went hard. Elfi had to wash it so he could start again.

6 March 1961 : Spent several hours showing Eric Wright, managing editor of the left-wing Sunday newspaper *Reynolds' News*, and his wife, around the Bonn area. *Reynolds'* circulation, of about 500,000, is being kept going – as it has been for years – by a subsidy from the cooperative movement.

Wright seems to be trying to be fair to the Germans, not seeking to exploit the insignificant signs of a neo-Nazi revival, as some British papers do. At the same time he is wary of what might happen in Germany in future years in view of the Berlin and reunification problems.

7 March 1961 : Averell Harriman had further talks in Bonn. He sought to reassure the Germans about reported American plans to withdraw nuclear weapons from NATO's front line, so as to avoid having to use such weapons in the first stages of a war. The West German military chiefs argue that you can't expect Germans manning NATO's front line to be deprived of such weapons when they know that Russians on the other side have got them. I accept that. On the other hand, it has been West Germany which has blocked plans for controlled disarmament on both sides of the Iron Curtain, knowing this would reduce West Germany's international political weight.

9 March 1961 : Special treat for Robin and me: we used two complimentary tickets from the Soviet Embassy press department to enjoy a performance of the Soviet State Circus in Cologne. Best of all was Oleg Popov, the famous clown, who did all the things clowns do with lots of verve and presence. I tried to imagine it was all happening in Moscow.

10 March 1961 : Adenauer was not in brilliant form today when he gave his first press conference for about two years; he lacked his usual sparkle. He also said something which I thought was a sign of bad judgement. He referred to the possible anti-German effect of the Eichmann trial on world public opinion, and said that only a very small proportion of Germans had been convinced Nazis. I don't think that was true in the early days of Nazism. And even if it was true, it's not likely to go down well abroad.

17 March 1961 : The *Bundestag* approved a record budget of 48,000 million marks, of which about one quarter is for rearmament.

I wrote about the decline of storks in northern and western Europe: a reduction of about a quarter in 26 years up to 1958 in 15 European countries, and a further fall since then, due to less swampy land and meadow and more hazards such as high-tension wires, radio waves which confuse the birds, and the use of insecticides in their winter haunts in Africa – insecticides sometimes strong enough to kill the storks.

Was surprised to hear from a Soviet diplomat tonight that censorship of foreign correspondents based in the Soviet Union has been lifted. I knew that this had been rumoured, but he insisted it had come about already. Other Soviet sources tended to confirm the story, but it is still unclear whether the measure has been introduced or is about to be.

18 March 1961 : The other day we were visited by Herr Pintz, an ethnic German formerly of Yugoslav nationality, and his wife, who is a farmer's daughter from Elfi's parish in former East Prussia. Pintz's story is amazing and amusing. When the Germans invaded Yugoslavia, he was faced with joining the German or the Hungarian Army, then allied with the Germans. (His home village in Serbia is near the Hungarian frontier and the people there speak Hungarian as well as Serbian. As an ethnic German, whose grandfather migrated to the area from Swabia, in south-west Germany, he also spoke German.)

Pintz, who had already done some military service in Yugoslavia, chose the German Army and was packed off to the eastern front after only a week or two's training. The Germans used him as a spy behind the lines, often dropped by plane and getting back by using his knowledge of Serbian and Russian, pretending to be a Russian who spoke a Serbian-like dialect.

After the war Pintz masqueraded as a former concentration camp inmate, changing his alleged nationality from Yugoslav to German or Hungarian, just as it suited him. He feared to return to Yugoslavia in the Stalin era, but has been on holiday there since. He was not harmed. He found the majority of his relatives and fellow-villagers were all for Tito and very anti-Russian.

19 March 1961 : Instead of going to church – rose too late – I read a first-class sermon by the famous British Methodist minister, Leslie Weatherhead, whom I once heard in London, probably during the war. On the character of God, he argued that God could not be a god if he were bad, because humans on the whole know the compelling power of goodness, i.e., most people know that to do good is better than to do evil, and if God did not know that, he would be morally inferior to us. Weatherhead admitted that he had often been discouraged by the seeming injustices in life. He explained these partly by saying that God really had given humans free will, and partly by saying we might have to pass through a number of existences before we realized the meaning of all that happened to us in this life.

[Today I don't think much of his argumentation. I prefer the view of our Unitarian minister, Rev. Ashley Hills, who said, roughly, 'If God is all-powerful, then – in view of such things as natural disasters – he cannot be good.' And I don't believe in reincarnation. Weatherhead also referred to the flashes of goodness, of godliness, that are seen occasionally in human life. I agree with that.]

We were the guests of German friends, elderly Willi and Lotte Krämer, in their vast modern house in a select area of Bad Godesberg. Willi told me how he had invented a welding machine for making wire mesh. He founded a business, with a co-partner who provided some capital, at about the time the Nazis came to power in 1933.

Willi, a Protestant, said he had been impressed at first by the Nazi Government, because unemployment disappeared and social strife appeared to end. It was not until the 'Crystal Night' pogrom of November 1938, when he saw a Jewish business being sacked in the Rhineland town of Emmerich, where he then lived, that he really had strong doubts about the system. The pogrom occurred soon after he had been persuaded to join the Nazi Party, but before he had received his party card. He said he had never been more than a nominal member.

Willi recalled how, in Berlin during the war, after discussions with a ministry official on the supply of barbed wire for the forces, the official told him, 'I am finished, without hope.'

The official said his son had told him he had been a member of an execution squad in Eastern Europe, and had shot dead Russians or Poles after they had been forced to make their own graves.

Emmerich was flattened in a raid in the autumn of 1944 – said to be revenge for the defeat of British airborne troops at Arnhem in Holland – and Willi's factory was destroyed. Since the war the Krämers have made an economic comeback. Willi's story is typical of many decent, but politically not very acute Germans.

20 March 1961 : Drove to Hemer, small Westphalian garrison town, to see ten British soldiers 'join' the West German Army in the first exchange of any size or duration between the two armies. These men of the Green Howards, a Yorkshire regiment, were marched in, as about 250 steel-helmeted men of the German regiment, in their field-grey, stood to attention on the parade ground.

Four German tanks, marked with large Iron Crosses, stood at the corners of the parade ground. The commanding officer of the German unit, Lieutenant-Colonel Bless, a jovial jackbooted figure, made a speech of welcome in German and English from a stand draped with the West German black-red-gold tricolour, and the German soldiers gave three cheers for their British comrades, who stepped smartly into the German formation to form the centre rank of an otherwise German company.

The British and German flags were hoisted as the national anthems were played, and the soldiers marched off to German and British military marches played by the German regiment's brass band.

The British soldiers are to stay in the German unit, doing some tough training, for ten days. All are volunteers. The idea sprang from a talk between British and German officers after the units had met at football.

A German Army public relations officer, Captain Rhein, enthused about this link, and asked me what I thought. I said I was all for it, but would have preferred to see Russians invited!

In fact I felt rather uneasy. True, I find the average West German soldier pleasant enough, just as I did when I met members of the East German Army on a conducted visit to one of their barracks in 1959. But I am still of the view that West German rearmament is regrettable, just like East German rearmament, and only tends to complicate the world situation and create new possibilities of clashes.

22 Moscow lifts censorship

23 March 1961 : Today came the official Moscow announcement that censorship of foreign journalists' despatches had been lifted. The advance news had been quite a scoop for me, as one does not often get this from Soviet officials.

Newspapers today were full of reminiscences about the censorship system, which had been in operation for most of the period since the 1917 revolution. Reporters never saw the censor who, officially, was not a censor at all, but someone helpfully provided by the Soviet Government to assist foreign correspondents in removing 'mistakes' and 'rumours' from their copy.

The correspondents had to send all their despatches through the Central Telegraph Office, handing in two copies of each story, marked at the top with 'corrections mine'. One copy was returned with any censored passages crossed out or cut out. And if the correspondent tried to telephone any of the deletions, he would be cut off and might be reprimanded.

Occasionally correspondents have got important stories through to their offices in the West by pretending to chat innocuously on the phone, but slipping in a few significant words. Some correspondents had been instructed to try this in the case of top stories – say, Stalin's death – even though it might have meant their expulsion.

Heinz Schewe, Moscow correspondent of the West German newspaper *Die Welt*, recalled in an article how, when he had visited the Baltic states, he had written: 'I met many people who were obviously pleased to speak German.' The censor changed this to: 'I met many people who could speak German.'

Schewe also mentioned an anecdote from the Stalin era, according to which a correspondent, describing a Moscow May Day parade, wrote: 'I stood only a stone's throw from Stalin.' The censor, so the story went, added: 'But nobody threw a stone.'

Some correspondents once became so furious at having to wait even several days for their stories to be returned to them that they tore out the telephone from its fitting in the Central Telegraph Office and flung it on the floor.

I had felt that Khrushchev would be bound to lift censorship sooner or later, partly because it only made correspondents more ill-disposed towards the Soviet Union than they might otherwise have been, and partly because he, I am sure, believes that, as a whole, Soviet society is superior to others and could thus, in the long run, bear a free comparison. Of course, it is not impossible that Khrushchev's successor will reimpose censorship, because it fits in with Soviet – and Russian – traditions.

24 March 1961 : Chris gave us much happiness today. Firstly, he came home bursting with joy, and hammered on the door so that Elfi would let him in. She guessed what was the cause of this behaviour: a better-than-expected school report, with not one bad mark. One less-than-middle mark was for his general behaviour. He tends to look out of the window too much, and to be a bit of a roustabout occasionally, but his teacher likes him a lot.

Not long after this news, Chris came across his missing teeth-regulating plate in the communal garden close to our house. For the rest of the day he preened himself for having pleased his parents so much. Robin added to this happy atmosphere by also coming home with a better-than-expected report. On the basis of a scale of rewards, Chris pocketed five marks and Robin sixteen: his report was better and he takes more subjects.

An important press conference with Selwyn Lloyd, one of those responsible for Britain's mad attack on Egypt in 1956. He was Foreign Secretary then and is now Chancellor of the Exchequer. He gave details of West German measures to aid Britain's balance-of-payments situation. They included the advance repayment of £67.5 million of post-war debts. West Germany is also expected to step up its arms purchases from Britain.

After asking one question – cursing myself inwardly for causing my heart to beat fast from nervousness – I managed to get in another one at the end. I asked whether West Germany had agreed to buy Britain's 105-mm tank gun. I saw that British Ambassador Sir Christopher Steel was annoyed by this question, as Lloyd had said earlier that such matters were the responsibility of the ministries concerned. However, Lloyd answered simply, 'Yes'.

This was a good story, as the order might in the long run be worth £30 million, which would be the largest West German arms order to Britain.

Tonight we watched another instalment of the 14-part West German television series on the Nazi regime. This one was about the war against the Soviet Union. Very fairly done, I thought. No wonder the Russians distrust the West Germans more than I think they ought to.

25 March 1961 : Off to Britain on leave, by car. With Elfi and me taking turns at the wheel, we passed our favourite (comic) Belgian place names – Odeur and Erps-Kwerps – on the way to Ostend. Some 220 miles in about five hours, mainly motorway and in good weather.

A pleasant crossing to Dover, which began in coastal fog, with the foghorns giving Chris the jumps, but continued mainly in sunshine. We put back our clocks, but will have to put them forward again tonight because Britain goes on to Summer Time during the night, and that's the same as Central European Time. In Ostend we had a delay of about 75 minutes, due mainly to false information from the West German motorists' club, ADAC, which had told me I did not need a triptyque – a kind of passport for the car – to travel to Britain. Had to have one made out.

The roads of south-east England seemed toy-like after the

Continent, perhaps because more things are fenced off, with one little house after the next, and neat little gardens, whereas the Continent seems to be on a bigger scale.

We bought petrol in Kent and were amused at the garage man's reaction when I asked him to wash our windscreen. He mumbled, in a friendly but surprised fashion, something like, 'Now, how do we do that?' (It is done without even being asked for at many petrol stations in Western Europe.) I suggested he bring some water and told him I had a sponge of my own, so he fetched some and we managed to accomplish this unusual task.

We crossed the Thames northwards from Tilbury on a British Railways ferry *[a service discontinued many years ago, and replaced by the Dartford tunnel-and-bridge Thames crossing]*.

26 March 1961 : After overnighting with friends in Essex, we drove about 200 miles to my hometown, Bradford – that chock-full bowl of mills, shops and houses. What happiness to come home to a dear mother and childhood surroundings! Feeling this joy makes me realize how much Elfi has lost due to the dismemberment of Germany.

Bradford, population about 300,000, now has a considerable number of Asian citizens. That led to the joke about the Bradford-ian who, like me, had been elsewhere for a long time. When he came back he commented, 'When ah were a lad, buildings were black and t'people were white. Nah it's t'other way rahnd.' (Many of the once soot-blackened buildings had been cleaned.)

Tonight we enjoyed fish and chips. The fish now costs eight-pence a portion, compared with about twopence in 1939, and a 1939 pennyworth of chips now costs fourpence. *[These figures are in old pence, abolished in 1975. Then 2¹/₂ old pence were converted to one new penny.]*

30 March 1961 : Called on my former boss, mercurial but human Oliffe Bryant Stokes (known as OBS), Welsh editor-in-chief of the Bradford and District Newspaper Co. Ltd, whose main prod-uct, the evening *Telegraph & Argus*, is booming as never before, thanks to masses of adverts. A double bonus was paid to the staff last year. We never had a single one when I was there between 1949 and 1954.

The minimum rate, agreed with the union, for a journalist in Bradford is about £16 a week, compared with about £24 in London.

While enjoying a five-course dinner – we were the guests of my sister Pat and brother-in-law, Derek – I quizzed one of the other guests, Dr Tom Priestley, about the effects of alcohol. His view is that 'a little of what you fancy does you good', the key words being 'a little'. After that I felt I could accept a glass of red wine with my duckling.

1 April 1961 : Was amused by the TV show *Candid Camera*, in which a reporter masquerading as a German tourist asked people in Stratford-on-Avon to take him to Mr William Shakespeare who, he insisted, still lived in the town. One obliging old gent went so far as to look in the telephone book, where he actually found the number of a Mr Shakespeare – unfortunately not the right one.

2 April 1961 : My family and I went to Sunday service at the church where Elfi and I were married, Tetley Street Baptist, in Bradford. We liked the clear and humorous style of the new minister, Mr Seddons. I tackled him afterwards about one aspect of his sermon which I had understood to mean that Jesus or God would take a hand in solving the world's political crises. (He referred to Laos, where right-wing and pro-Communist factions are feuding at present.) Would not that, I asked, infringe the Christian concept of free will? Mr Seddons said he had been thinking of what he called 'God's way of working within people'. Although he felt that he personally had free will, he wanted to do what he thought was God's will.

I do believe that the world is moving towards a higher plane and that God wants people to help in this process. This is not a belief based on logic, but on feeling about what is good and bad, and the wish not to believe that there is no point in the world. I was pleased Mr Seddons appealed to the congregation to see a film made by the nuclear disarmament campaign, as he said, to help people make up their minds on this issue. That seems to me to be practical religion.

Called on 70-ish, white-haired Stanley Bradfield, former assistant editor of the *Yorkshire Observer*, the Bradford morning paper, and something of a genial father figure to some of the young reporters. Stanley, a widowed Welshman, lives in an old terrace in central Bradford, with a Ukrainian family on one side and a Pakistani one on the other. *[Large communities of Eastern Europeans and Asians had settled in Bradford since the Second World War.]* He told me there is little colour trouble in Bradford, and he regards it as rather amusing that some original Bradfordians look down on the Ukrainians who, in their turn, look down on the coloured people. He disapproves of this, I'm happy to say.

4 April 1961 : This was the day we took our leave of Robin who, in three weeks, is to start at Ackworth, a mixed Quaker boarding school near Wakefield, some 15 miles from Bradford. He will be 13 in May. His granny will be able to take him out three times a term.

In a fatherly chat with him, I told him we would be looking forward to a weekly letter, that he should not be a tell-tale, that he should always own up if he did something he shouldn't have done, that he should be ready to tell us or his teachers about any worries and that he should be gentlemanly to the girls in the school. He said yes to all this.

Elfi has wept once or twice at the prospect of 'losing' Robin, while my feeling has been occasionally of semi-remorse that my job has made it necessary to send Robin away to school. (By next year we should be stationed in Moscow, where there are no suitable schools for Brits of Robin's age.) But I have also felt happy and thankful that we are able to afford to give him about five years of good English education – education in the real sense, I hope.

5 April 1961 : After consultations in Reuters head office about the Eichmann trial with several top people, we took the night

218

ferry from Dover to Dunkirk. Home by 1 pm to a Godesberg filled with warm summery air and fragrant with fruit tree blossom.

8 April 1961 : Have been preparing a background article on the Nazi concentration camp system, to be used in connection with the Eichmann trial at London's discretion. One interesting fact I dug up was that even Heinrich Himmler, head of the SS, had at times doubts about the rightness of exterminating the Jews.

Himmler was also responsible for introducing the gas chambers as a 'humane' method of killing Jews, after being terribly shaken by witnessing a mass shooting of Jews – the method used earlier. From what I have read, it seems that the Western countries could have done much more to save the Jews if they had been ready to allow more Jewish immigration earlier.

23 To Jerusalem for the Eichmann trial

9 April 1961 : With one of my Bonn colleagues, Lionel Walsh, I flew in a British-made Comet IV of the (Greek) Olympic Airways via Athens to Tel Aviv. We passed the ten-hour journey pleasantly, enjoying the excellent free meals, included in the £125 return fare, served daintily by pretty bronzed apparently Greek stewardesses.

After a half-hour break in Zurich, we had a glorious few-minute glimpse of the snow-covered and sun-bathed Alps, then, soon afterwards the blurred snake of the River Po and the lagooned sweep of the Gulf of Venice.

At more than 400 mph in the not-so-noisy jet, we could soon see the Greek islands. Then I recognized the large, triangular island of Aegina, south of Athens, near where I had seen service as an officer in a Royal Navy mine-sweeping flotilla in 1945.

After spotting the port of Athens, Piraeus, we were coming down over small, flat-roofed houses, looking fruitlessly for a glimpse of the Acropolis, hidden by a hill. After about an hour on Athens airport, where a minor engine defect was quickly fixed, we flew on for two more hours in the dark to Tel Aviv.

Our first sight in the Jewish state was of a bustling half-finished arrivals hall, with police in British-type uniforms. Fascinating to see the different skin colours of Jews who had come to live in their young state: from the pink of the ex-British to the dark brown of the ex-Moroccan.

All signs are in right-to-left Hebrew with English beneath – it looks like a kind of shorthand and, in fact, like some kinds of shorthand, it does omit most of the vowels. Many of the officials spoke English. All were polite and friendly, and there was a European air of efficiency, almost more European than some European countries – Italy, for instance.

Formalities were quick, and soon a government press office man had found us seats in one of the shuttle service taxis, mainly old American Plymouths, which run between Tel Aviv's airport and Jerusalem – a 66-kilometre *[41 miles]* drive which was bone-shaking more because of the temperament of the driver than the admittedly not-too-good condition of the road.

Our driver, born in Afghanistan, turned out to be a character, with a smattering of several languages. As our taxi was nearly run into by a luggage trolley while we were trying to leave the airport car park, he called out, 'Don't kill me, I'm not Eichmann.'

It was too dark to see what Israel looks like, except in the lighted streets of Jerusalem. That is, the Israeli (Western) part of Jerusalem – a New Jerusalem built outside the Old City walls. The Old City lies on the Jordan side of the armistice line drawn in 1948, after the abortive Arab attempt to strangle the young state at birth.

What we saw tonight revealed modern-style buildings of cream-coloured local stone, easy on the eye, often with the small windows of the sub-tropics, designed to keep out too much sun. It was pleasantly cool in this 2,455-feet-high *[750 m]* city, the jewel of Judaea. An awesome feeling to be here, even though what we saw tonight was not reminiscent of the Bible.

The elderly white-haired night porter in our hotel, the Eden, is a charming person, with a warm half-smile always flitting about his pink, slightly Semitic face. German-born, I think. He survived the Nazi concentration camp of Dachau, near Munich. I learned later that he has found it a hard job to learn Hebrew, since coming here four years ago.

10 April 1961 : Our correspondent in Nicosia, Cyprus, little, dark and bespectacled Shahe Guebenlian, an Armenian known as Gubby, took us to be accredited at the 'Russian Compound', an area of West Jerusalem with a Russian church and ancillary buildings, near the almost sealed-off border with the Old City. Some of the buildings are leased for use as Israeli Government offices. It is a historic quirk that this compound is now owned by the atheistic Soviet Government.

First impressions of Jerusalem in the warm sun today were of a somewhat quiet provincial city, with a plethora of signs in Hebrew, many of them duplicated in English, which helps one to learn the Hebrew letters. I noticed that one Hebrew letter, depicting the sound 'sh' as in 'shop', is similar to a Russian (cyrillic) letter standing for the same sound. Both look like an inverted 'm'. *[Decades later I read that when the Macedonian brothers Kyril and Methodius were devising the first Russian alphabet in the ninth century, they used mainly Greek and Latin letters, but also a small number from Hebrew. So I suppose that's where the similarity came from. I wonder if that Hebrew letter was based on the sight of teeth when one makes that 'sh' sound.]*

Jerusalem has a somewhat Italian, somewhat Maltese and a little Arab air – the new city, I mean. There are also little British touches, such as blue-uniformed policemen and red, round letterboxes. The air today in this hill city was warm but fresh, and with a faint scent hinting at the fruit blossom and the spring flowers which are ablaze on the surrounding stony hills.

Almost everyone is in European dress, but there are small numbers of Orthodox religious Jews, the men in broad-rimmed black hats and long sideburns. Quite a number of men, young and old, wearing the Jewish skullcaps. Occasionally a bearded rabbi passes by, for Jerusalem is still the heart of the Jewish religion and has the reputation of being a strait-laced place compared with some other Israeli towns, such as 'godless Haifa', the attractive northern port nestling at the foot of the garden paradise of Mount Carmel.

Today there was little time for us to steep ourselves in

Jerusalem's atmosphere. We had to be off to the Beit Haam, West Jerusalem's community centre, a flat-roofed building faced in white marble, which has been converted into a heavily guarded courthouse for the trial of Eichmann.

Gubby took us in past guards dressed like British policemen. Inside there were more guards, in RAF-style uniforms, and on the roof were others, armed with submachine-guns. We were not only thoroughly searched (mainly for bombs) in little cubicles, but my typewriter and handbag were taken off me for thorough scrutiny, which took about an hour.

Inside, where several hundred of about 700 journalists expected for the trial were busy preparing advance stories, I met the fourth member, and chief, of our reporting team: Arye Wallenstein, a 35-ish friendly but rather quiet Jew, our staff man in Israel, who has done all the complicated preparation for our coverage.

Also there were middle-aged East Londoner Reg A'Court, a senior teleprinter operator and news traffic expert, and Ted Hall, another teleprinter operator, also from London, who completed our staff at the trial.

The six of us have been allocated a cubicle about two yards by four, intended to hold four people – the fifth is expected to be in court and the sixth will have to find a place somewhere else. Our cubicle also has to hold two teleprinters, a TV set, two tables, four chairs, numerous files and books about Eichmann and the usual bric-a-brac of a news agency office.

This afternoon we worked on a final pre-trial story, with atmosphere, comments from prosecution and defence sources. (You can't do that in England, even though Israeli law is largely based on English and American practice.) We got our story moving on our 30-words-a-minute radio teletype transmitter to London: half the usual speed because we are sharing a channel with United Press, one of the American agencies. Each is using alternate 'beats' of the transmitter to send our messages winging to London.

Later we sent off a further story – in Reuter parlance a 'post-midnighter' – intended for early evening editions of newspapers in various countries tomorrow before the trial has really got under way. To bed after midnight in our pleasant Eden Hotel, with a cheerful good night in interestingly accented English from that delightful night porter who was in Dachau.

11 April 1961 : We have to be careful in our hotel not to ask for the wrong things, because it is kosher: that is, subject to the Jewish religion's food laws. Lionel put his foot in it by asking for bacon and eggs. The waiter diplomatically said, 'Yes, sir' and brought eggs without bacon.

It was soon my turn to break the kosher rules, by asking for some milk in coffee or tea after we had eaten meat. *[The kosher rules were adopted by the tribe of Israel under Moses, who lived in the fourteenth and thirteenth centuries BC. They are believed to have been imposed because of hot climate and hygienic conditions at that time.]*

The kosher rules include an absolute ban on pork and shellfish. Later we found that many Jews did not observe these rules any more, and that Israel is not a predominantly religious society at all. But the religious Jews, having their own political party, have influence sometimes going beyond their numbers, because of their usefulness in forming coalition governments, normally headed by Mapai, the moderate Labour Party led by white-haired David Ben-Gurion, 64. *[Ben-Gurion had been Prime Minister, and Defence Minister, since 1955.]*

Around 8.30 am, I was ensconced in my corner seat in our cubicle, ready to start sub-editing copy provided by my three editorial colleagues.

We had decided that, for a start, Gubby should sit in the courtroom, the converted auditorium of the community centre. This is an ultra-modern light-coloured room with walls of greyish bare stone. At the rear is the judges' bench, behind which in gilded relief on the wall is the symbol both of the tribes of Israel and the modern state of Israel, the seven-branched candlestick, the menorah, with the name 'Israel' in Hebrew beneath it.

Gubby had to watch like a hawk when Adolf Eichmann, 55, a former SS Obersturmbannführer (Lieutenant-Colonel), was escorted from a concealed door on the left, leading straight into a cubicle enclosed by bullet-proof glass (to prevent assassination attempts or bids to pass him poison).

Three Israeli policemen, burly men in British-style khaki uniforms with black peaked caps – men chosen because they had not lost relatives in the concentration camps – entered the cubicle with the bespectacled, sallow, sharp-faced accused, a clerk-like figure.

Eichmann sat down before a battery of microphones – for intercom in the court and for recordings of the trial for press, radio and history. Apart from Gubby, we were watching this from the closed-circuit TV in our cubicle, in a room underneath the court, packed by hundreds of journalists.

Eichmann stood to attention as an attendant barked out in Hebrew that the court was entering, and the three German-born judges, all refugees from the Nazis, walked in wearing their black gowns, hatless. Only about 20 ordinary members of the public had seats in the auditorium, which held about 750 press, diplomats, foreign official observers and Israeli high-ups. Six hundred more members of the public were watching on large-screen television in a hall a few hundred yards away.

Eichmann had to say but two words today – '*Jawohl*' twice: once when the presiding judge, handsome, balding 50-ish Mr Justice Moshe Landau, asked him if he was indeed Eichmann, and once when Judge Landau asked him if he had understood the 15-count indictment of about 5,000 words, which was read out at the start of the morning session.

The indictment alleges that Eichmann sought, together with others, to destroy the Jewish people by causing the murder of millions of Jews through slave labour, starvation, maltreatment and, finally, through mass extermination – first by shooting, then in lorries into which engine exhaust gases were diverted, and finally by the use of the cyanide gas, Zyklon B, in the extermination camps of Eastern Europe.

The most notorious camp was Auschwitz, in occupied Poland, where, according to the later-executed commandant of that camp,

Rudolf Höss, at least 2.5 million people, mainly Jews, were deliberately murdered and where a further half million died from deliberate maltreatment.

Subsidiary counts of the indictment allege the pillaging of Jewish property; the forced deportation of Jews, Poles and Slovenes; complicity in the murder of 100 Christian children in the Czech village of Lidice, which was razed by the Nazis as a reprisal against partisan operations; and membership of Nazi organizations declared illegal by the four-power Nuremberg War Crimes Tribunal after the Second World War.

Eichmann, who was outwardly calm except for occasionally twitching lips and twiddling fingers, did not have to plead today, as his square-headed jovial Rhineland lawyer, Dr Robert Servatius, immediately raised objections. Servatius, a Roman Catholic, submitted that in view of the sufferings of the Jewish people, an Israeli court could not fail to be prejudiced in a legal sense, and was thus disqualified from trying Eichmann who, he submitted, ought to be tried by an international court or a German court.

Dr Servatius further claimed that the court was barred from trying Eichmann as he had been illegally captured by agents of the Israeli state in Argentina last May, and illegally brought to Israel against his will. He also submitted that the Israeli law of 1950, on the punishment of Nazis and their collaborators, ran counter to normal legal practice and international law because it was retroactive and provided even for the prosecution of non-Israelis who had committed crimes against non-Israelis (i.e. European Jews), outside Israel and before Israel had existed.

The German lawyer's oral submissions did not take long, but the court, contrary to normal Israeli practice in a criminal trial, allowed him to put in 100 pages of written submissions.

It was then the turn of Israel's hawk-faced Attorney-General, Polish-born Gideon Hausner, to start putting the prosecution's lengthy counter-arguments. Mr Hausner, who lost relatives in the Nazi death camps, maintained that Israeli judges were trained to conduct a fair trial whatever might be their personal views on an accused, and that morally no country had a better right to try Eichmann than Israel.

Speaking mainly quietly, but with bursts of emotion, Mr Hausner made a strong impression on me, much more persuasive and moving than the older Dr Servatius who has, I think, taken on something a little too big for him.

12 April 1961 : The legal argument continued today. We sent lots of copy: 5,000–6,000 words.

13 April 1961 : The court took a day off today for Israel's annual day of mourning for the millions of Jews killed by the Nazis, an appropriate anniversary at this moment. I went with Wally Wallenstein in his battered green-grey British-made Hillman to the stony Mount of Remembrance outside Jerusalem, near the new Hebrew University, built to replace the original one which is now in Jordanian territory east of Jerusalem.

Pallbearers, some soldiers and some civilians, shuffled along sadly, carrying a yard-wide metal casket, draped with the Israeli flag – a blue Jewish star on a white background. The casket contained ashes from the crematoria of various Nazi death camps.

The procession, headed by a black-coated bearded rabbi wearing a wide-brimmed hat, had come from the nearby temporary burial place of the ashes. As the rabbi chanted a psalm to a mournful oriental melody, the procession, with hundreds looking on, moved past dignitaries, including the grey-haired Foreign Minister, Mrs Golda Meir, and entered an unusual new building, the door of which is covered with modernistic iron sculpture representing the implements of torture and death used in the concentration camps.

The building, some 30 yards by 30, is squarish. Its wall, of large rough brown boulders, supports a concrete roof, modelled inside to recall a desert tent. Called a 'memorial tent', the building is a traditional form of burial place for 'righteous Jews'. The procession had brought the casket to this place, dimly lit by daylight filtering through a single central skylight, for the symbolic burial of the six million Jews estimated to have been killed by the Nazis in their 'final solution of the Jewish problem' in which, the prosecution alleges, Eichmann had a major planning and directing role.

As psalms were intoned in Hebrew, and an elderly rabbi gave an address, I thought of the absolute in horror that had been suffered by those millions of Jewish innocents who died in the gas chambers, the execution ditches or the starvation-and-forced-labour camps of Nazi-occupied Europe. I am glad to say that I wept, along with many of the hundreds present, some of them former camp inmates themselves.

Rabbi Nurock, a member of the *Knesset* (Parliament) and former minister, who opposes Premier Ben-Gurion's policy of reconciliation with West Germany, made a speech in which he damned Germany as a whole. One may not accept that all Nazi-era Germans were guilty of these crimes – I do not accept that they were – but one can understand why a man who lost his whole family in the death camps should speak in this way.

As red-bereted paratroopers stood by, a silent guard of honour in a shadowy corner of the chamber, the casket was lowered by officers into a vault in the middle of the black mosaic floor, which is inscribed with the names of about 20 of the most notorious concentration camps, written both in the original languages and in Hebrew.

I was rather surprised to see only a few hundreds at this mourning ceremony. Wally explained that today, Thursday, was a working day and that large sections of Israel's 1,800,000 population (300,000 of whom are Arabs) have no personal link with the tragedy.

14 April 1961 : Last night there were larger gatherings of remembrance in various parts of Israel. Some of the speakers, committing what would be contempt of court in Britain, took it upon themselves to attack, at least by implication, Dr Servatius's contention that the court has no right to try Eichmann.

We heard further legal argument today. The court will give its decision after the long weekend adjournment, which began at midday. The Sabbath begins at sunset on Fridays, lasting until the same time on Saturdays. Out of deference to the Roman Catholic, Dr Servatius, the court does not sit on the Christian Sunday. We journalists are all in favour, for the grind is tough during the week.

Tonight I was a guest at a party in West Jerusalem given by an architect, Dr Ben Dor, and his wife at their home, number 29, Street of the Prophets, an Arab-built thick-walled and small-windowed house about 100 years old, only a few hundred yards from the wall of the Old City, which marks the Jordanian border. A wick was burning smokily in a large earthenware vase to light our way up steps into the house, which had whitewashed interior walls, setting off some excellent old furniture.

The atmosphere of modern Israel pervaded. I talked, for instance, with a Dr Salz, a Jew from New York, who had come to help Israel's hospital services in 1950. He told me that until he came to Israel, he had not realized that the United States was not his real home. In Israel, he said, he did not have to be on his guard in case someone made a wounding remark about Jews.

Dr Ben Dor, who served in the British Army, remains pro-British, but pronouncedly anti-Arab. He told me the Jordanians had refused to comply with a United Nations agreement under which the Jews should be allowed to visit the Wailing Wall in the Old City, on the site of the Jewish Temple, which was destroyed by the Romans in AD 70 after an abortive Jewish revolt.

The situation between old and new Jerusalem is worse than that between East and West Berlin, for there is virtually no circulation except for some United Nations and consular officials. People who have visited Israel may cross over to the Old City, into Jordan, but the Jordanians do not let them come back again. They have to return by some indirect route or continue their journey elsewhere.

15 April 1961 : Off duty, I joined a government-sponsored bus trip for journalists in a fairly elderly but not uncomfortable bus run by a large cooperative organization responsible for much of the country's transport. It is called, in Latin lettering, Egged. I can read it in Hebrew (from right to left) too now.

229

Through a loudspeaker an Israeli guide told us about many of the places we passed through on the daylong drive of about 400 kilometres *[250 miles]*. (Jerusalem itself stands some 75 kilometres *[47 miles]* from the coast.) We drove first through the stony but, on the Israeli side, well cultivated and increasingly tree-covered hills of Judaea.

At first, on either side of us, at most a few kilometres away, was Jordan, because Jerusalem forms a kind of bridgehead into Jordanian territory as fixed under the 1949 armistice, when the Arabs, for the time being, halted their attempt to squash Israel. Israel won some Arab territory during that war and lost less of its own.

We came through an area where Samson, the Bible's strong man, lived, then past two Crusader churches and near many kibbutzim, the collective settlements run on quasi-Communist lines by volunteers inspired by religion or idealism, and hailing from many countries.

The land descends towards the sea, the vegetation becoming more sub-tropical. Orange and banana plantations and palms mingle with the vegetation of more temperate climes. Occasionally we came through an Arab village, not so well kept as the others, with flat-roofed small houses, often with a blue colour-wash, believed to be a protection against the 'evil eye'.

We passed the airport of Lod (formerly Arab Lydda), where we landed six days ago, and then turned north through the narrowest part of Israel which, in places, is only ten miles wide – between the Mediterranean and the Jordanian border. In that area, we were told, Jewish pioneers of the last generation had reclaimed swamps and semi-desert to make fruitful fields and plantations. Our road was near the ancient Via Maris, the coast road leading from Egypt to Syria and Babylon.

Our first extended stop was some 35 kilometres *[22 miles]* north of Lod: the ruins of Caesarea, built by the Jewish King Herod for the Romans, and given that complimentary name in the period after the Romans conquered Israel in 67 BC (24 years before England became part of their empire).

Today Caesarea is an apparently uninhabited treasurehouse of history and archaeology. The remains of the Roman port, including dark basalt columns, were used as foundations for later cities in the Byzantine, Mameluke (rulers of Egypt), Crusader and Arab periods.

The Crusaders were in Palestine from 1099 to 1291 and, from what some Israelis have told me, they treated the Jews worse than the Arabs or Turks did. The Roman occupiers of Caesarea used to make the Jews fight lions and other animals, while the French Crusaders, centuries later, organized horse races.

A small minaret stands above ruined Arab and Crusader walls, and the Mediterranean laps on Roman breakwaters. I would have been content to stay there for the rest of the day, but our itinerary soon took us further up the coast to Haifa, Israel's beautiful modern port some 100 miles from Jerusalem, nestling at the foot of Mount Carmel.

The mountainside is covered with gardens, including the exotic garden shrine of the Bahai movement, a religion including elements of many others and stressing the oneness of mankind, regardless of race, sex, colour, class or creed. (I remember seeing its little office in Bradford in the forties.)

We ate in a pleasant café where the manageress spoke German – the lingua franca, incidentally, in the buffet at the courthouse.

We then drove eastwards into part of Israel which was won during the war with the Arabs – started by the Arabs – in 1948–49. We passed near a mountain where the Old Testament Israelites defeated an opposing force of Canaanites, thanks to advice from the prophetess Deborah who, it is claimed, performed a miracle. Historians now believe she had been able to see from a mountain that rain clouds were gathering, and advised the Jewish side to quickly attack the Canaanites, who were armed with the tanks of that day, chariots. The rain muddied the ground and made the 'tanks' useless, so the Jews won, the story goes.

We also passed through the beautiful hills of Samaria and entered 'Upper Galilee' – 'upper' because it has mountains up to about 2,500 feet *[760 m]*, with lots of apparently limestone outcrops making it look, for me, like a sub-tropical version of the

Yorkshire Dales, with beautiful moorland spring flowers on the uncultivated areas. (More land is uncultivated here, a relatively backward, Arab-inhabited part of Israel.)

Soon we saw Arabs in burnous, light-coloured long hooded cloaks, and the road signs were in Arabic as well as in Hebrew and English. Driving up a winding road, we were told that a stony cliff a mile or two away was the place where Jesus, according to the New Testament, escaped pursuers by jumping from the cliff top without being hurt. No doubt our guide, being a Jew, did not believe this and of course I, too, as usual, was sceptical.

I had been warned that Arab Nazareth would be a disappointment, and it was, though I wouldn't have missed it for words. It is a mainly flat-roofed town of about 24,000 people, mostly Christian Arabs. Beautifully placed on the Galilean hills, it looks like a colourful gem from a distance. But when you get inside the place you see it is dirty, at least in the centre, and that it is devoted to the worst sort of biblical tourism. The main street has lots of shops selling tawdry souvenirs (the kind of thing you can buy in Blackpool). Guides and trinket sellers importune as one walks up a hill to the two holy places of the town.

We went first to the cave which is the traditional site of the Annunciation. A little plaque states that this is the place where Mary was told by an angel that she would conceive of the Holy Ghost and bear the Saviour. When we came to the cave, it was partly blocked by scaffolding for a new large church being built on the spot to replace one which stands nearby.

A passage in the rock leads down a few feet to an altar commemorating the Annunciation, near which a brown-robed friar sat on a chair reading a book. An Arab guide gave us a few details in broken English, like a character from a comic BBC radio programme, 'Here … laydees, chentlemen, is place of Annunciation … where Holy Ghost told Mary she would be mother of Christ … Mind your 'eads and watch your step.'

None of us was greatly impressed by this spot. Our guide, his patter at full pelt, took us further up the hill to another, smallish church, built over the traditional site of Jesus' family home, where, it was said, his father Joseph also had his carpenter's workshop.

This home, too, is a cave beneath the church. Said the guide, 'Here lived Holy Family … Down this hole was store for grain … This was hook for rope to pull up things … Mind your 'eads and watch your step.'

I was much more taken with this second shrine, for while it may not be the actual site of Christ's childhood home – it was designated as such in about AD 600 – it does give an idea of how the people of Nazareth lived in those days.

It darkened as we drove back to Jerusalem, finally on the same road we had started out on, where there are still wrecked or burnt-out lorries and armoured cars from Israel's war of independence in 1948–49.

Tonight we had an instance of one of the problems facing Israel's leaders: the news that Austrian-born Israel Baer, formerly one of the country's top military planners, had been arrested on suspicion of spying for a Communist country. In this melting pot for Jews with widely differing backgrounds, the government has to take largely on trust the personal histories of citizens. Baer, apparently once a Communist who broke with the Reds in the Stalin period, seems to have been tempted back again thanks to Khrushchev's brand of Communism. The story was passed by Israel's military censorship (not a tough censorship, Wally tells me).

16 April 1961 : Had a fascinating chat this Sunday evening with an Israeli police inspector with the historically resonant name of Dryfus, aged about 40, born in Mannheim, Germany, and looking much like a friendly Himmler when he has his British-style flat cap on. *[The name of Dryfus made me recall the case of the French-Jewish army officer, Alfred Dreyfus, who was falsely accused in 1894 of having betrayed military secrets to the Germans and was imprisoned until 1899, when he was pardoned.]*

Inspector Dryfus is one of the officers in charge of Eichmann's guard. Eichmann, he told me, was at present reading in his cell Bernard Shaw's *Everyman's Political What's What*, a biography of

French Colonial General Lyautey by André Maurois, and a romantic novel. Dryfus also gave me the gruesome news that Eichmann's favourite food was mincemeat. But most interesting to me was the view of this Israeli police officer on Germany, which he visited a year or two ago. After a tough argument I had him admit that a large proportion of Germans had not known about the Nazi mass murders of Jews, which did not take place in Germany.

However, Dryfus then told me this story: 'Sitting in a railway carriage on my visit to Germany, I was together with a German couple and their boy. The boy expressed the hope that his father might give him some extra pocket money if it turned out to be convenient to leave the train one station earlier, thus saving on the fare. His mother was livid and said, "Only a dirty Jew would have an idea like that."

'I stood up and said, "Madam, I am a member of the race you referred to. If you were not a so-called lady I would knock you down."

'Just then the husband, who had been out of the compartment, returned and his wife related what had happened. The husband said, "I must apologize for my wife's absolute stupidity."

'I said that after what had happened I hardly felt we should stay in the same compartment, and they moved to another one.'

What a striking illustration of how a stupid – and probably not really intentionally anti-Jewish – remark can cause ill feeling and help to block reconciliation. However, I'm happy to report that Dryfus told me he felt the husband had been sincere in condemning his wife. My experience in Germany has been that anti-Semitism is no longer a force. Of course, as someone once said to me, it hardly needs to be, in view of the fact that nearly all the German Jews were murdered or fled the country. Anyway, after being in Israel, I feel like punching anyone on the nose who starts being anti-Semitic.

24 Eichmann pleads 'Not guilty'

17 April 1961 : The trial really got under way when the judges ruled they were competent and not prejudiced.

Next came Eichmann's pleas of 'Not guilty' to the indictment's 15 counts, 12 of them liable to the death penalty. They were headed by the charge that he caused the murder of millions of Jews by gassing, shooting, starvation, beatings and forced deportations.

Then the prosecutor, Israel's balding Attorney-General, Gideon Hausner, began a nearly ten-hour address which did not finish today. It was an impressive piece of work for a lawyer whose experience has been in civil cases, and it will undoubtedly go down in history.

'Oh, Judges of Israel,' he began, 'the history of the Jewish people is steeped in suffering and tears. Pharaoh in Egypt decided to "afflict them with their burdens" and to cast their sons into the river.'

After referring to other persecutors of the Jews down the ages, he went on, 'Yet, never down the entire bloodstained road travelled by this people, never since the first days of its nationhood, has any man arisen who succeeded in dealing it such grievous blows as did Hitler's iniquitous regime, with Adolf Eichmann as its executive arm for the extermination of the Jewish people. In all human history there is no other example of a man against whom it would be possible to draw up such a bill of indictment as has been read here.'

'Murder,' the prosecutor continued, 'has been with the human race since the days when Cain killed Abel. But we have had to wait till this twentieth century to witness a new kind of murder, the result ... of a calculated decision and painstaking planning, not through the evil design of an individual, but through a mighty criminal conspiracy involving thousands ... not against one victim but against ... a whole nation.'

Everyone who has ever had a nasty thought about Jews – not only Germans – ought to read this statement. One thinks of the South African white supremacist government in reading the following words of Mr Hausner, 'Hitler denied the existence of a common basis for all humanity ... In place of the injunction, "And thou shalt love thy neighbour as thyself," we find, "Crush him that is unlike thyself."'

The prosecutor said that although tens of thousands of Germans had resisted Hitler, the 'decisive majority of the German people made peace with the new regime and were phlegmatic witnesses of the most terrible crime ever perpetrated in human history'.

[No one knows what percentage of the German people genuinely 'made peace' with Nazism once the dictatorship had been imposed. Even small signs of opposition could bring the death penalty. Further, it is incorrect to state that the German people were 'phlegmatic witnesses' of the mass murder of Jews, as the mass murders were carried out in Eastern Europe and were treated as a state secret.]

Sketching Eichmann's biography, Mr Hausner said he was born on 19 March 1906 in Solingen, Germany. He reached technical school level. In 1932 (the year before Hitler came to power), Eichmann, then living in Austria, joined the Nazi Party security organization, the SS, on the suggestion of a boyhood acquaintance, Ernst Kaltenbrunner, who later became the head of Nazi Germany's security authority, the *Reichsicherheitshauptamt* (RSHA).

[Kaltenbrunner was found guilty by the four-power war crimes court in Nuremberg after the Second World War of complicity in the murder of Allied soldiers and of millions of Jews, and was executed.]

In 1933, after the Nazis had come to power in Germany,

Eichmann was moved to Germany for military training and, Mr Hausner said, at the concentration camp of Dachau, near Munich, was 'taught the doctrine of hate'.

Eichmann joined the RSHA in Berlin and became an expert on Jewish affairs. After Austria's forcible inclusion into the German Reich in 1938, Eichmann was put in charge of an office in Vienna which compelled Austrian Jews to emigrate. Those who refused were arrested. He moved on to do the same task in Prague. In Vienna and Prague, Mr Hausner said, Eichmann used 'oppression, terror and intimidation – and, at the same time, the deliberate cultivation of the impression that "perhaps the Devil is not so bad after all" – that, perhaps, it might be possible to come to terms with him somehow'.

Back in Berlin in 1939, Eichmann directed expulsions of Jews and Poles from parts of German-occupied western Poland, and the collection of Jews from various places near Nisko, Poland – where the Nazis planned to set up a kind of Jewish state, but dropped the idea after strong opposition from the Nazi Governor of Central Poland, Hans Frank.

In March 1941, the prosecutor said, Eichmann took over as head of department IVB4, the Gestapo (secret police) department for Jewish affairs in the RSHA. He thus became 'the official executor of the extermination programme, with enormous authority in the German Reich ... and all the occupied countries'.

The prosecutor said that Eichmann would claim he had been obeying superior orders, but the conscience of the world 'speaking with the voice of the International Military Tribunal [the Nuremberg Tribunal] has declared that orders contrary to the principles of conscience and morality ... constitute no defence, legal or moral'.

Mr Hausner: 'But that is by no means all. We shall prove to the court that he went far beyond his actual orders. Eichmann engaged in the work of slaughter, not in apathy but with a clear mind, was fully conscious and aware of what he was doing, and believing that it was the right and proper thing to do; that was why he acted with all his heart and soul.

'He did not repent; he still believes that he did what was right and proper in destroying millions. He knows that today it is regarded as a crime, and will therefore be ready to give verbal and insincere expression of this view. But we have every reason to believe that if the swastika flag were again to be raised with shouts of "*Sieg Heil*", if there were again to resound the hysterical screams of a Führer, if again the high-tension barbed wires of extermination centres were set up – Adolf Eichmann would rise, salute and go back to his work of oppression and butchery.'

The prosecutor said it was not known whether the Nazis had planned from the start to exterminate the Jews, but it was known that there were various phases in their actions. At the start there was forced emigration. 'But when they found it could be done, that for all practical purposes the world was silent … they went over to total extermination.'

In between there had been a transitional phase in which the Nazis had toyed with the idea of a so-called territorial solution. (Occupied Poland and Madagascar were considered for this.)

Mr Hausner detailed the waves of anti-Jewish acts by the Nazis before the war, including the 'Crystal Night' ('Night of Broken Glass') of 9–10 November 1938, when synagogues and Jewish shops were smashed and Jews were attacked and arrested, after a young Jew, Hirschel Grynspan, whose family had shortly before been deported from Germany to Poland, killed a German Embassy counsellor in Paris, Ernst vom Rath.

The prosecutor described how the Jews were systematically forced out of the German economy and segregated more and more from non-Jews. Hitler had fused the Jews with his two mortal enemies: the capitalist West and the Communist East.

The German invasion of the Soviet Union and the entry of the United States into the war were the turning points in developing the extermination plans. Mass shootings of Jews began in the summer and autumn of 1941, carried out by special 'operational groups' of SS and police. And in August 1941 Eichmann wrote to the Foreign Office that it would be advisable to prevent any further Jewish emigration in the light of 'preparations for the final solution'.

That summer Eichmann had gone to the Auschwitz death camp in Poland to arrange technical details. And in October 1941 an official of the ministry for occupied territories wrote that agreement had been reached with Eichmann for the use of gas chambers. Also in 1941, Jews were ordered to wear a yellow 'Star of David'.

Mr Hausner went on to describe the 'Wannsee Conference' in Berlin on 20 January 1942, when the head of the RSHA, Reinhard Heydrich – who was assassinated later that year in Czechoslovakia – outlined 'the final solution' in somewhat guarded words. Heydrich said that Jews capable of work would be made to build roads in the east, and added, 'No doubt a large part of them will be eliminated by natural decrease.'

Those who remained, the most resistant group, would 'have to be dealt with appropriately', otherwise they would be the germ of a new increase in the Jewish race. The prosecutor alleged that Eichmann was put in charge of this extermination programme.

Mr Hausner continued, 'We shall see him issuing detailed directives for the implementation of the deportations to Auschwitz. We shall trace the activities of his men concerned with the supply of gas for killing Jews. We shall find him negotiating with the representatives of the puppet governments in order to persuade, to stimulate, to spur on the work. We shall follow him as he travels in the autumn of 1941 to Globocnik, SS and police chief in the Lublin region (of Poland), in order to transmit to him personally the secret command for the physical extermination of the Jews.

'Then he was also in Treblinka and in Chelmo, where gases were used for extermination. He witnessed in Chelmo a parade of naked Jews who had been stripped of their clothing and were waiting for their turn for death by asphyxiation with gas.

'He looked on as gold teeth were extracted from the mouths of his dead victims. He inspected the system of extermination, by means of vans expelling gas from their exhausts [into the interior of the vans].

'He was sent to examine the exterminations carried out by shooting. He saw the murderers in Minsk [Byelarus] shooting their victims in the back so that they fell into prepared graves.

'But direct murder by shooting did not satisfy him. "Our men will become sadists," he said. At another place Eichmann said that the method was not "elegant" enough for the purpose. A new method … was found in the gas chambers and crematoria of the extermination centres.'

On one occasion Eichmann had simply said, 'Shoot' on the telephone when asked by a Foreign Ministry official for confirmation of an order that 10,000 Serbian Jews should be disposed of in that way.

Mr Hausner gave many examples of the care Eichmann took to stop any Jews slipping out of the Nazi net. He went on, 'But no part of this bloody work is so shocking and terrible as that of the million Jewish children whose blood was spilt like water throughout Europe. How they were separated by force from their mothers who tried to hide them, murdered and thrown out of trucks in the camps, torn to pieces before their mothers' eyes, their little heads smashed on the ground – these are the most terrible passages in the tale of slaughter.'

Later sections of the prosecutor's address traced the catalogue of horrors which swept through European Jewry in the wake of the Nazi advance, but also included some flashes of light: resistance in some places to the Nazi plans to 'cleanse' Europe of Jews, in particular in the Netherlands, Denmark and Bulgaria.

One section dealt with one of the major spheres of Eichmann's personal activity, in which he succeeded, by June 1944, in having more than 430,000 Hungarian Jews sent off to the death camps out of about 800,000. More were sent later, but exact figures were not stated. It was particularly in this phase, according to Mr Hausner, that Eichmann exceeded his orders in his burning desire to have Jews killed.

The prosecutor went on to detail the horrors of the concentration camps, both the so-called 'labour camps' and the extermination camps. He said, 'The railway wagon doors open and the people, to the lashings of whips, are ordered to get out. The instructions are relayed over loudspeakers.

'Everyone is ordered to hand over clothes and belongings –

crutches and spectacles as well. The women and girls then go up to a barber who, with two cuts of the scissors, shears off their hair, which is placed in potato sacks.

'After this the march begins. To the right and left there are barbed wire fences and, at the rear, scores of Ukrainians with rifles. Men, women, girls, children, babies, one-legged people, all of them naked as the day they were born, march together.

'At the corner, before the entrance to the building, stands a smiling SS man, who declares in an ingratiating voice, "No harm will befall you. All you have to do is to breathe in deeply. This strengthens the lungs. Inhaling is necessary as a means of disinfection."

'He is asked what will happen to the women and replies that, of course, the men will have to work at road and housing construction. The women, he says, will not have to work.

'For a number of men there still flickers a lingering hope, sufficient to make them march without resistance to the gas chambers. The majority know with certainty what is to be their fate.

'The horrible smell that pervades everywhere reveals the truth. Then they climb the small steps and behold the reality. Silent mothers hold babies to their breasts, naked. They hesitate, but nevertheless proceed toward the death chambers, most of them without a word, pushed by those behind, chased by the whips of the SS men.

'A woman of about 40 curses the chief of the murderers, exclaiming that the blood of her children will be on his head. Wirth, an SS officer, himself strikes her in the face with five whip lashes, and she disappears into the gas chamber.

'Many pray. The SS men squeeze people into the chamber. Naked people stand on each other's toes. The doors close. The remainder of the transport stand waiting, naked.

'The diesel engine is not functioning. Fifty minutes pass by – 70 minutes. The people in the death chamber remain standing. Their weeping is heard. Professor Dr Pfannestiel, SS Sturmbannführer (Major), lecturer on hygiene at Marburg University, comments, "Like in a synagogue."

'Only after two hours and 49 minutes does the diesel finally begin to work. Twenty-five more minutes pass by. Many have already died, as can be seen through the small window. After 32 minutes all of them are dead.

'Jewish workers open the doors on the other side. The dead, having nowhere to fall, stand like pillars of basalt. Even in death, families may be seen standing pressed together, clutching hands.

'It is only with difficulty that the bodies are separated in order to clear the place for the next load. The blue corpses ... babies and bodies of children, are thrown out.

'But there is no time. Two dozen workers occupy themselves with the mouths of the dead, opening them with iron pegs, "With gold, to the left – without gold, to the right."

'Others search in the private parts of the bodies for gold and diamonds. Wirth displays a full tin can and exclaims, "Lift it up and see how much gold there is."'

At the entrance to the gas chambers were inscribed the words: 'Washing and Inhalation Equipment'. More than 600,000 were killed at Belzec, and another 2,500,000 at Auschwitz, the 'largest and most terrible of the death camps', according to the estimate of its commander, Rudolf Höss, later executed by the Poles.

The prosecutor said the court must fulfil the dying injunction of an anonymous poetess, who wrote before being put to death at Auschwitz:

> *There is no more hope in the white skull,*
> *Among the barbed wire under the ruins,*
> *And our dust is scattered in the dust,*
> *Out of the broken jars ...*
> *Our army will go forth, skullbone and jawbone,*
> *And bone to bone, a merciless line,*
> *We, the hunted, the hunters, will cry out to you:*
> *The murdered demand justice at your hands.*

Mr Hausner concluded by reciting some of the great names of European Jewry and referring to the tragedy of the relations between the Jews – who adopted a Germanic tongue, Yiddish, as their folk language and wrote in German the standard works on Jewish history and philosophy – and the Germans.

For no other country, he said, had Jews displayed the same enthusiasm and devotion as for Germany. But all that, including Jewish valour in the German Army in the First World War, had only served to fire the anger of the Nazis, and the Holocaust unleashed by them had destroyed European Jewry's ancient communities.

The prosecutor added, 'By the mercy of Providence, which preserved a saving remnant, Adolf Eichmann's design was frustrated. Adolf Eichmann will enjoy a privilege which he did not accord to even a single one of his victims. He will be able to defend himself before the court. And the judges of Israel will pronounce true and righteous judgment.'

18 April 1961 : The prosecution gave evidence about how the piles of documents – well over 1,000 – which are to be exhibited in the case, were obtained: mainly from Western Allied collections, including the library of the German Foreign Office which was captured after the war and brought to Britain.

Lionel amused us by telling us how he went on a bus trip last weekend and sat by a blonde American woman, whose Jewish lawyer husband from California was an observer at the trial. The woman told Lionel at length how she hated all Germans.

Finally, Lionel said innocently, 'My wife is German.'

The blonde woman replied rather unconvincingly, 'I'm sure she's very nice.'

19 April 1961 : The other night I heard my room-mate Lionel say in English-accented German, twice, 'Not now, darling.'

Tonight it was my turn to dream, but my subconscious chose another subject: Eichmann. I dreamt Eichmann was showing me round an extermination camp, and I was scared to disagree with anything he said. All kinds of horrors were to be seen, such as people with wounds or looking emaciated. And we entered a room fitted with plush sofas. (A room like this was described by the prosecutor. It was an antechamber at one camp, where sick people were taken to await their turn to be shot in the neck by an SS man in the next room.) I saw no SS men waiting, so presumed there was no shooting going on that day, perhaps because visitors were being shown around.

Today the prosecution began to play tape-recorded extracts from the eight-month interrogation of Eichmann. The full transcript runs to about one million words.

Eichmann sat impassive most of the time, his face occasionally twitching, as his voice – sounding sepulchral because of an echo in the pre-trial interrogation room – boomed around the courtroom.

In the first extract he said that the Nazis had used the Jewish people as an issue to draw attention away from difficulties.

The second extract was an account of how, shortly after Germany attacked the Soviet Union in 1941, Reinhard Heydrich, the security police chief, called in Eichmann and said, 'The Führer has ordered the physical extermination of the Jews.'

Eichmann went on, 'In the first moment I did not grasp his meaning, because he chose his words so carefully. Later I understood and did not reply. I had nothing to say. I had nothing to reply to such words, to such a brutal solution.'

Heydrich had sent him off to see how mass shootings, which had already begun, were being carried out in the Lublin area of occupied Poland by Odilo Globocnik, the SS and security police chief in that area.

Eichmann said he was shown a hut, and a police officer told him, 'Everything has been made air-proof; the engine of a Russian submarine will be started and the gases will enter this hut and the Jews will be poisoned.'

Eichmann went on, 'This was something terrible. I am not so strong that a thing like this would not move me at all. If today I see a gaping wound I cannot possibly look at it.'

Later, Eichmann said, he was sent to a place in the Warthegau, western Poland, and saw naked Jews put into a van. He added, 'I couldn't even look at it. All the time I was trying to avert my eyes from what was going on ... the screaming and the shrieking – I was too excited to have a look at the van.

'Afterwards I followed the van. And then I saw the most blood-curdling sight I have ever seen in my life. The van made for an open pit. The doors were flung open and corpses were cast out as if they were animals. I also saw how the teeth were being extracted with iron bars.'

Eichmann said, 'Then I knew I was washed up. It was quite enough for me.'

Back in Berlin he told his chief, Heinrich Müller, head of the Gestapo, 'It is horrible. It is an indescribable inferno. I cannot stand it.'

Müller was taciturn, as usual.

Eichmann also described seeing people shot in anti-tank ditches near Minsk, Byelarus. He had told Müller later that this would make Germans into sadists, that it was 'not a solution of the Jewish problem'. Müller made no comment.

Eichmann asked to be excused further visits to extermination sites, but later was sent to Auschwitz death camp in occupied Poland three times. There he did not watch gassing, but saw corpses piled up afterwards.

At Treblinka, another death camp in occupied Poland, he saw a file of naked Jews enter a large hall to be gassed. The station of Treblinka was fitted out with all kinds of German railway signs, to make it look like a place where one changed trains.

Eichmann said he had been compelled to be present at the infamous Wannsee Conference in Berlin on 20 January 1942, when plans for coordinating the extermination of the Jews were discussed between ministerial officials. Eichmann said, 'I took part for the first time in my life in such a conference, where high officials were present, like state secretaries *[deputy ministers]*. It was conducted quietly, with much politeness and friendliness. Brandy was served as the meeting concluded.'

Gradually the taped extracts built up a picture of Eichmann's part in the Nazi actions to exterminate European Jewry.

This evening, as Lionel and I began to read, and later to transmit, extracts from the one-million word transcript, Jerusalem began to echo with the sounds of revelry, on the eve of Israel's own bar mitzvah – coming-of-age on the 13th birthday of the Jewish state.

20 April 1961 : Lionel and I transmitted long excerpts from the transcript. We had an 18-minute beat over the American agency, the Associated Press, with a lead point: a statement by Eichmann that he had never been an anti-Semite.

21 April 1961 : We sent still more extracts, some read in court and some dug out by Lionel and me. We sent lots more today, around 6,000 words. We had our best play report of the trial so far today, with big usage of our stuff in Britain, the United States, Canada and Japan.

25 With the Eichmann tourists

22 April 1961 – Though tired, I went on another government-sponsored bus trip today, not knowing how long I shall be in this absorbing country. I took with me a further book – about 179,000 words – of the six-volume transcript, leaving Lionel to work on another one on his day on duty in Jerusalem.

Our trip took us first of all to Nazareth again where, instead of visiting the shrines once more, I bought some rough and genuine Arab pottery in a colourful street market.

As we drove, I read more of the transcript, and also discussed the case with Mr Mandellaub, an American Jewish lawyer reporting the case for the *American Journal of International Law*. He was a member of the prosecution team at the four-power Nuremberg war crimes trials.

Mr Mandellaub told me did not think Eichmann ought to be sentenced to death, partly because it is a long time since he committed his crimes and he is now a different person. Mandellaub seemed to accept in the main Eichmann's claims that he was simply someone carrying out orders, and not a very high-up one at that.

Eichmann adds that he realizes that the defence of 'superior orders' was no longer acceptable today, and that he faces the death penalty. He also says that he would be prepared to hang himself publicly if that would help to atone. Before that he would write a book as a warning to other anti-Semites.

I have the impression at this stage that the prosecution has blown up Eichmann to a figure he never really was. A few days ago, though I normally oppose the death penalty, I regarded it as fitting because of the enormity of his crimes. Now I am not sure at all. It might redound to Israel's credit to give him life instead.

From Nazareth we descended the mountains to Lower Galilee, the region around Lake Tiberias (the Lake of Galilee), a fairyland reminiscent of some of the Swiss and North Italian lakes. Lake Tiberias, some ten miles by five, is roughly plum-shaped, and forms the north-eastern part of Israel.

On the eastern shore the Syrian border is no more than a stone's throw away at the most. Mountains rise to about 2,000 feet *[610 m]* near the lake, with higher peaks further away, particularly to the north in Lebanon. We glimpsed patches of snow on one of them.

The road took us near the Mount of the Beatitudes, a green hill topped by a chapel, where Jesus preached the Sermon on the Mount. We drove down into Tiberias, one of the few towns which remained a centre of Jewry during the Diaspora.

I had some tasty fish from the lake. It was a remarkable feeling to be eating fish from that lake, descendants perhaps of fish netted by the disciples, or those *[allegedly]* fed to the five thousand.

We drove north a few miles to the little village of Capernaum where, in 1925, the ruins of a large second or third-century AD Greek-style synagogue were unearthed. It is believed that on that same site there stood an earlier synagogue where Jesus did much of his early preaching.

On the south-eastern side of Lake Tiberias, we visited a kibbutz, a collective settlement with about 400 members. One member, a middle-aged man, told us that membership was voluntary. (About 100,000 of Israel's population of about 1,800,000 are kibbutz members.)

The kibbutzim are mainly agricultural, but some have factories. Members give up what capital they have to a communal fund and receive no wages – just a small amount of pocket money for little private purchases. This handsome bronzed man went on to tell us that the kibbutz supplies its members with housing, clothing and food, as well as communal facilities such as dining-rooms, laundries and kindergartens.

A minority of the kibbutzim are religion-based, while others follow some Jewish observances, such as eating kosher food, out of a feeling of national tradition. The spokesman said that the children were looked after communally from birth, and slept in communal bedrooms.

The children came to their parents from four to eight in the evenings, to be with them either in the communal dining and recreation rooms or in their family flat, usually consisting of two rooms and a small kitchen.

The communal element in the kibbutzim has been somewhat reduced in recent years. In some, I gather, all meals were formerly taken communally, but now some of them are eaten at home. Parents can go along to the communal nurseries to tuck in their kiddies and kiss them good night.

The spokesman said that when he had joined the kibbutz he had not been convinced that the communal life of the children, to the extent it was practised, was a good thing. But now he was.

We peeped into his neat flat, which included a well-stocked bookcase. (The kibbutz movement has produced healthy people, who are also noted for filling their leisure with a large amount of cultural activity. However, their appeal is limited to idealists, and they are finding it hard to maintain their level of membership. Earlier it was regarded as the done thing to go into a kibbutz rather than to university, but now that attitude is declining. Many immigrant Jews, often primitive people from North Africa or the Orient, don't understand why they should work without pay. They prefer to become small farmers, working for themselves, with some restricted cooperation in machine use and marketing).

As we talked, the sun went down behind the mountains, and the blue of the Sea of Galilee darkened. I picked up a handful of pebbles as souvenirs.

We stopped at a small café late at night for refreshments. No one spoke anything but Hebrew, so I drew a picture and clucked, then held up two fingers, and received two fried eggs in quick time. I did the same thing for blonde anti-German Mrs Hurwitz from California, and she was grateful.

23 April 1961 : The courthouse re-opened after the Sabbath break, and we sent final extracts from the Eichmann transcript, including his statement that he had known someone was on his track and had decided not to flee again, as he had a wish to atone, having heard that today's German youth felt guilty about what the Nazis had done.

24 April 1961 : Most of today's proceedings were occupied by a 'historical witness', Professor Salo Baron, Professor of Jewish history in Columbia University, New York, who depicted the Nazis' acts against the Jews as worse than anything in history. This kind of evidence appeared to many reporters (including me) to be out of place in court.

Among documents submitted to the court today were 127 handwritten pages of memoirs by Eichmann, of which I obtained a copy. Lionel and I had a tough job extracting something from them, because the handwriting was partly in German Sütterlin script – which I learnt at school but have almost forgotten – and was in parts not written clearly. It was almost like working on the Dead Sea Scrolls. In these memoirs Eichmann repeats his story that he was trained from the nursery to obey and that's why he did what he did. He says that his facial twitch dates from the time when he was forced to see the horrors of mass extermination himself.

We also heard today from little, bearded Mr Zindel Gruenspan, a Polish Jew who lived in Hanover from 1911 to 1938, when the Nazis expelled him and his family into Poland with thousands of other Polish Jews. A few days later his son, Herschel, then living in Paris, having received news of the Nazi action, assassinated a minor official at the German Embassy in Paris, Ernst vom Rath.

The Nazis used the murder as a pretext for their 'Crystal Night' wave of attacks on synagogues and Jewish businesses on 9–10 November 1938, their largest-scale measure against the Jews until then.

25 April 1961 : The court used its powers to waive normal rules of evidence, powers granted under the 1950 law on Nazis and Nazi collaborators, in order to admit a Nuremberg affidavit made by a former close associate of Eichmann executed in 1946 in Czechoslovakia. *[I did not note the name.]* Such evidence would normally be excluded as hearsay but, as in the Nuremberg trials, exceptions can be made, in view of the difficulties of proving certain things because of the time that has elapsed and the death (often through execution or suicide) of important witnesses who left written material.

Written statements by Rudolf Höss, the last commandant of Auschwitz, whom the Poles executed, were also admitted.

26 April 1961 : A living witness, Dr Franz Meier, a former Zionist official and ex-Berliner, drew a picture of a 'Jekyll-and-Hyde Eichmann'. He said that in 1936 or 1937 Eichmann was polite, seemed sincerely interested in Jewish affairs and helped to iron out some difficulties. In 1939 he was 'coarse and impertinent … a man who regarded himself as master of life and death'.

Documents being submitted are building up a picture of the means used by the Nazis to exclude the Jews from the German economy, to segregate them from Aryans and force them to emigrate.

27 April 1961 : The vile nature of the Nazi leaders is shown as well as anything by excerpts from a transcript of a meeting in about 1939, called to discuss further measures in excluding the Jews from the German body politic. Propaganda Minister Josef Goebbels expresses annoyance that it is still possible for a Jew to share a railway sleeping-car compartment with an Aryan. Another top Nazi, Hermann Göring, suggests – maybe this passes for humour – that a special part of the 'German forest' be set apart for Jews, and populated also with animals resembling them, such as elks with their hooked noses.

Today we had several witnesses of Eichmann's role in forcing the emigration to occupied Eastern Europe of Jews from

Czechoslovakia. Tribute was paid to a British consular official in Czechoslovakia who helped Czechoslovaks to obtain papers to travel to the West. There was a similar tribute the other day, to another British consul, in Berlin. In other evidence there appears criticism, direct and indirect, of countries which did not do as much as they could to grant entry permits for Jews.

28 April 1961 : Mrs Ada Lichtmann, a Polish-born Jew, gave her evidence in Yiddish – which means 'Jewish' and is largely a German dialect – once again showing the close links Jews had for centuries with the Germans. She told the court how her father was taken out, with 31 other men, and shot, for no reason, by Nazis. She also said that, on the order of German troops or police, paraffin was poured over religious Jews and set alight as they prayed.

We have also heard evidence about Eichmann's appearance in Poland in late 1940 during an abortive attempt to settle Jews in a 'state' of their own in occupied central Poland.

29 April 1961 : Wally Wallenstein, our Israel correspondent, kindly showed us Tel Aviv, where he lives, this Saturday. With him was his pretty German-born wife, Shula, who is an assistant district attorney specializing in tax cases. Her family left Nuremberg in 1933 after her father had been briefly under arrest. Although Wally's name sounds German, he is the great grandson of a Hungarian rabbi, who came to Jerusalem to die in the nineteenth century and managed to found a family there instead. Wally is not religious, neither is his father.

The religious party in Israel, representing about 15–20 per cent of the population, has much power, as it often holds the balance in parliament. As a result, various regulations are in force which are not wanted by the majority, though some other things which seem strange to Christians are supported by the majority out of traditional rather than purely religious reasons. Wally told us, for instance, that there was a ban on keeping pigs in urban areas, but they can be kept in the country. (The Jewish religion would ban them entirely.)

The toughest clash concerns religious education, where no one wants to compromise. At present around 15 per cent of pupils attend religious schools subsidized by the state, like Roman Catholic schools in Britain.

I found Tel Aviv, Israel's commercial capital and largest city, pleasanter than expected. Mainly concrete buildings, built on stilts to give ground-floor open-air shade, large balconies. About 500,000 of the total population of 1,800,000 live in Tel Aviv and suburbs.

Wally and Shula have a pleasant flat of, I think, three rooms.

On the sands near a beautiful beachside hotel, I asked Shula about her feelings concerning the Germans. She apparently does not blame all Germans for the Nazis' crimes.

She is not religious and does not believe that the Jews are a 'chosen people', but that they are no better and no worse than anyone else. She agreed that in a way the 'chosen people' belief was akin to the Nazi 'master race' belief, except that it was supposed to make the Jews behave better than others, not to oppress others.

South of Tel Aviv is the former Arab town of Jaffa, still with about 5,000 Arabs living there. We went to eat a fish lunch at an outdoor table on the seafront by a crumbling minaret and an orange-washed Franciscan church.

Later, at the Wallensteins', Shula served typically German apple cake and whipped cream. Her mother, whom we did not meet, speaks much more German than Hebrew.

We later drove to Dizengoff Street, a crowded boulevard. One sees few poor people, apart from the Arabs, in Israel, but the country continues to be subsidized from abroad to the tune of about £50 per head per year, according to some incomplete figures Wally showed me. Exports are going up, however.

Most people appear happy, like the Romanian-born Jew who saw me reading the Soviet newspaper *Izvestia* earlier today and started to talk to me. He said he was very happy here among his own people, and asked me, 'Are you a Jew?' (Just another proof that Jews have many different kinds of faces.)

Late in the evening Wally, our two teleprinter operators, Reg and Ted, and I went to an Israeli night club in a former Arab house, thick-walled and small-windowed. Here we heard a darkish Yemenite Jewish girl sing several songs. (The Yemenite Jews, mainly primitive and very religious people, were brought to Israel some years ago in an airlift. When the new state of Israel had been set up, they had believed that the Messiah had at last come, and that they were fulfilling a biblical prophecy which spoke of Jews returning to the Promised Land 'on eagles' wings'.)

30 April 1961 : I spoke to one of the assistant defence lawyers, 29-year-old Dieter Wechtenbruch, who told me it was not excluded that the defence would try to call Dr Hans Globke, Adenauer's State Secretary. Globke wrote the official commentary to the Nazis' Nuremberg racial laws, one of the first major steps to set the Jews apart from Aryans. This suggestion that Globke might be called upon to give evidence could be an indirect threat to the West German authorities to change their refusal, so far, to contribute towards the costs of Eichmann's defence.

I later spoke to spade-bearded Mr Yaacov Bar-Or, an assistant prosecutor, born in Frankfurt, Western Germany, who several times told me he could not understand why the Germans – or sufficient of them – had done what they did to the Jews. He told me his father had once said to him that only two peoples had a similarly tragic history – the Jews and the Germans.

Bar-Or agreed with my suggestion that the prosecution had blown up Eichmann beyond his proper importance, and said that this would encourage some Germans to say, as it were, it was 'all Eichmann's doing'. In his view some of the German Foreign Office people were more guilty than Eichmann because they were more intelligent.

1 May 1961 : Angry shouts shattered the courtroom hush today as Mr Yaacov Gurfein, a Polish-born Jew, described how his mother pushed him out of a train bound for the extermination camp of Belzec, in occupied Poland, and how, evading shots from

254

SS guards, he hid in snow and eventually escaped through Slovakia, Hungary, Romania and Turkey to Israel.

The shouts came from 46-year-old Mr Zvi Schaefer, who cried out, 'All my family was killed. Bloodhound. Murderer.'

Later, sobbing bitterly after police had hustled him out, Schaefer told a bunch of reporters, including me, that all but four of his 62 relatives had been killed in the death camps after they had been deported from his native Hungary.

'Why don't they kill him? Why do they try him?' he asked.

I can understand his feelings, but it is, of course, much better to try Eichmann. It is surprising there has been no earlier interruption in the trial, now entering its fourth week, as many victims of the Nazis have been in the public gallery.

Today we had some of the most gripping evidence of the trial from Dr Leon W. Wells, a New Jersey Jew born in Lvov, Ukraine, who was put into a concentration camp near his home, fell ill, and was earmarked for death. With 181 other prisoners he was marched to the planned burial place.

Two by two the victims dug their own graves and were then shot down in them. The next two covered up with earth the last two to have been shot and were then shot in their turn. As he was walking down into a grave to be shot, an SS officer ordered him back and told him to return to the concentration camp to fetch the body of a prisoner who had been shot there, and bring him to be buried.

As Wells went away, the shootings continued. He reached the camp, took the body of the dead man and, preceded by an SS guard, off back to the burial site again. On the way he spotted another group of prisoners, gave the SS man the slip and mingled with the group. He escaped from the camp after his death had been announced on the following day – thus removing the fear of reprisals against comrades or relatives because of his escape.

2 May 1961 : Dr Wells, continuing his evidence, said he was put in another concentration camp later and was made a member of 'Special Unit 1005', the so-called 'death brigade' used by the

Nazis to try to erase traces of mass executions in Eastern Europe. With an expression of disgust on his ruddy face, and occasional sobbing in the courtroom, he described how this unit collected scores of thousands of bodies and burned them on pyres. Anything not burned to ash was put through a grinding machine, 'like a cement mixer'.

The Nazis had lists giving the position and exact number of executed people in various places around Lvov. Dr Wells told how, one day, he was ordered to exhume what the SS thought was his own body, along with the 181 other corpses of the persons shot on the day he had escaped. When the SS found there were only 181 corpses, the unit searched for two days to find the missing body: Dr Wells' own.

Finally, Dr Wells said, when almost all the Jews in the area had been shot and cremated, he and a few comrades escaped, while others, sacrificing themselves so that the world would perhaps learn of the horrors, sang or played musical instruments in an attempt to mask the sounds made as the escapees overpowered guards. Just how he survived the rest of the war was not revealed in court.

Documents submitted showed the link between Eichmann's office and these and similar events described by other witnesses.

Tonight Wally, Lionel and I went to hear Dr Friedrich Kaul, a burly East German star lawyer and Communist, of Jewish race but not of Jewish religion, speak at a press conference staged – ill-advisedly in view of its propaganda nature – by the Israeli Journalists' Association.

Kaul's obvious purpose in coming here is to continue the – in itself, justified – East German campaign against Dr Hans Globke, Chancellor Adenauer's State Secretary (Deputy Minister), who has admitted playing a part as a Nazi Interior Ministry official, in preparing some Nazi racial laws and in writing, together with an SS officer who was also a State Secretary, a commentary on the 1935 Nuremberg Laws (passed by the rubberstamp Nazi *Reichstag* meeting in Nuremberg), which provided the ideological basis for the later extermination of European Jews.

Adenauer has stood by Globke, whose defence is that, as a Roman Catholic, he was asked by his Church and members of his former party, the Catholic Centre Party, to remain in his official post, which he had held in the Weimar period, so that he could tip off the Church about impending Nazi moves and do his best to ameliorate the worst measures which passed through his hands.

Most people who know the facts about Globke, whether they are Communist or not, think his case is at least sufficiently doubtful to make it imperative he quit his present post. Indeed, it is said that he has offered to do so, but Adenauer has asked him to stay on.

However, Dr Kaul, the representative of a dictatorial puppet regime, and with no great skill in holding a press conference for non-East Germans, was a poor advocate. The press conference, which produced nothing new about Globke, soon degenerated largely into a shouting match, with Kaul and members of the audience alternately losing their temper.

3 May 1961 : Two highlights today. The first: a Polish-born witness, Dr Adolf Bemann, produced in court a tiny pair of crumpled children's shoes, held them up reverently and said, 'They are very precious. They represent a million children.'

He said he had brought the shoes from the site of Treblinka death camp in occupied Poland.

The second: as Yitzhak Zuckermann, a ginger-haired hero of the Jewish uprising in the Warsaw Ghetto, told his story, the windowless courtroom suddenly blacked out when a lorry outside hit an electricity pylon. A split second later emergency lights in the courtroom roof snapped on, casting two beams through the bullet-proof glass of the dock and onto Eichmann's grim face.

There he sat, still, spotlighted, like the villain in a thriller play, while the courtroom audience, still in darkness, murmured at the eerie sight. I shan't forget that picture. It lasted for several minutes until the presiding judge decided to adjourn the court until the circuit was restored.

26 Orthodox – and other – Jews

5 May 1961 : Further evidence today about mass shootings of Jews in the Baltic states. One Jew said it was not until 1944 that he had learned that mass killings were going on in Auschwitz. This indicates that not many people knew about the killings then – including Germans, as this man was nearer and personally more concerned about the issue.

After the court had adjourned for our usual long weekend, Lionel and I walked a mile or so from our hotel to Mount Zion – a hill, really – the last bit of Israeli territory next to the roughly 25-feet high *[8 m]*, massive sandstone walls of the Old City, where Jordan begins.

Mount Zion is a holy place for Jews and, I suppose, for Christians too, for on it is the tomb of King David, from whom the Messiah had to be descended, according to scripture. From a guidebook, I learn that King David conquered Jerusalem in 1000 BC, around the time that the 'land of milk and honey' was shared out between the Jewish tribes.

One of the buildings on Mount Zion is the reputed site of the Last Supper. From a vantage point on a minaret-like tower, we looked down on part of the Old City, with its flat-roofed houses, domed mosques and the Holy Sepulchre church.

We saw no sign of Jordanian soldiers as we passed within a few yards of a rusty barbed-wire entanglement marked with signs in Hebrew, English and French saying: 'Frontier – Enemy Territory'.

6 May 1961 : Lionel and I set forth this Sabbath (Saturday) morn, intending to do some sketching in the Mea Sherim quarter of Jerusalem, where strictly Orthodox Jews live. We were fortunate in coming upon a friendly, middle-aged and non-Orthodox Jewish couple, Riga-born Boris Barkai and his Vienna-born wife Fanny. They walked with us to Mea Sherim.

As soon we entered the Orthodox quarter, half a dozen young boys, all wearing skull caps and sporting the traditional side curls – fulfilling a biblical instruction not to put a sharp knife to the face – came towards us. They started shouting at me, not menacingly, but loudly, 'Shabes!' This is the Yiddish word for Sabbath, and it was obvious after a few seconds that they were complaining about something. Barkai, knowing their dogmas, spotted it: it was the pencil I had in the outside breast pocket of my jacket. A pencil is a tool, and no work is allowed on the Sabbath, so they were objecting. Lionel and I had intended to stay in their quarter and sketch, so we gave up that idea for today.

After I had put the pencil away in my inside pocket, quietening the lads, Barkai had a conversation with them in Yiddish. Lionel and I understood part of the mixture of German and Hebrew, mainly the former.

Barkai told us that Orthodox Jews do not speak Hebrew as an everyday language, as they regard it as holy and not to be profaned by normal use. They read Hebrew newspapers, but don't use them for such profane purposes as wrapping paper, but burn them after reading them.

The young boys, wearing long stockings and otherwise fairly normal clothes – the stockings to cover up their flesh, regarded by Orthodox Jews as indecent, just like some Catholics – were a cheerful lot, continually chewing sunflower seeds as they chatted. Barkai asked them about Eichmann and they said he should be hanged because he had killed Jews.

In various nearby houses live Jews from several national groups. Their ancestors were sent a generation or two, or more, ago to live here – financed from their homelands – and occupy themselves entirely with learning the scriptures and praying.

Now, however, they work. Their children attend religious schools. The numbers of such people, only a small minority in Israel, remain about constant, Barkai told us.

At the entrance to this quarter is a notice in Hebrew requesting visitors to respect the religious feelings of the inhabitants and not to enter if they are 'indecently' dressed. For a woman, that means she should have her legs and neck covered, no short sleeves and, if she is married, her crowning glory should be covered up too, in case it may arouse the lust of someone not her husband.

Some of the Jewish men we saw in the Orthodox quarter wore black, silky coats and black hats with a thick 'halo' of fur around them, something which looked Russian to me but which, I read later, is supposed to have originated from Germany.

The reaction shown towards me by the lads who saw my exposed pencil is a frightening example of how bigoted religious teaching can affect children.

Later Lionel and I did get down to a spot of pencil sketching – with the Dormition Monastery and Mount Zion for our subject.

7 May 1961 : On this Sunday, thought it was about time I went to church in Jerusalem and persuaded Lionel to accompany me. We found out there was a service of the American Missionary Alliance, which occupies a small church, similar to many British Free Churches.

Soon we were sitting in a Sunday-school basement room, for all the world as if we were in my hometown, Bradford, with the usual plain wooden seats, a harmonium and somewhat grubby stained-glass windows. The young pastor, Mr Kroh, and his wife, greeted us warmly, telling us that the service was being held in that room because the congregation was too small to fill the church above. The church used to serve a congregation mainly of Christian Arabs, now refugees in Jordan, or residents of Jordan – which begins just up the road – who can no longer come there.

I enjoyed the rousing hymns, some of them Wesleyan, and it was a new experience to hear Mr Kroh quoting from the New Testament passages referring to places I have now visited. For instance, he spoke about Jesus' having healed someone on a Sabbath at Capernaum and how the Pharisees criticized him for that.

He referred to Jesus' insistence that he was the Messiah and, in an aside, about the obstinacy of the Pharisees, who were always studying the law but, according to Jesus, did not know the truth. Mr Kroh mentioned the Orthodox Jerusalem Jews, like the ones we saw yesterday. He said that even today one could see them studying the Old Testament all day long, rocking backwards and forwards. Later there was Holy Communion, which Lionel and I declined, not feeling that we had sufficient belief in the dogmas attached to taking it in this church.

This afternoon we did watercolours, at the same spot. I did the monastery again, while Lionel started to paint a broken-down house. I'm sure his effort would have been good had it not been for half a dozen friendly cheeky brown-eyed Israeli kiddies who crowded round and started feeling the wetness of the blue skies we had painted.

This did not disturb me much, but rattled Lionel sufficiently for him to stop work on his painting, which he allowed one of the kids to take away, and to start drawing the kids instead. I used one of my few Hebrew words to try to calm one of the girls: '*nudnik*' (a nuisance, bore or bother). I pointed at her, said the word, and one of the lads gave her a slight clout, which calmed things for a few moments.

They didn't beg, though obviously not well off; nearly all the children here look well looked after, unlike in the Arab countries I have visited. However, I gave them about one shilling and six-pence *[7¹/₂p]* to share.

8 May 1961 : I did not think there could be anything more horrible, or moving, than some of the evidence we had already heard in the Eichmann trial. I was wrong.

Today Mrs Rivka Yosselevski, a sad-faced brunette, told how she was driven by SS men to be shot with other Jews near Pinsk, Byelarus, on a small hillock where a pit had been dug. My pencil almost refused to write as the woman, fighting back her tears, said, 'And the four devils shot each one of us separately. They were SS men, armed to the teeth. While we had been lined up in the village my child had said, "Mother, why do you make me wear my Sabbath dress? We are being taken to be shot." As we stood near the pit, she said, "Why are we waiting, let's run!"

'Some of the young people tried to run, but they were caught immediately. They were shot right away. Children were taking leave of their parents. We were already undressed. Our father did not want to undress. We begged my father to undress, but he would not. He did not want to stand naked. And then they tore the clothes of the old man and he was shot.

'And then they took my mother. She said, "Let us go ahead." They got mother and shot her too. And then there was my grandmother, my father's mother, standing there. She was 80 years old and had two children in her arms.

'Then came my father's sister – she also had children in her arms – and she too was shot on the spot with the babies in her arms.

'My younger sister ... begged of the Germans. Naked, she went up to the German with one of her girl friends. They were embracing each other and, standing there naked, asked to be spared. He looked into her eyes, shot both of them and they fell together, still embracing.

'Then my second sister was shot, and then my turn came ... We turned towards the grave, and he asked, "Whom shall I shoot first?" I did not answer.

'I felt him take the child from my arms. The child cried out and was shot immediately. Then he aimed at me. First he took hold of my hair and turned my head round. I remained standing.

'I heard a shot. I continued to stand and then he aimed the revolver at me and ordered me once again to turn my head round, and shot at me. And then I fell to the ground into the pit among the bodies and felt nothing.

'I felt a sort of heaviness and then I thought, "Maybe I am not alive any more." Then I felt I was choking, people falling over me. I tried to move and felt that I was alive and that I could rise.

'I heard the shots and I was praying for another bullet to put an end to my sufferings, but I continued to move. I tried to save myself. I felt that I was climbing towards the top of the grave.

'I rose above the bodies and I felt the bodies pulling at me with their hands, biting me, legs were pulling me down, down. And yet, with the last of my strength, I came up on top of the grave.'

The Germans had gone.

Mrs Yosselevski, parting her greying brunette hair, showed the court the scars from the bullet wound on the back of her head.

She said that after climbing from the grave, not wanting to live, she saw from a nearby field how the Germans returned and rounded up a few other survivors, shooting them and then covering up the grave.

When the Germans went away, she tried feebly to scratch open the grave to die herself, but had not enough strength. Days later a farmer found her and took her in. She finally hid out in woods with Jewish partisans until the Soviet Army came.

9 May 1961 : Partly due to Mrs Yosselevki's evidence, we sent about 9,000 words yesterday, and were told by London today – the first instruction of this kind we have received – that it was excessive, and that we should aim at a maximum of 5,000 words a day unless things are sensational. The message, from Doon Campbell, the news manager, added that our stuff, in both timing and content, continued to be top and took nearly all the British play for agency material today.

The only witness to testify today was Georges Wellers, a French scientist, who revealed that René Blum, director of the Monte Carlo ballet and brother of pre-war French Socialist Premier Leon Blum, had been tortured before being killed in Auschwitz in 1942.

He also recalled the day when he and René Blum spoke in Auschwitz with a seven-year-old French-Jewish boy, Jacques Stern, one of 4,000 Jewish children who had been separated from their parents, put in Drancy concentration camp near Paris and were later sent to Auschwitz.

The boy had told them, 'My father goes to the office. My mother plays the piano. She is a good player.'

He asked when he would see his parents again. The two men knew it would be never, but Wellers told him it would only be a day or two.

The lad took from the pocket of his now-ragged jacket an army ration biscuit of which he had eaten half. 'I shall keep the other half for Mummy,' he told them. And as René Blum, 'a most sensitive man', bent down to take boy's head in his hands, the lad burst into tears.

The prosecution submitted documents showing how even the French puppet leader, the Fascist Pierre Laval, used delaying tactics to hold up the deportations of French Jews, even though he had not been concerned about foreign and stateless Jews.

Documents also showed how Eichmann and his subordinates would hardly ever let go of a Jew, whatever the reason. In one case, an inventor, Abraham Weiss, who had devised a new kind of electric bulb which could have been useful for the German war effort, was referred to by one of Eichmann's subordinates, who asked whether the man should be spared. Eichmann replied that, as the man had already patented his invention at the Reich Patents Office, there could no longer be any interest in him. 'Send him off with the next deportation,' he ordered.

Dr Hans Stercken, a senior official of the Federal Press Office, an observer at the trial, told me and two of my Reuter colleagues an interesting story about the Moscow talks in late 1955 of a West German delegation headed by Adenauer. During those talks the West Germans agreed to take up diplomatic relations with the Soviet Union.

Stercken, who was a member of the delegation, said he was sitting in a Kremlin reception room when Khrushchev came up to him and another official, who had only one arm. Khrushchev, speaking a little German, asked the one-armed man where he had lost his arm. He replied, 'In the war in Russia.'

Khrushchev replied that war was bad. Then he turned to the two men and, Stercken recounted, said in German, '*Deutschland*

... Russland ... zusammen (together) *... ganze Welt kaputt* (whole world done for).' Stercken said that was the line Khrushchev was putting to Adenauer, though Khrushchev had said he did not expect the West Germans to go Communist.

10 May 1961 : We heard evidence today from a Dutch-born official of the Israeli Education Ministry, Dr Josef Melkman. He and his wife were deported *[apparently early in the war]* to Belsen concentration camp near Hanover, not an extermination camp. They had a semi-privileged status as they had applied to emigrate under the auspices of a Zionist organization.

Before he was deported to Belsen, a Gentile woman had taken their 14-month-old son into hiding. But as the Germans had a document, prepared for the planned emigration, showing that they had a child, they obtained a child of the same age from a non-privileged Jewish deportee. The mother of that child was deported to the death camp of Sobibor in Poland and did not return.

Dr Melkman and his wife looked after the child until their liberation from Belsen in 1945. He is now a student in Israel. Their own son survived too.

Today's hearing ended with heart-warming evidence from the 35-ish son of Denmark's Chief Rabbi, a man called Melchior, who described how nearly all the 8,000 Jews of Denmark were saved from the Nazis by their fellow citizens, including King Christian. The Danes blocked the Nazis' efforts to round up Jews, and helped most of them to escape to Sweden.

In his first letter from his boarding school, Ackworth, in Yorkshire, Robin told us he was keeping in his purse a pebble I sent him from Galilee. He will be 13 tomorrow.

11 May 1961 : Evidence today about Italy where, until the Germans took over power after Mussolini was ousted in July 1943, the Nazis were not able to get far with their anti-Jewish measures. It seems that anti-Semitism was not part of the ideology of the Italian Fascist dictatorship.

A Jewish woman who lived in Italy, Mrs Hulda Campagnano, gave a moving account of how good-hearted Gentiles helped her and five children, her own and her brother's, to escape the clutches of the Jew-hunters.

12 May 1961 : Mordecai Ansbacher, born a German Jew in Würzburg, described life in the 'model' ghetto of Theresienstadt, Czechoslovakia, which the Nazis used as a front for visiting Red Cross delegations and the like. He described how the camp was prettified before visits by such delegations.

'The most appalling thing of all was a glass palace set up for the occasion as a "children's home", a beautiful structure complete with toys, wooden horses, tiny clean cots, good food.

'They had to take the children for "rehearsals", and the children swooped down on food they had never seen before in the camp.'

13 May 1961 : This Saturday morning I joined a party of about 20 journalists for a two-day trip to the Dead Sea. We drove in one of Egged's most elderly buses, evidently made in the thirties, long before the state of Israel was created.

First we drove south-west, through the stony but cultivated Judaean hills, until we reached the central north-south road and turned south-east into the Negev, the southern desert which forms more than half the land of Israel. Formerly part of Palestine, it was allocated to the Arabs when the British mandate ended in 1948 and was occupied by the Israelis during the war started by the Arabs in 1948.

Gradually fields of grain, grass or fruit trees give way to scrubland, and the dominating colour becomes the fawn of the stony, rather than sandy, desert. The good but not too wide asphalt road is mainly flat as it passes through the first stretch of rolling desert on the way to Beersheba, some 20 miles from the edge of the cultivated land.

This is Bedouin country. The typical scene has four or five patched black or brown tents, each apparently big enough to hold a family of a dozen or so. Goats – also black – graze nearby, with a mule or two as personal transport for the men, and a camel train wends its way over one of the hills.

Now that frontiers hem them in, these traditionally nomadic people are restricted in Israel to a comparatively small area, so that some of them – encouraged by the state – have become residents of certain areas (still in their tents). Some of their chiefs have houses.

Other Bedouins still wander within Israel's desert areas, and occasionally some of them cross the largely unguarded desert frontiers. The Bedouins belong to numerous tribes and sometimes feud among themselves, bronzed Joe Davis, New Zealand-born Israeli Press Office spokesman, our guide today, told me.

He said that Muslim tradition allowed them four wives each and unrestricted numbers of concubines, but Israeli law – itself diverging from the rulings of some Jewish sects which allow more than one wife – lays down monogamy. Bedouins who already have their four wives are allowed to keep them, but their religious leaders are liable to punishment, along with the Bedouins concerned, if they sanction bigamy.

There is no civil marriage under Israeli law – a concession to the religious minority who regard civil marriage as invalid. If there were civil marriage, this would make the children of civil marriages illegitimate, according to the religious Jews, and would cause complications in future generations, because religious Jews are not allowed to marry such people as a rule.

The nomadic Bedouins, whose dark robes looked rather ragged, live like the Jews did at the time of Abraham – about 2,000 BC, when the Jews lived in Chaldea, Mesopotamia, before they began their wanderings which eventually brought them to the Promised Land.

Goats feed on the sparse grass which grows here and there even in the desert proper, usually in depressions where the infrequent rain collects underground and keeps alive grass, bushes and small trees, such as tamarisks. As water pipelines are gradually extended out into the desert, and age-old drainage and water-storage systems are cleared of sand and brought into use again, settlements are springing up in the desert, where the soil is excellent, lacking only water and some manures.

In ancient times the Philistines farmed northern parts of the Negev. We passed a small squarish hill which was the site of their city of Gat where, according to the Bible, you are to 'tell it not'.

Near this spot today is a new small manufacturing township, Kiryat Gat, with trim flats going up and temporary huts for new immigrants. We were told that there are a few people from Manchester working there, helping to build up a textile industry. They certainly won't complain about too much rain.

Further south-east, well into today's desert, there lived around AD 300 the Nabateans, with their capital of Petra – now in Jordan. They used quite refined methods to conserve the desert rainfall in great underground cisterns. Later, when population fell in the area for various reasons, man retreated from the desert. Now he is going back again.

Prime Minister Ben-Gurion went to live in one of these desert settlements, a kibbutz at Sde Boker, near Beersheba, after he resigned in 1953. (He became Prime Minister again in 1955.) His main home is now in Tel Aviv, but he still keeps his wooden house in the desert.

Beersheba, which I believe was also a Philistine town, was an Arab town until 1948, when it was largely destroyed in the war. There remains a small Arab quarter, with a minaret we saw from afar. Around it a prosperous-looking new town of modern flats and factories is springing up.

From Beersheba we moved further south-eastwards, into a part of the desert where we no longer saw any Bedouins, just a very occasional settlement, supported by piped water. Warning notices in Hebrew and English, fixed to a wire fence, told us we were on the perimeter of Israel's second nuclear reactor, now under construction.

Across the desert, a mile or two away, we could see the dome of what is apparently the reactor building. There have been unconfirmed reports that Israel is to develop an atomic bomb. At a desert filling station and café, I was told that there were many French experts working at the new station.

I broached the subject of an atomic bomb with one of the café staff. While he said he knew nothing about it, he added, 'I *hope* they are making one.'

I can well understand Israelis feel they need an atomic bomb, in view of growing Arab strength and the openly-stated desire of the Egyptian leader, Nasser, to push the Jews into the sea. Spokesman David pooh-poohed suggestions about an atomic bomb, but he would most likely not know if one were being developed. *[Today Western arms experts are convinced that Israel has a sophisticated nuclear weapon which, however, unlike those of India and Pakistan, has not been tested.]*

We drove further south-eastwards, through largely uninhabited country which began to descend. The rolling rocky desert gradually gave way to canyons and weird windswept shapes of sandstone-like rock and, later, limestone.

About two hours' driving from Beersheba, we caught our first glimpse of the Dead Sea, which forms part of the Great Rift Valley, stretching southwards through the Red Sea and through most of Africa. Steep cliffs, dropping several hundred feet in places, mark the edge of the valley at the southern end of the Dead Sea. The sea is hemmed in by desolate fawn-coloured mountains on either side.

Soon we were down at Dead Sea level – about 1,300 feet *[400 m]* below 'normal' sea level. *[This is the lowest point on earth.]* We drove past salt flats, where water from this terribly salty sea is pumped in, largely evaporates in a few days, and then the strong salt solution is pumped into a refinery to extract the salt and other minerals.

At the south-western end of the sea is the little settlement of Sodom, near the traditional site of that biblical Las Vegas, the city of sin where Lot went astray and near where his wife, disobeying an instruction not to look back on the place where her husband was corrupted, allegedly turned into a pillar of salt.

There are many pinnacles of salty rock near the present-day

settlement, a cluster of wooden huts occupied partly by mine and refinery staff and partly by people who come to bathe in the health-giving salty water, and to plaster themselves with the blue-black mud at the seashore. One of the rock pinnacles is pointed out to visitors as being Lot's wife in person; it is near a prefabricated restaurant called 'Lot's Wife Inn'.

A stop for fruit juice and postcards – and two anti-malaria tablets made by ICI – and then we drove northwards along the Dead Sea's western bank for about 35 miles, a journey taking about three extremely bumpy hours on an unmade road between the blue sea and the arid heights.

We passed only one or two isolated settlements on the drive to Ain Geddi (Spring of the Kid), a mile or so short of the Jordan frontier. Ain Geddi is a green paradise of palms, maize, eggplant and other plants watered by the spring, which spurts from the heights above and is used partly for irrigation and partly to fill a series of four rock pools terraced down the brownish mountainside.

Most of us swam in one of the pools, a lyrical experience after our sweltering journey in the *khamsin*, the desert wind from Arabia which, unluckily, dogged us all day. Not far from Ain Geddi, in the wild hinterland, the second main batch of the Dead Sea Scrolls was found not long ago, relating part of the history of the Jewish survivors of the unsuccessful revolt against the Romans led by Bar-Kochba around AD 135. The survivors lived in caves in the rocky wadis until the Romans starved them out.

In the Ain Geddi kibbutz dining hall, we ate a simple meal of eggs, tomatoes, olives, cheese, tea and bread. Outside we had seen a cloud of locusts hovering over a green field of eggplant, and inside the dining hall were one or two of these creatures, much bigger than I had imagined, about four inches *[10 cm]* long.

Kurt Strumpf, burly German photographer working for the (American) Associated Press, managed to catch a locust and, holding its back, placed it on a small onion, two inches in diameter. The locust immediately grabbed hold of the onion with four of its (how many?) feet, and held on to the onion when Strumpf lifted the locust up.

Southwards for 45 minutes to our overnight resting-place, a modern youth hostel, the gift, like so many new buildings in Israel, of a Jew living abroad; this one a man in Trieste, Italy.

14 May 1961 : We had been given camp beds in mosquito-proof stone-and-wood shelters, but few of us could sleep in the terrible heat, which relaxed but a little during the night.

At the behest of our guides we rose around 4 am and, the two-thirds of us who felt up to it, set off in the bluish dawn light to climb the steep squarish table mountain of Masada, a reddish-brownish-yellowish block of rock rising behind the youth hostel.

The summit – 1,200 feet *[366 m]* above the Dead Sea – is reached by a good winding path. We had gone up perhaps 200 feet when a large yellow sun peeped over the Jordan hills across the sea. Very soon it was fully light again, though a gentle breeze made the going easier.

Masada is a phenomenally interesting archaeological site, where the Romans crushed the final resistance of the Jews after a revolt which broke out in AD 66 and lasted until AD 73. Flavius Josephus, a Jew who went over to the Romans and wrote a history of this war, said of Masada (see G.A. Williamson, *The Jewish War*, Penguin):

'A rock with a very large perimeter and lofty all the way along is on every side broken off by deep ravines. In two places … the rock can with great difficulty be climbed. *[It's easier now.]* After an agonising march of 3¹/₂ miles the summit is reached … a sort of elevated plateau.'

'On this the high priest Jonathan (161–143 BC) first built a fortress and named it Masada; later King Herod (acceded 40 BC and died in March AD 4), devoted great care to the improvement of the place. The entire summit, measuring ³/₄ mile round, he enclosed within a limestone wall 18 feet *[5.5 m]* high and 12 feet *[3.7 m]* wide, in which he erected 37 towers 75 feet *[23 m]* high; from these one could pass through a ring of chambers right round the inside of the wall.'

Josephus says Herod also built a fortified palace below the

summit and stocked it with abundant food and water. About a hundred years elapsed from the time when the provisions were laid down to the capture of Masada by the Romans, yet the Romans found what was left of the various foods in excellent condition. 'There was found too a quantity of weapons of every kind … enough for 10,000 men.'

In his description of the 11-month siege of the fortress, Josephus says, 'Against Eleazar and the Sicarii *[a Jewish sect most hostile to the Romans]* came the Roman general *[Flavius Silva]* at the head of his forces.'

Josephus describes how the Romans, to be able to bombard the fortress walls with their stone-throwing engines, built an enormous ramp of earth and stone, enabling them to get close to the fortress and breach its wall.

When Eleazar realized that the Romans were on the point of victory, he saw this as God's vengeance against the Jews for their sins. He called on the 960 Jews, men women and children, who had taken refuge in the palace, to choose 'death with honour' by slaughtering their wives and children and each other.

Josephus adds, 'When ten of them had been chosen by lot to be the executioners of the rest, every man lay down beside his wife and children, flung his arms around them, and exposed his throat to those who must perform the painful office. These unflinchingly slaughtered them all, then agreed on the same rule for each other, so that the one who drew the lot should kill the nine and last of all himself.

'The one man left till last surveyed the serried ranks of the dead … and finding that all had been dispatched set the palace blazing fiercely, and summoning all his strength drove his sword right through his body and fell dead by the side of his family.'

Two women and five children, who had hidden in water conduits, survived. They gave the victorious Romans an account of what had happened. Josephus adds, 'When they *[the Romans]* came upon the rows of dead bodies, they did not exult … but admired the nobility of their resolve. Masada having fallen thus, the general left a garrison in the fortress and returned with the rest of his army to Caesarea. For nowhere was there an enemy left.'

As we climbed the mountain – before I had read Josephus' account – our guides told us that the Romans had 8,000 soldiers, and 2,000 slaves with 500 mules used in building the gigantic ramp needed for their final assault.

It took us about an hour to reach the top of one of the two paths to the plateau. At this point the rock falls sheer for about 50 feet *[15 m]*, and steps with handrails have been made to enable one to reach the plateau.

The plateau still has a few remains of the fortress walls on its edge. Also standing is part of Herod's palace, including some mosaics. The palace section, which has been partly reconstructed, is perhaps 15 yards by ten.

Below the palace are the ruins of many dwellings, a confused mass of stones, but with the outlines of walls still apparent. Here and there are signs of the fire which the Jews started when they massacred themselves.

The whole hilltop is littered with broken pottery. We went into one of the ancient water cisterns and storehouses, a cool area.

From the plateau we could see, almost as if the siege had just taken place, the remains of the once six-metre-high wall built by the Romans to encircle the whole of the mountain top, except for one or two wadis through which water runs occasionally, but not at this season.

Heaps of stone at intervals along this ruined wall are the remains of regularly placed Roman watchtowers. One can also clearly see the ruins of eight or nine squarish walled Roman camps. I do not think I've ever seen a more fascinating historical site. The ramp built by the Romans has sunk 30 or 40 yards, but is still fully evident.

After breakfast at the youth hostel, our bus bumped southwards back to Sodom. The thing to do at Sodom is to lie – literally lie – in the over-salty water reading a newspaper; you can't sink. I was holding a copy of *Izvestia* as a colleague took my photo.

A fellow journalist told us later that a Russian-born French woman correspondent, whom he saw by the lake, appeared to have a bathing costume on, but when she dived in he realized the costume had only been mud.

Swimming in the Dead Sea is rather like lying on an airbed with not much air in it. The water gives, but not too far. I found it difficult to swim breaststroke as my legs were forced out of the water and my chin went in.

We'd been warned that the slightest cut would sting badly and, in fact, after about five minutes in the water we were stinging in various places. We fled across the whitish salt-strewn sand to freshwater showers in a hut. We did not feel any strong desire to bathe in the Dead Sea again.

Our return journey took us past the edge of the United Nations-occupied Gaza Strip, part of Egypt, which is demilitarized at present. This is a fruitful area of orange groves and fields, a relief after the unfriendly desert.

We called at the coastal town of Ashkelon, another once-Philistine town, now a mainly modern place with palms and greenery between the light-coloured flats and houses, and a beautiful beach – our magnet. By this time, 4 pm, we were all tired, but a swim in the Mediterranean invigorated us. Homewards to Jerusalem, up into the hills once again, to experience the delight of a cool breeze.

27 A fair trial for Eichmann?

15 May 1961 : There has been a lot of irrelevant evidence in the trial, irrelevant so far as the actual charges are concerned. However, I don't blame the Israelis for wanting to make a historical meal out of the trial, which may well be the only chance they have of trying a key Nazi official.

This desire seems to come from the government, represented in the trial by the Attorney-General, rather than from the judges, who are impressive. However, their impressiveness is marred by the fact that the law under which they are trying Eichmann allows all sorts of exceptions from the normal rules of evidence.

This is justified on the ground that Nazi crimes were committed a long time ago and are harder to prove, partly because many of those involved are dead. If these exceptions could not be made, it is possible that Eichmann might be acquitted on one or two of the counts against him.

What would that matter when weighed against the moral gain of having tried him according to normal procedures? However, it should be said that the Nazis who were tried at Nuremberg by the International Military Tribunal were subject to similar procedures as Eichmann, for a similar reason.

16 May 1961 : Today we had a truly inspiring man in the witness box, white-haired German Protestant church dean, Heinrich Grüber *[1891–1975]*. Grüber is a national figure in Germany, thanks to his fearless humanitarian efforts both in the Nazi era and, later, as the accredited representative of the all-German Evangelical (Protestant) Church to the Communist regime.

In the Nazi era he ran an office of the Bekennende Kirche (Confessing Church), that minority of the Evangelical (Protestant) Church which, during the Nazi era, split from the main body of the Church, which showed some loyalty to Hitler.

Grüber's office worked to save Jews and other anti-Nazis from the concentration camps and death. Grüber said he had a network of contact men in all the government ministries, some of them Nazis who had realized they were serving an evil regime and were impelled by their consciences to make amends in some way.

One of his contacts was Bernhard Loesener, a Jewish affairs expert in the Interior Ministry, who was brave enough to soften certain measures even at a late stage. Grüber said he had worked closely with Roman Catholic bishops.

The largely Jewish audience was so moved by the dean's account of how he was imprisoned in Sachsenhausen and Dachau concentration camps because of his efforts on behalf of Jews, that there was occasional applause, and some weeping.

Grüber attributed Eichmann's activities – he described him as 'like a block of granite' in dealing with intercessions – to the doings of the Devil, who had taken hold of that man and others, in spite of religious teaching in schools and elsewhere.

Grüber said that in one of the many interviews he had with Eichmann, the SS officer asked him why he helped Jews. In reply Grüber referred to the story of the Good Samaritan, the non-Jew who helped the Jew who had fallen by the wayside.

'My God tells me to do that,' the Protestant clergyman told Eichmann. Grüber did not indicate Eichmann's response.

Grüber said he hoped Eichmann would not hold against him what he said about the accused. With trembling voice, the elderly dean concluded his more than four hours in the witness box with a moving appeal that the Eichmann trial should contribute to understanding between Germany and Israel, and to the happiness of humanity. He said it was his plea that forgiving love – on the

Israeli side – and forgiven guilt – on the German side – should meet together 'before the throne of God'.

18 May 1961 : Today the trial dealt with Czechoslovakia. Evidence included the written report of a Red Cross official, Paul Dunand, a Swiss, about his visit to the Theresienstadt ghetto – the 'privileged' concentration camp in Czechoslovakia – about a month before the end of the war. Theresienstadt was used as a front by the SS chief, Heinrich Himmler, to mislead such visitors.

In his report Dunand said he had a long talk with Eichmann at a reception in nearby Prague after his visit to the ghetto. Eichmann had told him he thought Himmler was planning 'humane methods' for the Jews. While he was not entirely in favour of this, he would as an officer do as he was ordered.

20 May 1961 : Talked with a Jewish dentist, Dr Loje, who had visited Germany three years ago and found people there most friendly and doing their best to make amends to the Jews. He thinks the past should be forgotten and does not believe that most Germans wanted the Jews to be exterminated.

My new friends, Boris and Fanny Barkai, speak German to each other. Their 14-year-old son understands German but scarcely speaks a word of it, and addresses them in Hebrew, which they cannot speak as well as he.

21 May 1961 : This Whitsuntide Sunday I visited the Russian Orthodox church, a handsome sandstone building with greenish copper cupolas. No service was in progress. Instead I saw a few black-garbed old women, like Russian peasants from a nineteenth-century novel. On entering the church they crossed themselves, sometimes more than once. Then they walked to several icons, pictures of saints in ornate frames, kissed the pictures and then went on to an altar showing Jesus on the cross, depicted in flat cut-out pictures, with Mary and Mary Magdalene standing by.

At the altar the women took a candle from a holder, lit it from a hanging oil-lamp and placed it in a glass holder. The final and

277

perhaps the most important part of their observances appeared to be the kissing of two more holy pictures, placed amid flowers on a lectern in the centre of the nave, in front of the richly decorated holy of holies and beneath a great metal candelabra.

The wizened old women, whom I heard speaking together softly in Russian, were joined by two nuns, also in black from head to foot, and differing from the peasant types only because they wore hats shaped like plant pots.

As I sat on a bench, watching this colourful scene for some 15 minutes, I felt some understanding for the Russian Communists' damning of religion as 'the opium of the people', if this was the kind of religion they were used to, and because the Russian Orthodox Church allied itself with the despotic Tsars, helping them to keep just such wizened peasants in thrall.

This afternoon it was my duty to report on final hours of the largest international meeting yet to have been held in Israel: the World Pentecostal Conference attended by 2,500 'hot gospellers' from about 30 countries, about one-third of them from the United States.

This was an emotionally charged gathering, and the emotion was stepped up even more when a wavy-haired man acting as cheerleader announced that a man among a group of Pentecostals, who had today visited the Upper Room on Mount Zion, the traditional site of the Lord's Supper, had been granted the 'baptism of the Holy Spirit with the speaking of tongues'.

I decided I would write a Reuter story about this happening, which took place on Pentecost (Whitsuntide) Sunday, the day on which the disciples in the Upper Room were said to have received the Holy Spirit after the Crucifixion.

First I spoke to Gilbert Dean, pastor of the Pentecostal Holiness Church of Rahway, New Jersey. He told me that the man who had 'received the baptism' had been an elderly farmer called Williamson.

Dean said that about 35 Pentecostals had gone into the Upper Room, a first-floor room in the ancient complex of buildings. 'We gathered there to sing and pray. As we were praying, the Spirit of

God came on them and Williamson received the baptism of the Holy Spirit and began to speak in tongues. It was not understandable to any of us present. Others were speaking in tongues. In fact, practically everyone was, but the others had already received the baptism; this phenomenon occurs continually in life after one has received it.'

At my request Williamson was found. He is 71, with crewcut, almost grey hair, squarish horn-rimmed spectacles and a friendly, rather ascetic face. He told me his name was William Harvey Williamson, of Route Four, Washington, North Carolina.

I've never seen a happier man. He was absolutely bubbling over with joy, and he embraced one or two of the Pentecostal leaders before he began to tell me his story in his fairly simple, homely way.

'I don't have words to express it, just my feelings,' he said. 'I felt like I was flying in the air almost, when the presence of God came down on me, oh Glory Hallelujah to my God.

'They prayed for me last night. I knew it was going to happen in the Upper Room. I felt it when I left home. That is why I came here, to get the baptism of the Holy Ghost. And I got it.

'I am clear in my heart. I have been a member of the Church for about ten years, but I never had the baptism of the Holy Ghost and I have been striving for that. God told me to come to Jerusalem and I prayed to Him, "Keep me well."

'You know, I was sick the first week on the trip. I said to Him, "You know who I am. I want you to help me." And He helped, and today I am well inside and spiritually, I am well. Praise God, praise His Holy Name for it all. I am happy, happy as can be.'

Williamson said he had used up all his savings for the 1,500-dollar trip, and has his social security and army pension to live on when he gets home. His wife, a Methodist, did not want to come.

In order to 'balance' my story I asked the only bishop of the Pentecostal Holiness Church (one of the larger Pentecostal churches in the United States), Bishop J.A. Synan of Hopewell, Virginia, a jolly, well-built man, how one could know whether such experiences were genuine.

He replied, 'Baptism with the Holy Spirit is a great and real spiritual experience, which we can know ourselves by the fact that we receive it in harmony with the teachings of Christ and the apostles, and by the initial evidence of speaking with other tongues as the Spirit gives utterance.

'And when we have the experience and witness others receiving it, in accordance with the same principles, and observe the same evidence and discern the same spirit, we can be satisfied ourselves that they have received it.'

The bishop referred to a passage in the Bible, stating that the disciples at Caesarea were convinced that the Gentiles had received the Holy Spirit because they spoke with tongues and magnified God.

I told these Pentecostal leaders I was sceptical about such things. One of them, I think it was Bishop Synan, said he had always thought a lot of Doubting Thomases and hoped that one day my doubts would be resolved. This kind of religion – though it may well improve and brighten the lives of its adherents – is not for me.

22 May 1961 : Went for a drive this morning with 40-ish Golda Zimmermann, Jerusalem correspondent of the London *Jewish Chronicle* who, owning a new Morris Minor brake, needs someone to give her confidence while driving.

We stopped for a walk in the most lovely cemetery I've ever seen, on Mount Herzl, the main Israeli military cemetery, where each soldier has been laid to rest in a tasteful grave covered with hand-hewn sandstone, with the soldier's name on a kind of sandstone pillow.

The graves are terraced on the rocky slope, and brilliant reddish sub-tropical flowers are dotted about between the terraces, as well as olive and cypress trees. Nearby, Theodor Herzl, founder of Zionism, is buried under a slab of black marble, on the hilltop.

Golda told me she was looking forward to returning to London, after about nine years in Israel, because she felt that Israel had largely lost its original idealism, and that its leaders were spending their time concerned with their personal power and party fortunes instead of with the common good.

The court hearing resumed this afternoon after the Pentecost (Jewish) and Whitsuntide (Christian) recess. Our main point today was an announcement, following a *New York Times* report that Eichmann had suffered two heart attacks, that he had in fact – during his 13-month imprisonment – suffered two attacks of irregular pulse caused by nervous tension. Servatius's secretary told Lionel that one of the attacks had been about a week ago.

We noticed – coincidence? – that Eichmann was looking particularly nervous today, eyes blinking frequently, mouth contorting, and so on. I really cannot feel sympathy for this man, though I suppose I really ought to, for it was partly fate that put him into the situation he occupies today. For instance, if he had been born British, he would not have joined the SS at all.

Evidence today concerned Bulgaria, where there was considerable opposition to Nazi attempts to have Bulgarian Jews deported to the death camps. King Boris himself was among those who managed to thwart the Nazis to a large extent.

The court then turned to Salonika, northern Greece, where the Germans were in direct control and managed to deport the majority of the area's 55,000 Jews. Again and again the name of Eichmann crops up in documents concerning anti-Jewish measures in various countries.

23 May 1961 : Today it was the turn of Romania, where there was some wavering by the country's authorities, but by no means as much opposition as in Bulgaria. We were told about a dramatic journey to the Vatican by the Papal Nuncio, Cassulo, at the request of the Chief Rabbi of Romania, Dr Alexandre Safran, now the Chief Rabbi in Geneva.

In a written statement, Dr Safran said he had appealed to the Nuncio 'in the name of the respect he owed to the Creator and His creatures' to make this last effort to save Jews from deportations to the death camps.

The Nuncio had tried several times to persuade the dictator, Ion Antonescu, and Vice-President Mihai Antonescu to stop anti-Jewish measures, which had included deportations to labour and concentration camps. When the Nuncio came back from Rome, in autumn 1942, the Antonescus were finally swung over, and halted most anti-Jewish measures.

We also heard of events in Slovakia, where about 70,000 of the 90,000 Jews living in that German-dominated puppet state were killed by the Germans, mainly by sending them to death camps in Poland.

Later today we had a blow: an order from Doon Campbell, Reuters editorial chief, to cut daily maximum wordage from 5,000 to 3,000 until further notice. We all think this too little, particularly as the story is likely to warm up within a day or two.

24 May 1961 : Quite a battle to hold down the wordage, even today when the story was not really top-line, dealing mainly with a largely unsuccessful attempt by Slovakian Jewish leaders to bribe the Germans to stop deportations to the death camps. *[This was, I think, in 1944 or early 1945.]*

25 May 1961 : Things hotted up today with evidence on Eichmann's activities in Hungary, where he played an important role in the deportation of about 600,000 of Hungary's 800,000 Jews. Most of this was done with the help of the Hungarian fascists, between March and early July 1944.

After the Hungarian leader, Admiral Horthy, had ordered a halt to the deportations under Western Allied pressure, Eichmann got one of the last trains away, by summoning Jewish leaders and keeping them talking all day while the train holding 1,220 Jews was sent over the border, bound for Auschwitz.

The most touching evidence today was that of elderly frail Mrs Margot Reich, a Hungarian-born Jew, who identified copies of a postcard and a letter written on toilet paper which her husband threw out of a death train. The documents expressed the hope of a man who was doomed, but held on to the hope that God might spare him to rejoin his family. She never heard from her husband again.

Evidence from Pinhas Freudiger, the bearded former leader of the Budapest Orthodox Jews, was interrupted by screamed abuse from a Hungarian-born Jew, Szalaki, who was in the public gallery. Szalaki alleged that Freudiger had turned Jews over to the Nazis in order to save himself and his family.

It seems to me that Freudiger did what he could for his people in negotiations with the Nazis, and could not be blamed for slipping into Romania with his family when warned by a Nazi he had bribed that Eichmann was about to deport him.

One of several charming Israelis I have met during the trial is Yaacov Bar-Or, assistant prosecutor, born in Frankfurt/Main, where his name was Breuer. He amusingly told me that when he informed his father, while they were still living in Germany, that he was getting engaged to a Jewish girl from Breslau, then in German Silesia, his father said disgustedly, 'What, marrying a Polak!' (a pejorative German word for a Pole). His wife does not like to think that Breslau is now in Poland. These loyalties linger on, in spite of what the Nazis did to the Jews.

28 Eichmann 'took part' in murder of Jewish youth

26 May 1961 : Today we heard evidence indicating that Eichmann himself took part in the murder in mid-1944 of a Jewish youth, known only as Shalomon, who was in a group of Jews who were forced to dig ditches in the garden of Eichmann's Budapest villa.

A 35-year-old Hungarian-born Israeli, Abraham Gordon, who was in the group digging ditches, said it appeared that Shalomon was killed in a toolshed which had been entered by Eichmann and a man called Slawik who, he believed, was Eichmann's bodyguard. Eichmann's driver, Teitel, had accused the youth of stealing cherries, which he had denied.

Teitel drove away what appeared to be the dead body of Shalomon in an amphibious car. When he returned, he said to the diggers in Hungarian, 'I have thrown the stinking corpse into the Danube, and your fate will be the same.'

Although Eichmann is not specifically charged with this murder, the prosecution has argued that it is the only known instance of the 'desk killer' murdering with his own hands.

27 May 1961 : Glorious Saturday recreation by the sea at Herzliya (called after Herzl), a few miles north of Tel Aviv, with two other members of the Reuter team and two Associated

284

Press men – five 'Eichmann tourists' as we are called at weekends. We swam in windswept surf, with a hot sun occasionally moderated by welcome cloud, and visited the ruin of the little Roman fortress and harbour of Apollonia, 20 minutes' walk northwards along the beach. Felt grateful to God for sun, sand, surf and good companions. *[Today I would add: but God – if there is one – created Eichmann too.]*

28 May 1961 : I pressed Lionel and our two teleprinter operators, Reg and Fred, into acting as bit players in an 8-millimetre colour film of Jerusalem, which I shot with a hired cine-camera. One of the best shots, I think, will be of us all climbing up Mount Zion wearing regulation Jewish skullcaps.

We were able to get into the traditional site of King David's tomb, once a mosque and now a synagogue, where a yellow inscription on a wall proclaims: 'David, the King of Israel, lives on.'

On an altar stand three silver or golden vessels containing the Law and the Commandments, flanked by thirteen crowns made of goldlike metal, brought to Israel from synagogues which formerly existed in the Diaspora – one crown for each year of the existence of modern Israel.

Upstairs is the traditional site of the Upper Room where the Last Supper was held and where the disciples are said to have received the Holy Spirit at Pentecost. The arched and colonnaded room is actually of Crusader construction, with some earlier and later elements, such as apparently Roman plinths from the Byzantine era, a Muslim prayer niche and Arabic inscriptions.

The recent removal of wall plaster, by the Israeli Department of Antiquities, has revealed a coat of arms of Regensburg, Germany, probably mediaeval work.

A persuasive and friendly Jesuit, Father Calderoni, from the United States, who was showing around another priest, told us that Israeli Jews were banned by the Israeli authorities from visiting the Christian shrines on Mount Zion in order to prevent possible incidents – anti-Christian desecrations. Evidently the prohibition does not extend to foreign Jewish tourists.

Near the Upper Room is the (Christian) Dormition Abbey, built by the Germans in 1924 and still staffed by Germans and Austrians. Some wonderful shimmery golden mosaics inside, one showing the Madonna; this is the place where Mary is supposed to have fallen asleep before her Bodily Assumption, her reception bodily into heaven – according to a Roman Catholic dogma laid down in 1950. *[Dormition, from Latin and French, means 'falling asleep'.]*

One mosaic showing the Madonna has a few bullet-holes in her face, the work of Israeli soldiers when they captured the building in the 1948 war.

Doon Campbell, Reuters editorial chief, a 41-year-old Scot and former war correspondent, called on us in Jerusalem this afternoon, taking a few hours away from Tel Aviv, where he is to attend the conference of the International Press Institute (IPI), starting in two days. He praised our work so far, but warned us to keep wordage firmly in hand this coming week because of big competition internationally.

Doon told me I may be posted to Moscow, as holiday relief, starting in July and I should learn more about this within a few days. I am, of course, very bucked about this. (Doon confirmed by phone from Tel Aviv on 1 June that I am to go to Moscow for about two months on holiday relief.) *[Campbell's memoirs,* Magic Mistress, *were published in 2000 by The Tagman Press. He died in 2003.]*

29 May 1961 : Cheerful letter from Elfi, who is very pleased because I promised to buy her a new sewing machine to mark our 14th wedding anniversary the day after tomorrow. *[That sewing machine became a memento of the Eichmann trial, as it was partly financed from my* per diem *expenses].* Elfi told me that, for obvious reasons, Robin has been nicknamed Fritz at his boarding school.

Wally has been removed from our team this week to report the IPI conference, so Lionel and I decided not to work in the courtroom but to report from our closed-circuit TV and use our transistor receivers giving translations of the proceedings. In order to make our coverage still quicker, we did not use shorthand, but, working in relays, typed out the evidence as it came, using abbreviations.

Particularly absorbing evidence this morning from a psychology professor from Long Island University, New York State, Dr Gustave M. Gilbert, who was a US Army psychologist at the Nuremberg War Crimes Trials. A sidelight showing the utter stupidity of Nazi racial theories was that Gilbert did not initially reveal to the top Nazis that he was a Jew. When he did reveal that, Julius Streicher, the lewd Jew-baiter, said he had been impressed by the courage of the Jews in building a new homeland in Palestine, and would like to become a leader of the Jews.

The main reason for calling Gilbert was to hear him say that many of the Nazi leaders mentioned Eichmann as a kingpin of the extermination machine.

This afternoon, burly red-faced Joel Brand, who was one of the Jewish leaders in Budapest, spoke about his leading role in the abortive 'blood for goods' deal. This was a proposal which came from Himmler, but was initially proposed by Eichmann, under which one million Jews were to be spared from the gas chambers in exchange for 10,000 lorries to be supplied to the Germans for the Russian front.

Brand made Eichmann grin when he said that if he had sat opposite to him in a coffeehouse today he would have recognized him within five minutes and would then have 'exploded'. He made the Nazi smile again by imitating the staccato barking used by Eichmann during their meetings in Budapest.

At those meetings Eichmann had instructed him to go abroad to try to conclude the deal. Eichmann had called himself an idealistic German and had said he knew Brand was an idealistic Jew. Eichmann had told him, 'One hundred Jews for one lorry, that is cheap.'

He had added that Brand must return within about a fortnight, and promised that if he returned bringing acceptance of the deal, Auschwitz would be blown up and the first hundred thousand Jews handed over. Brand left from Vienna on 18 May for Turkey, taking with him Bandi Gosz, a Jew who was a Gestapo agent, who was to keep an eye on Brand.

30 May 1961 : Today Brand, as well as documents, highlighted the role of the British Government, working in concert with the Americans, in blocking Brand's return to Budapest.

As, each day, Eichmann sent off 12,000 more Hungarian Jews to the death camps, Brand, who had been arrested by the British while trying to reach Palestine, was interrogated in Cairo. Top-level negotiations went on for weeks in London between Jewish Agency leaders and British ministers, including Foreign Secretary, Anthony Eden, while the British consulted with the United States and the Soviet Union.

The Soviet Union's attitude was not stated in court, but the upshot was that Brand was held by the British for $4^{1}/_{2}$ months, while 600,000 of Hungary's 800,000 Jews were sent to the death camps. (Eichmann actually accomplished this by 12 or 14 July, and then had to stop because of the ban imposed by Admiral Horthy, the Hungarian regent, under Western pressure.)

Eden's concern, as indicated in a memorandum, was not to be seen to be negotiating with the enemy, but it seems to me that the Western Allies – if they had received Soviet approval – could have pretended to start negotiations in order to try to halt the flow of trains to the gas chambers. Britain also turned down, on technical grounds, a Jewish proposal that Auschwitz, or the railway station leading to it, should be bombed. Mr Hausner, the Chief Prosecutor, said his personal view was that there were no such technical grounds.

According to a memorandum from the late Chaim Weizmann, Israel's first President, the British military authorities approved a plan for the dropping of several hundred Jewish paratroopers into Hungary in an attempt to disrupt deportations, but the British Foreign and Colonial Office had the idea dropped for 'political reasons'.

Brand's well-built wife, Hansi, who was left behind in Budapest with her children as a hostage, also spoke of meetings with Eichmann, who was pleased when the deal fell through, but angry that her husband had slipped through his hands.

31 May 1961 : Today Brand spoke of his meeting with Lord Moyne, British Deputy Minister of State in the Middle East, in Cairo, where Brand was held. He said Moyne had asked him, 'What shall I do with one million Jews? Where shall I put them?'

Brand had already said yesterday that he had the impression that the British did not want to receive even thousands of Jews.

Documents which, the prosecution says, show that Eichmann was more extreme than Hitler, were put to the court today. They stated that Eichmann had said he would consider asking Himmler to ask Hitler to change his decision, made in July or August 1944, agreeing to the emigration from Hungary of several thousand Jewish families to Palestine, plus 1,000 children, on condition that Hungarians agreed to the deportation to the death camps of the 200,000 Jews still remaining in Hungary at that time.

1 June 1961 : Failed to get through to Elfi last night, our 14th wedding anniversary, on the radio-telephone link, but raised her this morning. She had received 15 roses, arranged for me by Lionel through his wife, Veronika. I had asked for 14 for 14 years, but Veronika had worked out that with the wedding and 14 anniversaries it was worth 15. I can hardly believe that we have been married 14 years. I used to think that people who reached their silver wedding anniversaries were so old, and we now have only another 11 years to go to reach that.

Today's trial evidence was about the November 1944 'death march' of an estimated 50,000 of Hungary's remaining Jews from Budapest to the Austrian border 220 kilometres *[138 miles]* away, and the successful efforts of the Swiss and Swedish consulates to save many thousands of the Jews by issuing them with protective passports of those countries. In many cases this enabled them to drop out of the marching columns guarded by Hungarian gendarmes.

A leading figure in the Swedish efforts was Raoul Wallenberg, a Swedish diplomat who disappeared when Soviet troops reached Budapest in January 1945. He is credited with having saved the lives of between 20,000 and 100,000 Jews. *[It was learned later that*

Wallenberg, born in 1912, was arrested as an alleged spy. For decades the Soviet Union said Wallenberg had died in 1947 from a heart attack while in prison in Moscow. However, there were reports in the sixties that he had been seen in a Soviet labour camp in Siberia in the 1950s. But in November 2000, Alexander Yakovlev, the liberal ex-Communist chairman of the Russian presidential commission on the rehabilitation of victims of political repression, said the commission had no doubt that Wallenberg had been shot at the main KGB prison, the Lubianka, in Moscow in 1947. A month later the Russian Prosecutor-General, using some of the findings of the Yakovlev commission, stated that Wallenberg had been 'repressed' by Soviet authorities – a term referring to arbitrary arrest, torture or murder by the secret police. The Prosecutor-General's statement said Wallenberg had been held for nearly three years as a suspected spy and had died in the Lubianka.

In 1981, although it was not known whether Wallenberg was still alive, he was made an honorary citizen of the United States, the second person to receive that honour; the first was Sir Winston Churchill.]

So that Lionel and I are aware at all times which one of us is actually responsible for taking notes from the transistor radio transmissions, we have devised the system of wearing a white nebbed cloth cap which I bought some time ago to protect me from the sun. When one wears the cap, one is on note-taking duty. There are also two bits of paper on the cap, one saying, 'Taking shorthand, do not disturb,' and the other stating, 'There is no snow on this peak, though below lies an ice-cold brain.' That latter was contributed by Ted.

This evening I enjoyed a few hours as the guest of an Israeli couple, the Doblins, in Jerusalem. Mr Doblin, born in Mannheim, Germany, brought out a picture of his matriculation class at school in 1933 or 1934, after Hitler had come to power. In the centre of the group of 15 boys is a little man in Nazi stormtrooper's uniform – their class teacher. Doblin, then a left-winger, recalled how this teacher had said before Hitler became Chancellor, 'If you get in, you will probably hang us, and if we get in we shall probably hang you.'

In fact, that teacher allowed Doblin to be elected as class prefect even after the Nazi era began.

Doblin told me had held the post of prefect more or less alternately with a classmate called Gemes, who was an early member of the Hitler Youth but, after a journey abroad in 1937 when he learned what other countries thought about Nazism, became an anti-Nazi.

Doblin read us some extracts from recent letters from Gemes, who is now a pacifist suspicious of the aims of the Bonn Government and unhappy about the attitude of many Germans, who blame all the world's ills on the Communists and forget about Hitler.

Another boy in the class, a handsome lad called Müller, became an SS officer and deputy to a senior official, Fritz Sauckel, who was in charge of the Nazi forced labour organization. But this former classmate, Doblin said, later developed a conscience and was put into prison by the Nazis. Doblin also showed us a letter signed by several former members of his class at a class reunion recently, sending him greetings.

29 Visit to an Israeli Arab – and to Israel's south

2 June 1961 : Some ten miles west of Jerusalem lies the Arab village of Abu Gosh, perhaps the best-known Arab village in Israel. Boris Barkai, who took Lionel and me there today, with his wife Fanny, had told me earlier that some of the citizens of this village of 1,600 had fought alongside Israeli underground fighters, including terrorists, to get the British out of Palestine. When the Arab countries attacked Israel in 1948, as the British mandate ended, the muktar, or Muslim chief of Abu Gosh, Abu Ali ('the father of Ali'), urged the villagers not to flee to nearby Jordan, and they obeyed.

Barkai took us to call on Abu Ali, who lives in a 2¹/₂-storey flat-roofed house, with sheep in the lower floor. We climbed up a staircase to reach a balcony fitted out with old couches covered with somewhat disreputable-looking mattresses. There Abu Ali, looking rather like a Franciscan in a brown belted robe rippling over his ample figure, and with a brown apparently knitted skull-cap, stood to shake hands and say in Hebrew, '*Shalom*.' He ushered us through a room lined with more sofas and a kind of cocktail cabinet of tasteless modern design, with carpets on the walls, and into a room beyond, similarly furnished, with garish decorations on the walls showing in places that the wall carpets did not cover.

We were joined by one of Ali's numerous sons-in-law, a handsome dark-haired man in European working clothes, a fruit farmer, who translated Ali's Arabic into Hebrew, which Barkai then put into his slightly accented melodious English.

Abu Ali, a balding round-faced man with a rather sad face occasionally creased by a half-smile, told us how, before the Second World War, he had bought arms for the Jews' defence organization, not thinking then that there would be a Jewish state.

Then he told us the sad story of his gun. He did not tell us what kind of gun it was, but it was evidently a rifle. It had been presented to him in about 1936 by Moshe Sharett, then a leader of the Jewish Agency and later Israeli Prime Minister.

'It was given to me after I had bought arms for the Jews,' Abu Ali explained. 'I did not need a gun, I had plenty of arms. But this gun was special, a present. My name was engraved on it in golden letters. I kept it all the time during the mandate. Then about six years ago – I remember it was the same day that Moshe Sharett became Prime Minister – I was walking with the gun in Ben Yehuda Street in Jerusalem, and the police took it off me. They would not give it back.

'After a time they offered to give me money for it instead, but I told them, "Money is not equal to a present." It was a slur on my honour. I, Abu Ali, had worked with the Jews. So I wrote to Moshe Sharett, I wrote 50 times. I asked that at least the gun be given back to me for a day, just a day, so that I would be free to return this present with dignity. But he never answered.'

Boris Barkai said that Abu Ali had only one wife, like all the villagers of Abu Gosh, which makes it peculiar in the Muslim world. Barkai added that Abu Ali had lost much of his money by signing cheques in favour of a mistress while in his cups.

3 June 1961 : With three German media colleagues and a driver-guide from the Israeli Government press office, we left in a nicely-sprung 1958 Chevrolet Brookwood estate car for a journey of about 200 miles to Israel's southern extremity, the port of Eilat at the northern end of the Red Sea.

There was a slight morning haze, betokening the *khamsin*, the hot dry wind originating in the Sahara, but the nearby stony hills, mainly planted with fruit trees or vines, were crystal clear. The beauty of the scene made me feel that God intended men to live together in happiness and peace or, at least, they should strive for it. *[At 78, I no longer believe in a personal God, but it is pleasing to read what I thought then.]*

As far as Beersheba, capital of the Negev, the southern desert, the road was familiar to me from my trip to Sodom. In Beersheba, our driver-guide, Polish-born Schmuel Becker, who fought with the British Army 'desert rats' in North Africa, pointed out some of the former Turkish buildings in the town which, in its modern form, was founded about 200 years ago. The Philistine city of the same name was found not long ago by archaeologists to have been sited about a mile outside the present city. *[The Philistines, a non-Semitic people, fought the Israelites in the eleventh and tenth centuries BC.]* In this area one can see the embankment of the Turkish railway line which, I suppose, led towards Baghdad and which the British pulled up in the First World War. This was no doubt to stop the Turks from recapturing it or the Germans from using it.

South of Beersheba, in the desert, we approached three Bedouin men clad in dirty white robes, one of them wearing a brown pullover over his robe in spite of the temperature, which was much hotter than on an English summer's day. However, it was a dry heat, which was bearable.

We wanted to snap a group of camels, but it was made clear to us in Arabic, interpreted by Schmuel, that we were not allowed to click our shutters until we provided a quid pro quo. I gave one of the Bedouins half an Israeli pound, worth about 1s 9d *[about 9p]*. That was enough for our first shots.

Then we wanted to snap a trio of camels, which were hitched together and were being led round and round a flattish heap of desert grain, about ten yards across, to thresh it. The person leading them was a veiled Bedouin woman in black, with metal bangles showing beyond the fringes of her robe.

Bedouins don't like their women to be photographed. Schmuel

suggested we snap them anyway, but I was against this. So, for another half Israeli pound, we persuaded one of the men to take over as the camel driver. Somehow we were relieved of a further half-pound as we took more snaps, but we drew the line at paying a further half-pound to take a shot of three reporters and three donkeys. So we took it anyway, thinking we had paid our due, which Schmuel emphatically confirmed.

The Bedouins came for a couple of hundred yards to our car and smilingly said goodbye. I suggested they might have stationed themselves near the road in order to combine grain threshing with selling photo concessions. We drove south through the beige, mainly rocky desert, where the oil pipeline from Eilat to the northern port of Haifa runs close to the road. This is the Israeli way of bypassing the Suez Canal.

One of the kibbutzim we saw – green fields and orchards amid the wilderness – was Sde Boker, the country home of Ben-Gurion, where he lived for some years in temporary retirement in the fifties in a Swedish-made prefabricated wooden house – still there, with its sun-heated hot-water boiler on the roof.

Onwards, into the wasteland again, with an old camel caravan route a few hundred yards to our left for a while, and then a stop at Avdat, the ruins of a hill city of the Nabateans, an ancient Arab people who, in 312 BC, founded an independent kingdom with its capital at Petra, in present-day Jordan.

We half drove and half climbed up the hill and went into caves and ancient grain storerooms. One of the storerooms had an inscription in Byzantine Greek asking a saint to keep away evil spirits, and ending with the injunction, 'Lead a righteous life.' The Nabateans riddled mountains with vast water storage systems, enabling them to make the desert fertile.

The hilltop has a citadel dating from the Byzantine era. *[The Byzantine Empire was formed in AD 395 from the eastern part of the Roman Empire, and had its capital in Constantinople, now the Turkish capital, Istanbul. The loss of Constantinople to the Ottoman Turks in 1453 was the end of the empire.]* Also in the citadel are the quite well preserved ruins, partly restored, of two Christian

295

churches. An inscription on one of them begins with the cross and ends with the menorah, the Jewish seven-branched candlestick.

At the bottom of the hill a professor of the Hebrew University, Jerusalem, lives in a little house near a reconstruction of a Nabatean farm, worked without irrigation, but instead using the dew precipitated at night in the desert and collected in small fields with trenches around them, and with heaps of stones which attract the dew.

Twenty miles further south one reaches a desert township, Mispe Ramon, population 2,000 at a guess. It lives mainly from mining around the Makhtesh Ramon, a great rock fault – evidently part of the edge of the Great Rift Valley.

The road snakes down about 1,000 feet *[305 m]* to the bottom of the Makhtesh Ramon. It then drops, more gradually, over about another 60 miles, to the middle of the floor of the Rift, the parched valley which was once a sea connecting the Red Sea to the Dead Sea.

A former inmate of a German concentration camp, a cheerful little moustached man, makes a living painting oddities on pieces of flint, a much-mined mineral in that area, or making crazy creations from pieces of wood and rocks he finds while pottering about. We bought some.

A little further south we came across a real-life horror: a kind of lizard, about two feet long, dead and almost headless in the middle of the road where it had been left by two white-and-red vulture-like birds as we approached. No one knew the name of the lizard, not even Schmuel.

Down in the bed of the Rift we passed through a vast dried-out riverbed, where winter rains leave enough moisture for desert acacia, a flat-topped dusty green tree, small bushes and some kind of grass.

Here we saw groups of camels, owned by Bedouins who live in Jordan a mile or two away. The camels wander across in search of forage, then wander back again. The frontier in this almost uninhabited area is marked by occasional white-painted posts.

296

We also had a glimpse of a lightning gazelle, used by the Israeli post office as its symbol.

About 30 miles north of the Red Sea, we stopped at a kibbutz, Yotvata, existing thanks to a well. There, after some hesitation, we were allowed to have a delicious dip in their freshwater swimming pool, the water from which runs away to irrigate land or operate sprinkler systems placed around the shelters, roofed with palm leaves, where their poultry – thousands of white leghorns – and their horses stand in the heat, apparently thriving.

Modern flats are replacing the wooden huts in which the founders of the kibbutz, army personnel, lived when the place was first settled about ten years ago. About 100 people live there, and the young couples have brought into the world seven children up to now, and are about to open a kindergarten. They offered me a job.

After a drink of cold water, handed to us by a mournful-looking girl, we drove our last lap, glimpsing the Red Sea a few miles north of Eilat, after we had seen on our right the modern workings of King Solomon's Mines, a rich source of copper.

King Solomon (King of ancient Israel from about 970 to 930 BC, son of David) used thousands of slaves to exploit these deposits. The slaves had to carry the wood for smelting the ore from the other side of the roughly 5,000-feet-high *[1,525 m]* arid brown mountains, which are today in Jordan.

Today Israelis get high wages and tax reliefs to work there and live in Eilat, which has had a record temperature of 48° Celsius (about 115°F). When we reached Eilat, around 5.30, we were told it had been just a few degrees cooler than that. We were glad we had not been there at midday, for the desert was cooler.

I think Schmuel said that about 9,000 people now live in Eilat, founded in 1948. It has some handsome hotels and public buildings and rows of trim flats. *[Eilat began to grow after 1956, when the Egyptian blockade on the Gulf of Aqaba was lifted. The resumption of the blockade in 1967 led to the six-day Israeli–Arab war. Today Eilat has about 20,000 inhabitants.]*

After a very much needed fruit juice and soda, Schmuel drove us to the Coral Beach, the main bathing beach, about two miles west of the little port, which is being rapidly expanded.

Altogether Israel has about eight miles of coastline here.

Standing on the shore, in the centre of this coastal strip, one sees to the left (east) the Jordanian port of Aqaba, and half-left is the mountainous desert of northern Saudi Arabia. About four miles to the south-west lies the Egyptian frontier, where Yugoslavs are currently manning the demilitarized tone set up after the Suez War of 1956, when Israel invaded the Sinai desert.

Before the Sinai campaign of 1956, the Egyptians were preventing Israel from using Eilat, as their guns commanded the approaches to the port from nearby heights. Israeli now ships oil from Iran, and maybe other places, to Eilat and pumps it about 250 miles to Haifa, for refining there. Other cargoes are moved by road in 40-ton American-made lorries.

Eilat is having its off season at the moment (too hot), so we found only a handful of people on pebbly Coral Beach, where there is a modern bar and restaurant, changing cubicles for hire and overnight accommodation fitted with 'desert coolers'. These – an Israeli invention, I believe – comprise a fan which forces air through a box, of about one cubic metre, filled with a kind of sea grass impregnated with slowly running water from the mains. The resulting air is both much cooler and more humid than normal air. Traditional air conditioning is no good here, as the climate is too dry.

Borrowing a snorkel, I swam out a short distance to a coral reef, which is a few feet underwater. I was staggered by what I saw. I've seen lots of underwater films, but to see the real thing is a tremendous experience. Hundreds of fish, some of them brilliantly coloured, gambolled about, above and alongside the reef of sponge-like coral, while black sea urchins, like baby porcupines, nestled in their lairs. Then there were other colours: the greeny-blue of the sea, the fawn of the coral, sometimes shading into pink or brown, the greyish-brown of the seabed.

I could also see the torsos and feet of my companions, and all so clearly. Raising my head out of the water, I exploded with delight, and no one would believe me until they, too, had taken their turn with the snorkel.

Soon it grew dark, so we adjourned to the modern Eilat Hotel for drinks, to be captivated by a Los Angeles Negro called Powell, bearded and handsome, who was playing jazz for fun.

Also in the bar lounge was a woman of perhaps 45, a somewhat fading beauty in a blue costume, wife of a *Time-Life* executive and once the spouse of Ernest Hemingway in his Spanish Civil War period. She was reading an Eichmann trial transcript to prepare an article for the Atlantic Monthly.

Later we ate scrumptious local fish in a café which was so well air-cooled that we felt chilly after the hothouse outside. To bed in a small hotel, with a desert cooler in each room. I thought it was too cool at first and switched it off, but after 90 minutes I was sweating madly and so switched it on again.

4 June 1961 : Schmuel drove us to a small factory where a Yugoslav-born Jew, the owner, and three North African Jewish girls were working at grinding and cutting machines, making jewellery from blue-green copper ore from King Solomon's Mines, which they fixed in silver settings made by Jews from Yemen. Such little factories are built by the government and then rented to immigrants, who have little capital.

The owner and the girls wore no masks while working, but two of the girls held handkerchiefs to their noses. The jewellery was beautiful and we all bought some.

In Eilat's little marine museum a young man, described by Schmuel as Israel's best skin diver, showed us specimens of tropical fish, including stuffed sharks caught in the Gulf of Eilat – but nowhere near Coral Beach, we were relieved to hear. Some specimens were in tanks, including crabs which protect anemones living on their backs and, in return, obtain food sucked in by the anemones.

After a fish lunch, off to the airport to sit sweating madly in a Dakota of Arkia, Israel's internal airline, till it took off some ten minutes later and gradually cooled down. I was exhilarated by this flight amid the sunshine, with at first the parched desert beneath and later the green areas of Israel near Ashkelon, as we flew out over the blue of Mediterranean, among translucent wisps of cloud, to land at Tel Aviv's internal airport.

Back to Jerusalem by train, a pleasant two-hour trip up into the hills on a one-track railway, the train having a bar where we enjoyed some fruit juice. We saw a magnificent view of gorges, pock-marked by ancient caves. We four agreed this had been our most absorbing trip to date, in spite of the heat. Tonight we felt our sunburn and were unable to sleep on our backs, but it was worth it.

30 Horrors of the death camps

5 June 1961 : It was stark horror at the trial again this Monday, with accounts of the death camps of Maidanek and Sobibor, where shooting and gas from diesel engines were used to kill thousands. Several witnesses who testified are among the handful of survivors from these places.

6 June 1961 : More about the death camps, this time Treblinka and Belzec. There was no survivor out of 600,000 victims at the latter. At least 750,000 are said to have died at Treblinka. One man told us that 10,000 people were gassed within 45 minutes in 13 gas chambers filled with diesel exhaust fumes.

7 June 1961 : One of today's witnesses was Jehuda Bacon, a 30-ish artist whose pictures of melancholy beauty Lionel and I admired at an exhibition some weeks ago. Bacon was taken to Auschwitz aged about 14, with his family, and lived with them for some months in a 'family camp', the only one in the vast complex of camps known as Auschwitz.

Bacon and his family came to Auschwitz from Theresienstadt, Czechoslovakia, the Nazis 'model' ghetto for 'privileged' Jews. According to the files of the Bacon family, they were earmarked for the gas chambers after six months.

In the meantime they were ordered to send postcards, post-dated March 1944, to relatives who were still in Theresienstadt, saying they were well. Bacon said he and some others began their cards with the words '*Liebe Mutti*' (Dear Mum), because the German word *Mutti* is like the Hebrew word for death.

In fact his family was spared for a few more months, but were all gassed in mid-1944, after he had been separated from them and put to work with other imprisoned boys, hauling carts loaded with blankets and fuel and spreading the ashes of the dead on roads to prevent them becoming too slippery.

At times, when it was cold, the boys were allowed to warm themselves in the 'cloakrooms' where the doomed stripped before entering the gas chambers, which they were told were showers. Sometimes the boys were even allowed to shelter in the gas chambers.

8 June 1961 : As part of the concluding Auschwitz evidence, a British-born former British Army doctor, Mordecai Chen, now living in Israel, identified photographs of Belsen concentration camp, near Hanover, taken in his presence about 18 days after the camp was liberated in 1945.

More interesting, and even more horrible, was a 90-minute film shown by the prosecution as evidence: documentaries taken by the Soviet, American and British armies in various concentration camps. We saw the piles of emaciated bodies, spider-like survivors deliriously happy that they were still alive – many of them died a few days after liberation – row on row of artificial limbs and false teeth taken from victims, a bale of cloth made from human hair, German guards burying victims at Belsen under the orders of British soldiers.

Eichmann, a ghostly figure in the half-light of the glassed-in dock, was affected by the film. I watched him on our closed-circuit TV, which gave a close-up of his face. He often bit his lips or contorted his mouth. He swallowed heavily and occasionally opened his mouth like a fish, apparently trying to get breath. Once, as the film showed Supreme Allied Commander General Dwight Eisenhower and other American officers viewing a liberated concentration camp, he scribbled a note for his counsel.

As Reuters is shortly sending me to Moscow – about which I

am enthusiastic – I am to leave Israel in a day or two. Today I took round a large bouquet of gladioli for the Barkais as I went to say goodbye to them. Barkai told me I'd got into the Israeli press: he'd mentioned me in writing an article about Abu Ali and the gun which was taken away.

The Barkais gave me a handmade Bedouin bracelet made of an alloy produced in the desert, and then made me feel rather embarrassed by insisting I also take a small Arab-made brass coffee pot, from Nazareth, which had been standing on their radio set. I told them I felt like an American tourist who, according to Barkai, took traditional Arab hospitality so seriously that when Abu Ali offered him all sorts of things out of courtesy, he accepted them all, denuding the old Arab's collection of guns and so on.

9 June 1961 : This Friday was my last day at the trial, which was concerned with some procedural matters. The court adjourned until 19 June, to give the defence more time to prepare Eichmann to give evidence in his own defence.

Said goodbye to several of the trial lawyers, all most pleasant people, like so many Israelis I've met. I've never been to a foreign country which has appealed to me so much.

As for Eichmann, my dominant question is: how could it all have been possible? My view is that it was a historical accident, due largely to Hitler's personality, that made it happen in Germany, not that it was caused by particularly strong anti-Semitism among the German people. The evidence has shown that, in some ways, other countries, such as Poland, Ukraine and Hungary, were worse in that respect.

Of course, British people may say – and I think it myself – that even if there had been a dictatorship in Britain, such things would not have been possible, at least to such a degree. *[Today I take a critical view of the German élite in the 1930s, particularly the generals, who had the means to remove Hitler as soon as he had shown himself responsible for the murders, in late June and early July 1934, of at least 85 and possibly more than 150 people: mostly members of the Nazi paramilitary organization, the SA, including its leader, Ernst*

Röhm, but also including some conservative politicians, officers and clerics. Hitler had accused Röhm of planning 'a second revolution' and seeking to place the SA, with its four million members, above the army. But he provided no proof and, instead of putting Röhm on trial, had him shot.]

I'm basically against the death penalty, but in the case of Eichmann I waver from day to day, some days thinking it is the only right penalty, to remove this thing from human ken, and then on others I try to make excuses for him, saying it was not his fault that he was born German, that he joined the SS in its early days, was transferred to the Jewish Affairs Department and indoctrinated with the nauseating nonsense which led him to send millions of Jews to their deaths. At the moment the feeling that he should be executed predominates in me. But I would not like to be the judge.

This evening I said goodbye to our hotel staff with a short piano recital of old favourites, Lionel groaning some of the words with me, shortly before *shabbat* (Sabbath) clamped down (6.07 pm in Jerusalem and 6.23 pm in Tel Aviv). Five of us shared a taxi down the Judaean hills, with a last nostalgic look at Jerusalem before we reached Abu Gosh. Then past Tel Aviv to the coastal resort of Herzliya, about nine miles north of the sprawling commercial metropolis.

No doubt, I'd prefer Jerusalem to Tel Aviv if I lived in Israel, even though the latter has more of what is called culture, in the way of concerts, theatres etc. Ted, one of our teleprinter operators, who also leaves for home tomorrow, shared a Hollywood-style suite with me in the Sharon Hotel, overlooking the lovely beach. (About £5 each for bed, breakfast and a main meal.)

Lionel, Reg and a German reporter of the Associated Press, Hans Neuerbourg, are staying at the hotel for several days during the court recess. We all dashed down to the beach for an immediate plunge, except Reg, who cannot swim. We worried about Lionel when he went out of sight in the dark, being a little reckless as usual because he is a strong swimmer. But it was a silly thing to do, as there is a strong undertow there.

Dinner included my last portion of *shabbat gefillte* fish, a mixture of fish and bready stuff served ready-made on the Sabbath, when certain kinds of work are forbidden in kosher hotels. All Israel's good hotels are kosher, as religious Jews would otherwise not patronize them, for they are not even allowed to eat kosher in a non-kosher hotel, I'm told.

It was the 40th birthday of Hans – an ex-Afrika Corps anglophile, who received his *Daily Telegraph and Morning Post* in a Siegfried Line bunker up to 3 September 1939. I presented him, the AP man, with a diver's mask and snorkel on behalf of the Reuterians present.

10 June 1961 : Ted and I slept little, scratching ourselves; he thanks to some kind of fly and I mainly with peeling skin from last Sunday's Red Sea scorcher. Up nevertheless at 7.30 am, to swim again, well greased, in that wonderful warm sea. Hotel filled mainly with elderly American Jews.

We five spent most of the day near the remains of the Roman harbour of Apollonia, which we visited a fortnight ago. Though the somewhat agitated water was not as clear as the Red Sea, I was able to watch lots of not-so-garish fish and hermit crabs. As my back was feeling the sun, I put on a shirt for my last swim. It filled with water and made me look like a 'Michelin Man', that bulbous advert for tyres.

Wally, who's been grand to work with, and his wife, Shula, a judge, joined us for a farewell dinner, at which I bought a bottle of champagne to pay off a bet I lost to Wally; I'd bet that Eichmann would be giving evidence by today.

Wally has given me as a farewell present a new edition of Theodor Herzl's *Altneuland*, a novel written by the Budapest-born Zionist leader around 1895, forecasting the creation of a Jewish state. This new edition has pictures showing to what extent Herzl's prophecy has come true. Shula inscribed the book: 'Here is the story behind the story.'

I intend to send them something from Moscow, but tonight handed Shula a bouquet of carnations bought in a typically

German flower shop in Jerusalem, run by two German Jews. Seeing such shops moves me a lot, makes me think how crazy it was that the Nazis did such things to the Jews.

11 June 1961 : After saying goodbye to Lionel and Hans, who will be reporting on the rest of the trial, Ted – who flew with me as far as Rome – and I boarded a Bristol Britannia of the Israeli airline, El Al, at Tel Aviv airport. We'd taken our last look at the palms, the cacti, the fruit trees and the modern settlements on our way to the airport at Lydda.

'*Shalom*' (peace) was the first word on the cabin loudspeaker. I learned only recently that Jerusalem means 'city of peace', 'salem' being a corruption of '*shalom*', the most frequent Hebrew greeting.

Soon we were at 20,000 feet *[6,100 m]* having breakfast – still kosher – in this wonderfully quiet plane. Had a glimpse of brownish Cyprus, with a few streaks of snow on its peaks, and before long the Italian coast near Catanzaro was in view.

The flight to Rome took about 4^1/$_2$ hours. We landed at the new airport of Fiumicino, on flat land near the coast. Each plane taxis up to a seemingly endless arrival hall. One then walks along a rubber-coated corridor to reach one's connecting plane in another arrival bay, thus saving the use of buses.

The flight northwards in a French-made Caravelle jet of Alitalia took us above the Italian coast. The sea was clear of clouds, the land covered. I could identify the port of Leghorn (Livorno), where, in late 1944 and early 1945, I was a sub-lieutenant in a Royal Navy motor torpedo boat flotilla.

I also spotted – some 20 miles west of Leghorn – the small island of Gorgona, between which and the coast the Germans had laid mines. Then I saw the great harbour of La Spezia, not far north of Leghorn, which was German-held until shortly before the end of the war.

We flew close to coastal resorts, such as Santa Margherita and Portofino, from where German coastal batteries used to have a go at us, ineffectively. Glimpses of the Alps through clouds and then nothing but clouds over Germany, until we came down at

Frankfurt to be met by Elfi and Chris. I've never seen Chris looking so radiant. So was Elfi, through some tears.

The intermittent rain which fell as we drove the 100 miles home was the first I had seen for about seven weeks. The greenery seemed overpowering, because in Israel it is not such a dark green nor so ubiquitous.

31 The case for Eichmann

On 29 June – by then I was in Moscow – Dr Servatius opened the defence case for Eichmann. He argued that the SS officer only became involved in the extermination of European Jews because he was made head of Department IV-B4 of the Gestapo and could not, therefore, escape being implicated. But Dr Servatius added that Eichmann would be able to show that the real responsibility lay with the political leadership of Germany at that time. Dr Servatius further argued that, as Eichmann was not a member of the Nazi leadership corps, he was on the lowest rung of the ladder of responsibility. Eichmann, in his evidence, argued that he was nothing more than an expert in the emigration of Jews. He claimed that as 'chief railway transport officer for the deportation of Jews from the German-occupied territories', he had eased the sufferings of the deportees by ending the transport chaos and establishing some order. He said he had been concerned 'strictly with timetables and technical transport'.

It had been impossible for him to take any independent action in his official capacity.

Eichmann said that, before Himmler had issued his order in 1940 for the deportation of Jews to ghettos in Eastern Europe, he – Eichmann – had favoured the settlement of Jews on Madagascar, and had worked together with numerous other government departments on that project. It was, however, never implemented.

Eichmann said that the first occasion on which he heard mention of the 'final solution' of the Jewish problem – the mass murder of the Jews – was at the Wannsee Conference in Berlin in January 1942. He felt that he was not guilty because the decisions of the Wannsee Conference were made by the élite, and he had had to toe the line. Eichmann told the court that he had asked many times to be relieved of his post and given another, more congenial one. He had reluctantly visited extermination camps, but had had to obey orders.

Asked by his counsel whether he felt guilt, Eichmann said the actions he took had been ordered by the Head of State. He added, 'Ethically I condemn myself. I have regret and condemnation for the extermination of the Jewish people, which was ordered by the German rulers, but I myself could not have done anything to prevent it.'

Questioned by the Attorney-General, Eichmann confirmed that he had said to an Israeli police interrogator, 'I am aware that I shall be found guilty as an accomplice to murder. I am aware that I face the death penalty, and I am not asking for mercy because I do not deserve it.' He had also said he was prepared to hang himself in public as an atonement for 'these terrible crimes'.

However, Eichmann added that he did not consider himself guilty from the legal point of view, as he had only carried out orders. But he felt guilty from the human point of view.

Eichmann denied being an anti-Semite. He described himself as a 'fervent nationalist'. He said he had not wanted the Jews to be exterminated, but to be given a country of their own.

Under further questioning, he said, 'I regard the murder, the extermination of the Jews, as one of the most hideous crimes in the history of mankind.'

Asked if he had felt the same at the time the crime was committed, he said, 'When, for the first time, I saw dead Jews, I was utterly shattered. But I was in the iron grip of orders. Many times I asked the Head of Section IV to release me from these duties.'

After an adjournment, the closing speech of the prosecution began on 8 August.

The Attorney-General alleged that Eichmann had murdered 'with fervour and insatiable lust'. He asked the court to find that Eichmann had been involved in a conspiracy to commit crimes against the Jewish people and against humanity, and that he had occupied a central position in the conspiracy and was therefore responsible for all the acts committed by himself and by others in furtherance of the conspiracy.

After a three-day adjournment, the court sat again on 14 August to hear the closing speech for the defence.

Dr Servatius said that the main issue before the court was to what extent Eichmann bore responsibility for having sent Jews to the death camps, knowing the fate that was in store for them.

Dr Servatius stated that the death camps were under the control of the SS Head Office for Economy and Administration and not under the Reich Security Head Office, in which Eichmann worked. He put forward the defence of 'superior orders' – that at all times Eichmann had been acting on orders received from above. He argued that the court should not seek revenge for deeds which were, in fact, committed by Germany's political leaders.

The court's judgement, delivered on 11 December 1961, after a four-month adjournment, found Eichmann guilty of committing crimes against the Jewish people and against humanity, of committing war crimes and of being a member of criminal organizations – the SS, the Gestapo and the SD (the Nazi security service) – as defined by Article 10 of the Nuremberg Charter, issued by the four-power Allied War Crimes Tribunal.

The court rejected the defence claim, put forward earlier, that it had no jurisdiction to try Eichmann, as the state of Israel had not existed when Eichmann's crimes were committed. It also rejected another defence claim, that the law under which Eichmann was tried, the 'Nazi and Nazi Collaborators (Punishment) Law' of 1950, was illegal because it was retroactive.

The court found that all Eichmann's crimes were recognized as crimes in the laws of all civilized nations, including Germany before and after the Nazi era. The 1950 Israeli law did not conflict with the rules of natural justice.

The court rejected Dr Servatius's major argument, that Eichmann's crimes had been committed in the course of duty and were therefore Acts of State for which only the German state, not Eichmann, could be held responsible. The plea of an 'Act of State' had been rejected by the Nuremberg International Military Tribunal and in a resolution of the United Nations General Assembly passed on 11 December 1946.

The judgement also rejected the defence claim that, because the kidnapping and abduction of Eichmann was illegal, this invalidated the right to bring him to trial. In support of this view, it quoted a number of English and United States precedents.

The court stated that Eichmann's chief task had not been to obtain the necessary railway wagons to send the deportees to the extermination camps, but to obtain the Jews with which to fill the wagons. The judgment added: 'He was not a puppet in the hands of others; he was one of those who pulled the strings.'

The court said the evidence had shown not only that the accused knew of the Nazi Government's intent to destroy the Jewish people, but that he personally shared that intent.

The court found Eichmann guilty as an accomplice in the general crime of the 'final solution' in all its forms.

It also found him guilty, from August 1941, of causing serious bodily harm to Jews as part of the efforts intended to exterminate those Jews who still remained alive. He was also found guilty of devising methods intended to prevent child-bearing among Jews imprisoned in the Theresienstadt ghetto.

Eichmann was also found guilty of crimes against humanity, which included all or any of the following: murder, extermination, enslavement, starvation, deportation of the civilian population, plunder of Jewish property and persecution on national, racial, religious or political grounds.

The court found Eichmann guilty of the war crime of ill-treating and deporting Jews from German-occupied territories during the Second World War. He was also found guilty of organizing the deportation of over half a million Polish citizens from their homes, with intent to settle German families in their stead, and guilty on a similar count referring to more than 14,000 Slovenes.

Although the court found that Eichmann had caused the deportation of tens of thousands of gypsies to extermination camps, it stated that there was no reliable proof that Eichmann knew that the gypsies were to be exterminated.

The court rejected Eichmann's principal defence of 'superior orders', stating that the rejection of that defence had become general, if not universal, in all civilized countries, and had also been rejected by the General Assembly of the United Nations. Even the Nazis had not repealed a section of the German Military Criminal Code stating that whoever committed an offence against the criminal law, by obeying a superior's order, was punishable as an accomplice to a crime, if he knew that the order was to commit an act which was a crime or an offence under military law. That section also applied to the SS.

The court stated that Eichmann knew that the order for the physical extermination of the Jews was manifestly unlawful. He had said in court that he regarded the extermination of the Jews as one of the gravest crimes in history.

Eichmann had acted within the general framework of the orders which were given to him, but within that framework, the court said, he 'went to the very extreme to bring about the speedy and complete extermination of all Jews in the territories under German rule and influence'.

After the Attorney-General had asked for the death penalty to be imposed, and Dr Servatius had called for a more lenient punishment, Eichmann addressed the court.

He said the murders of Jews were committed against his will. He had tried to get away from his desk and go into the front line. His guilt, he said, lay in his obedience.

He argued that the 'ruling circles' of Nazi Germany deserved punishment, not underlings like himself. He added, 'Today, of my own free will, I would ask the Jewish people for pardon and would confess that I am bowed down with shame at the thought of the iniquities committed against the Jews.'

On 15 December, after an adjournment, the presiding judge

sentenced Eichmann to death for what he called 'crimes of unparalleled enormity in their nature and their extent'. The aim had been to blot out an entire people from the face of the earth.

The judge added, 'The dispatch by the accused of every train carrying a thousand souls to Auschwitz, or to any of the other places of extermination, amounted to direct participation by him in one thousand acts of premeditated murder, and his legal and moral responsibility for those murders is in no way less than the measure of liability of him who, with his own hands, put those persons into the gas chambers.

'Even had we found that the accused acted out of blind obedience, as he alleges, we would still have said that one who had participated in crimes of such dimensions, for years on end, must undergo the greatest punishment known to the law, and no order given to him could be a ground even for mitigating his punishment. But, in fact, we have found that, in acting as he did, the accused identified himself in his heart with the orders received by him and was actuated by an ardent desire to attain the criminal objective.

'The court sentences Adolf Eichmann to death for the crimes against the Jewish people, the crimes against humanity and those war crimes of which he has been found guilty.'

Eichmann exercised his right to appeal to the Israeli Supreme Court against the court's verdict and sentence. On 29 May 1962 the Supreme Court rejected his appeal.

Just before midnight on 31 May, after Israeli President Isaac Ben-Zvi had rejected an appeal for clemency lodged by his wife, Eichmann was hanged in Ramleh prison near Tel Aviv. One of four journalists who were among the witnesses was my Reuter colleague, Wally Wallenstein. Eichmann was the first person to be executed in the Jewish state since it was set up in 1948.

Eichmann declined a final meal, but drank half a bottle of red wine before the hanging. Although originally a Protestant, Eichmann turned down a suggestion from a Canadian missionary, Pastor William Hull, that he again commit himself to Christianity. But Eichmann, who had been reading the Bible with

313

Pastor Hull, described himself as '*gottgläubig*' (a believer in God), a term used by those Nazis who had left the churches but who were not agnostics or atheists. Pastor Hull's wife, who acted as interpreter, said Eichmann 'showed no sign of confession or repentance'.

Eichmann rejected the offer to place a black hood over his head before the hanging. His last words were, 'Long live Argentina, Austria and Germany. I obeyed my mission in war. Remember me to my wife, family and friends.'

Eichmann's body was cremated, which he had asked for in his will. His ashes were scattered in the Mediterranean – outside Israeli territorial waters, about eight miles from Jaffa. Under Israeli law the body of an executed criminal had normally to be handed over to the person's family, but in this case the Minister of Police amended the regulation, evidently to prevent there being a grave of Eichmann which could have become a shrine for anti-Semites. The cremation and the dispersal of the ashes mirrored the methods adopted in the cases of Nazi criminals executed after being convicted by the four-power International War Crimes Tribunal.

32 Off to Moscow as new Berlin crisis looms

13 June 1961 : When Elfi had taken some trouble to obtain some envelopes of different colours, which Chris needed for school, he said, 'Oh Mummy, I love you. I can't do without you.' (He was eight in March.)

Mum attended the open day at Robin's Quaker boarding school, Ackworth, near Pontefract, Yorkshire. She wrote to us: 'You need have no worries about him, and must rejoice that you are able to give him this wonderful opportunity of attaining an excellent education.' *[For this we were indebted to Reuters, which made a large contribution to the school fees.]* Robin was 13 in May.

14 June 1961 : Have read G.K. Chesterton's short biography of St Francis of Assisi, that Christian Communist. A theme which struck me was Francis's thankfulness to God for having been granted a life at all. I was not convinced by Chesterton's argumentation in favour of believing that Francis had really performed the many miracles attributed to him, though I'm not saying that some of them did not happen.

15 June 1961 : Berlin is in the forefront again, now that Khrushchev has once more, and most seriously, in a long memorandum, called for a peace conference on Germany.

20 June 1961 : To Cologne-Bonn airport to see off the unimpressive, cherubic West German President, silver-haired Dr Heinrich Lübke, for the first state visit to France of a German Head of State in modern times. (The last such visit was paid by the Holy Roman Emperor, Sigismund, to Charles the Mad, King of France, in the early fifteenth century. Stephanie Roussel, correspondent of the important French evening newspaper, *France Soir*, told me she had decided not to use the name 'Charles the Mad' in view of the fact that there is a Charles ruling in Paris today.)

Adenauer was there to see off Lübke for this historic trip, so I asked him to say something for two other pressmen and me. He answered in a friendly fashion, describing the visit as proof of the close links, indeed the friendship, between the two peoples whom he said were now 'inseparable'. When we grabbed Lübke as he made his way to his Lufthansa Viscount, he said that France and Germany, who had long been at each other's throats, could now be an example to others by getting along with each other.

After a visit to Cologne Zoo, Chris asked to be taken into the great Gothic cathedral *[begun 1248, completed 1880]*. He was awed by its size and beauty. Looking at the stained glass windows, he several times asked me to show him God – meaning Jesus– and was pleased when he was able to spot the infant Christ in Mary's arms.

In Jerusalem today Eichmann began to speak in his defence. To try to recapture the atmosphere of our cubicle in the courthouse, I bought a tin of Jaffa orange juice, canned in Tel Aviv. Have learnt that this name is a free Hebrew translation of the title of Herzl's book *Alt Neuland (Old New Land)*. *Tel* means 'ruin' and *Aviv* means 'spring', the idea being that a onetime ruin is experiencing a new spring.

21 June 1961 : Have enjoyed ordering and filing some of the letters I sent to Mum during the war. Perusing them, was amazed to see how many girls' names cropped up before the arrival on the scene of Fräulein Elfi Kowitz in 1946.

Sub-edited part of a highlight version from East Berlin TV, covered by our West Berlin office, of a Khrushchev speech in

Moscow on the eve of the twentieth anniversary of the German invasion of the Soviet Union in 1941. Khrushchev, in the uniform of a lieutenant-general, said in the clearest way yet that the Soviet Union will sign a separate peace treaty with East Germany by the end of this year unless the West agrees to join the Soviet Union in signing a peace treaty with the two Germanys.

22 June 1961 : Official news that my Soviet visa can be issued has reached the Soviet Embassy here, one of its diplomats, Mr Siborov, told me today – in Russian, on the phone. I replied that I was most pleased, and thanked him for the news, later breaking into German because I could not understand all he said. Told him I hoped that, after my planned two-month stay in Russia, I would not need to change over from Russian in future telephone talks. He said he was always pleased to give someone cheering news.

How do I feel? Excited, and a little apprehensive as to whether I shall be able to hold down the job. Also feel sorry at leaving Elfi and the boys again, but console myself with the argument that, if we go to Moscow later for some years, Elfi will see much more of me than in the past few years.

In a letter from Dad, which arrived today, he praised my admiration for Israel, saying he had thought my 'warmest admiration' was for Russia. This misreads my viewpoint. I think there are both horrible and hopeful things in the Soviet system; I certainly do not admire it more than all others. More about this when I've actually seen it!

Extracts from my horoscopes for this week: from the British newspaper, *Today*: 'Unexpected opportunities for travel make this a busy week.' From the German magazine *Hör Zu*: 'A new aim, a new idea. That does you good, even though it turns out that there are some diversions.' And Elfi's from *Today*: 'New friendships blossom while older ones fade. Revolutionary changes are fore-shadowed. Be ready to embrace them.'

23 June 1961 : Nearly finished *Alt Neuland*, which gives an amazingly prophetic picture of modern Israel which is, I think, as near Utopia as any race has reached – still a long way from it, of course. *[Today, my view of Israel is much more negative. I still think that it was right that the United Nations granted the Jews part of their ancient homeland – particularly after the Holocaust. And it was wrong of neighbouring Arab countries to try to eradicate Israel by war. Equally, it was wrong of Israel, backed by the United States with its influential Jewish lobby, to occupy large areas of formerly Palestinian Arab land in the wake of its military victories in several wars, turning hundreds of thousands of Palestinian Arabs into refugees. In the end, I think, Israel will have to withdraw from all or nearly all of the territory it occupied in the 1967 war in order to bring an end to Palestinian suicide bombings and the like.]*

After a small drinks party we gave tonight, marking my impending departure for Moscow, my Russian friend Boris Yurinov, TASS correspondent, took me aside and urged me to do my best to give a fair picture of life in the Soviet Union. *[Perhaps his embassy had told him to say that.]* He said there were Western correspondents who seized on shortcomings – 'and we have some'– without explaining the reasons for them. (I thought: the reasons are in dispute.)

I told Boris I would do my best, that it was in my interest for relations between the Soviet Union and the West to be good. I said that my attitude towards Russia had already caused some of those close to me to dub me a near-Communist, 'which of course,' I told Boris, 'is nonsense'. He grinned; he evidently thinks it's nonsense too.

I'd shown Boris and his wife, Ina, a book of photographs of the Soviet Union, published by the American magazine *Life* and sent to us by Dad. They thought some of it was typical American propaganda, but were amused by a picture of a middle-aged man wearing pyjamas outside at a holiday resort. 'That, unfortunately, is typical,' Ina said, 'though mainly of the older generation.' She laughed heartily at a shot of a backwoods couple, in padded winter clothing, the man half-shaven, standing at the counter of a Ukrainian village store. 'They would have to choose a picture like that,' she commented.

24 June 1961 : Took Elfi and Chris for a small farewell outing, a visit to a new children's playground in Godesberg and tea in the open air at the Stadthalle restaurant.

I know, of course, that going to Moscow will be a wonderful experience for me but, this evening, the thought of going away again so soon was saddening, although, if I get a long-term assignment in Moscow next year, Elfi, Chris and I will see more of each other than for a long time.

25 June 1961 : The day I flew to Moscow! Up at 5 am to Rhineland sunshine. Rice Krispies, bacon and tomatoes, lemon cheese on a white roll, and a cup of tea. I'd said goodbye to Chris last night – showing him Moscow on Robin's small globe, incidentally it's almost as far east as Israel – and he was still asleep as, just after six, we drove away to nearby Godesberg station.

Elfi came on to the platform to say goodbye, looking very young and a little weepy as I stood in the corridor of an Italian carriage, part of a long-distance south-north train which took me in about an hour to Düsseldorf.

An SAS Caravelle flew me to Copenhagen in just over an hour – incredible – with a look down at Hamburg, the Baltic coast of Schleswig-Holstein and the Danish mainland. We turned eastwards over the large Danish islands in the Baltic, and came into land at Copenhagen from the Kattegat, the sea between Denmark and Sweden, with the Swedish coast about ten miles away.

Lunched in the Tivoli, Copenhagen's large city-centre pleasure garden, with the local Reuter correspondent, Australian Geoffrey Dodd. Neat idea at the modern airport – children's rubber-tyred scooters, for use by pretty hostesses on the long corridors of the departure bays.

Enjoyed the Danish signs – like corrupted Dutch, which is like corrupted German! – and the trim city with its respectable-looking, well dressed citizens about their Sunday morning pursuits.

After the scheduled four hours in Copenhagen, an SAS Convair took us in about 90 minutes, over forests, lakes and farmland, to another smart-looking city, Stockholm, set beautifully by the north-eastern Baltic and near a string of lakes.

Chatted with Swedish merchant navy captain, L. Nilsson, of the MS *Arvidsjaur*, which sails regularly to Middlesborough, Yorkshire, for the Swedish Iron Ore Company. He takes a few passengers sometimes – might be a nice way to go home one day.

Stockholm's airport is smaller, more homely, than Copenhagen's. After a 20-minute wait I was in the air again, in a less than half full 55-seater Douglas 6B. Below, the well-ordered suburbs of Stockholm, with many small detached houses. And then we were over lakes, with yachts and motor boats furrowing through the dark greeny-blue.

Soon came the Baltic, and a member of the crew told us in several languages, including Russian, that our flight would last two hours and fifty minutes and would take us over Riga, the Latvian capital.

11.58 pm – As this red-letter day draws to a close, I am sitting at a large mahogany desk in my palatial Edwardian- (or Stalin-) style suite on the 28th floor (four from the top) of the pre-Khrushchev postwar skyscraper hotel, the Ukraina.

The suite costs eight roubles a night – about three pounds at the official rate of exchange, which is highly unfavourable to Westerners. Breakfast, I think, is not included. The actual purchasing power of eight roubles is probably about 30 shillings *[£1.50]*. However, even at three pounds, for a room in one of the biggest hotels in the capital of the Soviet Union it is not terribly dear.

The suite has a large sitting-room, a double bedroom, a hall and a bathroom. No smaller room available tonight, and we did well to obtain this one – we being mainly 28-year-old Londoner John Miller, the second of our two correspondents in Moscow, Norwich-trained ex-provincial reporter, slim, bespectacled with hornrims. His humour and street-wiseness are helping him to survive Moscow.

I'll go back to where I left off. As we approached Moscow I could see, through breaks in the clouds, Russian soil beneath, rolling woodlands alternating with fields and some small lakes.

The fields often looked like large sausages – the main fields of the collective and state farms – and then I could distinguish in places the small strips, of an acre or two, which each collective farmer is allowed to work for his own keep and profit.

All the roads looked unpaved from above. Bumpily we came through the clouds and over a snaky yellow river (the Moskva?) to land at Moscow's Sheremetyevo airport, some 15 kilometres *[10 miles]* from the city centre. Scores of large Tupolev jets, red stars dominant in their markings, lined the tarmac. MOSKVA in big Cyrillic letters greeted us from the top of the neo-classical sandstone terminal building.

An English-speaking official in brown uniform took our passports as we left the plane, and we were given them back, stamped, about 15 minutes later in a waiting room, where arriving passengers watched a jolly music-hall show booming forth from an old-fashioned-looking TV. Displayed in showcases were Edwardian-looking wares: dancers made of china, dolls, boxes of chocolate, bottles of brandy. Above us, a crystal candelabra. The TV produced waltz tunes as we waited. Women in blue uniforms with red armbands let us out of the waiting room as soon as we had our passports.

By then John had slipped in and identified me. He laid his hands on an elderly taxi while I filled in a customs and currency declaration and collected my bags, which were not searched.

I found that the currency I had on me was 46 Danish crowns, one shilling and twopence sterling *[almost 6p]*, two West German marks and 35 pfennigs and half an Israeli pound. Quite a collection, mainly souvenirs!

It was darkening as we were driven into the centre of Moscow along wide roads, dual carriageways for most if not all of the way, at first past small houses, some wooden, later past great blocks in over-decorated Stalin style.

My hotel overlooks an arm of the river and a sea of lights. Up here it is quiet. I have identified across the water what looks like the high tower of the new university building. My brain is dull with fatigue, but I am very happy to be here.

26 June 1961 : 6.47 pm – I am in the five-yards-by-five Reuter office on the second floor of no. 24, 3rd Tverskaya Yamskaya Street, adjoining the pleasant three-room flat of Bob Elphick, the chief correspondent, who is on leave. *[Altogether there are five Tverskaya Yamskaya streets. Tverskaya is the adjective for the city, about 100 miles north-west of Moscow, which used to be called Tver and is now called Kalinin after the former titular President of the Soviet Union, Mikhail Kalinin (1875–1946), a slavish henchman of Stalin. His name was also given to the former capital of German East Prussia, Königsberg, where Elfi lived for some years; it became Kaliningrad in 1946 and is still Kaliningrad as I write in early 2002, though Tver regained its old name in 1990.*

When I came to Moscow in 1961, Kaliningrad and the region around it, the former northern part of East Prussia which had been annexed by Russia in 1945, were a closed military area on the Soviet Union's western frontier, and – with few exceptions – were not opened to Westerners until 1990. Elfi and I visited the area in 1991 in a group of German 'nostalgia tourists'.

It was a shattering experience for her to see how a once prosperous region of Germany had become a run-down, impoverished Soviet province. She never wanted to go there again. But for me it was of unique interest both journalistically and personally, as my by then good command of Russian enabled me to establish friendly contacts with its new, Soviet, citizens.

I paid three more visits to Kaliningrad – some German friends were understandably but unrealistically critical when I used that name – the last one in 1996. I hope to write about Kaliningrad in a future book.

As for the other half of that street name, Yamskaya, that is easier to explain. It is an adjective meaning 'coachman', indicating that coach-men, yamshchiki, lived there, no doubt with their coaches and horses. In English, a mews.]

After a good night's sleep in my skyscraper, beneath a some-what impressionistic flower still-life, I bathed in the spotless bath-room, tried unsuccessfully to get something on the TV in my room – only radio was transmitting at the time, I think – and emerged into the dignified carpeted corridor.

I handed my room key to an elderly woman in light blue over-alls, who watches over my floor, sitting at a desk opposite the high-speed lift. I asked her how she was this morning. She said not too good, pointing to a boil on her nose. She told me she worked a 24-hour shift, then had three days off.

A pretty young woman with red fingernails had replaced last night's lift woman, who was elderly. I breakfasted in a ground-floor self-service restaurant on some dark-red fruit juice, an open ham sandwich and a large sweet biscuit or cake; about 5 shillings (at the official rate) *[25p]* for the lot.

Tourists from abroad, and a smaller number of Russians, milled around the vast foyer which, like the rest of the place, looks Edwardian or Victorian. As I waited for a taxi outside, I spoke to an Italian architect, here with several colleagues. His verdict on Moscow's modern architecture, 'No good.'

Appreciable traffic in the city, with buses and cars not as old, on average, as I had imagined they might be. Many wide roads. Streets in general well kept and clean. Here and there, even in the centre, some wooden houses. The taxi driver told me he earned 120 roubles a month – about £600 a year at the official rate, but appreciably less in purchasing power – and told me he had TV at home.

3rd Tverskaya Yamskaya Street, at the point where our office is, has five-storey stuccoed flats with balconies, evidently pre-war, with dark streaks on the stucco. Not a very pretty prospect, but it could be worse, and trees lining both sides of the street brighten things up.

Behind the office flat is a flagged yard with a volleyball court marked on it. The flat itself is quite large, with two living rooms rather larger than ours, one bedroom, a kitchen and hall each larger than ours. The flat will soon have an extra room, for the one-room office is shortly to be made part of the flat, as new office rooms are being provided by the authorities. This should make the flat adequate for Elfi, Chris and me. However, the furniture has been supplied by Reuters, which would mean we would have to store much of ours in Britain.

Met Brian Gardner, visiting *Sunday Express* journalist and

historian, who had been impressed by the intellect and aghast at the dogmatism of some Soviet historians he had just met.

I read some files, and John took me to lunch in their first-floor two-room flat in a larger 'foreigners' block'. As at the office building, a red-capped policeman in blue uniform keeps watch from a kind of sentry box. *[I learned later that the policeman watched comings and goings and forbade entrance to unauthorized Russians.]*

John's pretty, Norwich-born wife, Brenda, was depressed because they had had to postpone their move to a three-room flat, planned for tomorrow, because the lift in the other building, where they are to live on the eighth floor, is not working.

Brenda told me that meat is not always available on the nearby 'private enterprise' Russian market. When there are long queues she sometimes jumps them. If she takes along their seven-months-old son David – *Dodik* in Russian – people often make way for her; Russians love babies, she said.

The Millers buy some of their groceries through a Western import firm, which sends the stuff from Copenhagen. Reuters has supplied their quite attractive Finnish furniture.

A quiet day for news from Moscow today. Most hot news comes on the radio or on the TASS (Telegraphic Agency of the Soviet Union) news agency service, both of which can be picked up by Reuters radio monitoring station near London. Our Moscow correspondents then follow up with additional material and interpretative.

The correspondents also send news from the papers and from interviewing people, mainly foreign delegates or visitors, as Russians are pretty tight as a rule, believing many foreign correspondents to be spies or, in any case, warned not to associate with such elements.

We dropped into the nineteenth-century British Embassy, conveniently sited just across the Moskva river from the walled Kremlin. *[Built between 1891 and 1893, the embassy was the former residence of a rich merchant family, the Kharitonenkos. I learned later that in the fifties Stalin had been putting pressure on the British to move somewhere further away from the Kremlin – perhaps he was worried about bugging and the like. However, he died before a move was arranged. Today the embassy is in a new building, and the former embassy is the Ambassador's residence. A beautifully illustrated book about the former embassy,* The British Embassy Moscow, *by* Kathleen Berton (now Kathleen Berton Murrell), *who served in Moscow as first a Canadian and later a British diplomat, was published in 1991 with the support of the Foreign and Commonwealth Office and the Moscow offices of some British firms.]*

On the way to the embassy, we drove through Red Square – so named before the Communist era; *krasnyi*, the word for 'red', has the archaic meaning, 'beautiful'. I had my first glimpse of the low black-and-red marble mausoleum, close to the high redbrick Kremlin wall, housing the embalmed bodies of Lenin and Stalin. Today's top Soviet leaders stand on the flat roof of the mausoleum during ceremonial parades.

Behind the Kremlin wall I could see the gilded onion-shaped cupolas of several churches inside the Kremlin – made into museums since the revolution. In Red Square itself is the crazy garish but, to me, highly attractive cluster formed by the also onion-shaped domes of the former Cathedral of St Basil, another museum.

Altogether today I was in a kind of dream, perhaps due to the flight yesterday, but more probably because of the effect on me of at last being in Moscow. Strangely for part of the day I was slightly depressed, perhaps because there were no news stories.

I dined this evening with *Daily Telegraph* correspondent, Jeremy Wolfenden, charming university-educated, bespectacled son of the life peer, John Wolfenden, author of the liberal 1957 Wolfenden report on homosexuality. *[I learned later that Jeremy, who became a good friend in Moscow, was himself a homosexual.]*

As Jeremy was 27 today, I agreed to drink 50 grammes of vodka with him, accompanying some excellent sprats, followed by *solianka* – a soup with meat, olives, herbs, onions, sour cream and a slice of lemon. We ate in the comfortable 1902-built National Hotel, close to the Kremlin. Lenin used to stay there. I could still hardly believe this was all real.

Jeremy considers that the Khrushchev regime is doing great

things to improve the Soviet standard of living, and that most citizens, though they grumble at shortcomings, are behind the government. My impression of Moscow, after one day, is that it is in better fettle than I had expected.

Jeremy, who was first here in 1956, has been able to note changes: vast building programmes and much better clothing, for instance. We travelled back to the Ukraina in a spotless underground train, its lower half dark blue and top half light blue.

We set off from Revolution Square station, where bronze figures of 1917 fighters stand in marble archways. We went through several other palatial stations until we alighted at one named after the Ukrainian capital, Kiev. I found this station really impressive, with murals of Ukrainians in national dress, more marble columns, and ventilators masked by intricate plaster tracery.

Jeremy told me a joke about a Soviet guide who was told by a Western visitor that Soviet underground lines went down very deep, and was not sure whether this was criticism or compliment. So he did not know whether to say, 'Yes, they are deeper than anywhere else', or, 'But there are deeper ones in London.' This kind of thing is all part of a kind of Soviet gamesmanship, known to British residents as 'unasmanship'. *U nas* means 'here' or 'in our country'.

I learned that the National Hotel almost always displays a sign saying 'Restaurant closed', even when it is open. Jeremy thinks this is to deter Russians. The hotel caters mainly for its own foreign hotel guests and people who have found out that 'closed' does not mean 'shut'.

[Jeremy Wolfenden had imbibed his excellent Russian on an intensive Royal Navy course. His life and tragic early death in December 1965, due to chronic alcohol abuse, is described in The Fatal Englishman: Three Short Lives *by Sebastian Faulks (Hutchinson 1996, Vintage 1997).]*

During the day I met two members of the Reuter staff. The first was Grisha Zaitsev, burly cheerful middle-aged driver, in dark suit, open-necked shirt and soft grey or fawn flat cap. Grisha, who survived the wartime siege of Leningrad as a sergeant in the Soviet Army, is in charge of the office car, a brown Humber Hawk – known in Russian as a '*Gumber*' as there is no exact 'H' sound in the Russian alphabet – and looks after various technical needs of our correspondents, such as transformers for their electrical equipment. (Most of Moscow is on 120 volts instead of the West's usual 220 or so.) The other member of the staff I met was Viktor, a handsome man in his early twenties who is standing in for one of our two women translators and secretaries, who is on holiday.

33 Getting to know some Russians

27 June 1961 : This morning I was introduced to one of our translators, pretty brunette, 33-year-old Lena Yengyboryan. When I asked if she had needle and cotton to mend a hole in an inside pocket, she went out and bought what was needed with her own money and would not take the money back.

As my pending long-term appointment to Moscow, from next year, was already known to one of the Associated Press men, I thought it only right to tell John, who took it calmly. He might well have been expecting the job himself, as an inducement to stay on in Moscow after his normal two-year term expires at the end of this year.

Girls waiting to have their photos taken in a shop where I had 12 passport photos made – 10 shillings *[50p]* at the official rate – were pretty well dressed. The usual street scene in this season is colourful: most men in shirts and trousers, women in bright-coloured dresses of generally not bad-looking material. Some older women wear peasant-like headscarves.

A small minority of Mongolian faces. I got proof today that foreigners do not stand out too much when a half-shaven man in a blue suit, a fag in his mouth, asked me the way to the nearest metro station. I could not help him, but learned that he was from Novosibirsk in Siberia and that he earned 200 roubles a month as a building worker.

In a garden near the Bolshoi Theatre, a giant new statue of Karl

Marx, hewn from a 200-ton block of stone, is nearing completion. Moscow's very wide main roads continually impress me; scarcely any traffic congestion. *[This was due partly to the relatively small numbers of vehicles compared to Western Europe.]*

Interviewed two Russian journalists who are acting as spokesmen for the second Moscow International Film Festival starting on 9 July. One of Britain's delegates to the festival is to be Diana Dors, whose reputation as a star of slapstick films rests not a little on an ample bosom. She provided the angle for a mailed advance story on the festival, the first story I have written in Moscow.

A taxi-driver laughed when I asked him if he had enough to eat. I knew he had, but wanted to get his reaction. He put his monthly wage at 120 roubles. He told me he lived in two rooms with his wife and student-teacher daughter. He said in his block of flats 17 people lived in six rooms; six families shared one kitchen.

I was not sure he believed me when I said that standards in Britain were somewhat higher, adding that I realized Russia had lagged behind for a long time and had much to catch up.

He said of his flat, 'I like living there. It's very convenient for the centre of town.'

The Russian word for a speech is pronounced 'retch', so one can hear a British correspondent say, 'Khrushchev made a *bolshoi* (big) retch tonight.' I think Khrushchev would appreciate the joke.

Intourist – the 'In' comes from *inostrannyi*, 'foreign' – the official, monopoly travel agency dealing with foreigners, is a butt of old Moscow hands. One of them told me the true story of the Glasgow correspondent who came to Moscow wanting to see a football match. Intourist said there would be one on Friday at 6.30 pm and they would provide a car and interpreter.

On Tuesday, when he dropped in to the Intourist office to confirm matters, they said they were sorry could not provide the interpreter as they finished work at 7 pm, but the car would be there. When Friday came there was no car – but an interpreter turned up. After phoning furiously for transport, they reached the stadium half an hour late to find there was no match on that night after all.

Lots of kiosks and stalls on the streets selling ices and fruit juices. No Coca-Cola, thank goodness. *[The ice cream was tasty and creamy. I learned later that First Deputy Prime Minister Anastas Mikoyan, that sharp Armenian, somehow obtained the rights to have American-type ice cream made in the Soviet Union when, as Trade Minister in the fifties, he visited the United States. I also found later that ice cream was to be had on the streets in Moscow even in midwinter.]*

At dinner in the Ukraina, sat opposite an East German official and had the usual argument about the meaning of freedom and democracy. Though a Communist, he seemed to have quite some respect for British institutions. He said that democracy in the Communist countries was developing increasingly inside the parties and in industry.

This man, who said he was concerned with economic matters, apologized for not giving me his name – few Russians would have apologized – but said it could cost him his job if I were to exploit it. I understood. He told me his father had been a Social Democrat, but he himself had been conscripted by the Nazis and had fought in Russia. He had only gradually become pro-Communist in the last years of the war and immediately afterwards. He told me he was not even allowed to make personal friendships with his Soviet comrades. When I asked him if he thought this was right, he said, 'I am too small a cog to assess that.'

Western correspondents find it difficult to be invited into Russian homes in Moscow; it's somewhat easier in the provinces. Apart from political and security reasons, there is another in Moscow: Russians don't want to invite foreigners to flats where they have hardly room to turn round. However, ordinary people don't seem at all unfriendly.

28 June 1961 : Most of the time I am in near-ecstasy at being here. I think the main reason for this is the exceptional interest aroused in me by being in the capital of the Communist world and of Russia, for I strongly desire to know more both about Communism and Russians. It also gives me great pleasure to practise my Russian. In addition, of course, there is the challenge of Moscow as a journalistic assignment.

Censorship of foreign correspondents' despatches finished some weeks ago – I'd have liked to have seen it in operation, just for the experience. The door covered with a green curtain in the comfortable press room of the Central Telegraph Office, behind which the – unseen – censors used to work, still remains.

In the days of censorship all news messages had to be handed in at this office for approval, before being either cabled or telephoned from there. This meant that correspondents spent a large part of their lives there, waiting for stories to be cleared, which could take from a few minutes to days.

We still file stories by cable and phone. Cables have to be handed in at the same office, with no wait for a censor, and we can phone from the office or elsewhere.

Our main news sources are the newspapers, the radio and the TASS news agency. But radio broadcasts and the radioed TASS news transmissions are picked up by Reuters radio monitoring station north of London, so we cannot compete on hot breaks from them. Our task is to add descriptive and interpretative material and, of course, to obtain other types of stories where possible, through interviews.

Official bodies, I'm told, are not very productive for Western journalists, but I believe that will improve. I had an object lesson about our work today when a 'friendship meeting' for the visiting North Vietnam Prime Minister, Pham Van Dong, was addressed by Khrushchev for an hour in the Great Kremlin Hall. The event was televised.

Lena took full notes while John, whose Russian is a deal better than mine, and I took notes of important passages as far as we could. We also tape-recorded the speech. When it was over Lena dictated to us in English the passages we wanted. On doubtful passages we checked the tape-recording or John's or my notes.

Then we put in a phone call to London, which took about 45 minutes to come through. By then, a basic report of the speech would have long been issued by London sub-editors, who would have received it from our monitoring station. It was for us to provide a 'top' for the story, comprising the main points of the speech, some descriptive of the scene and the applause, and a little interpretative stating that the speech had maintained the firm tone of recent Soviet speeches on Berlin.

Khrushchev said additional measures would be taken to maintain fighting capacity if the West mobilized over the Berlin crisis. He added that there would be no blockade of West Berlin, but that the West must respect East Germany's rights as a sovereign state after the Soviet Union had signed a peace treaty with it. The Soviet Union has said that it intends to sign such a treaty alone if the West refuses to join in.

The arrival in London of our story enables London to change the dateline of the story from London to Moscow, and drop the attribution to Moscow Radio. If we had known in advance that this was going to be a major speech, we would have booked our phone call in advance.

Changed my room tonight from the 28th to the fourth floor because the first one was too expensive and took longer to reach. Perhaps I should just have taken a smaller room on the 28th floor, for on the fourth floor I found traffic noise disturbing, while it had hardly been noticeable on the 28th.

My new room, with bath, shower, lavatory, radio and a large desk – also decorated with an impressionist print of a landscape – costs only $3^1/_2$ roubles which, even at the unfair official rate, works out at only 28 shillings *[£1.40 in today's money]* without breakfast. A similar room in West Germany would cost about the same.

As on the 28th floor, there is a bath plug but no plug for the washbasin. Down here (not upstairs) the lavatory float has a hole in it, causing the water to start running at times. I shall report both these faults.

One cannot have newspapers delivered to rooms. Service in the main restaurant is slow, but there are several smaller restaurants, called buffets, on various floors and here service is quick.

I have decided that the vast pile of the Ukraina, topped by a thin spire rather like that of St Martin-in-the-Fields on Trafalgar

Square, reminds me most of the kind of building that can be made from an old-fashioned box of children's bricks. The decorative bits are terribly excessive and are now officially frowned upon.

29 June 1961 : The Ukraina must have the most international clientele of any hotel in the world because, as well as Westerners, there are Communist foreigners and all the races of the Soviet Union. Two brown-faced men in maroon robes, wearing sandals, whom I took to be Burmese monks, were – I was told by a hotel attendant – Soviet Uzbeks from Central Asia, in their national costume. I also came across a bearded Russian Orthodox priest, with a gilded chain around his neck.

John took today off to move into their new flat, three living rooms instead of two. It's on the eighth floor and the lift was still out of order, though he'd been promised it would be working. It was fixed by 7 pm. He had to walk up the stairs eight times, while his Russian removers had to carry furniture up all the way. *[That reminds of me a cartoon I saw in the Soviet satirical magazine,* Krokodil. *Under the heading 'Final touches', it had a drawing of a lift, with a notice on it saying: 'Lift not working.']*

Strawberries at street stalls cost $1^1/_2$ roubles a kilo – nearly half my hotel room price.

This evening to a British Embassy reception for the Royal Ballet, headed by prima ballerina Dame Margot Fonteyn and choreographer Frederick Ashton. They have appeared in Leningrad, and open in Moscow on 2 July. The reception was certainly more appealing than a normal diplomatic function, with all those pretty ballerinas sprinkled around the dignified room with its pictures of several British monarchs, including a rather austere one of our present Queen.

Through a window I could see the Kremlin across the river. I noticed that a Christian cross on one of the gilt-domed churches is still the highest object in the Kremlin, beating the Red Star, which surmounts some smaller towers and blocks.

Met some of Moscow's Western press corps, including Ed Stevens of *Time* and *Life*, Seymour Topping of the *New York*

Times, and the unofficial doyen, moustached Henry Shapiro, chief of the United Press International bureau for about 20 years, and his Russian wife.

The ballet folk have preferred Leningrad to what they have seen of Moscow. But one of them told me Moscow looked better than they had expected. I had the same reaction from an Austrian interior decorator, here for several months to decorate the Austrian Embassy. He agreed with me that parts of Moscow are reminiscent of Vienna, with brownish-yellow colour-washed façades and a somewhat olde-worlde air.

Apart from the piles of building bricks like the Ukraina and four or five other such edifices which tower over the city, and the many minor Stalin-style buildings, there are now also lots of blocks of simple, functional style as in the West. They are gradually replacing the old wooden houses with their quaintly ornamented window frames. In the parts of the city I have seen, the wooden houses are now well in the minority.

30 June 1961 : I was taken back to tales told by my maternal Grandad, Joseph Brierley, when I read in our office files about the recent sale to the Soviet Union of textile machinery worth several million sterling by Mather and Platt of Manchester. I believe it was for this firm, or a similar one, that a friend of Grandad's, Peter McGuire, used to work. He was for me a legendary figure because he had gone to Moscow around the time of the First World War as a textile machinery salesman. He used to call on Grandad, a foreman bleacher, for tips on how to overcome certain snags.

Pravda announced that Yaacov Sharett, a second secretary in the Israeli Embassy, had been asked to leave the Soviet Union because he had caught red-handed at an espionage meeting and had been circulating Zionist literature.

When I phoned Sharett, son of former Israeli Prime Minister Moshe Sharett, he would at first say only that he completely dissociated himself from the charge. When I rang him again he unbent far enough to say it was a frame-up. It had happened in Riga, Latvia, on 27 June when he was holidaying with his wife and children. I asked him if he had had Zionist literature with him and he replied, 'That's a question of definition.'

Chatted with two Nigerians studying at Moscow's Patrice Lumumba University, where about 600 students from the developing countries are studying with about 60 Soviet citizens. The university has only been open a year or two. It is regarded in the West as an arm of the Soviet efforts to persuade Third World countries that Communism is the panacea for all.

One of these two students is to leave his course after less than a year. He was studying international law, and he told me that he did not think one could learn that and other non-technical subjects in a country where, he said, teaching is one-sided. Along with their chosen subjects, students have to study Marxism-Leninism.

The student who is leaving complained that the foreigners were being treated like children by the Communist administration of the university who, for instance, organized a mass meeting at which the students were told that thousands of letters had come in asking that the original name of the university, 'The Friendship of the Peoples University', be changed to 'The Patrice Lumumba University'. *[Patrice Lumumba became the first Prime Minister of the Congo in 1960, after it had achieved independence from Belgium. He was deposed in a coup and murdered by Congolese rivals in January 1961, aged 34.]*

Although the Moscow students had spontaneously demonstrated in protest at the murder of Lumumba, many of them had opposed changing the university's name, my informant said. They argued that this would bolster Western charges that the university was a political rather than an educational institution.

The mass meeting made no decision, but the Rector, Sergei Rumantsev, asked the students to think the matter over. However, a few days later it was announced that the authorities had decided to change the name.

This student was also bitter about some of his Russian fellow students who, he said, had molested Africans who had been going out with Russian girls. *[The Africans evidently had more money than the average Russian students].*

335

My informant said he believed that scarcely any of the 120 Africans at the university were Communists. However, most of them were too poor and too badly educated to speak their minds. Some had come to the university to get square meals for the first time in their lives – a nice comment on the Western colonial system.

Others had been attracted by Communist propaganda which, this student said, gave an untrue picture of life in Russia. However, the two students agreed with me that the Soviet Government was improving the standard of living, though the one who was leaving criticized what he called the 'sputniks before housing' policy.

Both students paid tribute to their university lecturers, all women I believe, whom they described as 'very, very kind' and ready to take all pains to help them in their studies. The two students forecast that quite a number of the Africans would break off their studies and leave Moscow within a few months.

Resident British correspondents – four of us were in town at the moment – were received by the British Ambassador, little greying Sir Frank Roberts, for a background briefing. *[Sir Frank, born in 1907, had a brilliant Foreign Office career. During the Second World War he attended the 1945 Yalta conference, where Churchill, Roosevelt and Stalin met. From 1945 to 1947, Sir Frank was minister at the British Embassy in Moscow. He was Ambassador in Moscow from 1960 to 1962. He later held several other senior posts, including Ambassador to West Germany from 1963 to 1968. His memoirs,* Dealing with Dictators *(Weidenfeld & Nicolson), appeared in 1991. He died in 1998.]*

Sir Frank expounded the often stated Western viewpoint that the Soviet Union has created the Berlin problem, is not ready to compromise, but merely wants to have a first bite at Berlin, to be followed by others later if the West gives in. I asked what Khrushchev could do to convince the West that he only wants the recognition of the actual situation in Central Europe.

Sir Frank said nothing Khrushchev did could convince him of that because it was implicit in Communist actions that they would be wanting to take further measures later. He said he hoped

Khrushchev had realized that the West was not ready to compromise on the essential matter in Berlin: the protection of the freedom of the Berliners on the basis of the rights acquired by the West in the occupation agreements.

I asked whether the West would accept a peace treaty between the Soviet Union and East Germany if Western Allied rights, based on the occupation agreements, were expressly recognized by East Germany. I did not get a clear answer, but Sir Frank referred to the Allied offer to accept the East Germans as agents of the Russians in checking Allied convoys and air traffic to and from Berlin through East German territory or air space.

34 Drinks with Khrushchev in the Kremlin

1 July 1961 : The Ukraina, I have learned, is Moscow's largest hotel, with 1,000 rooms, and is claimed to be the largest in Europe. An Irishman I bumped into in the hotel's post office told me that, like me, he had better first impression of Moscow than he had expected. Apparently he had expected the people to be semi-ruffians. Evelyn Enz, German-born wife of one of the Associated Press correspondents, also told me that her first impression had been better than expected. For housewives, she added, things usually become tougher when they leave hotels and have to obtain their needs on the Russian market. But, of course, correspondents' wives have diplomatic facilities and can import what they need additionally from Scandinavia.

To the Lenin Stadium for the first day of a two-day international sports meeting, attended by about 500 competitors from 23 countries (about 150 from abroad), an annual memorial for two famous Soviet pre-war sportsmen, the Znamensky brothers, now dead.

With me at the stadium today was Chris Chataway, former crack runner and TV interviewer, now a Tory MP for a North London constituency; a most appealing type and – I asked him – a self-confessed Tory left-winger. He visited Moscow first in 1955 and told me the improvement since then had been immense. Today he was working for the *Sunday Telegraph*. He is in favour of the Common Market and thinks Britain will be trying to enter shortly.

In the restaurant 'Sport' at the stadium, a gramophone was blaring out a hotted up version of *La Paloma* with a modern text sung in American. The restaurant was in a new room with up-to-date chandeliers but old-fashioned crockery, chairs and plush curtains, reminiscent of pre-revolutionary rich men's clubs. There are lots of contrasts like that here.

Moscow restaurants close around midnight these days, an hour earlier than they used to. Reason: the working day has been shortened by an hour.

2 July 1961 : As well as all the other forms of public transport, Moscow has a special kind of large taxi called a *marshroutnoye*, which follows a definite route and waits until it is filled with six or seven people before moving off. It costs only about 10d *[about 4p]* at the official rate for a journey of up to about two miles.

Lena tried to help me buy flowers for the Millers' new flat this Sunday lunchtime, but shops were closed. So she said we could look on a street corner for 'speculators' who sell flowers there without permission, i.e. without paying any market rent. None was in attendance at the time.

Reported on a *Pravda* article which managed to blame Britain for the dispute between a number of Arab countries and Iraq, which has claimed the oil principality of Kuwait after the recent ending of the British protectorate there. Those other Arab countries are supporting Kuwait's independence.

Finished the day with a post-midnight repast in the large flat of *Daily Express* correspondent, Dennis Pitt, together with Chataway and Terry O'Connor, *Daily Mail* sports news editor. We ate tinned sausages, iced asparagus (asparagus which had been preserved in ice and was now thawing out on the table), potatoes and Heinz tomato sauce – all stuff brought in from abroad.

3 July 1961 : Investigated lack of wash basin plug and was told it is not usual to use them here; only in baths. Reported defect in toilet for second time today and they promised it would be fixed.

Visited GUM (the letters stand for 'State Universal Shop'), Moscow's famous department store on Red Square opposite the Kremlin. (Someone once quipped that it was the biggest shop in the world specializing in ... GUM.) It has about 80 departments. It's an old building, architecturally over-decorated. It looked like a vast version of the pre-war building of the large Bradford drapers, Lingard's, which also had an olde-worlde air.

I went there to buy flimsies on which to make copies of my diary. They had none. I made do with some thin coloured paper in large sheets. Virtually all the shops I have seen use the abacus for counting. I'm told some Russians are so used to it they cannot add two and two without its aid.

In my one week here I have been stopped on the street three times by Russians asking me to show them the way. (Up to now I've not been able to help them.) This again indicates that foreigners' clothes do not stand out so much these days.

4 July 1961 : Toilet defect still not repaired by this morning. Had my first glass of kvass yesterday – 3d at the official rate *[1p]* – a very slightly alcoholic ferment made from rye flour or bread, with malt. It is sold in the street from vehicles which look like tar boilers, but are cleaner.

Many drainpipes here issue straight onto the pavement instead of into grates. As a result, pavements are swamped in heavy rain.

A thunderstorm cooled down the city a little – temperature about 27°C – but wet my trousers so much as I waited for a taxi that I nearly gave up the idea of attending my first Kremlin reception. However, I took courage and, when I'd got a taxi, tried to restore my creases by gripping the sodden bottom half of my trousers between thumb and finger and running them along the right area a few times.

Actually it turned out not to be a proper taxi which took me to the Kremlin, but a car driven by a city employee trying to make a bit on the side.

I hurried in through one of the public gates in the redbrick

Kremlin wall, past several ancient buildings, mainly former churches – now museums – with onion domes now being re-gilded, perhaps for the 22nd Party Congress, and past the enormous 'Czar's Bell', lying on the ground. *[Made for Czar Ivan the Great (1440–1505), it is said to be the heaviest church bell ever cast, weighing over 200 metric tons.]*

I walked into the Great Kremlin Court, a series of halls used for receptions and conferences. The reception, given by Khrushchev for Pham Van Dong, the little North Vietnamese Prime Minister, was held in the formerly Czarist St George's Hall, about 80 yards long and 20 yards wide. *[St George, as well as being the patron saint of England, is also one of the major saints of the Russian Orthodox Church. He is said to have been martyred in Palestine in AD 303.]*

I was told that this hall had been kept as it was under the Czars. Plaques on the interior walls bear the names of Czarist regiments. Intricate white plasterwork covers much of the walls, columns and ceiling with tracery and reliefs, including St George killing the dragon at one end above a stage.

The top leaders stood near the stage, beyond two tables placed across the hall, with a small gap between them, a gap one does not go through if one is not of the 'requisite' rank. The 'requisite' rank includes members of the diplomatic corps, among whom today were who several African and Asian men, with their dusky wives in colourful dresses, some of African design, some Western.

Long tables lined each side of the hall, loaded with small goodies, such as caviar in pastry boats, salad in pastry, small pieces of meat and lots of wine and juices. Khrushchev and Pham Van Dong spoke between the eating and drinking.

I took a glass of champagne along with Igor Witsinos, correspondent of the West German news agency DPA, who said that though he was not a Communist he admired Soviet foreign policy as an impartial observer because of its effectiveness. He said the foreign policy exchanges between East and West were like a chess grand master (the Soviet Union) opposing an idiot. I wouldn't go so far as that. *[I learned later that Witsinos was descended from a Soviet-Greek family domiciled near the Black Sea.]*

It's about a year since I was face-to-face with Khrushchev. He has aged noticeably. I agreed with Witsinos that he has become more like an elder statesman. Witsinos and I left during a concert – Russian songs accompanied by violins – in order to be in time for our next engagement, a 6 pm reception in the palatial American Embassy residence, marking US Independence Day.

I arrived at the residence at about 6.35, to be told that Khrushchev and a bevy of other Soviet leaders had turned up for the first time in three years; six marshals of the Soviet Union were somewhere in the place too.

Khrushchev stayed for 90 minutes of non-political banter with diplomats and journalists, and was in his usual jolly, appealing form, seen so often on such occasions. A great press of guests (including me with my ears cocked) had him hemmed in on a colonnaded balcony until Mrs Jane Thompson, wife of Ambassador Llewellyn Thompson, led him by hand into the garden, with guests following at a more or less discreet distance.

Mrs Thompson showed Khrushchev the kitchen garden of one of her daughters, 11-year-old Jenny, who sells vegetables at the market price to the embassy cook and has already earned a dollar. Khrushchev said he approved of the use of the garden to teach the girl about nature.

Back on the balcony, Khrushchev told a story of how he went to Kazakhstan and was guest of honour at a ceremonial sheep banquet. He knew the local custom of giving the guest of honour the eyes, but he took both the eyes and the ears and gave them to the local party secretary, telling him he needed them. Then he had taken the brains and given them to an academician.

When Henry Shapiro asked whether an academician hadn't enough brains already, Khrushchev said, 'He knows he never has enough.'

Shapiro then asked, 'What was left for you?'

Khrushchev replied, laughing so much that the three Orders of Lenin on his chest shook, 'I am Prime Minister of the Soviet Union. I do not need anything.'

342

Khrushchev drank hardly any of the whisky he was given, and raised laughs by offering it to his well-rounded wife, Nina, and making her try it, and later giving another glass to one of the senior members of his party, Anastas Mikoyan. When someone offered another glass of whisky to Khrushchev, he waved it away, saying, 'I want to live.'

It will be a long time before I can understand enough of such conversations at parties, but I was pleased I could grasp it here and there. Fortunately the news agency corps in Moscow has an arrangement to pool what they hear at such events, in order to get the most accurate account of what has been said. I phoned about 600 words to London.

5 July 1961 : Funny, after the Eichmann trial, how Israel keeps cropping up. London cabled me saying that the Israelis had sent up a space rocket, and asked for reaction. Lena achieved this from a deputy director of a Soviet planetarium, who said it was very small cheese. The rocket weighed 250 kilos and went up 80 kilometres *[50 miles]*.

Have now met our second translator, Alla Nusinova, 35-ish, just back from a holiday on the Black Sea, with a conch shell for the Millers' baby.

6 July 1961 : Am finding our two women translators fun to work with, and don't know what I'd do without them. Thank goodness I learned some Russian before I came here, unlike some of my predecessors.

Good story today: Khrushchev announced the signing of a treaty of mutual aid (in case of attack) with North Korea, which puts North Korea more firmly in the Soviet orbit and can be seen as part of the Soviet–Chinese rivalry.

To another Kremlin reception in St George's Hall, for North Korean Prime Minister Kim Il Sung. *[One of the main buildings in my hometown, Bradford, is St George's Hall, a concert hall.]* The Chinese Foreign Minister, Chen Yi, was present, smilingly drinking toasts with lots of Soviet leaders. I thought at my first

Kremlin reception, and again today, that I knew a smallish auburn-haired man of about 50, so I asked him who he was. He turned out to be Sergei Lapin, Foreign Minister of the Russian Federation, the largest political unit in the Soviet Union, former Ambassador in Vienna and before that a journalist.

I realized I had seen him abroad – probably with Khrushchev.

7 July 1961 : One of the delights of Moscow, paradoxically, is to be able to get more British food specialities than in Bonn – through the embassy shop here, which is open to Western journalists.

My toilet has still not been repaired. Have now reported it about five times. The usual conversation, with the manageress in charge of our vast floor, is, 'My toilet is still not right.'

'But the plumber was there and he said there was nothing wrong with it.'

'Well, please tell him there is a small hole in the float, which lets air in, and thus the float sinks every few hours.'

'Very well, I'll tell him again.'

This conversation I have had several times and have also left a drawing of the fault. Tonight the manageress obviously didn't believe me because the plumber had been again during the day and had told her everything was all right. I was able to convince her by taking the lid off the lavatory cistern to show her the air escaping from the float when I put it underwater.

She asked me, 'Are you an engineer?'

I told her, 'No, but I have mended toilets before, at home.'

The blonde, middle-aged manageress then said of the plumber, 'He's a fool.'

I've been alone, in charge of the whole Soviet Union (!) these past three days, as John has been covering a sports meeting in Helsinki. He returned tonight, I'm happy to say, though, I've been coping, helped of course by our translators and by other correspondents.

8 July 1961 : By last night it appeared that my toilet had been fixed. But after a party at John's tonight, I returned home to find

344

it gurgling merrily away. It was around 1 am but, having given up hope of having it fixed by the plumber, I got out my screwdriver and fixed it myself in about ten minutes. I did not tell our floor manageress, but might do some day.

I've been in Moscow's largest toyshop, Dyetskyi Mir (Children's World), which is more impressive than GUM, as it's in a modern building. I was pleasantly surprised by the variety of toys on offer, many of them of the instructional type, but also lots of 'just toys'. The place was crowded. I bought a compass for Chris – his request – a gramophone record about Yuri Gagarin's space flight, and a sailing boat kit for Robin. *[Gagarin's epoch-making space flight, one orbit of the earth at up to 30,000 kph (18,750 mph), had taken place on 12 April. Born in 1934, Gagarin died in a plane crash in 1968 while training for the Soyuz III space mission.]*

A Western diplomat told me that this year's harvest, dogged by bad weather, is not likely to be better than last year's, which was behind the plan. The increase in farm output, he said, had virtually stopped since 1957, whereas between 1953 – when Stalin died – and 1957, there had been a big increase.

Khrushchev today called on the West to get round the conference table on the Berlin question. In the same speech, to officers passing out at a military academy, he announced that the defence budget was being increased by one-third. We interpret this as mainly a tactic to show the West he won't back down about signing a German peace treaty.

Had my first swim in Russia, in Moscow's – and perhaps Europe's – biggest open-air bath, circular, about 60 yards in diameter, which opened some months ago and can take 2,000 bathers. *[It was built on the site of a Russian Orthodox cathedral, called Christ the Saviour, which was demolished for political reasons. After the collapse of Communism, the bath was closed and the cathedral rebuilt.]*

In spite of Moscow's bitterly cold winters, the bath is open all the year round. The water is heated with natural gas from the supply which feeds Moscow. In winter one goes into the pool from the changing room through a covered passageway.

The roof and sides of the passageway project for a few feet over the pool, like a canopy. The sides and closed end of the passageway are just below the surface of the water. One walks into the water, still protected by the canopy, and dives under the end of it to reach the main expanse of the bath.

Even in winter, I'm told, one can swim comfortably there because the warmth from the heated water keeps the cold away sufficiently, and great clouds of steam rise from the bath. Men and women change in separate open locker rooms, with elderly women attendants present in the men's changing room.

A swim is expensive – four shillings *[20p]* at the official rate – and you must be out within 90 minutes. As I was swimming around I felt this was just a foretaste of what the Communist world might be like in all spheres in another generation or two. I know, of course, that such facilities are already common in some Western countries, but when one considers how primitive Russia was in 1917 the advance has been great. I hope that more such advances will bring with it greater political tolerance. There have, I think, already been signs of that.

9 July 1961 : One naturally tends to think about the existence of God when one is in a country where God is officially not recognized. No Communist has yet been able to explain to me how the world began. For me, the world is too intricate, too wonderful, too incomprehensible to have come about by a kind of accident.

The conclusion, to me, is inescapable: that there is some kind of directing power, which we call God. Of course, this does not explain how it all started, that is something that we, I believe, are not able to grasp.

The Soviet Union today displayed its air power – another tactic in the Berlin crisis, we think – in its first major air display for three years, held at Tushino outside Moscow. John attended while I picked up additional data from a television broadcast.

Some new aircraft were shown, including a supersonic bomber carrying missiles, which could be the supersonic airliner of the future, and a 'convertiplane' which takes off vertically, thanks to a rotor on each wing, and then flies horizontally with two turbo-props. May hold 150–200 people – bigger than anything of its type elsewhere. Britain's Fairey Rotodyne uses a similar principle.

There was also a giant lifting helicopter which deposited a small prefabricated house – the kind of thing used by geological surveys in remote places – gently on the airfield. Khrushchev was there with Gagarin.

Tonight I covered the opening of the 2nd International Moscow Film Festival, at which the main event was the première of the first documentary about Gagarin's space flight on 12 April. The film gives away little new. For instance, it still keeps silent about how Gagarin landed, whether by parachute or in the space-ship, *Vostok* (East) 1, itself, and gives only a brief glimpse of what is stated to be the launching rocket.

As a film I found it technically good, and Gagarin is an attrac-tive person, with a charming smile. The film also shows the American space shot in which the monkey, Ham, was sent into the ether. The Russian commentator, speaking as a shot of American candidate astronauts is shown, says, 'Ham excellently carried out what one of these brave young men will have to do in the near future ...' *[That part of the film was evidently made before the United States' first suborbital space flight on 5 May, called the Mercury-Redstone 3 mission, in which Alan Shepard piloted the* Freedom 7 *capsule. As the commander of the* Apollo 14 *lunar landing mission in 1971, Shepard was the fifth man to walk on the moon.]*

I was particularly moved by the scenes of Gagarin's arrival back in Moscow after his space flight. He was hugged by Khrushchev, who then took out a handkerchief to wipe his eyes. I believe that was genuine. There was lots of applause in mid-scene for the film. Khrushchev was present at the showing.

Later they screened the British film, *Saturday Night and Sunday Morning*, an earthy 'kitchen sink' drama about a Nottingham factory worker who sleeps with his mate's wife and carries on with an unmarried woman at the same time. Russians are reputedly somewhat puritan about sex and some of them in the audience, listening to the simultaneous translation, made lots of 'oohs' and 'aahs'. I could not forbear to tell a Russian girl sitting next to me, 'It's not always like that in England.'

As well as its sex angles, the film has some social criticism, which is perhaps why the Russians decided to accept it for showing here – not as part of the competition, but within the framework of the festival. It made me a little homesick because the Nottingham scenes and accents were much like Bradford's. (The English dialogue could be heard when the Russian translator did not obscure it.)

10 July 1961 : Interviewed the famous – in Britain – allegedly Abyssinian-born horseracing tipster, 'Prince' Monolulu, who was wearing his gaudy green, blue and gold outfit with ostrich feather headdress. He told me – one does not have to take him seriously – that he had come on a personal mission to achieve peace through horseracing.

He'd been to the *Pravda* office to submit an article, which they had turned down. He had told them horseracing would bring peace, because as soon as a man won a bet he became a capitalist. They did not quite fall in with his ideas. This morning I watched him walk round the public area of the Kremlin, patting babies, shaking hands, saying, '*Russkiye khorasho!* (good)' and drawing crowds of several hundreds.

Many Russians went up to him to have their pictures taken at his side, and some asked me where he came from. Few of them, if any, noticed that in golden letters on the back of his green cloak was his famous motto: 'I got an orse.' Or was it: 'I gotta orse'?

To a Yugoslav reception for Foreign Minister Koca Popovic, who was making the first high-level contact with the Soviet Union for about six years. Soviet attacks on 'Yugoslav revisionism' have been dampened down recently. Maybe we shall learn later what it all means.

35 Exclusive interview with the first cosmonaut

11 July 1961 : To Moscow's Sheremetyevo airport to see off to London 27-year-old Yuri Gagarin, the Soviet air force major and former foundry worker who, on 12 April, made the first manned space flight, when he orbited the earth in 108 minutes.

I was allowed to interview Gagarin in an airport lounge – the first interview, I believe, he has given to a Western journalist. Also there were two Soviet Foreign Office officials, a journalist from Pravda and a stream of foreign and Soviet well-wishers who kept coming in for him to sign autographs.

He is rather more slightly built than one would think from pictures. I made him laugh by saying I didn't want to know any secrets; my purpose was to have a few lines for the British evening papers' early editions before Gagarin arrived in London, where he is to visit the Soviet industrial exhibition being held there.

When I asked him what he most wanted to see, he gave a good party-line answer, 'The British people'. He spoke in a friendly, almost bantering manner, occasionally flashing his famous smile. When I asked which building he would particularly like to see, he said there were so many, but added that he thought the Houses of Parliament beautiful.

The nearest Gagarin had been to Britain during his space flight was over the Atlantic, and he'd not been able to see the

British Isles from there. After a few more questions, it was time for him to board a gleaming Tupolev 104, so I shook hands with the man who has been where no one else yet could.

On my way back to the city, I swam in a wide canal at the village of Chimki, where there is a well organized bathing beach on the sandy canal bank, fitted with wooden chairs and loungers with headrests. With me were Walter Lister of the *New York Herald Tribune* and his wife Sue. They decided to swim in their underwear which, they said, was often the custom in Russia. But the Russians at this spot all wore costumes, some of the girls even being in bikinis.

The road from the airport to the city centre has some of the most impressive new blocks of flats, built in modern utilitarian styles. The usual form is a block of about eight to ten storeys, with a square ground plan, leaving a large courtyard in the middle, with a garden. In the suburbs there are still little villages of the old (and some new) wooden houses, occasionally with an old church in their midst.

A sign on the road says: 'Two hours to the Crimea, four hours to Central Asia' – by air, of course.

Did a mailer story on a *Pravda* article arguing that, though so much needed to be done on earth, Soviet space science was worthwhile because it produced new techniques which, in the long run, would repay more than was being invested. The article instanced the fiery jet of a space rocket which, it said, could be converted into a chemical laboratory, producing various substances at various points in the jet by inserting cooling devices into the flames at the right points.

However, the writer did not go into the costs of rocket development, which could have made it clear how many more houses could have been built instead. Still, he has half an argument, I suppose, and the Soviet Union could hardly keep out of the rocket race in present political conditions.

12 July 1961 : Have had some instances of 'clever' reporting by unscrupulous colleagues. Won't mention names, but one of them sent a phony, saying that the Italian star, Gina Lollobrigida, had walked out of the film festival opening when, in fact, she had done the festival the honour of attending the opening, though very tired after having just flown in. She had left after the opening ceremony, but before the showing of films began.

Tonight another colleague wrote that the British film star, Peter Finch, had rescued Elizabeth Taylor from a crowd when, in fact, the correspondent knew that Finch was merely present when Taylor entered the Moskva hotel to cash a cheque. She was pursued by fans, but there was no question of anyone saving her. This sort of thing goes on all the time among a certain set of journalists who try to squeeze just that much more out of a story by inventing something.

Westerners I have met in Moscow have very varied attitudes towards the Soviet Union. (I don't mean Communist Westerners.) They vary from absolute rejection of the system and criticism of virtually everything, to much admiration for what has been achieved. The average attitude is one of annoyance at petty troubles, such as shortages of this and that, and the bureaucracy, coupled with a recognition that things are going ahead here. I haven't met one person yet who thinks the Soviet Union will have caught up with the United States by, say, 1970.

The visit of Koca Popovic, the Yugoslav Foreign Minister, seems to have gone well so far as inter-state relations are concerned, but there has been no rapprochement ideologically, I understand.

13 July 1961 : A visiting 'White' (emigré) Russian man told me that Muscovites now spoke like animals. A woman official from the West German Embassy, who has toured many areas of the Soviet Union, told me she had found friendliness everywhere.

I think that the Muscovites, like the inhabitants of some other large cities, are in too much of a hurry and are not terribly polite. But if you speak to them in the right way, they respond in a friendly fashion. Found that my inside pocket, where I keep my wallet, had been slashed. Lena said it might have been someone in a crowded bus or train, trying to rob me.

Attended a film festival party with Liz Taylor present; not my type, but she was pleasant.

Then to the showing of Britain's main entry, *The Trials of Oscar Wilde*, starring Peter Finch. The Russian subtitles were perhaps not so clear, for a Russian sitting next to me asked, about half way through, what exactly was the relationship between Wilde and Lord Alfred Douglas. Mind you, the Russian had got that clear by the end. The film certainly reveals the tragedy of Wilde, and the problem of homosexuality, and pulls no punches.

Shirley Ann Field, the red-haired star of *Saturday Night and Sunday Morning*, which has been praised as very realistic, told me she'd been overcome by the reception. She described herself as a socialist, said she had received only £1,000 for a year's work on *Saturday Night* and could have earned more by making other kinds of films.

Moscow faces, older people, especially, show signs of having had a hard life. There are certainly not as many pretty women as in Israel. One sees more people reading in buses than in Germany.

Quite a number of people ignore the police when they blow their whistles to order people not to cross the road against the lights or contrary to a policeman's signal. The standard of driving is bad; our temporary office driver, Victor, is no exception.

The wider roads have two white lines in the middle, about a car's width apart. You are not allowed to drive in that space, which tends to be a refuge for pedestrians. In some cases, I'm told, it is used by high-ups when traffic is heavy.

14 July 1961 : Had a glass of grape juice, 1s 4d *[about 7p]* at the official rate. I buy this occasionally in a bar which does a roaring trade selling glasses of Soviet champagne, which is supposed to be matured in three weeks by a new process, and does not taste bad at all. I'm off alcohol at present, find it affects my work capacity.

15 July 1961 : Many small boys here have shaven heads. *[An anti-lice measure, I believe.]*

To Sheremetyevo to see Gagarin return from London tonight.

He's had a really triumphal and warm reception in Britain, and was received by both Prime Minister Harold Macmillan and Queen Elizabeth after initial arrangements had made it look as though official Britain was going to be rather stand-offish, by sending only a minor official to meet him at the airport.

Gagarin, who'd already given a press conference before leaving London, would only say tonight, in answer to my question, that he had best of all liked the British people. However, he gave me a second autograph. The first one, given to me when I saw him off, I had given to Lena, who seemed so keen on it. The second one is for Robin and Chris.

Gagarin, who was met by air force officers, drove off in a black limousine piled high in the back with British bouquets. After phoning my story to London, I was back in town, at the Bolshoi Theatre, in time for the last act of *Sleeping Beauty* danced by Britain's Royal Ballet on the last night of their Soviet tour, which has been a great success. The audience shouted 'Bravos' and clapped for nearly 25 minutes, with a break for speeches on stage.

Galina Ulanova, the Soviet Union's top ballerina, who is not too well, came back from leave specially to see the performance. She went on stage to give a bouquet to Dame Margot Fonteyn. Scores more bouquets were flung down onto the stage by well-wishers in the six gilded balconies of the theatre, rebuilt in 1856 and redecorated after the 1917 revolution.

The red-and-gold curtain is decorated with a mixture of hammers-and-sickles and harps. while Lenin, who appears somewhere in almost every public building in Moscow, is pictured on the proscenium arch, together with red flags and the musical notes of, I suspect, the 'Internationale'.

I spoke to Dame Margot and other leading members of the company. All were most gratified by the reception. And Dame Margot and the leading male dancer, Michael Somes, commented that the ballet had had to come to Russia, the home of the male dancer, to receive real recognition for its male dancers who, at home, are often not regarded as top class.

This has been quite an Anglo-Russian week, I reflected this Saturday night.

16 July 1961 : Lunched in the Sofia, the usually crowded workaday restaurant near our office. A couple of Russians, one of them a newspaper photographer, helped me to choose *Okroshka Bulgarska*, a cold soup with cucumbers and other vegetables floating in a creamy mixture, most tasty, followed by kebab with chips and gherkins, washed down by an oversweet fizzy drink. Total cost about one rouble *[eight shillings, or 40p]*.

I complained to the men about the terribly slow service in the Ukraina restaurant, of which they were aware. One suggested I should write to a Soviet paper about it, but that wouldn't do for a Reuter man.

I told them that the poor service in the Ukraina restaurant was most damaging to the Soviet Union because so many tourists and foreign delegates stayed at that hotel. They said restaurant service was slowly improving, and argued that the bad service was due to the fact that Russia had been so backward at the time of the revolution – 44 years ago!

One of the men was critical (in talking to me) of our waitress in the Sofia, in that she forgot to give me a knife and fork, and then brought my fruit drink in its bottle, without a glass. He said the standard was improving by sending young catering staff to technical schools.

Out to the Lenin Stadium, in a suburb, to see Valery Brumel, Soviet high-jumper, increase his world record from 2.23 to 2.24 metres in a match against the USA. The USA and the USSR each broke three world records during the meeting. The US men won and so did the Soviet women. Overall the Soviet team was ahead, as usual these days.

17 July 1961 : Can't say that, up to now, I've found the work here harder than in Bonn, though it's much more rewarding. One has to be more elastic about the hours worked, ready to jump in at any time the need arises.

354

Today the Western powers handed over their Notes replying to the Soviet Union's latest (and, no doubt, final) call for a German peace treaty to be signed by the Soviet Union and the Western powers. The Notes were not published, but we understand they leave room for negotiation.

Praise in a letter from Reuters editor, Doon Campbell, congratulating us on our work in the past week or two and enclosing some cuttings – in particular, a splash in both the London evening papers for my story of Gagarin's departure for London, and some good credits for the Monolulu piece.

Dinner at the flat of Keith Oakeshott, First Secretary at our embassy, along with several other guests. Impeccable meal served by a Russian maid on a beautiful mahogany table decorated with lace mats.

For the first time in my life I experienced that high-class British custom of the men staying behind to smoke, drink or chat at the table, before joining the ladies. I don't think it's a bad idea, as it gives both sexes the chance for their own kind of conversation for a time.

This time the men spoke about Gagarin's visit to London, which an American guest rather disapproved of as allegedly helping Communism, while I and other Britons felt that it had helped relations and we should try by all means to do this without, of course, surrendering to the Communists. I think that more Britons than Americans – who tend to see Communism more starkly – hope that both the world systems will change and become more like one another.

One of the Oakeshotts' daughters, aged ten, has been at a Russian school, where Lenin, instead of Christ, is held up as an example to children – as a good scholar, for instance, and a lover of children.

Once this girl came home and asked Mrs Oakeshott, 'Mummy, what is a capitalist? They called me that and they all laughed.' Mrs Oakeshott replied that it had to do with the way you produce things, but was not very important though the Communists thought it was.

Mrs Oakeshott said her daughter had been met with the greatest kindness by other pupils, and teachers. The Oakeshotts have managed to make a number of Russian friends, something virtually impossible ten years ago here. (It is still very difficult.)

Eddie Bolland, one of our diplomats present, who has returned here after about ten years elsewhere, is amazed by the relatively freer atmosphere, and also by the amount of building that has been done.

18 July 1961 : Talked to John J. McCloy, burly genial adviser on disarmament to President Kennedy, leading the American side in talks with the Soviet Union which restarted here yesterday after a fortnight's earlier session in Washington. The talks are aimed at settling the forum for disarmament negotiations.

Instead of the previous ten-nation commission, the Russians have proposed five neutrals, five Communists and five Westerners. Of course, the five neutrals they want may well be those nearer to Communist thinking – the names have not yet been released.

McCloy said the Americans had responded by proposing a geographical basis and an 'interested party' basis – i.e. countries with a particular interest in disarmament – which would bring in some neutrals, but not necessarily those whom the Russians want. McCloy said that during the talks, which are supposed to be about procedure, the Russians keep trying to start discussion on their overall disarmament plan, tabled by Khrushchev last year, but the Americans are rejecting discussion of it at this stage.

The more I learn about disarmament talks, the more I think both sides are unreasonable. They just do not seem to realize the enormity of what faces us in a few years if there is no success in getting a disarmament agreement with controls. It's extremely difficult to say which side is most to blame.

I have been critical of the West's rejection of ideas like the Rapacki Plan for arms control in Central Europe. And in the talks on nuclear tests I think the Soviet Union has been to blame for suddenly changing its position – calling for the 'troika' system in supervising tests when agreement had seemed near.

My talk with McCloy took place at an American reception for film festival people, including the 33-year-old Italian film idol, Gina Lollobrigida. As I gazed into her eyes, I felt this was much more my meat than Elizabeth Taylor, though Gina looks as though she could spit fire on occasion. (All this purely academic, I maintain.)

Tonight I also interviewed Lord Casey, former Australian Minister of External Affairs (1951–60), in the beautifully furnished Australian Embassy. I liked the drift of a press statement issued by this dignified grey-haired and very English Australian at the close of his first visit to the Soviet Union, which has lasted for ten days. He has spoken to Western ambassadors and Soviet officials, including Foreign Minister Andrei Gromyko, and toured part of the country.

He thinks that most Russians are behind their government, that the terror of Stalinism has gone and that what is most needed is increasing contact between the West and the Soviet Union to achieve greater understanding. He described Soviet foreign policy on disarmament and Berlin as 'hard to understand' and told me he had tried to impress on Gromyko how seriously the Berlin question was regarded in London and Washington. How did Gromyko react? 'He just nodded,' Lord Casey said.

19 July 1961 : Again interviewed 'Prince' Monolulu, who left today after achieving no success yet in his 'peace through horse-racing' mission. However, he has enjoyed drawing the Russian crowds with his weird costume.

As I spoke to him at the entrance to the Leningradskaya hotel, a Russian asked him if he was a worker. The tipster insisted that he was. Another Russian then asked him why he was carrying a copy of the *Daily Mail*, which the questioner described as a capitalist newspaper. Several people asked me what delegation he belonged to, and one Russian seriously wanted to know 'what was his function' in Abyssinia.

20 July 1961 : Interviewed some Cambridge students who've been here for a fortnight studying education and youth. They thought Moscow looked better than they'd expected, but said they'd been surprised at the wooden houses which remain here and there.

They described the educational system as 'highly efficient'. In talks with about 25 Russian students, they found two who, though Communists, were 'anti-establishment'. When they visited a Russian student's home, the student's father was informed by neighbours, who took the number of the Cambridge students' British car. The father, a general, gave the Russian student a blast.

36 Post Office red tape, Foreign Ministry obstruction

21 July 1961 : Sent off a small parcel to my family in Germany – quite a rigmarole. The woman assistant at the Central Post Office, where gold letters on red banners exhort the postal workers to give ever better service, took each article and examined it carefully. She then packed the parcel for me, providing the necessary carton, paper and string. Meanwhile I filled in four copies of a form. Total cost about 6s *[30p]*.

The Foreign Ministry would not allow us to send John to accompany President Ibrahim Abboud of the Sudan on a trip round the Soviet provinces. This was in spite of the fact that we had an important request from the Sudan to cover the visit. We are trying to scrape up this and that by phone – a difficult task when you don't know where the delegation is staying.

22 July 1961 : President Kwame Nkrumah, the dictator of Ghana, was absent from a reception today at which he was to have been host. His Foreign Minister, Mr Ako Adjei, explained this in a speech by referring to the thousands of miles covered during the Ghana delegation's tour of the Soviet Union, lasting 13 days.

After Adjei's speech, I asked him if Nkrumah was ill. He did not reply, but instead called out 'Audience, audience, audience!' – apparently part of Ghana ceremonial – and made another, shorter speech in which he said Nkrumah was resting. He stated three times, 'He is not sick'. And then he added, 'He is never sick.'

Judging by his published comments Nkrumah, the apostle of African union, has been greatly impressed by his Soviet tour. I enjoyed the bare-chested male dancers and the dusky ladies in gaudy sarongs, who danced to the hot music of a Ghana band during the reception.

I received my first compliment from a Soviet woman today, a student working at the film festival press centre. She is on a five-year journalism course. When I told her of my interest in the Soviet Union and the Russian language, she called me a *molodyets*, which means something like 'fine chap' or 'stout fellow'.

Had my second plunge in the great circular swimming pool today, and was again slightly disturbed by the elderly women attendants walking through the men's changing room, but suppose that is what equality between the sexes means. Delightful to be swimming in the warm water at 9 pm – still quite light – with swallows overhead and some of the gilded Kremlin onion domes visible a few hundred yards away. Everyone must wear a bathing cap and bring along soap for a compulsory wash before their dip.

In a trolleybus on my way to the bath I was reading a booklet containing the Communist Party programme, when a tipsy man sitting behind me poked me in the back and asked if I was reading a breviary. He was evidently trying to make fun of religion, and a man sitting next to me told him to shut up.

I asked the man behind me if he believed in God. In reply, he took out his wallet and opened it to show me his Communist Party card; party members are supposed to be atheists. It was a pity I had to get out at that juncture, for I felt the conversation might have become interesting.

A taxi driver told me petrol costs only about 2s 6d *[12¹/₂p]* a gallon, but a 1,500 cc car, the Pobyeda (Victory), costs about £1,000 compared to about £550 for a similar car in West Germany. He told me about 200,000 people were waiting to buy cars *[perhaps he meant in Moscow, rather than in the whole Soviet Union]*, and the wait lasted from one to four years.

Cars can be hired – the two-litre Volga costs 10 roubles *[£4]* a day plus 5 kopecks *[5d or 2p]* per kilometre.

A young Communist woman, acting as a guide for a 20-ish Norwegian, here for a Communist-sponsored World Youth Forum starting later this week, told me that in her hometown, Ufa, east of the Urals in the small Soviet republic of Bashkiristan, there were not so many queues as in Moscow – because there were not so many people! This pretty woman, with Mongolian features, told me that Ufa got its name because Muslims used to go up a nearby mountain, and when they reached the top used to say in wonderment, 'Oof Allah!' This, she maintained seriously, was shortened to 'Oofa'. *[My Russian dictionary confirms, at least, that a word sounding like 'oof', spelt 'uf' in Russian, can mean 'phew' or 'gosh'. Evidently the Muslims who went up that mountain were Russian-speaking ones.]*

This woman told me that young Russians, quartered in the Ukraina for the forum, had been critical of the slow restaurant service. As a result, a meeting of the restaurant staff had been held in an attempt to improve matters – so far not very successful.

I said I hoped further meetings would be arranged so that guests at the Ukraina who remained after the forum would benefit from the hoped-for improvement. She replied soberly that meetings alone would not do the trick. However, I was pleasantly impressed that something had been done about the situation, even if it had been fairly ineffective up to now.

The young Norwegian, Guenderson, told me he was a Conservative, but was interested in meeting different kinds of people. He speaks some Russian.

23 July 1961 : Sunday, still a day of rest for most people here. As I came to work early in the afternoon, two couples were dancing on the pavement near our office, while a seated man played an accordion and several old people sat outside on chairs, watching. And tonight in the Metro I again heard accordion strains as a young man with his squeezebox approached the escalator on which I was travelling, playing for the benefit of two or three friends.

I feel that being in Russia is like beginning a long, long course at some university. After one month here I feel my Russian is becoming fluent enough to make it really worthwhile asking questions! *[I had been learning Russian since the mid-fifties. I am still learning it – and enjoying it – today, in 2003.]*

Had quite an argument with a young Englishman, a student with considerable knowledge of Russian history, who appeared unable to see anything positive in *(a)* the Bolshevik revolution and *(b)* the Soviet Union today. I argued that there were many positive points, such as the economic development, which is tending to bring with it some political liberalization, and the lack of racial discrimination. I recommended him to visit a few factories instead of concentrating mainly on museums, which he had been doing.

24 July 1961 : Letter from head office quite severely criticising a story I'd done a couple of weeks ago, summing up incompletely the progress of Nkrumah's visit after its first few days. There had been a misapprehension on the part of both John and me about what London had wanted. With the same mail came praise for two other stories I had done, beating the Associated Press.

Listened to the live transmission of a speech by Nkrumah at a 'Friendship Meeting' held in the Kremlin Palace – the Soviet way of honouring the Head of State of a very friendly country. Nkrumah speaks in a very English way, quite impressively, and seems to be fired by his (in my opinion, justified) bitterness towards the old colonialists. *[Ghana had become independent only in 1957.]*

Nkrumah sees himself as an apostle of African unity. And today he held up the Soviet Union as an example of how African unity could be achieved. He also spoke of his reverence at visiting the bedroom of Lenin in Leningrad, and spoke of Lenin's ideas as having changed the course of history for the better. I don't think that he is a Communist, though he tends in that direction. Perhaps now, after his visit, he will tend even more so. *[Nkrumah's policy of 'African Socialism' led to links with the*

Communist bloc. He was overthrown in a coup in 1966 and went into exile in Guinea. He died in 1972 and was rehabilitated in 1973.]

25 July 1961 : One sees rather more drunks here than in Bradford, so far as I can judge. *[I now think that was an understatement.]* There are frequent newspaper articles about drunkenness, including criticism of people who do not pay the fees at the 'sobering-up centres' staffed by medical personnel.

Paid my first visit to the permanent exhibition of Soviet economic achievements, on Moscow's northern outskirts. The site of about 530 acres *[215 ha]* is said to be larger than that of the Brussels World Fair. Most of the pavilions are in ornate neoclassical styles.

I was there to follow around friendly-looking Ibrahim Abboud, Sudan's President and (Sandhurst-trained) military dictator. I found there was a wide variety of exhibits, but they have not the finish or modernity of comparable items in a Western exhibition.

Abboud is said not to be a left-winger, and his relations in public with the Soviet leaders have not reached the same level of cordiality as Nkrumah's. I find the Sudanese, most of whom speak English as well as their native Arabic, more gentlemanly than the often-temperamental Ghanaians.

Abboud seems to be a moderate dictator, like Ayub Khan of Pakistan, trying to improve his country's economy after competing political parties had not proved very successful in the first years after it became independent in 1956. *[Between 1899 and 1955 Sudan was a condominium jointly ruled by Britain and Egypt.]*

Bob Elphick, the present chief correspondent in Moscow, whom I am to succeed next year, returned from leave tonight with his pretty and charming wife, Eve. Bob told me he had been asked to stay on in Moscow to see out the Berlin crisis which, he expected, meant about six months. So it looks as though I will be taking over in about February. Eve served us a delicious pile of bacon and eggs, about all they had in their larder on return from leave.

26 July 1961 : To a *Herrenabend* (male evening get-together) with about a dozen West German and German-speaking correspondents, given by Alfred Reinelt, the 55-ish press attaché at the West German Embassy, in his flat.

Fascinating conversations. An interesting point was made about the economy: that there is no proper way of comparing Soviet and Western statistics, as they are differently based, the former on the cost of labour and certain other factors, and the latter on the market system.

One German who's been here about two years told me he was most depressed with the Soviet Union, while another one, Hermann Pörzgen, of the conservative *Frankfurter Allgemeine Zeitung*, who's been here on and off for 25 years – including several years as a prisoner-of-war! – took some comfort from the political and economic improvements he had observed over a long period.

One cannot expect Russia to be like Britain, and one cannot expect things we regard as evil to disappear overnight. If there are signs – as there are – that some of these things are disappearing, then we ought to be thankful for that.

One very disappointing thing for foreigners, and even more so for diplomats and journalists, is the difficulty of making friendships with Russians. The Russians are warned that foreign diplomats and journalists are often spies – true, I imagine, but no truer here than anywhere else. As a result, Russians very rarely invite foreigners into their homes. However, I understand that even in this respect things are improving slowly.

27 July 1961 : Found I could do an acceptable shorthand note (in English translated in my head) of a radio speech in Russian without help from John or our translators. Of course, it was partly due to the fact that the speech was made up of political clichés. *[Much Russian political and economic vocabulary comes from Western European languages.]*

One tip concerning my later Moscow stint, from Bob and Eve: don't bring heavy underwear or you will boil in Moscow's winter, because hotels and flats tend to be overheated. What one needs is heavy outer clothing, a hat and boots. You carry a bag of shoes round with you to wear inside.

Snow usually starts falling in October, and sets in firmly in November. We've had close, thundery weather for some days, with showers almost every day, but now we have wonderful breezes plus sunshine, most exhilarating.

28 July 1961 : Just to show me that – after some five years of trying – I haven't really learned enough Russian yet, one of the papers had a complex article about the profession of artist's model (apparently regarded as shameful by some Russians). In reading this article I had to consult the dictionary or Lena scores of times.

Most Russian workers receive one month's holiday – apart from statutory public holidays – several of them have told me. Most Reuter correspondents receive only three weeks.

Today I had my first meal as the guest of a British Ambassador. Sir Frank Roberts had included me at a luncheon for about 12 persons held in the dignified embassy. From my seat in the middle of the long mahogany table I could see large oil paintings of King George V and Queen Mary.

[In her book, The British Embassy Moscow, *Canadian-born ex-diplomat Kathleen Berton says that Soviet guests were often taken aback by the portrait of King George because it was so like Nicholas II, the last Russian Tsar, who was King George's first cousin.]*

Embassy servants in khaki uniforms flitted about, ensuring that guests had enough on their plates, marked with the Royal crest. The Ambassador at one end of the table and his pretty Egyptian wife, Cella, at the other, were the centres of the loudest conversation.

I chatted with Leslie Metcalfe, one of the top engineers of the National Coal Board, here in a delegation. He is a Quaker who led the first post-war Quaker delegation here in 1951. *[I learned later that he had first visited the Soviet Union, as an engineer, in the 1920s, and after the Second World War had been the chairman for many years of the Quakers' East–West Relations Committee.]*

Metcalfe told me that, since 1951 the Russians had made many advances, but there were still many insufficencies, not least in Intourist, which had arranged the delegation's visit. I admired Metcalfe for not taking any wine; I did.

On my other side was 55-year-old Gerald Severn, a Moscow-born American who lives in London, member of a onetime Moscow manufacturing family, grandson of a mayor of Moscow and a former director of Russian ballet companies in the West.

Severn, born Sevastianov, told me he'd been frightened to return to Russia until after Khrushchev came to power. In 1958 Severn had made his first visit. He's never been scared since and does not think a return to a terror regime is likely.

He comes here mainly to sell films from the West or to buy Soviet films. He told me he has good relations with culture officials here, who know that his family, though capitalists, were also patrons of the arts.

He spoke highly of Khrushchev's efforts gradually to liberalize things more, but said that in view of the peculiar nature of the Russian people – one Russian is a genius, two are a disgrace and three are a revolution – the authorities dare not go too fast. He attributed the fact that few Russians invite foreigners to their homes largely to an ingrained xenophobia which the Communists had exploited for security reasons.

He, with many relatives in Russia, has no difficulties in that respect and, anyway, seems to be accepted by the authorities as trustworthy. He had been told today that the Russians were going to buy Britain's Oscar Wilde film, which won several awards at the film festival, even though when he brought the film, with its homosexual aspects, over here last September, officials had said, 'Very beautiful, but we cannot show it to the public.'

37 Scoop on new Communist Party programme

29 July 1961 : Enjoyed interviewing on the street five persons, taken at random, and asked what they thought, or hoped, the building of Communism – to be detailed in a new party programme to be issued tonight – would bring them. Was happy to find that, when I showed these people my press card issued by the Soviet Foreign Ministry – they did not clam up, but answered my questions in a friendly way. From what I have heard, it is doubtful whether they would have reacted like that ten years ago.

A naval officer said there would be no classes, and 'everyone would have equal rights'. It would eventually be possible to get everything without paying for it, 'but not immediately'.

He added, 'We are still some way behind America, but we shall catch up. If there was not the threat of war it would all happen much more quickly.'

An engineer, who said he was a party member, forecast there would be restrictions on the ownership of dwellings by party members. They would not be able to own even their own home, but would have to rent it from a public authority. He added, 'I cannot say exactly when Communism will come about. It depends partly on outside conditions.'

A minor state official, not very smartly dressed, said, 'Money won't be abolished yet. When that will be depends on whether we can maintain peace.' Two pretty teenage girls didn't know what to say, giggled, then one of them said, 'More of us will go up into space.' Our translator, Alla, said she hoped working hours would be reduced from seven to five per day, and the working week from six to five days.

All that was heart-warming, and so it was this evening when I dined in the Hotel Sovietskaya: an excellent meal which would not have disgraced any Western restaurant – three courses, with grape juice and mineral water. The price, at the unfair (to us) official rate, 27 shillings [£1.35].

At my table in the plush surroundings were two young men in white shirts and grey trousers, engineering students in their early twenties, on leave from their college in Leningrad. They receive 40 roubles a month, plus free food and lodging.

They were apparently 'on the town', having ordered vodka, port wine, beer and a cocktail (*kokteil* in Russian, and at this hotel there is even a large bar with a sign in Cyrillic letters saying, *Kokteil Holl*). One of these lads, who made me drink some vodka with them, told me he was a party member and gave me the classic definition of Communism: 'From each according to his ability, to each according to his needs.'

I asked him long it would take to achieve that.

'From five to seven years.'

I suggested he was optimistic, and that, for instance, the drunks one sees in Moscow would probably get worse if they got free vodka so soon. His burning faith prevented him from accepting that argument.

Tonight I got the biggest scoop so far in my journalistic career, which began in 1947. This was the night in which the new programme of the Soviet Communist Party was published. As we were certain that it would appear in *Pravda*, I went in the late evening to the Ulitsa Pravda (Pravda Street) and, by a stroke of luck, came across a printer who was walking home with a proof copy of tomorrow's paper, increased from its normal four to six pages to ten, nine of which were devoted to the programme of about 30,000 words.

I told the *Pravda* printer that the whole world was waiting to know what was in the new programme, and pleaded with him to give me the paper, which he did. He didn't ask for payment, nor did I give him any.

After phoning a few main points to our office from a telephone box, I rushed back to the office where it was a thrill to phone London excerpts from the programme and to be told, again and again, 'No opposition sighted yet.' Bob and I took turns in phoning material until about 3 am.

I phoned some passages straight from the paper, and when I got stuck for translations of some difficult words Lena stood at my elbow and whispered them to me. We had a 45-minute 'world beat' over the nearest opposition.

Because we have an unofficial, restricted cooperation agreement with the local staffers of the American agency, Associated Press (AP), directed partly against their and our important competitor, United Press International (UPI), we tipped them off after we had been on the phone for about 20 minutes. Two AP men, Stanley Johnson and Reinhold Enz, joined us. They were happy that we had given them a lead of about 45 minutes over UPI.

We were also joined by Jeremy Wolfenden. I had all present, including the AP translator, a pretty Russian called Mila, sign the historic copy of Pravda.

The hottest news in the new programme was its claim that by 1980 the Soviet people would be receiving about half their goods and services free of charge which, it said, would mean that by then, 'Communism would be substantially built.' Things earmarked to become free of charge during that period include rent, public utility services, public transport on the local level, medicines – at present there's a sort of prescription charge in the otherwise free state health service – meals in factories, offices, schools and other institutions.

The Soviet people were also promised an abundance of well-made consumer goods, 'including contemporary furniture' and well-designed clothes and shoes, and an increase in personal real income of from three to four times by 1980, with a fivefold increase in the national income during the same period.

The United States, according to the programme, is to be overtaken by 1970, and is described as being past its zenith. The programme repeats early Marxist tenets, such as the claim that the working class becomes poorer, either absolutely or compared with the richer classes, as capitalism enters its monopoly stage.

It makes the important pronouncement that the 'dictatorship of the proletariat' in the Soviet Union has now completed its historic task, and asserts that Soviet rule today represents all the people, though it adds that the working class 'still has a leading role' to play during the period in which Communism is to be built. No final date for the establishment of Communism is stated.

The programme lays down that 'a proportion of government and party leaders at the various levels shall retire at each election'. That measure is intended 'to train more people for democratic responsibility' and responsibility in government. In the case of 'top leaders or officials of recognized authority and qualities', they may be kept in their jobs by a 75% vote in the bodies which elected them, the ballot to be in secret.

According to Communist theory, during the period ahead 'the work of state institutions should be gradually transferred to elected bodies' such as the soviets and the trade unions, because, in theory, when Communism has been established, the state should no longer exist. Instead, it is said, there is to be a free association between highly developed, industrious and collegial individuals.

Irrespective of how much of this programme is in fact achieved, I have no doubt that it is of immense historical importance and will be a great propaganda weapon for the Communists in the under-developed countries.

Anyone foolish enough to equate Communism with Nazism ought to read this document. While there are points in it which, in my opinion, do not hold water, it gives a coherent view of the world. And it is not directed towards evil goals, however bad some Communist practices may appear to Western democrats.

One American correspondent commented to me that, if the programme is successful, it will give the Soviet people the things which the working class in some capitalist countries have already. That is true, but it is not the whole truth, for it will give the Soviet people more than workers in some capitalist countries, without the fear of unemployment and slumps. And it will, if the theory becomes practice, give the Soviet people a greater share in the running of their own affairs than is the case in capitalist countries.

The programme underlines 'the declaration of last November's Communist summit', stating that war is not inevitable because, in view of the 'increased strength of the Socialist camp' capitalism is no longer the danger it used to be.

I think that during the implementation of this programme the Soviet people may well receive more of the old 'bourgeois' freedoms, such as the right to read a greater variety of non-Communist literature and to travel freely abroad, perhaps even to emigrate. *[Those things did not happen until the Gorbachov era, which began in 1985 and was followed by the collapse of Soviet Communism and the break-up of the Soviet Union in 1991.]*

In a service message London thanked us for a 'tremendous beat'. Feeling elated at our night's work, and at being in on such an event, I retired to bed at about 4 am after a nightcap of watered whisky in Jeremy's room at the Ukraina.

30 July 1961 : When I rose at noon I was able to point out to women staff of the Ukraina the most interesting passages in the new party programme, which some of them were by then reading in *Pravda*. One woman expressed delight when I told her rents and public transport were to become free. Another said glumly, 'Promises for the future. I shall be in my grave by then.'

During the afternoon I interviewed a few people on the street near our office, asking what they hoped the next 20 years would bring. Several men said they hoped we would have peace and friendship. These chaps were playing dominoes at a table in a yard.

I chatted with them warmly for a while. As I walked away, a policeman, who had evidently been waiting and watching, asked me for my documents and wrote down my details.

I asked him, 'Why are you taking my name?'

He replied, 'I have the right to do so.'

I said, 'Am I allowed to talk to people?

He, 'Yes.'

When he had finished making his notes – the men looked on in silence, indicating sympathy with me, I thought – he said, 'Excuse me, it is my duty.'

I replied, 'It's my duty, too.'

He was polite and friendly. I suppose that, when Communism comes, this sort of thing will die out too.

Tonight, like half the audience, I wept while watching *Clear Skies*, a celebrated new Soviet film directed by Grigori Chukrai. In some respects hackneyed, due to its use of clever-clever techniques, the film is nevertheless noteworthy as an example of what can be shown on the Soviet screen today. It tells the story of a Soviet air force pilot who, during the Second World War, falls in love with a girl just out of school, who has a child by him before they are married. This alone is a daring breakthrough in a Soviet film.

The pilot is taken prisoner by the Germans and, on his return home in the Stalin era, is treated by the authorities as an outcast. (Stalin regarded such servicemen as either cowards for having surrendered instead of going to their deaths, or possible collaborators with the Nazis.) His wife stands by him.

One day a boy dashes into their house to say, 'Stalin is dead.'

The scene changes to a shot of the sun breaking through clouds, followed by scenes of a spring thaw. After this the pilot is rehabilitated and goes on to become a top test pilot.

31 July 1961 : Yesterday, thinking about the coming of Communism, I decided to try out some Russian shaving cream. I took a tube and squeezed a bit on my chin, moistened the brush – and found it did not lather. I took rather more cream. Still no success. That's Communism, I was saying to myself when I noticed I'd taken toothpaste instead of the shaving cream. The cream worked perfectly.

A Russian architecture student asked me what I thought of the new party programme. I said that even if only part of it – as I think likely – materializes within the planned 20-year period, it will represent a great advance both economically and politically.

I have only found one reference to religion in the programme, a phrase attacking 'clericalism', but no further reference to the atheist party's attitude to religion as a whole, about which there were a paragraph or two in the old, 1919 programme. Alla suggested that the omission was because the question of religion – 'supersitition' as the Communists call it – is no longer an important one in this country.

38 Encounter with the second cosmonaut

1 August 1961 : My first complete day off since I came to Russia. Had a chance to observe something about religion here. I hired a smart Volga limousine, with an Intourist driver, and was driven to Zagorsk, about 70 kilometres *[44 miles]* north-east of Moscow, after obtaining the necessary permission from the Foreign Ministry. Foreign journalists must stay within 40 kilometres *[25 miles]* of the centre of Moscow unless they obtain permission to travel further away. *[Very large areas of the Soviet Union were completely closed to foreigners.]*

The driver told me he was in the top of three classes of Intourist drivers. He received 120 roubles a month – about £48 at the official rate – compared with 80 for a third-class driver. He was a good driver, too.

Out of his 120 roubles, he said, he spent about 90 on food for himself, his wife and their small son and daughter. A further six went in rent. The rest was for all other needs.

If they wanted to go on holiday, they could go for two weeks for a total of 35 roubles, under a trade union scheme. He said he had three suits. For a workaday suit he paid about 70 roubles (£28).

Usually his wife worked as well, but was at present kept at home with a baby. At Intourist he was sometimes offered overtime, bringing his pay up to 200 roubles (£80) a month.

Outside Moscow almost all the houses are wooden, many of them log-cabin style. Most of the houses have radio or television aerials. I saw people drawing water from a roadside well.

Here and there, by the mainly flat road, leading past fields and forests – rather like the outskirts of Berlin – there are billboards exhorting the 'comrade maize growers' or the 'comrade milk-maids' to step up production. Few of the houses look well cared for, and a minority appear to be falling to bits.

There's fair amount of traffic – less, of course, than on a comparable road in Britain, but more, I think, than in East Germany. Trucks predominate. We passed a number of churches, some evidently 'working', as the Russians say, others which had obviously been converted into flats or stores.

We drove past a giant duckpond, swarming with white duck or geese. A special project, the driver said. Then a high concrete television relay tower, dwarfing some trim modern wooden houses, reminiscent of Austrian Alpine chalets.

Occasional holiday camps or children's 'pioneer camps', generally well-kept hutted encampments. Saw some stone buildings in small towns on the way, and again in Zagorsk, a largish town. I'd come to see the monastery, a kind of religious Kremlin behind a high rectangular wall on a hill.

Was stunned by the beauty of the five onion domes of the Uspenskiy (Assumption) Church – a central golden onion surrounded by four blue ones decked out with gleaming golden stars.

First I entered the Trinity Church, where prayers were being said and hymns sung in front of the silvery sarcophagus of St Sergei, who founded the monastery in about 1340.

As the bearded priest, in long black robe, intoned the prayers, members of a congregation of about 25 crossed themselves, went up to the sarcophagus, knelt to kiss the stone floor in front of it, stood to kiss the sarcophagus itself and then a holy icon on the wall.

Most of the believers were elderly women with black or whitish headcloths, and poor well-worn frocks, sometimes touching the ground, often of dark material. But I noticed several younger people, including a teenage girl, a 35-ish man and a youth of perhaps 19, who also carried out the observances.

Several other Russians stood some distance away, as I did, watching and occasionally whispering to each other. Behind an altar rail several of the evidently peasant women had placed their worn bags containing enamel tins filled with milk, country loaves and other food. Within the monastery wall I saw about 200 such people, eating, sleeping or admiring one or other of the 11 churches built there down the centuries.

Near the Trinity Church is a state museum about the history of the monastery. In the museum a selection of anti-religious books were on sale, along with pictures of the monastery and its churches. I heard a man near me mutter, 'Religion just over there, anti-religion here.'

I bought a couple of the anti-religious books for later study. One had several clerics depicted on its cover, pointing to the heavens. The title said, *Do morals come from God?* I also saw a notice stating that the museum ran a travelling exhibition on the Marxist attitude to religion; that's what I'd call an anti-religious exhibition.

In the historical section of the permanent museum the role of the Zagorsk monastery is depicted from a non-religious point of view. The monastery is described as a positive force in that it took part in efforts to unify Russia, first because its community fought against the Mongols in the battle of Kulikovo, south-east of Tula, in 1380, which was the first Russian defeat of the Mongols. It was also praised for its role, around 1610, in a battle against the Poles and Lithuanians.

There is even a quote from Stalin, displayed in the museum, showing that such monasteries, because of their military efforts, were regarded as a positive factor by the Communists. There is also a chart according to which about one third of the territory of Russia was owned by the Church in the seventeenth century.

After lunching quite well in a rather dingy café called 'Rest' in a peeling old building, I interviewed at the monastery 33-year-old Stepan Kostyuk, who has just completed about six years' religious instruction, first in a seminary elsewhere and for the past two or three years at Zagorsk which, he told me, houses one of the Soviet Union's two Orthodox Church academies. The other is in Moscow. There are seminaries, which are rated lower, in several cities, including Minsk and Odessa.

This handsome young Ukrainian laughed when I remarked that Mr Khrushchev comes from somewhere down that way – from southern Russia, near the Ukrainian border – and said, 'Fancy linking me with such a high personality.'

Kostyuk said he had done his army service before deciding to train for the Orthodox Church priesthood.

While in the army he had a small prayerbook with him, and some of his friends knew he was a believer, but he did not tell all his comrades. His father was a believer too, he said. Kostyuk told me that the monastery had been closed in 1922 and reopened in 1946.

Before then – I think he meant during the war – courses to train young men for the priesthood had been restarted. This was an aspect of Stalin's partial reconciliation with the Church, part of his wartime efforts to strengthen patriotism.

Kostyuk said that although young men training to become priests – there are about 200 at Zagorsk – were taught the Soviet constitution, there was no state interference in the curriculum. It was obvious, he said, that the Church did not agree with the Communists, as the Church was trying to work for a world 'guided by God and for the life hereafter' while the Communists were concerned with life on earth.

'But we, too,' he went on, 'exhort the faithful to work well, to be good to one another, and we, too, pray for peace in the whole world.'

This young priest told me there were daily services in four of the 11 churches inside the monastery wall, while the others were used for special services on holy days. He took me into the Refectory Church, built in the seventeenth century on the order of Peter the Great, and showed me two gilded altars in baroque style. He said they had been made only five years ago.

When I asked him how many believers there were in Russia, he said he did not know, and then added smilingly, 'When people are unhappy, then they are believers.'

This friendly and handsome young man, who told me he was at present considering whether to become a celibate monk or a married priest, took me into a church office and asked me to write in the visitors' book. I expressed my thanks for his patience in answering questions about religion in Russia today.

He showed me a booklet he had been trying to translate from the English. I was surprised and pleased to see it had been issued by an Anglican order of monks, the Community of the Resurrection, whose headquarters at Mirfield, near Bradford, I had once visited as a reporter. He had not realized that Mirfield was a place name and had translated it as 'something like mire field'.

3 August 1961 : Like Brenda and John, Eve and Bob have been most hospitable to me – I seem to have been eating in their flat about once a day.

I saw Khrushchev emerging from the Italian Embassy where he had lunched with visiting Italian Prime Minister Amintore Fanfani. Khrushchev, not so tall but a head taller than Fanfani, led the Italian leader across the road to a crowd of clapping Russians. I was told he said to Fanfani, 'Let's go and meet some of them. See how happy they are.'

The impression we were given after these two leaders' talks last night is that Khrushchev is treading softly but firmly on Berlin and that the West will be ready to start talks before long.

4 August 1961 : Interviewed, in the street, a couple of Americans from New York who were driving a Land Rover from Amsterdam to Singapore. One of them, a Mr Zipkin from Yonkers, a plastics manufacturer, told me that Russians, who had crowded round their vehicle in many places, had seemed unable to believe that a capitalist society could offer much apart from misery to its citizens.

The Russians had been in most cases incredulous when told about social welfare schemes in the United States. That kind of ignorance about the real state of present-day capitalism is unfortunately reflected in the new Communist Party programme too, which I am now reading again in Russian in detail, intending to read it in English later.

I know very few Russians, and there are about six million in Moscow. But tonight, on a street corner, I bumped into one I know, Gubanov, East Germany correspondent of *Pravda*, whom I'd got to know in East Berlin. Over a drink in the *Kokteil Holl* at the Sovietskaya, we argued about who started the Berlin crisis.

I agreed with him that the semi-panic reaction in the United States was bad, but argued that in the last analysis Khrushchev was to blame for this. I conceded that the Soviet Union had the right to sign a peace treaty with East Germany, but had no right to claim that Western Allied rights in West Berlin, including access rights, would then lapse. In return I received the usual Soviet arguments.

Up till about 1.30 am, working with Bob on the new rules of the Communist Party, which contain proposals to bring in more new blood compulsorily by retiring a section of the officials at each election, and one or two more democratic formulations of the rules.

6 August 1961 : There had been rumours that a second Russian cosmonaut was about to go up, and as I walked along wide Gorky Street on my way to the office this Sunday morning, I realized that rumours were about to be confirmed or had been, for the street loudspeakers – which are switched on for big events – were relaying the Moscow Radio interval signal, part of the melody of the 'Internationale' played on some kind of chimes.

When I got to the office around 11.00, Bob, who lives in the adjoining flat, and Lena were taking down the first announcement which started at 10.40, telling the world that Major German Stepanovich Titov, born in 1935 in the Altai region, bordering on Outer Mongolia, had been launched on an extended space flight, taking about 88 minutes to whirl round the world.

Titov, an air force major like Gagarin, had reported that everything was working normally and that he was fine.

Titov's spaceship had been launched at 09.00 Moscow time from, we (correctly) believed, the cosmodrome at Baikonur in Kazakhstan, north-east of the Aral Sea. As is usual on all big Moscow stories of this nature, the first break for Reuters came through our radio monitoring station at Green End, north of London.

I phoned a 'flash' (top priority) around 11.20 to one of our excited German women teleprinter operators in Bonn, while a journalist rushed into that office to take more copy. We had television and radio on constantly.

The former soon showed us a picture of Titov, handsome, with a longish face, bushy hair and eyebrows, in a major's uniform. The radio reports gave periodic reports of Titov's orbits, taking him, as the day wore on, over most of the world's largest cities.

Thanks to a local contact, I was able to quote informed sources as saying that the flight would end some time tomorrow morning after between 15 and 20 orbits. Bob had already put out a piece stating that the flight was expected to end after 17 orbits, as this would bring the spaceship, *Vostok II* – Gagarin's was *Vostok I* – into a convenient position over the Soviet Union. (In fact it ended after 17^1/$_2$ orbits, so Reuters did well on that.)

Before long the radio gave us recordings of Titov himself, talking from space as he zoomed on at 18,000 miles an hour. Eve kept us supplied with meals, some of them on our desks, as we worked through the day, evening and night with Titov still going round and round, after having lunch, supper and eight hours sleep in his spaceship.

7 August 1961 : To bed finally at 4 am on the Elphicks' couch. Up again around 08.30 as we continued our stint. A good thing (for us) that the Russians brought Titov down after 17^1/$_2$ orbits. He had travelled further than any man in one journey, more than 700,000 kilometres *[437,500 miles]*, which is close to the distance to the moon and back.

He did all that in 25 hours and 18 minutes. What vistas this opens up, not only of inter-planetary travel before long, but of amazingly fast world travel – Britain–Australia in 45 minutes, perhaps.

Titov, 26, a career pilot, seems to be another Gagarin so far as his good looks, smiles and his loyalty to the party and government are concerned. His spaceship landed in a field near Saratov, about 700 kilometres *[438 miles]* south-east of Moscow, in the same pre-determined area as Gagarin's. Whether Titov landed inside the spaceship or by parachute we are not sure.

I managed to get the news through a contact a few minutes before the official announcement, but United Press had it a few minutes earlier, not surprisingly, as their chief correspondent, Henry Shapiro, has been in Moscow about 25 years.

If all this had happened in the USA, we would have had reporters at the launching site and in the landing area, but here only Soviet journalists have that privilege, and their reports are carefully edited for security reasons. Still, I have hopes that, as time goes on, Western pressmen will be invited to a Soviet space launch and landing. I hope I'm one of them.

8 August 1961 : We learned through devious channels, later confirmed by the evening paper *Izvestia*, the government organ, that Titov was resting in a cottage near the Volga while doctors made further tests on him; so far, his condition was said to be perfect.

With him was Gagarin, who joined him last night after cutting short a visit to Canada. The second Soviet cosmonaut is handsome, like Gagarin, but his smile is not quite so attractive. Reports in Soviet papers said Titov listened to Strauss waltzes he picked up from earth as he spun round the globe in a state of weightlessness, which he described as 'unusual' but not detrimental to work.

We have now seen pictures, too, of his pretty, petite, brunette wife, Tamara, 23, a medical student, and his 50-ish parents who live in the Altai region where his father is a teacher, of German among other things. Soviet press reports praise both Titov as a person and the Soviet system for having made his flight possible. The achievement is hailed as 'another proof' that the Soviet system is superior to all others and will eventually spread (without war, of course) to the rest of the world.

9 August 1961 : A bulky Ilyushin 18 airliner, escorted by seven MiG jets, put down at Moscow's Vnukovo airport at 1 pm. Then, engines off, it stood silently for some minutes before the main door opened and out popped a rather small chap in a khaki jacket, peaked cap and dark-blue trousers.

As soon as he came out, Titov found he was standing on the start of 30 metres of red carpet. He put on a broad grin and walked quickly along the carpet with a sailor's rolling gait. Several thousand people, waiting with flowers, balloons and placards, cheered and clapped.

At the end of the red carpet the smiling young man found he had reached a flower-decked platform. He went up the steps and saluted before a burly man slightly smaller than himself – Khrushchev.

He said, 'Comrade First Secretary of the Central Committee of the Communist Party of the Soviet Union, Chairman of the Council of Ministers of the USSR. I report that the task of the Central Committee and the Soviet Government has been fulfilled. In the spaceship *Vostok II* on August 6 and 7, 1961, a space flight of 25 hours was completed. I flew more than 17 times round the globe and landed safely and exactly in the predetermined area. All the equipment of the spaceship worked faultlessly. I feel excellent. I am ready to fulfil any tasks of the party and government.'

Khrushchev smiled broadly, put his brawny arms round Titov and kissed him three times on his cheeks, in the Russian fashion. Then the cosmonaut turned right to face a pretty, shapely woman who stood, in blue figured dress and white high-heeled shoes, her eyes on the man who had come back to her from space.

They kissed for a moment, bringing tears not only to my eyes. And as his wife hung her head – either in embarrassment in front of the crowd or merely to weep with joy – Titov turned to hug his black-suited father and his bulky mother, who wore a peasant's

382

black-and-white headscarf and a rather shapeless black-and-white dress.

Next in line for Titov's kisses were two unidentified elder members of his family and his teenage sister, Zimfira. Then the crowd's roar boomed more loudly as the two cosmonauts did a delighted bearhug.

Titov's kissing was not done by a long chalk. Next came 13 more members of the Communist Party presidium on the platform. Then, after a walk past workers' delegations with Khrushchev, Titov was taken along to kiss other government and party dignitaries, first of all a motherly, elderly woman – Mrs Nina Khrushcheva – then more politicians, followed by half a dozen Soviet marshals.

For me, this scene at the airport was the best of the day, far more moving than the vast official demonstration which followed on Red Square, amid a sea of flags. Although the several hundred thousand marchers who paraded past the Lenin-Stalin Mausoleum, where Titov stood with Khrushchev and Gagarin on the roof, were cheerful, and occasionally cheered and clapped, the enthusiasm, I was told, was nowhere near as great as when Gagarin returned from the first manned space flight in April.

Khrushchev's speech in Red Square repeated the familiar theme that the Soviet Union wanted peace, but was strong enough to defeat any aggressor, and tonight he said it again at a Kremlin reception for Titov, which Bob covered for us. The drift of Khrushchev's speech tonight was that if the Soviet Union signed a peace treaty with East Germany that was no excuse for the West to commit an aggressive act against East Germany.

If the West did so, he said, that would be suicide. Of course, that is not the real point. The West knows it cannot stop the Soviet Union signing a peace treaty with East Germany, but until now Khrushchev has linked this with his claim that the signing will end Western rights in West Berlin. From his latest utterances, it now appears he is willing to negotiate with the West on their rights if they will, at least tacitly, accept the planned Soviet treaty with East Germany.

10 August 1961 : Our driver, Grisha, a great character, baffled me by telling me about his 'harazh' which, because he cannot say the letter 'g', was his way of pronouncing the (also Russian) word 'garage'. On another occasion he referred to the first cosmonaut as 'Haharin'.

Interviewed Professor David Green, of Wisconsin University Enzyme Institute, who had given the plenary address at an international conference of 5,000 biochemists, held in Moscow. For me, the journalist, he put his findings into simple language. He said that in the past couple of months he and his associates had found what they believe to be the ultimate in the 'power stations' which produce energy in human cells.

Scientists already knew that virtually all body cells – usually about one-hundredth of a millimetre in diameter – contained a 'cake' known as the mitochondrion, which is one ten-thousandth of a millimetre in diameter. This 'cake' was known to be the cell's power station, but research in past weeks had shown that the power is produced within 'raisins' embedded within the cake.

Improved electron microscope techniques, devised by H. Fernandez-Moran, a Venezuelan working at Massachusetts General Hospital in Boston, have enabled scientists to see the 'raisins' – 17,000 inside each 'cake'. The scientists have also been able to see faintly that the 'raisins' are subdivided into five complexes, within each of which energy is produced by the burning of sugar in oxygen to produce carbon dioxide – water plus energy.

'We think the complexes are the ultimate unit,' Professor Green said.

The team has found that these 'machines' in the cells have a similar build-up whatever the type of cell: muscle, brain, heart or kidney, for example. They have also been able to take the 'machines' to pieces and put them together again. Though it was hard work, I enjoyed doing this bit of popularization – which made things more understandable to me too – and hope it is printed.

To a Romanian Embassy reception tonight, in honour of the visiting Romanian Communist leader, Georgi Gheorgiu Dej, at which Khrushchev appeared to be in the best of spirits, never mentioning

Berlin in his speech, contrasting with his grim mood of last night. He drank toasts with several reporters, signed autographs for some of us, including me, and exchanged occasional quips.

When I knocked over a glass while standing near Khrushchev, he said, 'What's he doing, breaking glasses.'

Denis Ogden, correspondent of the London Communist paper, *Daily Worker*, quipped, 'Oh, he's from Reuters, they're always doing things like that,' while an Indian journalist, who's been in Moscow for four years, said, 'He's a beginner.'

Several of us had a chat with Titov, who dropped some of his shyness tonight, and his wife. He told us he had not seen Britain during his space flight, because of cloud. Mrs Titova said she thought husbands should get permission from their wives before going into space. But Titov smilingly disagreed, saying he believed in the 'good old days'.

Mrs Titova said she would have liked to have gone into space with her husband, but Titov said it was so comfortable in the cosmos that one did not want one's wife with one. A pleasant couple. In a way I find Titov more appealing than Gagarin, because Gagarin never shows shyness.

11 August 1961 : Am dying to get home after so long away but now, only two days before I am to leave Moscow, I am sorry we are not going to move here soon. However, the two months' experience, including almost every type of Moscow story, will be invaluable for me when I return.

In a colonnaded marble-walled auditorium of Moscow State University, I attended Titov's first international press conference; he had spoken earlier to Soviet reporters. Once again, I was charmed by his mixture of shyness, forthrightness and humour.

He said the right things about party and government, and no doubt meant them fully, but his answers were very human and warm. At some moments he reminded me vaguely of a childhood friend, John Baguley, a member of an RAF bomber crew who was killed in the Second World War.

Titov revealed that he had landed by parachute after ejecting his capsule from the spaceship, whereas Gagarin, we believe, landed in the ship. Titov said that when weightlessness set in he felt he was upside-down for a while, but the feeling passed.

A professor who also spoke said that Titov had suffered discomfort in his vestibular system (in the inner ear, affecting balance) during weightlessness, particularly when he was moving round the cabin. It was not known whether this was due to some peculiarity of Titov or whether it was something others would suffer. More tests were needed.

Young girl students and overalled men carrying arc lights and camera stands were delighted with a chance to listen to Titov, and were tickled with many of his answers. This space-age stuff is only gradually becoming reality to me. We have crossed not only the sound barrier but the science fiction barrier. I can now see Reuter men going on space flights within the next ten or twenty years.

In a restaurant at 10 pm – it was not due to close until 11 pm – I was told there was only one main course available – beefsteak – which I did not want, so I asked for some cheese. The waitress came back to say there was no cheese – 'too late'.

I made do with a tomato salad, a lemonade and some ice cream. When I came to pay the bill the waitress had no change. That's the kind of thing that wears down foreigners – and, no doubt, Russians too – in Moscow. In such matters the Russians have a long way to go before they can reach capitalism, never mind Communism.

12 August 1961 : Did my last interview of this Moscow stint, with Mr Hasegawa, a pleasant and, as one would expect, very polite Japanese Embassy First Secretary, who detailed the programme for First Deputy Premier Anastas Mikoyan's visit to Japan, starting next Monday – the first visit to Japan by such a senior Soviet leader.

I was luncheon host at the National Hotel; about 30 roubles for six of us (£12 at the official rate). Guests were Bob and Eve, British Embassy First Secretary, Keith Oakeshott, and his wife, Jill, and Leonard Parkin, visiting BBC man who was one of my colleagues on the *Bradford Telegraph & Argus* in the early fifties.

39 I witness start of Berlin Wall

13 August 1961 : I was dying to get back home, but at the same time sorry to be leaving Moscow after my first taste of the Soviet capital. I should have arrived home this Sunday evening after a flight via East Berlin, but world events decided otherwise.

Before I left Moscow, at about 10.45 local time, we learned by service message from London and from the BBC short-wave news (received without jamming) that early today the East Germans had begun to seal off West Berlin, both from East Berlin and from surrounding East Germany. Tanks and armoured cars were patrolling as soldiers and members of the 'armed factory fighting groups' set up new barriers. *[Until 13 August, it had been easy for East Germans, including East Berliners, to flee into West Berlin, usually by travelling on the still unified city overhead railway, the S-Bahn, or the underground, the U-Bahn. There were only occasional East German checks of passengers on these two railway systems, which ran between the two halves of Berlin and from some outlying East German districts through West Berlin into East Berlin.]*

Bob drove me out to Sheremetyevo airport, where I bought a Russian gramophone record with the popular (and beautiful) song, translated as 'Midnight in Moscow', before I stepped into a TU-104 jetliner which, with about 50 passengers, was about half full.

On the plane I had a frank but friendly discussion about the Berlin situation with an East German lawyer, returning from a holiday on the Black Sea. After a flight of about two hours and 25 minutes we landed at East Berlin's Schönefeld airport, which was ringed by East German troops carrying submachine-guns.

Instead of flying on to Bonn, as originally intended, it was agreed with London that I should stay in Berlin to help our East Berlin correspondent, Adam Kellett-Long. I was not prevented from travelling from Schönefeld, which lies just to the south of East Berlin, to Reuters East Berlin office near the centre of East Berlin, in the Schönhauser Allee, which I had opened in 1959 as the first non-Communist Western correspondent accredited in East Germany. *[I describe this assignment in my previous book,* Reuter Reporter among the Communists 1958–59, *The Tagman Press, Norwich, 2000. ISBN 0-9530921-7-8, 252 pp., illustrated, £10.]*

I found Adam tired out after 30 hours on the go. *[He had received phoned advice last night from an unidentified (apparently Communist) source not to go to bed – and had heeded it, putting Reuters ahead with an eyewitness report about the start of work on what soon became known as the Berlin Wall.]*

After snatching a spot of lunch with Adam, I took the new orange-coloured office car, an East German Wartburg, to look at the scene. (Adam had earlier reported East German police and 'factory fighting groups', armed with rifles and submachine-guns, forcing back sullen crowds from some sector border points which had been closed.)

Until early today there were about 80 road crossing points between East and West Berlin. There are now only 12, and ordinary East Berliners have been entirely forbidden by the Communist authorities from going to West Berlin which, apart from a few exceptions, they were free to do up to now.

The crossing points which have been closed are being blocked with barbed wire or barriers. I found ten East German tanks parked in a square not far from the sector border in the Swinemünde Strasse, a drab working-class area about a quarter of a mile from our office. I asked to see an officer and was presented with a stern-faced young blond captain wearing battle overalls over his grey-brown uniform.

I asked him what the tanks were doing and he said, 'You'll find it in the newspapers and on the radio.'

He refused to answer any more questions except to tell me his rank.

The tanks had been roped off. Small groups of people stood around, talking about the situation. One man said to me, 'It's outrageous.'

An elderly woman told me, 'I was absolutely staggered when I heard about it.'

Some people looked on from house windows.

I spent much of the evening on the two sides of the colonnaded Brandenburg Gate, the main East–West road crossing point, just inside East Berlin. On the Western side a crowd of several thousand had collected and, for a time, got partially out of hand.

Some groups from the West made dashes onto the road – East Berlin territory – in front of the gate and were driven back by water cannons mounted on East German armoured cars. Later the West Berlin police confined the crowd behind ropes.

A section of the crowd, perhaps two or three hundred strong, composed mainly of rough-looking youths, shouted rhythmically such slogans as, 'Berlin stays free!' and 'Down with the goatee beard!' – Walter Ulbricht, the top East German leader, sports one.

The area west of the Brandenburg Gate is part of the British sector. A British Army corporal, keeping watch in a radio-equipped jeep, was critical of the West Berliners in the crowd who, he said, were causing the tense situation at this spot. So were West Berlin police officers and the left-wing Social Democratic mayor of the West Berlin borough of Kreuzberg, Willi Kressmann, who asked a police officer to move back the crowd to reduce the danger of a clash. One police officer, I was told, said that a member of the West Berlin city government had been to the spot and had said, 'Let the people stay. It's good like that.'

While I fully understand genuine feelings of anger at the East German action, I think it is wrong to let it be expressed in this dangerous way, and mainly by louts who have little political sense.

My main feeling about the sealing-off of West Berlin is that it is a terrible advertisement for Communism, but something that was to be expected and which the West cannot stop without war, which would help no one. Western mouthings about 'counter-measures' will, I'm convinced, amount to little or nothing.

I think the Soviet Union and the Western Allies tacitly admit each other's right to control events in 'their' parts of Germany and of Berlin, a right born of conquest. The Western Allies began accepting Soviet rights in this respect when they bowed to the Communist moves which split the Berlin administration in 1948, and when they did not use force to break the Berlin Blockade of 1948–49.

It is too late now to do more than express chagrin at the Communists' use of force to prevent people from exercising the elementary freedom to live where they want. For West Berlin, paradoxically, the new East German measure may have some advantages: because it may mean that the Kremlin is preparing for an agreement with the West on maintaining real guarantees to West Berlin, including the continued presence of Western troops for an indefinite period.

From the Communist standpoint, it will be easier to do such a deal once the 'problem' of East German refugees, escaping through West Berlin, has been dealt with. Further, the use of East German forces to prevent East Germans from reaching West Berlin demonstrated the power that the Communist regime can bring to bear on its own population. By tonight there was no evidence of Soviet participation in the military measures in East Berlin.

14 August 1961 : More trouble near the Brandenburg Gate. The West Berlin police had ill-advisedly allowed a small crowd to approach the Soviet sector border. One of several youths threw a 'Molotov cocktail' – a bottle filled with ignited petrol – onto the road in front of him, which is in the Soviet sector.

Such weapons were used in profusion during the abortive anti-Communist revolt of June 1953, and the one thrown today could have provoked a savage reaction from an East German policeman.

No wonder the West Berlin police were not so gentle in hustling the youths away.

Early today the East Germans decided, wisely I think, to close the 'gate' – several openings between the columns – to traffic for the time being. During the day, apparently on the order of the British occupation authorities, the West Berlin police pushed back the crowds for about half a mile, thus relaxing the situation.

Brigadier Godfrey Hamilton, the British troop commander, who came to make observations later through a battered field glass, told me he thought the crisis was completely over.

East Germans continue to flee, in small numbers, mainly at night, some of them swimming rivers or canals which form the sector border in places.

I managed to spend an hour at the house of Elfi's aunts – as many as four lived there at different times – in the West Berlin suburb of Friedenau. The two old aunts who were there today did not seem really worried about the Berlin situation. Usually the most worrying things during such crises are the headlines in the London papers.

15 August 1961 : The East German authorities clamped on a couple of new restrictions today. Shortly after midnight they announced that West Berlin cars would be banned from East Berlin without special permits because, they alleged, such cars had been used for 'spying' and so on.

Doubtless some cars have been used for smuggling out refugees and goods, for – until 13 August – so many West Berlin cars routinely crossed into East Berlin that only a minority could be checked.

This new restriction shows how worried the East German leaders are about the atmosphere among their own population, and are determined to go to extremes in their efforts to stop people fleeing.

The other new restriction forbade East German citizens to use identity cards or passports issued to them by other states or authorities, including West Berlin. Penalty: at least three years' imprisonment or a fine, or both. This is designed to prevent people from fleeing by showing the identity card or passport of another country, for at present foreigners, West Germans and West Berliners can still move into and out of East Berlin after showing their documents.

Adam, his 22-ish East German secretary, jolly Erdmute Behrendt – whom I had hired in 1959 – and I had the honour to be placed temporarily under arrest by the East German People's Police, the Vopos, ably assisted by three members of the khaki-uniformed 'factory fighting groups' – pro-Communist workers who have been given infantry training.

Adam had been worried because Erdmute had not returned as soon as expected from the borough town hall of Prenzlauer Berg, where he had sent her to inquire about the large numbers of East Berliners who, until now, had worked in West Berlin and had now been ordered to register at the town hall for work in East Berlin.

Adam and I went to the town hall, showed our documents and explained who we were.

A young man in plainclothes showed us into a room where people were registering for work in East Berlin. He invited us to put questions to them. Just then we saw Erdmute, who was waiting to see a senior official, who was at lunch. Another man offered to take us to the mayor on the floor above.

We walked up the stairs and were waiting outside the mayor's room when three green-uniformed Vopos came up to us, with several of the 'factory fighters'. One Vopo snapped, 'You are temporarily under arrest.'

He immediately told us to get moving and, to reinforce his order, gave me a push. I protested at his rudeness. He grabbed my passport and hit my hand when I tried to get it back, saying he had no right to take it. He barked, 'Don't lay hands on me.'

The Vopo took us back to the town hall entrance, while Adam and I were explaining that we were accredited to the East German authorities, and all he need do was to ring the Foreign Ministry to check. Instead, after he had phoned someone, we were placed in an elderly black EMW (East German successor of the old BMW) police radio car, where we giggled and joked for about ten minutes. Once I wound down a window a little, but one of the policemen standing outside made me wind it up again. Then, with two policemen in the front seats and us in the back, we were driven at breakneck speed to the borough police headquarters, a few doors down the road from our East Berlin office.

After some furious cornering, I asked the driver if he was a racing ace. He replied with a grin, 'I always drive like that.'

In the police headquarters, we were ushered into a room with barred windows, already occupied by a platinum blonde, a West German girl from the Ruhr, who told us she'd been there since 8 am – it was by then 2.30 pm – after being arrested for entering East Berlin without one of the new permits.

They had not offered her a chair, but they brought three for us. I asked them to give the girl one too, but she said she would rather stand. The door of the room was left open. Through its barred window we could see onto a small yard, and beyond that a Jewish cemetery.

I passed some time reading inscriptions on graves – *Meine liebe Frau* – and then Erdmute pointed out a coiled rope in the yard – according to her the hangman's rope. None of us had brought a nail file, so we could not go to work on the bars.

Instead I spent some time convincing the police that they should ring up the Foreign Ministry, and in asking them repeatedly to give us something to eat. At first I was told, 'You have to be here eight hours before you are fed,' but after they had become tired of my nattering, or had received instructions from higher up, we were told we would get something.

Then, about an hour after we had been brought to the police station, an elderly police officer came in with our passports and said, 'You are free. It was a mistake.'

We asked him, what kind of mistake, and he mumbled something about their having to be vigilant in the present situation.

Just at that moment our lunch arrived – three large white porcelain bowls full of meat-and-noodle soup. We stayed to eat it up, and Erdmute even congratulated the white-overalled police cook, who had been working overtime to supply the Einsatzgruppen, the operational police squads brought in to stem the refugee flow and stand by in case of disturbances.

On the East Berlin side of the new barriers there have been some clashes between civilians and police, but no one has been hurt, so far as we know. The clashes happened when police cleared away crowds of East Berliners standing near the sector borders, looking sullen. There have also been minor brushes with people openly complaining about the new clampdown.

[According to Soviet-bloc documents which became available to Western researchers only in the early nineties, Ulbricht flew to Moscow on 31 July. Khrushchev told him that the planned peace treaty between the Soviet Union and West Germany would not be signed yet, but he authorized Ulbricht to seal off West Berlin.

Very few East German officials knew that West Berlin was about to be sealed off. Years later the former East German espionage chief, Markus Wolf, said that even he had not been informed. During the first 12 days of August, about 16,000 East German refugees had reached West Berlin; 2,662 were registered on the 12th. But on 13 August only 150 got through.

Initially the Berlin Wall was made of rolls of barbed wire, mainly held in position by concrete posts up to six feet (2 m) high. West Berlin's governing mayor, Willy Brandt, who was campaigning for the Social Democrats in the West German federal election campaign, flew into Berlin from Hanover on the morning of the 13th. He said later, 'We were very unhappy when it became obvious that our friends, our protecting powers, were not able to change anything as far as the other part of the city was concerned.'

In The Wall, *by Christopher Hilton (Sutton Publishing, Stroud, 2001), Dean Rusk, who was the United States Secretary of State in 1961, is quoted as saying in an interview with Hilton, 'The wall was a monstrous monument to the nature of the East German regime, and we knew at once that its purpose was not to keep people out but to keep people in, that it was directed against the Easterners rather than the Westerners. So we did not take any military action against the wall – it was defensive on their part. No member of NATO, including West*

Germany recommended that that action be taken because it might have been World War Three, oh yes.' Rusk conceded that the Western Allies had been taken by surprise tactically by the East German measures.

US President John F. Kennedy, who reacted calmly to the Berlin events, approved a US statement saying that the East German authorities had taken 'severe measures to deny their own people access to West Berlin'. It added, 'The refugees are not responding to persuasion or propaganda from the West, but to the failures of Communism in East Germany. The pretence that Communism desires only peaceful competition is exposed ... Limitation on travel within Berlin is a violation of the right of free circulation throughout the city.'

That right had been laid down in the Four-Power Agreement signed in Paris on 20 June 1949, after the Berlin Blockade, which had ended in May 1949.

Western leaders were relieved that the Communists did not block Western Allied access to East Berlin. If that had been done, it might have led to military clashes. An unknown section of the East German population, in my view a minority comprising members and supporters of the ruling Communist Party, the SED, welcomed the building of the wall as it ended the crippling Westward brain drain and made it easier to achieve economic growth.

At 7 pm on Sunday an East German Trabant car was apparently the first vehicle to break through the barbed wire and get to West Berlin.

The enormity of the wall was underlined by the fact that, before 13 August, about half a million people crossed between East and West Berlin daily and that the overground and underground city railways ran between the two parts of the city. Until 13 August, 53,000 East Berliners were working in West Berlin.

At 2 pm on 14 August the Brandenburg Gate crossing point was closed. An East Berlin police order said this was 'because of Western provocations'.

Although the Western commandants in West Berlin protested to their Soviet opposite number at the Communist measures, it soon became clear that they would not try to remove the beginnings of the wall. The Soviet commandant, Colonel Andrei Solovyev, replying to the Western Allied protest, said that the Soviet Union 'did not interfere in the internal affairs of the sovereign state, the GDR'.

Within a few days of 13 August, the East Germans began building the wall proper, made partly of slabs and pillars used normally for building prefabricated blocks of flats.

Within 12 months, a wall nearly eight miles long had been constructed in the built-up city-centre area. Along West Berlin's less populous border with the rest of East Berlin, and its border with surrounding East Germany, a total of nearly 92 miles, two parallel rolls of barbed wire were laid, with a 'death strip' of varying width between them.

Later, in most areas, the barbed wire was supplemented or replaced by a wall. Within a year 116 watchtowers, manned by armed East German soldiers, were erected at intervals around the whole of West Berlin. The East German top leaders, headed until 1971 by Walter Ulbricht and then by Erich Honecker, became guilty of complicity in murder by ordering their soldiers to shoot at would-be refugees who disobeyed shouted orders to halt – the so-called 'Schiessbefehl' or 'order to shoot'. East German soldiers who failed to carry out the order to shoot, without an acceptable explanation, were punished, usually by imprisonment, and those who, by shooting, prevented escapes, were rewarded or promoted, or both.

The first recorded shooting was on 15 August, when a couple swimming across the Teltow Canal, which formed the border between East and West Berlin in the south-east of West Berlin, were fired at. It was not known if they were hit.

In the early days after 13 August, some East Berliners reached the West by clambering over rolls of barbed wire or by simply walking out of the front doors of their East Berlin houses onto the streets in front of them – which were in West Berlin! Within days the 'Western' doors and windows of such houses were bricked up.

In a telegram to Kennedy shortly after 13 August, Brandt suggested that the American garrison in West Berlin be reinforced – for psychological rather than military reasons. On 17 August Kennedy decided to send Vice-President Lyndon B. Johnson to Berlin, by air, and to order an armed American Battle Group from West Germany –

1,500 men – to travel along the East German autobahn to West Berlin.

Some senior American military officers opposed sending the Battle Group, as they felt it could lead to war. But the Communists did not try to prevent the Battle Group from reaching West Berlin, where large crowds welcomed it.

The troop reinforcement, increasing the American force in West Berlin to 6,500, was militarily pointless in view of the immense superiority of the Soviet and East German forces in and around Berlin. But, together with Johnson's visit, it gave new reassurance to the worried West Berliners. Johnson reaffirmed the United States' guarantee for the freedom of West Berlin and for Western access to it.

Johnson was accompanied by a man who was a hero to the West Berliners, retired General Lucius D. Clay, who had been the US Commandant in Berlin during the Berlin Blockade of 1948–49.

In its 28-year history, the wall had four generations, each one more 'refined' than the last. The final one, made of reinforced concrete, was 11 feet 8 inches (3.5 m) high and more than three feet (0.9 m) thick. It was more difficult to scale because it was topped by cylindrical sections of concrete, making it harder to attach a hook thrown over on a rope.

In time the East Germans constructed a 'death strip' on their side of the wall – a sandy roadway which showed up refugees' footprints. Next to the 'death strip' was a tarmac road on which military vehicles patrolled. Fierce Alsatians ran along the 'death strip' attached to long leashes, the ends of which slid along wires. To make it still harder for escapers to reach the wall, an electrified fence was erected on the East Berlin side of the 'death strip'. If touched, it set off an alarm in a watchtower.

The most serious East–West incident concerning the wall began on 22 October 1961, when the head of the United States mission in West Berlin, Allan Lightner, a senior official of the state department, was refused entry into East Berlin by East German border guards. He was driving his wife's Volkswagen Beetle and, as usual, refused to show his identity card.

The incident may have been caused by a misunderstanding, as an official car of the United States mission, which entered East Berlin just before Lightner tried to so, was admitted without trouble when its occupants showed their identity cards. Whether a misunderstanding or not, this incident escalated to such an extent that the Americans and the Russians soon had several tanks facing each other on each side of Checkpoint Charlie.

But, according to an American source, Kennedy and Khrushchev quietly defused the situation by agreeing that the Soviet tanks would withdraw first.

While the Berlin Wall still stood, many East Germans, sometimes helped from the West, showed great ingenuity in means of escape, including tunnels, the use of fake Western Allied uniforms and cars, a gas-filled balloon and even a train with eight carriages. But escape attempts were often fatal: an estimated 140 would-be refugees were killed or died – for instance, by drowning – during escape attempts; the exact number will never be known.

For the Western Allies it remained an essential that, whatever happened in East Berlin, they continued to have free access to West Berlin along the 110-mile East–West autobahn from West Germany.

On 26 June 1963, President Kennedy was given a wildly enthusiastic welcome in West Berlin, where he made his historic speech in which he said that, two thousand years ago, the proudest boast had been, 'Civis Romanus sum.' ('I am a Roman citizen.') He went on, 'Today, in the world of freedom, the proudest boast is, "Ich bin ein Berliner." ("I am a Berliner.")'

But Kennedy's much praised speech did not alter the fact that the wall had come to stay. However, the unhappiness inflicted on millions of Germans in East and West, who could no longer visit each other, was gradually mitigated when the Communist authorities, in exchange for West German subsidies for their faltering economy, and for international diplomatic recognition, gradually allowed visits by West Germans and West Berliners to East Germany (including East Berlin) and visits by limited numbers of East Germans to the West. From November 1964 East German pensioners were allowed to make visits to the West or to stay there permanently – a financial saving for the East German regime.

In February 1969 it was the turn of another American President,

Richard Nixon, to win much applause during a visit to Berlin, after telling a West Berlin audience, 'We are with you.' He added – in an echo of Kennedy, 'In the sense that the people of Berlin stand for freedom and peace, all the people of the world are truly Berliners.'

In October 1969 West Berlin's former governing mayor, Willy Brandt, who had become chairman of West Germany's moderate left-wing Social Democratic Party, was elected Chancellor (head of government). His policy of détente towards the Soviet bloc played an important role in bringing about the Quadripartite Agreement on Berlin, signed on 3 September 1971 by representatives of the United States, the Soviet Union, Britain and France.

In that agreement the Soviet Union recognized that certain political and economic links existed between West Berlin and West Germany. As a result, there was a virtual end to the previous occasional harassment by the Soviets and the East Germans of Western traffic along the autobahn between West Germany and West Berlin.

The Berlin Agreement, which came into force in 1972, also contained some Western concessions, including the statement that West Berlin was 'not a constitutive part' of West Germany. Also in 1972, the two German states effectively recognized each other, by concluding what was called a Basic Treaty. This, too, took some of the tension out of the Berlin problem.

However, the murders of East Germans trying to go West continued. Although Honecker stated in June 1988 that the 'order to shoot' had been rescinded, except in cases of self-defence, there were a few cases in which escapers were shot at after that. The last person to be shot dead – on 5 February 1989 – was a 20-year-old waiter, Chris Gueffroy.

In June 1987, another US President, Ronald Reagan, came to West Berlin. Speaking from an observation platform near the Brandenburg Gate, two years after the reformer, Mikhail Gorbachov, had become the top Soviet leader, he said, 'Mr Gorbachov, open this gate. Mr Gorbachov, tear down this wall!'

The wall was opened for free movement in both directions on 9 November 1989, on the orders of the weakened East German leadership which, by a historic irony, had lost scores of thousands of its citizens who had reached the West by way of the relatively liberal

Communist countries, Hungary and Czechoslovakia, to which East Germans had normally been allowed to travel.

The East German regime was also faced with increasingly large peaceful anti-Communist demonstrations in its major cities. And – crucially – the East German leaders were told by Gorbachov that he would not commit Soviet forces to save the German Communist regime, as the Soviet Union had done in the face of workers' disturbances in June 1953.

When Gorbachov appeared at an official parade in East Berlin on 7 October, marking the 40th anniversary of the East German regime, there were even calls from bystanders of 'Gorby, help us!'

On 12 November 1989, I flew from London to Berlin on a journalistic assignment, and briefly joined a group of wall 'woodpeckers' who, using a variety of implements, were enthusiastically chipping small concrete souvenirs out of the wall near the Brandenburg Gate. When I told a German woman that I wished I had a hammer, she produced a small one from inside her fur coat, but the East German concrete was too tough for it. Later I bought souvenir pieces of the wall from dealers.

That evening, in the vast Deutschlandhalle in West Berlin, I joined several thousand exuberant 'Ossis' (Easterners) and 'Wessis' (Westerners) at a moving all-German pop concert, with stars from both Germanys. Many 'Ossis' gained admission by selling jars of jam or pickles they had brought with them through the wall.

Most of the East German leaders responsible for the 'order to shoot' on the wall escaped severe punishment. Ulbricht, who had been ousted as SED chief in 1971, had died in 1973. His successor, Honecker, emigrated to Chile to join his daughter there, after a West Berlin court controversially freed him on the ground of ill-health. He died in 1994.

The first free Volkskammer elections, held on 18 March, produced a large majority for parties favouring German reunification. The most important were the conservative Christian Democrats, who won 40.6 per cent of the vote, and the moderate left-wing Social Democrats, who won 21.8 per cent. The reformed SED, renamed as the Party of Democratic Socialism, won 16.3 per cent. Even that party, while defending some aspects of the Communist regime, did not expressly oppose reunification, which came about on 3 October 1990.

Most of the wall was demolished within months of its opening, but a few stretches were kept for historical reasons. Now, in most places, it is hard to see where the wall stood, and it is equally hard to believe that what is now the capital of reunited Germany could really have been divided by force for 28 years.]

Tonight I was able to return home to Bonn at last. While once again captivated by the heavenly beauty of clouds seen from the plane, I was saddened as I looked down onto the lakes, fields and forests of East Germany through the gaps in the clouds, thinking of the unhappiness of people there, forced to live under an alien system.

It was dark when we landed at Wahn, Bonn's home airport. It took Elfi and the boys some time to see that I was the first in the queue, led by the stewardess to the terminal building, but when they did there was a flurry of waves from their shadowy figures. Soon we were all chatting excitedly in our neat little blue Beetle, and I was driving us home along the familiar Rhineland roads.

I intend that my next (fourth) book, though starting in Germany, will deal mainly with my two years (1962–64) as Reuters chief correspondent in that strange but fascinating country, the Soviet Union.

Bibliography

Berton, Kathleen *The British Embassy Moscow* (published with the support of the Foreign and Commonwealth Office and the Moscow offices of some British firms 1991)

Chesterton, G.K. *St Francis of Assisi* (International Publishing Group 2001)

Faulks, Sebastian *The Fatal Englishman: Three Short Lives* (Hutchinson 1996, Vintage 1997)

Hemingway, Ernest *A Farewell to Arms* (Arrow 1994)

Herzl, Theodor *The Old New Land* (Markus Wiener 1997)

Hilton, Christopher *The Wall* (Sutton Publishing, Stroud 2001)

Huddleston, Trevor *Naught for your Comfort* (Fontana 1971)

Kantorowicz, Alfred *Deutsches Tagebuch* (Kindler, Munich 1961)

Roberts, Sir Frank *Dealing with Dictators* (Weidenfeld & Nicolson 1991)

Seghers, Anna *Das Siebte Kreuz* (Aufbau-Verlag GmbH 1996)

Sholokhov, Mikhail *Virgin Soil Upturned* (Picador 1988)

Peter Johnson in 1965

Biography

Peter Brierley Johnson, born in 1925 in Bradford, Yorkshire, England, served in the Royal Navy from 1943 to 1946, latterly as a sub-lieutenant, Royal Naval Volunteer Reserve. His last naval appointment, in mid-1946, was to the Royal Naval Headquarters in Germany. At the headquarters, in Hamburg, he became engaged to his future wife, Elfi Kowitz, a refugee from former German East Prussia. They have two sons.

From 1947 to 1954 Johnson was a reporter on British provincial newspapers, mainly in Yorkshire. In 1954 he joined Reuters, one of the world's leading news agencies, as a sub-editor in its London headquarters. From 1955 to 1965 he was a Reuter correspondent, successively in Bonn and Communist East Berlin, and then chief correspondent successively in the Soviet Union and Germany.

In 1965 he was appointed BBC Berlin correspondent. From 1971 until his retirement from the BBC in 1985, he was a London-based commentator for BBC External Services (now the World Service), specializing in German and Soviet-bloc issues. Since then he has been a freelance journalist, author and translator, living in London.